SECTARIAN POLITICS IN THE PERSIAN GULF

LAWRENCE G. POTTER
(*editor*)

Sectarian Politics in the Persian Gulf

Published in Collaboration with
Georgetown University's Center for International and Regional Studies,
School of Foreign Service in Qatar

HURST & COMPANY, LONDON

First published in the United Kingdom in 2013 by
C. Hurst & Co. (Publishers) Ltd.,
41 Great Russell Street, London, WC1B 3PL

Printed in the United Kingdom

A Cataloguing-in-Publication data record for this book is available from the British Library.

ISBN: 9781849043380

This book is printed using paper from registered sustainable and managed sources.

www.hurstpublishers.com

CONTENTS

LIST OF TABLES

ACKNOWLEDGMENTS

This book, the first scholarly treatment of sectarian politics in the Persian Gulf, grew out of two workshops initiated by Professor Mehran Kamrava, director of the Center for International and Regional Studies at the Georgetown University School of Foreign Service in Qatar. Recognizing the importance and timeliness of the subject, CIRS convened the workshops in Doha, Qatar, in October 2011 and May 2012. A selection of the papers presented at these meetings, thoroughly critiqued, revised, and updated, is provided in this book. We greatly benefitted from the comments made by the other workshop participants, and by invited outside experts, which are reflected in the final versions. Although I participated in the workshops and edited this volume, all along the way I had the full support and encouragement of Professor Kamrava and his able staff, especially Zahra Babar, Suzi Mirgani, and Nadia Talpur. Dr Mirgani prepared the bibliography with the assistance of CIRS students, for which I am very grateful. I must also thank my wife, Haideh Sahim, for her forbearance during the editing process, for assisting with transliteration, and providing helpful advice throughout.

The topic has taken on increasing saliency and urgency since the project began, and today sectarianism is widely recognized as a key—some would say the key—obstacle to peace and progress in the Middle East. We believe that this book is an important step forward in clarifying this phenomenon, and will be of value to all those who work in and care about the Persian Gulf states.

Lawrence G. Potter

ABOUT THE CONTRIBUTORS

Lois Beck is Professor of Anthropology at Washington University in St. Louis. She has lived in Iran and conducted cultural-anthropological research there over a span of five decades. She is the author of *The Qashqa'i of Iran* (Yale University Press, 1986), *Nomad: A Year in the Life of a Qashqa'i Tribesman in Iran* (University of California Press, 1991), and *Nomads Move On: Qashqa'i Tribespeople in Post-Revolutionary Iran* (Routledge, 2014), and the co-editor of *Women in the Muslim World* (Harvard University Press, 1978), *Women in Iran from the Rise of Islam to 1800* (University of Illinois Press, 2003), and *Women in Iran from 1800 to the Islamic Republic* (University of Illinois Press, 2004).

Kristin Smith Diwan is Assistant Professor in Comparative and Regional Studies at the American University School of International Service where she specializes in Arab and Islamist politics. She received her PhD in Political Science from Harvard University and holds an MA in International Affairs from the Johns Hopkins School of Advanced International Studies. Diwan has written on the politics and political economy of the Arab Gulf states for publications such as *Geopolitics, Middle East Report, Foreign Affairs, and Foreign Policy*, and is currently completing a manuscript on the politics of Islamic finance.

Khaled Fattah holds a PhD in International Relations from the University of St Andrews. His research interests include Yemen, state–tribe relations in the Middle East, state-building in fragile states, nationalism, political violence, intercultural communication, and the role of emotions in terrorism. He has taught at three European universities and worked as a consultant for the GIZ, the EU, and various UN agencies. He is presently at Lund University, Sweden, and a visiting scholar at Carnegie Middle East Center.

Justin J. Gengler is a senior researcher at the Social and Economic Survey Research Institute of Qatar University. In 2009 he completed the first-ever mass survey of political attitudes in Bahrain as part of his doctoral dissertation for the University of Michigan, titled "Ethnic Conflict and Political Mobilization in Bahrain and the Arab Gulf." This project forms the basis of a forthcoming monograph on group conflict in the rentier state. Other recent publications include "The Political Costs of Qatar's Western Orientation," *Middle East Policy* (Winter 2012); and "Royal Factionalism, the Khawalid, and the Securitization of 'the Shi'a Problem' in Bahrain," *Journal of Arabian Studies*, 3, 1 (Spring 2013).

Fanar Haddad is Research Fellow at the Middle East Institute, National University of Singapore. He previously lectured in modern Middle Eastern politics at the University of Exeter and at Queen Mary, University of London. Prior to obtaining his DPhil, Haddad was a research analyst at the Foreign and Commonwealth Office where he worked on North Africa. He has since published widely on issues relating to historic and contemporary Iraq. His main research interests are identity, historical memory, nationalism, communal conflict, and minority politics. He is the author of *Sectarianism in Iraq: Antagonistic Visions of Unity* (London/New York: Hurst/Columbia University Press, 2011). His current research focuses on historical memory and narratives of state in the Middle East.

Laurence Louër joined the Center for International Studies and Research (CERI) at Sciences Po in 2003. She served as a permanent consultant to the Policy Planning Department of the Ministry of Foreign Affairs (CAP), and has been the editor-in-chief of the French peer-reviewed journal *Critique Internationale* since 2006. Her most recent publications include *Transnational Shia Politics: Political and Religious Networks in the Gulf* (London: Hurst, 2008) and *Shiism and Politics in the Middle East* (London: Hurst, 2012).

J.E. Peterson is a historian and political analyst specializing in the Arabian Peninsula and Gulf. He has taught at various universities in the United States and has been associated with a number of leading research institutes in the United States and the United Kingdom. Until 1999, he served in the Office of the Deputy Prime Minister for Security and Defence in Muscat, Sultanate of Oman. He is the author or editor of a dozen books, the most recent of which are *Defense and Regional Security in the Arabian Peninsula and Gulf, 1973–2004: An Annotated Bibliography* (Gulf Research Center, 2006); *Historical Muscat: An Illustrated Guide and Gazetteer* (Brill, 2007); and *Oman's Insurgencies: The Sultanate's Struggle for Supremacy* (Saqi, 2007). He has also published some forty scholarly articles in such journals and annuals as: *American Historical Review, Arab–American Affairs, Arabian Studies, Asian Affairs, Encyclopædia Britannica, Encyclopædia of Islam, Hoover Institution Yearbook on International Communist Affairs, Mediterranean Quarterly, Middle East Journal, Middle East Policy, Orbis, RUSI/Brassey's Defence Yearbook, Survival,* and *Washington Quarterly,* as well as over twenty contributions to edited works. He is presently working on a book on Oman since 1970, a historical biography of a major Saudi Arabian personality, and a modern history of Arabia.

Lawrence G. Potter is Adjunct Associate Professor of International Affairs at Columbia University, where he has taught since 1996. He also serves as Deputy Director of the Gulf/2000 Project, based at Columbia, which is the largest research and documentation project on the Persian Gulf states. A graduate of Tufts College, he received an MA in Middle Eastern Studies from the School of Oriental and African Studies, University of London, and a PhD in History from Columbia. Potter was a Visiting Fellow for 2011–12 at the Center for International and Regional Studies, Georgetown University School of Foreign Service in Qatar. From 1984 to 1992 he was Senior Editor at the Foreign Policy Association. He has edited four volumes on the Gulf, most recently *The Persian Gulf in History* (Palgrave Macmillan, 2009), and published "The Persian Gulf: Tradition and Transformation," for the Foreign Policy Association's *Headline Series* (December 2011).

Marc Valeri is Senior Lecturer in Political Economy of the Middle East and Director of the Centre for Gulf Studies at the University of Exeter. He is the author of *Oman: Politics and Society in the Qaboos State* (London/New York: Hurst/Columbia University Press, 2009) and co-editor of *Business Politics in the Middle East* (London/New York: Hurst/Oxford University Press, 2013).

INTRODUCTION

Lawrence G. Potter

In the wake of the Arab Spring and the US withdrawal from Iraq, sectarianism has taken on an increasingly ominous role in the Middle East. By 2013, sectarian conflict had reignited in Iraq and spread to Syria, where ruling Alawites were locked in bitter civil war with a Sunni resistance which dragged in the neighboring states of Turkey, Lebanon, and Jordan. The conflict in Syria, indeed, became regarded as a proxy war between Iran and Saudi Arabia and between Shiʿis and Sunnis. Nervous Sunni rulers sought to consolidate power in the face of a rising assertiveness on the part of the Shiʿi and other groups long prevented from participating fully in the life of the state. In the Persian Gulf monarchies, there was a continuing standoff between Sunni and Shiʿi in Bahrain and Saudi Arabia, and a widespread fear of Iranian irredentism. The political constellation of the region was clearly changing, and Western powers and regional states were at a loss for how to respond.

This book explores the relationship between politics and sectarian identity in the Persian Gulf states.[1] Here the theme of sectarianism is

[1] I would like to thank colleagues who read earlier versions of this chapter and offered helpful suggestions and corrections: Zahra Babar, Lois Beck, Richard Bulliet, Justin Gengler, Michael Izady, Mehran Kamrava, Karen Rohan, and Haideh Sahim. Naturally, they are not responsible for my interpretations or errors.

taken broadly and may include ethnic and tribal as well as religious groups. It can alternatively be thought of as the politics of identity, which in recent years has gained increasing prominence in the Middle East in general and the Gulf in particular. In the 1970s the question used to be why we were witnessing a religious revival among Muslims and indeed throughout the world; today the question is why we are witnessing a resurgence of sectarian identity, often with harmful implications. This book aims to contribute to a framework for understanding this issue.

Defining sectarianism is notoriously difficult. It goes back to the idea of sect, a group with distinctive religious, political, or philosophical beliefs. Most often the term has a religious connotation, in Christendom meaning a small group that has broken away from mainstream "orthodox" beliefs. In the Middle East, Western writers typically, and mistakenly, characterized Sunnis as "orthodox" Muslims, while the Shi'i were regarded as "heterodox." Sectarianism has come to have a negative connotation, denoting a group that sets itself off from society and thereby raises tensions. Haddad notes that the term "sectarianism" does not have a definitive meaning, and prefers to view such groups in Iraq as "competing subnational mass-group identities. As such, the dynamics are in essence very similar to other such competing groups, be they racial, national, ethnic, or even ideological."[2] Sectarian identities, like ethnic ones, are constantly changing and being renegotiated.[3] The term "sectarian conflict" is typically applied to religious or political struggles such as those between Protestants and Catholics in Northern Ireland, Sunni and Shi'i Muslims in Iraq, or Hindus and Muslims in India.

One question is whether sectarianism is a modern phenomenon or one that has persisted throughout history. This is difficult to answer, due to a lack of historical research on the subject in the Middle East and especially the Persian Gulf. In the view of Haddad, "an approach that insists on either a sectarian or a non-sectarian Iraq misses the point: identity, sectarian or otherwise, is ambiguous both in its meaning and its salience, hence the abundance in Iraqi history of episodes of both sectarian harmony

[2] Fanar Haddad, "Sectarian Relations and Sunni Identity in Post-Civil War Iraq," this volume, p. 67, note 1 and p. 71.

[3] Anthony D. Smith, *The Nation in History: Historiographical Debates about Ethnicity and Nationalism*, Cambridge, UK: Polity Press, 2000, p. 24, and Haddad, "Sectarian Relations and Sunni Identity," p. 75.

and, less commonly, sectarian division."[4] The issue of sectarianism is intertwined with that of ethnicity, minorities, identity, religion, and nationalism, which complicates any analysis. For example, should the series of wars fought between the Persian and Ottoman empires between the sixteenth and nineteenth centuries be regarded as conflicts between Sunni and Shi'i, or as purely political disputes?[5] What about radical religious movements, such as the Shi'i Carmathians (Qarmatis) in Bahrain in the tenth and eleventh centuries, or the Wahhabi movement which arose in Arabia in the mid-eighteenth century and aggressively sought to impose its radical version of Sunnism on the region?

There are numerous examples of factional strife in medieval Islamic society, often based on ethnic, religious, and tribal differences. For example, the Shu'ubiya movement of the eighth and ninth centuries promoted the superiority of Iranians over Arabs. This was, however, primarily a literary, not a political dispute, and eventually petered out.[6] The fact that Sunnis were in the majority in pre-Mongol Iran, especially in Khurasan, did not prevent bitter quarreling between adherents of the different law schools. Geographers and historians, indeed, identified cities by their religious affiliation. (Hanafi cities included Ray, Nishapur, and Bukhara, while Shi'i cities included Marv, Qazvin, Shiraz, Ardebil, and Kazerun).[7] The bitter warfare that erupted in Nishapur between the Hanafis and Shafi'is led directly to the city's destruction by invading Turcic tribesmen.[8] In the pre-modern era, fighting between quarters or factions in cities was not uncommon.[9] After the advent of the Safavids

[4] Fanar Haddad, "Sectarian Relations and Sunni Identity in Post-Civil War Iraq," p. 70.

[5] For an interesting discussion, see J.R. Walsh, "The Historiography of Ottoman–Safavid Relations in the Sixteenth and Seventeenth Centuries," in Bernard Lewis and P.M. Holt (eds), *Historians of the Middle East*, London: Oxford University Press, 1962, pp. 197–211. I am grateful to Prof. Neguin Yavari for this reference.

[6] Roy P. Mottahedeh, "The Shu'ubiyah Controversy and the Social History of Early Islamic Iran," *International Journal of Middle East Studies*, 7 (1976), pp. 161–82.

[7] I.M. Lapidus, "Muslim Cities and Islamic Societies," in I.M. Lapidus (ed.), *Middle Eastern Cities: A Symposium on Ancient, Islamic, and Contemporary Middle Eastern Urbanism*, Berkeley: University of California Press, 1969, p. 52.

[8] Richard W. Bulliet, *The Patricians of Nishapur: A Study in Medieval Islamic Social History*, Cambridge: Harvard University Press, 1972, esp. Chapter 3.

[9] Hossein Mirjafari, "The Haydari–Ni'mati Conflicts in Iran," trans. J.R. Perry, *Iranian Studies*, 12 (1979), pp. 135–62.

and the imposition of official Shi'ism in the early sixteenth century, it appears that religious differences were heightened.

Scholars working on recent times, however, tend to regard sectarianism as a modern phenomenon that should not be projected back into the past.[10] This perspective is bolstered by recent research on modern Lebanese history. For example, Ussama Makdisi, who reconstructed the history of sectarian identity in Ottoman Mount Lebanon, found that "sectarianism as an idea and as a practice belongs to the realm of the modern."[11] A good case can be made that many of the present-day conflicts that the popular press depict as having existed since time immemorial, such as that between Israelis and Palestinians or Arabs and Iranians, are in fact products of modern times.

The debate whether sectarianism is eternal or modern parallels the debate on the antiquity of nations. Some historians make a distinction between nations, which may be ancient, and nationalism, which is a product of modernity.[12] Most see modern nations and nationalism as not arising before the late eighteenth or nineteenth century. At least since the end of World War I and the creation of the League of Nations, "the legitimate international norm was the nation state."[13] However, other experts are not so sure: according to Anthony Smith, "put simply, modern nations are not as 'modern' as modernists would have us believe. If they were, they could not survive."[14] Smith criticizes scholars who "overplay the rupture with premodern societies and cultures."[15]

In reviewing the history of the Middle East, what is obvious is that while society was self-consciously Islamic, it was in reality a mosaic containing many groups, religions, languages, and ethnicities.[16] Most coun-

[10] Fanar Haddad, *Sectarianism in Iraq: Antagonistic Visions of Unity*, New York: Columbia University Press, 2011, p. 3.

[11] Ussama Makdisi, *The Culture of Sectarianism: Community, History, and Violence in Nineteenth-Century Ottoman Lebanon*, Berkeley: University of California Press, 2000, p. 166. I am grateful to Elizabeth C. Smith for suggestions on sources and insights about sectarianism in Lebanon.

[12] See the helpful discussion in Smith, *The Nation in History*, Chapter 2.

[13] Benedict Anderson, *Imagined Communities: Reflections on the Origin and Spread of Nationalism*, rev. edn, London: Verso, 1983, p. 113.

[14] Anthony D. Smith, *The Ethnic Origins of Nations*, Oxford: Blackwell, 1986, p. 212.

[15] Smith, *The Nation in History*, p. 58. Here he is referring to Anderson and Hobsbawm.

[16] There is a large literature on minorities in the Middle East. See, for example,

tries in the region have heterogeneous societies, made up of multiple sectarian groups, which were carved out of multinational empires. These groups, while sometimes clashing, managed to live together and coexist in the same space without erupting in the kind of clashes we have seen in the last few decades. In many Middle Eastern cities minorities lived in their own quarter or *mahallah*, and dealt with the wider world mainly through their own leaders.[17] This may have lessened the likelihood of conflict. However, the supposedly unifying effect of Islam sometimes broke down and sectarian strife erupted.

In the Ottoman Empire, people lived in their own *millets*, or religio-political communities, and were largely self-governing. As Lewis notes, the basic identification was religious, although this sometimes coincided with ethnicity, such as for the Greeks, Armenians, and Jews. "It was not until a very late date, and under the influence of European nationalist ideas, that separate ethnic *millets* began to appear."[18] Although the *millet* system was ended with the founding of the Turkish republic, "the *millet* mentality continued to control the relations between Muslims and non-Muslims. Despite the secularization of the government, Turkish-speak-

---

A.H. Hourani, *Minorities in the Arab World*, London: Oxford University Press, 1947; Richard Tapper (ed.), "Some Minorities in the Middle East," *Occasional Paper*, no. 9, London: Centre of Near and Middle Eastern Studies, June 1992; Andrew Whitley, "Minorities and the Stateless in Persian Gulf Politics," *Survival*, 35, 4 (Winter 1993), pp. 28–50; Xavier de Planhol, *Minorités en Islam: Géographie Politique et Sociale*, Paris: Flammarion, 1997; "Minorities in the Middle East: Power and the Politics of Difference," Special issue of *Middle East Report (MERIP)*, no. 200 (July–Sep. 1996); Anh Nga Longva and Anne Sofie Roald (eds), *Religious Minorities in the Middle East: Domination, Self-Empowerment, Accommodation*, Leiden: Brill, 2012; and Rasmus Christian Elling, *Minorities in Iran: Nationalism and Ethnicity after Khomeini*, New York: Palgrave Macmillan, 2013.

17 The subject of quarters in the "Islamic city" has been a staple for historians. See Masashi Haneda and Toru Miura, *Islamic Urban Studies: Historical Review and Perspectives*, London: Kegan Paul International, 1994, pp. 258–9, and two key works, Lapidus (ed.), *Middle Eastern Cities*, and A.H. Hourani and S.M. Stern (eds), "The Islamic City: A Colloquium," *Papers on Islamic History I*, Philadelphia: University of Pennsylvania Press, 1970.

18 Bernard Lewis, *The Political Language of Islam*, Chicago: University of Chicago Press, 1988, pp. 38–9. See now Maurits H. van den Boogert, "Millets: Past and Present," in Longva and Roald (eds), *Religious Minorities in the Middle East*, pp. 27–45.

ing Muslims remained the only citizens who, in practice, possessed full civil and political liberties."[19]

According to Longva:

> The twentieth century has been described as the century of minorities, or more precisely, the century when concern with the need to provide a legal framework to protect minorities gained unprecedented attention ... By the late twentieth century, minorities no longer accepted tolerance as an ideal value; instead they were demanding the right to recognition, and there are no signs that these demands will diminish.[20]

The concept of minority groups emerged after World War I and is linked with the idea of representative government, as White explains in his study of French Mandate Syria.[21] Instead of living in multinational empires, many people found themselves minorities in newly created states, and laws were introduced to protect "minority rights." "In many ways, the history of the nation-state is the history of minorities: that is, the history of the processes that lead certain groups to be defined as 'minorities.'"[22]

Due to its location as a crossroads linking East and West, with a maritime economy and cosmopolitan population, the Persian Gulf region was different from other parts of the Middle East. Because of this, society there has perhaps been less afflicted by sectarian conflicts than other parts of the region.[23] Therefore, the sectarian experience in areas such as the Ottoman Empire may not be very relevant. One characteristic of sectarianism in the Gulf is that many groups are transnational, and are often located in border areas where in the past they enjoyed considerable

[19] J.C. Hurewitz, "The Minorities in the Political Process," in Sydney N. Fisher (ed.), *Social Forces in the Middle East*, Ithaca, NY: Cornell University Press, 1955, p. 216.

[20] Anh Nga Longva, "Introduction: Domination, Self-Empowerment, Accommodation," in Longva and Roald (eds), *Religious Minorities in the Middle East*, p. 1.

[21] Benjamin Thomas White, *The Emergence of Minorities in the Middle East: The Politics of Community in French Mandate Syria*, Edinburgh: Edinburgh University Press, 2011, Chapter 1.

[22] Ibid., p. 210.

[23] Lawrence G. Potter, "Introduction," in Lawrence G. Potter (ed.), *The Persian Gulf in History*, New York: Palgrave Macmillan, 2009, pp. 1–24; also M.R. Izady, "The Gulf's Ethnic Diversity: An Evolutionary History," in Lawrence G. Potter and Gary G. Sick (eds), *Security in the Persian Gulf: Origins, Obstacles, and the Search for Consensus*, New York: Palgrave, 2002, pp. 33–90.

autonomy. This applies for example to Iranian ethnic and tribal groups such as the Baluch, Kurds, Arabs, and Turkomans. Before the modern era, peoples along the Gulf littoral shared a common maritime culture, and religious and linguistic groups were intermingled, with many Arabic speakers and Sunni Muslims located on the Persian side of the Gulf, and a Shi'i, Persian-speaking community on the Arab side. This causes difficulty when speaking of identity, for in this region people have multiple, overlapping identities that may be activated at different times.

In modern times, as noted in the chapter by Gengler, the region's unique lack of political institutions or an economic basis for class-based politics (due to the rentier economy) makes ethnic and sectarian categories the most viable bases for political coordination. This means that political coalitions in the Gulf will naturally tend to form along these same group-based distinctions. "If sectarianism is to be defined as the politicization of ethnic or religious identity, then this politicization is best understood not as a *cause* of this or that political malady afflicting Persian Gulf states, but rather as an *effect* of their particular institutional characteristics."[24]

While in the past many ethnic groups adopted a quietist stance to protect themselves, today there are powerful political and economic motivations to make themselves heard. As Beck suggests, Iran's national minorities have politicized their identities to defend their interests.[25] According to Anthony Smith:

> In the modern era, *ethnie* [ethnic communities] must become politicized, must enter and remain in the political arena, and must begin to move towards nationhood, even if they have no intentions of becoming full nations themselves. That is to say, they are forced to forsake their former isolation, passivity, and cultural accommodation, and become activist, mobilized, and politically dynamic.[26]

This leads to a number of questions. What is it about modern times that so often activates exclusivist sectarian identities, so that ostensibly religious or ethnic differences—as in the Balkans, Bahrain, Iraq, or Afghanistan—threaten to tear countries apart? To what extent is the rise of the modern state responsible for the strengthening of sectarian identities? Clearly, years of warfare have politicized identity groups,

[24] Gengler, "Understanding Sectarianism in the Persian Gulf," this volume, p. 42.
[25] Lois Beck, "Iran's Ethnic, Religious, and Tribal Minorities," this volume.
[26] Smith, *Ethnic Origins of Nations*, p. 157.

especially those based on ethnicity.[27] It has been argued that "an important 'ethnicisation' of the world is taking place and … this process is linked with modernisation—it is what we could also describe as the politicisation of culture."[28] How does identity move from a passive to an assertive state?[29] What are the triggering mechanisms that set off conflict? Should we conclude that sects are a threat to national unity? How much have major movements such as the Islamic revival or the Arab Spring served to obscure the continued salience of religious and ethnic cleavages?[30] Do outside powers play a role, and how does their response color the outcome?

Historical background

World War I destroyed balance-of-power politics as practiced in the nineteenth century, which was based on a consensus of interests. In Europe this was accompanied by the growth of secularism, the eclipse of religion, and the rise of radical ideologies such as Bolshevism and fascism. In the Middle East and Asia, the colonial rulers were committed to secularization, and they expanded the powers of formal institutions to include what had formerly been in the domain of religion, notably law and education. They did not, however, succeed in eradicating the influence of religion, especially in two key aspects: its role in legitimizing political power, and in politicizing and mobilizing the masses.

After World War II the West faced growing anticolonial revolts. Religious leaders and groups played a key role in bringing the masses into the political process in the colonies. They spearheaded opposition to colonial (often Christian) rule and led many of the nationalist movements. The British faced opposition from the Muslim Brotherhood in

[27] Timor Sharan and John Heathershaw, "Identity Politics and Statebuilding in Post-Bonn Afghanistan: The 2009 Presidential Election," *Ethnopolitics*, 10 (2011), p. 301.

[28] Thomas Hylland Eriksen, *Ethnicity and Nationalism: Anthropological Perspectives*, London: Pluto Press, 1993, p. 125.

[29] For more on this see Haddad, *Sectarianism in Iraq*, pp. 25–9.

[30] Ali Banuazizi and Myron Weiner, "Introduction," in Ali Banuazizi and Myron Weiner (eds), *The State, Religion, and Ethnic Politics: Afghanistan, Iran, and Pakistan*, Syracuse, NY: Syracuse University Press, 1986, p. 2.

Egypt; the French battled Islamic resistance in Algeria; and the Soviets put down a revolt by the Basmachis in Central Asia.

The political boundaries many new nations inherited from colonial administrators often bore little resemblance to geographic or demographic realities. Here we are reminded of the definition of the nation provided by historian Benedict Anderson as "an imagined political community."[31] In Africa, for example, the borders of many states are the same as those drawn at a conference of European diplomats in Berlin in 1884–5. These borders cut across tribal and ethnic groups, which continued to clash with each other after independence. The British carved up the Middle East and South Asia in such a way as to divide many peoples who might have opted to form national states, such as the Palestinians, the Kurds, and the Pashtuns.

As the process of decolonization gained momentum, the newly independent states faced the problem of a loss of the political order, and, in some cases, the stability provided by the old empires. The patronage of specific minority groups by colonial and later, post-colonial external actors, led to serious fissures in societies. In Lebanon, for example, Weiss found that "the Lebanese Shi'i community became sectarian under French rule,"[32] which may be partly attributed to "French colonial privileging of sectarian and subnational modes of identification."[33] Minority elites often adopted the viewpoint of their patrons on political, social, and religious issues which was not shared by the majority population. After independence, minority groups formerly favored by colonial rulers, such as the Maronites in Lebanon, Sunni Arabs in Iraq, and the Tamils in Sri Lanka, found their privileged status challenged by previously neglected majorities. Religion now became a divisive force that diverted the new nations' energies from tackling social, political, and economic issues.

With the old power systems destroyed by two world wars, there was a proliferation of new states. (The United Nations, which consisted of fifty-one countries at its founding in 1945, today consists of 193 member states.) Many of these states lacked a coherent national identity, and

[31] Anderson, *Imagined Communities*, p. 6.

[32] Max Weiss, *In the Shadow of Sectarianism: Law, Shi'ism, and the Making of Modern Lebanon*, Cambridge: Harvard University Press, 2010, p. 3.

[33] Ibid., p. 231.

people found themselves in a political centrifuge, according to political scientist Harold Isaacs. He notes that in the postwar global shakeout of power, there have been no new "larger coherences" to hold people together as in the past. Additionally, he explains: [34]

> These systems [the Ottoman, Habsburg, and Romanov empires] created a certain order in which the differences and divisions were not so much submerged as held in their orbits by the gravity of the center. The force of this gravity was physical, economic, cultural and—most heavily—psychological.[35]

Neither overarching ideologies, such as communism or Islam, nor international organizations, such as the United Nations or the Organization of Islamic Cooperation (previously Organization of the Islamic Conference), have been able to establish order. The main power blocs of the twentieth century, led by the United States and the Soviet Union, had a more difficult time enforcing discipline than did the old empires. In the present-day European Union, there is increasing ethnic tension as members assert their national interests and identities over a European one.[36] This trend is also reflected in the Persian Gulf: "instead of the GCC [Gulf Cooperation Council] becoming more inclusive and developing as an institution, it appears that the GCC leaders are growing more inward looking with, in fact, a high degree of skepticism about too much integration," according to Christian Koch, director of the Gulf Research Center Foundation.[37]

While modernization has contributed to global homogeneity, paradoxically the spread of modern communications and the shrinking of the globe (globalization) have caused political fragmentation. This has reinforced a sense of separateness and a need for security. The individual has become more aware of his group identity and those factors—such as religion, ethnic group, nationality, language, tribe, and history—that mark him out from others. Because impersonal governments have not

[34] Harold R. Isaacs, "Power and Identity: Tribalism and World Politics," *Headline Series*, no. 246, New York: Foreign Policy Association, 1979, pp. 15–18.

[35] Isaacs, "Power and Identity," p. 15.

[36] Nicholas Sambanis, "Has 'Europe' Failed?" *New York Times*, 27 Aug. 2012.

[37] Christian Koch, "A Union in Danger," Gulf Research Center Analysis, 10 Dec. 2012 (http://www.grc.net/?frm_action=view_newsletter_web&sec_code=grcanalysis&frm_module=contents&show_web_list_link=1&int_content_id=79778).

been able to fulfill this need for security, there is a longing for the reassurance of community structure, traditionally supplied by religion.

A major objective of post-colonial states was to cultivate a sense of nationalism, which would subsume differences of religion, tribalism, and ethnicity. For when national identity is weak, sectarian identity may surge. "The Middle East and Central Asia offer the most striking early twentieth-century examples of how political structures were created first and a national consciousness underpinning these new political units was constructed afterwards," according to van Schendel and Zürcher.[38]

The educational systems in Iraq and Iran since the 1920s, for example, aimed to instill such a sense of nationalism. In the Gulf Arab states, many of which achieved independence following the departure of the British in 1971, ruling families have tried to create a historical memory to reinforce their legitimacy to rule, and have given priority to stressing cultural heritage (*turath*). In the process they have emphasized their Arab, Bedouin heritage at the expense of the other groups—such as Africans, Indians, Baluch, Persians, and the Hawala[39]—who played important roles in the hybrid society that characterized the Gulf before oil. Since the founding of the GCC in 1981, another broader regional identity, that of "Khaliji" (from *khalij*, Gulf), has arisen in the Arab states of the Persian Gulf.[40]

The invention of tradition

The project of states to "invent traditions" to legitimate themselves and promote nationalism has for some time been noted by historians.[41]

[38] Willem van Schendel and Erik J. Zürcher, "Introduction: Opting Out, Opting In, Exclusion and Assimilation: States and Nations in the Twentieth Century," in Willem van Schendel and Erik J. Zürcher (eds), *Identity Politics in Central Asia and the Muslim World: Nationalism, Ethnicity and Labour in the Twentieth Century*, London: I.B. Tauris, 2001, p. 7.

[39] The Hawala were Sunni Arabs who migrated from the Arab side of the Gulf to Iran, probably starting in the eighteenth century, and later returned. They have played an important role in some of the GCC states.

[40] Madawi Al-Rasheed, "Introduction: Localizing the Transnational and Transnationalizing the Local," in Madawi Al-Rasheed (ed.), *Transnational Connections and the Arab Gulf*, London: Routledge, 2005, p. 4. Also Fred H. Lawson, "From Here We Begin: A Survey of Scholarship on the International Relations of the Gulf," *British Journal of Middle Eastern Studies*, 36, 3 (Dec. 2009), p. 351.

[41] Eric Hobsbawm and Terence Ranger (eds), *The Invention of Tradition*, Cam-

Nations, Eric Hobsbawm points out, "rest on exercises in social engineering."[42] Even if artificially constructed, however, "it is useful to remind ourselves that nations inspire love, and often profoundly self-sacrificing love."[43] State projects designed to invent national identities and traditions are a significant factor affecting sectarian relations. In the region under discussion, Iran alone retains a well-established historic identity, on a par with a few other countries like Egypt, China, India, and Japan.[44]

In the GCC states, governments are keen to distinguish one state from another and construct histories that reflect this. The Gulf monarchies all have national flags, anthems, emblems, and official narratives aimed at promoting loyalty and national identity. Yet the traditions they are honoring, like camel racing, are largely newly created.[45] In Qatar, "the writing of national history and the presentation of history to the world is almost completely monopolized by the state and the Emiri Diwan (executive council)."[46] Gengler gives a pertinent example in the celebration of National Day in Qatar, designed to show allegiance to the ruling Al Thani family.[47]

In the Gulf states, minorities are routinely excluded from the governing process. According to Andrew Whitley, "the idea that minorities should be accorded separate status remains a foreign presumption on much of the Arabian Peninsula. That their vulnerability demands protection from the state—against discrimination, exploitation or violence—is even harder for most local rulers to understand."[48]

---

bridge: Cambridge University Press, 1983. However, Anthony Smith is uneasy with this concept, as it does not explain why so many of these "cultural artifacts" are so successful (Smith, *Nation in History*, p. 57).

[42] Eric Hobsbawm, "Introduction: Inventing Traditions," in *The Invention of Tradition*, pp. 12–13.

[43] Anderson, *Imagined Communities*, p. 141.

[44] Abbas Amanat, "Iranian Identity Boundaries: A Historical Overview," in Abbas Amanat and Farzin Vejdani (eds), *Iran Facing Others: Identity Boundaries in a Historical Perspective*, New York: Palgrave Macmillan, 2012, p. 20.

[45] Sulayman Khalaf, "Poetics and Politics of Newly Invented Traditions in the Gulf: Camel Racing in the United Arab Emirates," *Ethnology*, 39, 3 (Summer 2000), pp. 243–61.

[46] Allen J. Fromherz, *Qatar: A Modern History*, Washington, DC: Georgetown University Press, 2012, p. 14.

[47] National Day was celebrated for the first time in 2007. See Justin Gengler, "Understanding Sectarianism in the Persian Gulf," p. 54.

[48] Whitley, "Minorities and the Stateless in Persian Gulf Politics," pp. 28–9.

History is usually written by the majority, and "by writing 'national' history they affirm the majority's existence in the present and project it back into the past; in doing so, they also assimilate the history of the state to that of the nation."[49] In the Gulf monarchies, the Shi'i, despite their numbers, have been written out of the official narrative. In Saudi Arabia and Bahrain, Shi'i communities cherish the memory of a "golden age" before their conquest by Sunni or Wahhabi outsiders in the eighteenth and nineteenth century.[50] They are not permitted to serve in the police and army, which has opened a role for neighboring Sunnis, especially the Baluch, in Gulf militaries.[51] In Bahrain, the ruling Al Khalifa family established a strong tradition of "differential treatment" of Bahrain's communities.[52]

The way the majority treats minorities is also an issue in Iran. For example, according to Beck, "Persians have often seemed oblivious to other ethnic peoples in Iran, or they disregarded them, considered them inconsequential ..."[53] The problem of identifying uniform traits among the ill-defined "Persian" community in Iran is difficult, and the same could be said had our analysis been extended to Afghanistan for the large but somewhat artificial category of "Tajik."[54]

As Smith observes, "central to the concept of the nation is citizenship."[55] The fact that the majority of residents in the GCC states are not citizens and probably never will be is worrying for the region's future stability. The groups that are not of Najdi heritage, such as the Swahili, Indians, and Baluch in Oman, the Africans and Persians in the UAE, and the native Baharna in Bahrain, have been alienated by the newly created nationalisms. In Iran, Sunnis and many tribal groups, not to

[49] White, *Emergence of Minorities in the Middle East*, p. 211.

[50] Laurence Louër, *Transnational Shia Politics: Religious and Political Networks in the Gulf*, New York: Columbia University Press, 2008, Chapter 1, "Imposed States," pp. 11–44.

[51] The most prominent examples of this are in Oman and Bahrain. See J.E. Peterson, "The Baluch Presence in the Persian Gulf," this volume, pp. 234–38.

[52] Kristin Smith Diwan, "Royal Factions, Ruling Strategies, and Sectarianism in Bahrain," this volume, p. 161.

[53] Beck, "Iran's Ethnic, Religious, and Tribal Minorities," p. 293.

[54] See the illuminating discussion in Beck, "Iran's Ethnic, Religious, and Tribal Minorities," pp. 260–66; Thomas Barfield, *Afghanistan: A Cultural and Political History*, Princeton: Princeton University Press, 2010, p. 26.

[55] Smith, *Ethnic Origins of Nations*, p. 165.

mention the religious minorities, recall a history of discrimination which reinforces their estrangement from the Tehran government. The clerical regime even tries to control the Sunni seminaries there.[56]

Recent developments

The alienation that had begun to emerge in the 1960s sparked a religious revival in many countries in the 1970s, notably Liberation Theology in Latin America and the Islamic revival in the Middle East.[57] This led to the rise of charismatic religious and political figures such as Ayatollah Khomeini in Iran. Since the Iranian Revolution of 1978–9, violence has increasingly been carried out in the name of religion in the Middle East and South Asia. The Islamic revival alarmed the United States and other Western countries, which had associated Islam with stagnation and regarded it as a fatalistic faith which impeded progress. The West associated the new "political Islam" with revolutionary activity and violence. Shi'ism became a feared ideology among Sunnis, and tensions rose in Gulf states with Shi'i minorities. In Saudi Arabia, the Shi'i of the Eastern Province abandoned the traditional quietism they had adopted after the conquest by the Al Sa'ud in 1913 to launch the intifada of Muharram 1400 [November 1979].[58]

Iran's efforts to export its revolution to the Gulf coincided with the brutal Iran–Iraq War, which lasted for almost a decade (1980–8) and, aside from the horrendous casualties and damage that resulted, poisoned political discourse and served to accelerate sectarian discord in the region. In both Iran and Iraq, but especially the latter, the demonization of the opponent led to a stronger sense of national identity. Iran's calculation that the Shi'is in southern Iraq would rally to its cause and Iraq's conviction that the Arab citizens of Khuzistan would welcome the Iraqi army as their liberators were both wrong. The war helped the revolutionary government in Tehran to consolidate power and distracted attention from pressing social and economic problems. It was only when the leadership feared the revolution was in danger that Khomeini

[56] Hossein Aryan, "Clerical Regime Looks to Impose Control over Iran's Sunni Seminaries," RFE/RI, 12 Aug. 2011, http://www.rferl.mobi/a/24295121/p3.html

[57] Lawrence G. Potter, "Religion in World Politics: Why the Resurgence?" in *Great Decisions 1986*, New York: Foreign Policy Association, 1986, pp. 75–85.

[58] Louër, *Transnational Shia Politics*, pp. 161–7.

decided to "drink poison" by accepting the UN ceasefire proposal that had been on the table for a year.

Aside from the military encounter, Iran and Iraq waged a fierce struggle on the ideological and propaganda fronts. They invoked several broad themes: Arab against Persian, Sunni against Shi'i, and pan-Arabism against pan-Islam. Such discourse served to reinforce mutual hostility even after the war had ended.[59] The hardening of negative mutual perceptions between Sunni and Shi'i was thus a direct outcome of the Iran–Iraq War.[60] Frequent bickering over the proper name of the Gulf in the period since, whether Persian or Arabian, has continued to sour the atmosphere.[61] In times of Arab–Iranian tension, old disputes about sovereignty over the Shatt al-Arab and Abu Musa and the Tunb islands predictably heat up.[62]

The political priority for Iraqi governments from 1920 to 1990 was to create a national identity that would subsume differences of ethnicity, religion, and tribe. An Iraqi nationalism arose that was tested and reaffirmed by the war with Iran, in which Iraqis fought for their country and were not swayed by the religious appeals of Ayatollah Khomeini. However, in the wake of war and the violent uprising of Kurds and Shi'i Arabs in 1991, Saddam's government, in an attempt to divide his opponents, instituted a process of "retribalization," in which subnational identities were emphasized and Sunni Arabs were firmly on top. This policy went against everything Ba'thism stood for and has contributed to the unraveling of Iraq in the post-Saddam era. A key turning point in Iraq was the Shi'i revolts in the south in the spring of 1991 after the war ended, when Saddam's forces reportedly arrived in Karbala with banners declaring "no more Shi'i after today."[63]

[59] Lawrence G. Potter and Gary G. Sick, "Introduction," in Lawrence G. Potter and Gary G. Sick (eds), *Iran, Iraq, and the Legacies of War*, New York: Palgrave Macmillan, 2004, pp. 1–9.

[60] See Abdullah K. Alshayji, "Mutual Realities, Perceptions, and Impediments Between the GCC States and Iran" and Bijan Khajehpour-Khoei, "Mutual Perceptions in the Persian Gulf Region: An Iranian Perspective," in Potter and Sick (eds), *Security in the Persian Gulf*, pp. 217–37 and 239–51.

[61] Potter, "Introduction," *Persian Gulf in History*, pp. 15–16.

[62] Richard Schofield, "Anything but Black and White: A Commentary on the Lower Gulf Islands Dispute," in *Security in the Persian Gulf*, pp. 172–3.

[63] Haddad regards this as a key development, although he questions its historical accuracy. See *Sectarianism in Iraq*, p. 73.

A Shi'i revival?

The fall of the Saddam government in 2003 led to a major change in the status of Shi'is throughout the region and enhanced the power of Iran. For the first time Iraq had a Shi'i-led government, and Sunnis in Iraq, as well as the Gulf monarchies, were on the defensive. In the opinion of Vali Nasr, "by liberating and empowering Iraq's Shiite majority, the Bush administration helped launch a broad Shiite revival that will upset the sectarian balance in Iraq and the Middle East for years to come."[64] Furthermore, the post-Saddam Middle East "will not be defined by the Arab identity or by any particular form of national government. Ultimately, the character of the region will be decided in the crucible of Shia revival and the Sunni response to it."[65] Nasr sees a contest for power between the Shi'i and Sunni, first in Iraq, and later throughout the region.[66] By 2013 these warnings seemed prescient.

The sudden ascendance of Iraq's Shi'is, while gratifying to Iran, frightened Sunni governments who were apprehensive about the loyalty of their own Shi'i minorities. Clearly, the old familiar order was changing. In December 2004 King Abdullah of Jordan warned that if the new Iraqi government fell under Iranian influence, a "crescent" of Shi'i movements would emerge, threatening Sunni governments as well as posing a problem for US interests.[67] Former Egyptian President Hosni Mubarak, reflecting usually unstated anxieties, said in April 2006 that "Shiites are mostly always loyal to Iran and not the countries where they live."[68] As noted in the chapters by Gengler, Louër, and Diwan, the Shi'is were now perceived as a security problem, not just a religious group.[69]

Other experts disagree on the nature of the Shi'i revival. The Shi'i, they note, do not constitute a united bloc, and the Shi'is living in the

[64] Vali Nasr, "When the Shiites Rise," *Foreign Affairs* (July–Aug. 2006), p. 58.

[65] Vali Nasr, *The Shia Revival: How Conflicts within Islam Will Shape the Future*, New York: Norton, 2007, p. 22.

[66] Nasr, *The Shia Revival*, p. 24.

[67] *Washington Post*, 8 Dec. 2004.

[68] Cited in Vali Nasr, "When the Shiites Rise," p. 67. This is reminiscent of the question of the loyalty of Catholics to the pope in medieval Europe.

[69] Gengler, "Understanding Sectarianism in the Persian Gulf," p. 58; Louër, "The State and Sectarian Identities in the Persian Gulf Monarchies," this volume, pp. 124–25; Diwan notes the rise of a "security state" in Bahrain in "Royal Factions, Ruling Strategies, and Sectarianism in Bahrain," pp. 162–68.

Arab states of the Gulf are divided over their allegiance to Iran. Najaf is now a competitor with Qom for students and influence in the Shiʿi world. As Louër puts it, "the time is over when the Islamic republic could claim unconditional allegiance from all the Shia Islamic movements. Hence, the time is over when one could analyse them as mere proxies of Iranian foreign policy."[70] Louër found that the 1990s and 2000s "could be described as that of the failure of the transnational project and the triumph of the states."[71] In contrast to Sunni groups like al-Qaeda, Shiʿi groups are focused on local and not transnational issues.[72] The implication is that despite the multiple identities of people in states such as Iraq or Afghanistan (not to mention Iran or Saudi Arabia), they are not likely to break up.

According to Valeri, "the variety of situations encountered by Shiʿa in the Arab world suggests that delimiting a transcendent 'Shiʿi agenda' is hazardous. To be more specific, the 'crescent' thesis contributes to an obscuring of the complex social dynamics of Shiʿi Islam in the Arabian peninsula."[73] In contrast to the oppositional role of the Shiʿi in Bahrain and Saudi, in Kuwait, Qatar, Oman, and the UAE the Shiʿi are more recent arrivals and are largely loyal to Sunni ruling families. Some Shiʿi in the Gulf states have proclaimed their loyalty in hopes of escaping persecution, while others are successful merchants with a stake in the status quo. In Oman, for example, the Lawatiyya group sought to demonstrate its allegiance to the sultan so as not to be tarnished with an Iranian brush.[74] Such expressions were rewarded. In Saudi Arabia during the 1980s, the government permitted displays of Shiʿi religiosity and promoted some development in Shiʿi-majority areas, mostly in the Eastern Province.[75] However, the events of the Arab Spring, the GCC invasion of Bahrain, and the prospect of the permanent subjugation of the Baharna once again has set back inter-communal relations.

[70] Louër, *Transnational Shia Politics*, p. 218.

[71] Ibid., p. 223.

[72] Ibid., pp. 299–300.

[73] Marc Valeri, "High Visibility, Low Profile: The Shiʿa in Oman Under Sultan Qaboos," *International Journal of Middle East Studies*, 42 (2010), p. 251.

[74] Marc Valeri, "Identity Politics and Nation-Building under Sultan Qaboos," this volume, pp. 196–98.

[75] Louër, *Transnational Shia Politics*, p. 166.

Role of outsiders

It is important to note the role of outsiders in activating and sustaining sectarian identity. The United States, for example, played a significant role in promoting sectarian identity after the wars to "liberate" Iraq and Afghanistan. According to Adnan Pachachi, veteran Iraqi diplomat and politician, "perhaps the most serious mistake the United States made was to organize the new political system in Iraq on a sectarian basis."[76] The Iraqi Governing Council appointed in July 2003 by the Coalition Provisional Authority, and the cabinet it appointed in turn, each contained thirteen Shi'i Arab members, five Sunni Arabs, five Kurds, one Turkoman, and one Christian (Assyrian, Chaldean or Armenian). Subsequent Iraqi cabinets had a similar breakdown, and excluded former Ba'athists who were Sunni. This practice, along with the identification of political parties with ethnic or religious groups, has led some to wonder whether Iraq was a viable state or could break up.[77] The United States took a similar approach in Afghanistan: "the task of rebuilding Afghanistan from its earliest stages was an exercise in institutionalization of the role of ethnicity in the state, rather than building the institutions in such a way that they would de-ethnicize politics by design gradually."[78] Such practices mimic the sectarian structure of governance in Lebanon established in the unwritten National Pact of 1943, modified by the Taif Agreement of 1989. Under this pact, the president must be a Maronite Christian, the prime minister a Sunni Muslim, and the speaker of parliament a Shi'i Muslim.

The Arab Spring

The Arab awakening that began in early 2011 and rapidly spread throughout the Middle East again called attention to sectarian issues. Interestingly, the calls for change in the leadership of Arab states were

[76] Adnan Pachachi, "The Road to Failure in Iraq," War Blog, *New York Times*, 4 Apr. 2013, http://atwar.blogs.nytimes.com/2013/04/04the-road-to-failur-pin-iraq/?smid=fb-share

[77] Lawrence G. Potter, "The Persian Gulf: Tradition and Transformation," *Headline Series*, nos. 333–4, New York: Foreign Policy Association, 2011, p. 56.

[78] Shayeq Qassem, "Afghanistan: Imperatives of Stability Misperceived," *Iranian Studies*, 42, 2 (Apr. 2009), p. 264.

largely of secular, not religious, inspiration. Whereas demands by the opposition in the past were often fueled by slogans like "Islam is the solution" and advocated the creation of Islamic states, this time a religious agenda was conspicuously absent. Nevertheless, in countries such as Egypt, partly due to their superior organizational resources, religious groups like the Muslim Brotherhood initially emerged as the big winners of the Arab Spring.

The fall of dictators, however, has also reignited sectarian tensions as people seek to settle old scores and reach for power. "Sectarianism is an old wound in the Middle East," according to Nasr. "But the recent popular urge for democracy, national unity and dignity has opened it and made it feel fresh. This is because many of the Arab governments that now face the wrath of protesters are guilty of both suppressing individual rights and concentrating power in the hands of minorities."[79] In Egypt, following the overthrow of President Hosni Mubarak, there was an escalation of attacks on Coptic churches and the tombs of Sufi saints: "the increasing Islamization of politics in post-Mubarak Egypt has badly damaged the democratic credentials of the revolution by deepening the inequities between Muslims and Christians—and creating new ones."[80] Conflict is not only inter-confessional—it has also broken out between strict Islamic groups influenced by Salafis and Wahhabis and more moderate expressions of Islam such as Sufism. In Libya and Mali, Islamic militants have destroyed Sufi shrines.[81]

In Iraq, with the departure of US troops, the Shi'i government of Prime Minister Nuri al-Maliki became increasingly authoritarian and continued to question the loyalty of Sunnis. "Not since the worst days of Shia–Sunni warfare in 2006–08 has sectarian polarization presented such a threat to the country's integrity," according to analyst Rend al-Rahim.[82] In April 2013 the UN warned that Iraq was at a "crossroads"

[79] Vali Nasr, "If the Arab Spring Turns Ugly," *New York Times*, 28 Aug. 2011.

[80] Mariz Tadros, "Sectarianism and Its Discontents in Post-Mubarak Egypt," *Middle East Report*, 259 (Summer 2011), p. 27.

[81] "Militants Seek to Destroy Mali Shrines," *New York Times*, 1 July 2012; David D. Kirkpatrick, "Libya Officials Seem Helpless as Sufi Shrines are Vandalized," *New York Times*, 29 Aug. 2012, p. A5.

[82] Rend al-Rahim, "Iraq is still held back by sectarian violence and politics," *The Guardian*, 19 Feb. 2013 (online). Available at Available at http://www.theguardian.com/commentisfree/2013/feb/19/sectarianism-divides-iraq-again

and appealed for restraint.[83] According to the International Crisis Group, "the war in Syria also plays a significant part: as the conflict intensifies, Sunni Arabs experience mounting solidarity with their brethren next door and share feelings of hostility toward a purported Shiite axis linking Hizbollah, Damascus, Baghdad and Tehran."[84]

The Gulf monarchs responded to the Arab Spring with fear and indecision, and attempted to buy off or co-opt potential opposition. It also led to the novel idea that Jordan and Morocco might join the Gulf Cooperation Council, highlighting its nature as a club of Sunni monarchs. The GCC's military intervention in Bahrain in March 2011, which featured a Saudi-dominated ground force of several thousand troops, led to a significant heightening of sectarian tensions. While the Gulf rulers have always stuck together, this was the first time the GCC Peninsula Shield Force had been sent to intervene in a member's internal affairs. "The consensus [of GCC countries] is that no popular uprising in the Gulf can be allowed to succeed, that no concessions will be made because of public protests, and that under no circumstances are Shi'ites to be accorded greater influence," according to Bernard Haykel of Princeton University.[85]

The possibility that the Sunni monarchy in Bahrain could be overthrown by its Shi'i majority was a red line for the Saudis, who feared that their own Shi'i community would be encouraged to revolt should the Al Khalifa fall. Saudi Shi'is have carried out anti-regime protests since 2011 which have been met with state repression.[86] Although opposition to the Bahraini government was not strictly a sectarian affair—Sunnis also took part and in some cases even led demonstrations—Shi'is were at the forefront of protest activity as they have suffered the brunt of discrimination. The government, moreover, acted quickly to frame the conflict as one

83 "UN Warns Iraq at Crossroads as 195 Killed," *Kuwait Times*, 27 Apr. 2013, reprinted in *Gulf in the Media*, Gulf Research Center.

84 International Crisis Group—Conflict Alert, "Iraq After Hawija: Recovery or Collapse?," 26 Apr. 2013, http://www.crisisgroup.org/en/publication-type/alerts/2013/iraq-alert.aspx

85 Bernard Haykel, "Saudi Arabia and Qatar in a Time of Revolution," *Gulf Analysis Paper*, Washington, DC: Center for Strategic and International Studies, Feb. 2013, p. 4.

86 Toby Matthiesen, "A 'Saudi Spring?' The Shi'a Protest Movement in the Eastern Province 2011–2012," *Middle East Journal*, 66, 4 (Autumn 2012), pp. 628–59.

pitting loyalist Sunnis against Iranian-backed Shiʿis, thus demonizing the Shiʿi-led opposition and dissuading Sunnis who had their own political grievances from joining the revolt. A new, more ideological discourse now arose, reflecting Wahhabi anti-Shiʿi attitudes.[87]

The politics of identity: a framework for understanding

Despite the daily headlines of ethnic and religious conflict, there is a glaring absence of analysis of sectarian strife in the Persian Gulf region.[88] According to Gengler, "this lack of an objective analytical framework with which to study the politicization of ascriptive group identities across country contexts has given rise to … a tendency toward description or narration of the phenomenon of sectarianism, rather than explanation." At the same time, there is "the opposite tendency: to deny the independent significance of ethnic or religious distinctions, and indeed to avoid altogether the word 'sectarianism,' now criticized as simplistic, derogatory, and smacking of Orientalism."[89]

Governments do not encourage and may even actively hinder investigating such topics; in pursuing his research in Iraq, Haddad found that sectarian politics was a taboo subject.[90] The same applied to Gengler's research in Bahrain even before the uprising of 2008–9. In Iran, researchers will not receive visas if they want to study the Baluch or Kurds, or Sunnis in general. A recent book on Iranian minorities had to be written without the benefit of fieldwork, and is mainly based on articles in Iranian newspapers and academic journals.[91] Studying the Shiʿi community in Bahrain at this time is hazardous and it is very hard for foreign scholars to obtain visas. As a result, there is a lack of reliable demographic data for many of these states, and some basic facts are

[87] Diwan, "Royal Factions, Ruling Strategies, and Sectarianism in Bahrain," p. 170.
[88] Two major studies have just been published: Toby Matthiesen, *Sectarian Gulf: Bahrain, Saudi Arabia, and the Arab Spring that Wasn't*, Palo Alto, CA: Stanford University Press, 2013 and Geneive Abdo, "The New Sectarianism: The Arab Uprisings and the Rebirth of the Shiʿa–Sunni Divide," *Analysis Paper*, 29, Washington, DC: Brookings Institution, Saban Center for Middle East Policy, Apr. 2013. Forthcoming is Frederic M. Wehrey, *Sectarian Politics in the Gulf: From the Iraq War to the Arab Uprisings*, New York: Columbia University Press, 2014.
[89] Gengler, "Understanding Sectarianism in the Persian Gulf," p. 33.
[90] Haddad, *Sectarianism in Iraq*, p. 1.
[91] Elling, *Minorities in Iran*, p. 11.

disputed—for example, many Sunnis in Iraq and Bahrain think they are in the majority.

It is clearly risky to generalize about groups such as the Sunni or Shi'i. Such branches of Islam are too large to be meaningful indicators of behavior, which is why alarm over a rising "Shi'i crescent" is misplaced and may be confused with fear of Iranian irredentism. As Haddad found in Iraq, using these terms is inescapable, but many factors affect their meaning and relevance, including class, geography, and degree of piety.[92] His research revealed that sectarian identities are constantly changing and being renegotiated. Rather than unified, the Shi'i communities in Iran and Iraq are divided, with many clerics competing for leadership. The most prominent cleric outside Iran at present is Ali Sistani in Iraq, whom many Arab Shi'i in the Gulf emulate. But Sistani does not endorse the Iranian version of *velayat-e faqih*, according to which clerics rule directly, and Shi'i in the Gulf are likewise split in allegiance.

The factors that trigger sectarian conflict, especially wars, are also important to understand. There appears to be a pattern of challenge and response in which increased activity on the part of one group stimulates activity by another, often counter group. Thus in Iraq, "the more Baghdad imposes its will on Sunni areas, the greater the chances for wider sectarian unrest."[93] The rise of the Shi'is in Iraq since 2003 and the recent troubles in Bahrain have stimulated interest on the part of Sunnis in their own identity, and have led to a search for cultural symbols with which they can identify.[94] In Lebanon also, this has led to a "Sunni awakening."[95] Likewise, relentless government-promoted Shi'ism in Iran and Wahhabism in Saudi Arabia have led to greater popularity for Sufism in both states.[96]

[92] Haddad, *Sectarianism in Iraq*, p. 4.

[93] Ned Parker, "The Iraq We Left Behind: Welcome to the World's Next Failed State," *Foreign Affairs* (Mar.–Apr. 2012), p. 109.

[94] Haddad, "Sectarian Relations and Sunni Identity in Post-Civil War Iraq," pp. 107–11; Justin Gengler, "Are Bahrain's Sunnis Still Awake?" in *Sada: Analysis of Arab Reform*, Washington, DC: Carnegie Endowment for International Peace, 25 June 2012.

[95] Abdo, "The New Sectarianism," pp. 48–50.

[96] Beck, "Iran's Ethnic, Religious, and Tribal Minorities," p. 290. There reportedly has been a resurgence of Sufism in Hijaz.

The role of the state

According to Professor Eric Davis, "the ethnoconfessional model has yet to grapple with the problem of weak states in many Middle Eastern countries. It fails to recognize the extent to which 'sectarian entrepreneurs' exploit the political vacuum created by an absent state that is either unable or unwilling to deliver necessary social services or protect its citizenry."[97] A recurring observation in this volume is that sectarian differences and competition are encouraged and manipulated by states in order to further their own political interests. In the absence of alternative options to form civil society groups and political parties which could threaten the government on ideological grounds, people are driven back into primordial identities such as tribe and religion. Gengler finds that "electoral laws, bans or limits on political parties, and other legal regulations organize how citizens may interact with the state, but they also exert a decisive influence on how citizens cooperate and vie with each other. In the Gulf context, these institutions privilege and in many cases are designed precisely to encourage political competition on the basis of latent social distinctions—especially religious and tribal affiliations—a fact that helps explain further the region's tendency toward sectarian and other identity-based politics rather than cross-societal, issue-based coalitions."[98]

In Oman, the state blatantly manipulates tribal and other differences and has prevented the emergence of non-sectarian identifications, such as social class or ideology, which have broader capacities to gather support and challenge the current order, according to Valeri.[99] In Bahrain, Diwan argues that "sectarian strife is not simply the product of entrenched communal divisions; rather it is contingent upon choices made by the ruling elite."[100] In Iran, especially since the media freedom of the Khatami years (1997–2005), "ethnic politics have gained a new salience." According to Kaveh Bayat, "contemporary ethnic politics in Iran is, in a sense, the offspring of the Islamic Republic."[101]

[97] Eric Davis, "A Sectarian Middle East?" *International Journal of Middle East Studies*, 40, 4 (Nov. 2008), p. 557.

[98] Gengler, "Understanding Sectarianism in the Persian Gulf," p. 44.

[99] Valeri, "Identity Politics and Nation-Building under Sultan Qaboos," pp. 179–80.

[100] Diwan, "Royal Factions, Ruling Strategies, and Sectarianism in Bahrain," p. 143.

[101] Kaveh Bayat, "The Ethnic Question in Iran," *Middle East Report*, 237 (Winter 2005), pp. 42–5; quotes are on pp. 43 and 45.

Interference with and manipulation of sectarian groups also extends beyond the state. According to Fattah, "the dynamic interactions of local, national, regional, and international politics has made sectarian conflict in Yemen less localized and increasingly internationalized."[102] This also applies elsewhere in the region. Alluding to Qatar and Saudi Arabia, the Iraqi prime minister complained in September 2012 that "some governments" were spending a great deal of money providing assistance to Syrian rebels, thus heightening Sunni–Shi'i tension.[103] An Iranian parliamentary committee, for its part, referred to its option of "interfering" in Kuwait to protect the country's Shi'ites.[104] In May 2013 a leading Sunni cleric, Shaikh Yusef al-Qaradawi, who is Egyptian but based in Qatar, issued a fatwa calling on Muslims everywhere to assist the rebels in Syria.[105] Some analysts have discerned the rise of a new Sunni bloc linking Egypt, Qatar, and Turkey, led by Islamists and funded by Gulf Arabs, to resist the Shi'i upsurge and counter Iranian influence.[106] However, the religious aspect of this should not be overestimated.[107]

Outside powers are also implicated in stoking regional turmoil. In the case of Baluchistan, for example, "external support thus plays an important role in determining the outcome of secessionist movements, including why so few ultimately succeed," according to Rajshree Jetly.[108] According to a Yemeni scholar, "in many parts of the Arab Middle East,

[102] Khaled Fattah, "Yemen: Sectarianism and the Politics of Regime Survival," this volume, p. 228.

[103] "Some Regimes in ME Funding Sectarianism, says Maliki," *Gulf Today*, 21 Sep. 2012, posted by Gulf Research Center.

[104] "Iran to 'Protect Kuwait Shiites,'" *Kuwait Times*, 15 Sep. 2012, posted by Gulf Research Center.

[105] Anne Barnard and Hwaida Saad, "Sunni Cleric Issues Appeal for World's Muslims to Help Syrian Rebels," *New York Times*, 2 June 2013, p. 8.

[106] Neil MacFarquhar, "Mideast Shift: Sunnis Gain," *New York Times*, 28 Nov. 2012.

[107] According to Mehran Kamrava, "there is little evidence to suggest that at least in their mutual interactions, Iran and Saudi Arabia use religion for anything other than instrumentalist purposes." See "Iranian Foreign and Security Policies in the Persian Gulf," in Mehran Kamrava (ed.), *International Politics of the Persian Gulf*, Syracuse, NY: Syracuse University Press, 2011, p. 195.

[108] Rajshree Jetly, "Baluch Ethnicity and Nationalism (1971–81): An Assessment," *Asian Ethnicity*, 5, 1 (2004), p. 21.

particularly in countries with pro-Washington regimes, the consequences of the War on Terror resulted in further delegitimization of the ruling elites, further radicalization of opposition groups, and the surfacing of decades-old accumulated feelings of frustration and anger."[109] At the same time, as Davis points out, "the ethnoconfessional model enables external actors, particularly the United States, to avoid taking responsibility for their contribution to the region's problems."[110]

Conclusion

The upsurge of sectarian and ethnic conflict in the Persian Gulf states is likely to continue since the factors that foster it persist: heated rhetoric as reflected in the media, conflict or potential conflict, the questionable political legitimacy of rulers, and a longing for security and participation that is not being met. Such tensions are being exploited by governments which seek to divide in order to rule, and in the misguided attempts by outside powers to redress sectarian discrimination. Today, human rights organizations and diasporic communities, as well as extensive Internet and blog activity, continuously shine a spotlight on abuses.[111]

The problems in the Gulf more often arise from political, security, and economic concerns than for religious reasons. Rami Khouri, editor-at-large of *The Daily Star* (Beirut) writes:

> It is easy and convenient to speak of Bahrain as a Sunni–Shiite conflict, or Syria as a problem of a ruling Alawite minority … [but] that misses the main point, which is that the common Arab governance problem is not ethnicity- or sect-specific, but is more about curtailed and denied rights for all citizens, whether in Syria, Bahrain, Sudan, Iraq under the Baathists, or any other modern Arab state.[112]

The background to current sectarian tensions includes political events such as the Iran–Iraq War, the fall of Saddam Hussein and the ensuing civil war in Iraq, and most recently the Arab Spring. At present, the standoff over Iran's nuclear program has raised tensions in the Persian

[109] Fattah, "Yemen: Sectarianism and the Politics of Regime Survival," p. 227.
[110] Davis, "A Sectarian Middle East?" p. 555.
[111] Eliz Sanasarian, "Nationalism and Religion in Contemporary Iran," in *Religious Minorities in the Middle East*, pp. 309–10.
[112] Rami G. Khouri, "The Case of Bahrain," Agence Global, 7 May 2012, http://www.agenceglobal.com/index.php?show=article&Tid=2790

Gulf to dangerous levels. Regional states believe they are in a vulnerable position and are threatened by transnational forces they cannot control. Over the last decade the information revolution has had a powerful effect on people living in the Gulf states by informing them much more quickly and fully about developments in their own as well as neighboring states. Governments have lost their monopoly on controlling information. The start of broadcasting by Al Jazeera in 1996 has changed the regional discourse with many formerly forbidden subjects discussed, sometimes heatedly, including religious and sectarian issues.

Ethnic and sectarian conflict is not inevitable; part of the problem is that the literature focuses on conflict situations rather than peaceful cooperation and gives the impression of religious minorities as passive victims.[113] Diversity does not have to lead to conflict, and the term "sectarianism" is invoked too readily as an explanation for various problems. Haddad maintains that "'sectarianism' is viewed with profound disdain by the vast majority of Arab Iraqis" and could be mitigated if governments moderated discrimination against minority groups.[114] The overt use of symbols by the state—such as those associated with Shi'ism in Iraq—should be reconsidered so that other groups are not offended. Where some see this as merely an assertion of identity, others regard it as a provocation which encourages competing narratives of victimhood.[115] Participation in government is also important to reduce tensions; thus Sunnis in Iraq and Shi'is in Bahrain and Saudi Arabia should be accorded greater voice. Likewise the universal exclusion of Shi'is from militaries in the GCC states deprives them of jobs and makes them feel untrusted. Much of the reason for their protest, even if expressed in religious idiom, is actually economic; this is something in the power of the state to improve. Louër demonstrates that in the past Bahraini governments, even if they discriminated against Shi'is, could show flexibility—what she calls "pragmatic sectarianism"—if necessary.[116]

Government policies have served to inflame sectarian and ethnic identities, and different policies could mitigate the situation. States

[113] Longva, "Introduction: Domination, Self-empowerment, Accommodation," in *Religious Minorities in the Middle East*, p. 3.

[114] Haddad, "Sectarian Relations and Sunni Identity in Post-Civil War Iraq," p. 77.

[115] Ibid., pp. 84–93.

[116] Louër, "The State and Sectarian Identities in the Persian Gulf Monarchies," p. 142.

need to be persuaded that it is better for them, and will increase their security, to include rather than exclude minority groups in economic, social, and political life. After all, the demand of groups such as Saudi Shi'is or the Iranian Baluch is not for separate states, but for recognition and respect in the state in which they find themselves. Governments also need to be sensitive to the fact that minority groups resent being marginalized and excluded from the "official version" of history. If not corrected, competing historical memories and narratives will continue to foster resentment.

Multiethnic states are the historical norm in the region and it seems unlikely that they will break up. Although outsiders have speculated whether Iraq will remain a unified state, this has not been a question for most Iraqis (or Afghans for that matter), who are secure in a national identity and have not sought secession. (The Kurds may prove to be an exception.) Created over decades, such identities have progressed too far to go back. Nationalism is indeed compatible with sectarian identity, as shown by the Arab Shi'i in Iraq.

Because of its history and location, the Persian Gulf will always remain a region characterized by transnational religious, ethnic, and political groups. An inability to acknowledge the Other is at the root of many problems. In a region with great disparity in the size and wealth of states, all will feel vulnerable in some ways at different times. States will feel threatened by forces they cannot control. In recent times, identity groups that long remained passive have become activated, often in the wake of conflict or upheaval (Iraq, Bahrain, Syria). In "normal" times such groups coexisted peacefully. The goal must be to reduce the reasons for their activation. The key for governments is to manage differences without allowing them to become politicized or violent. Here the state is not neutral and can make a positive difference.

The roots of ethnic and sectarian conflict are not obscure, and a range of confidence-building measures can easily be taken to reduce tension and avoid, manage, or resolve conflict. The chapters in this volume shed considerable light on this little-explored problem and why solutions cannot wait. It deserves to be read by all students and policymakers of the region.

* * *

The book at hand is the first extended examination of sectarianism in the Persian Gulf, which despite its importance has been avoided by scholars until now. Recognizing the increasing significance of sectarian identification and conflict in the region, in the fall of 2011 the Center for International and Regional Studies, part of Georgetown University's School of Foreign Service in Qatar, under the leadership of Professor Mehran Kamrava, launched a research initiative on the subject. Although there are no recognized experts, the project brought together a renowned group of scholars to examine the issue of religious, communal, and ethnic identities in the Persian Gulf, and how these affect its domestic and international politics.

The central aim of this study is to examine the dynamic ways in which evolving sectarian identities and politics in the Gulf region, encompassing Iran, Iraq, and the states of the Arabian Peninsula, intersect. Due to the lack of sources on sectarianism in the region, the insights in the chapters below were critical to drafting this introduction, and have been extensively cited. Although authors worked on different countries, there was a surprising amount of agreement on the role that sectarianism has played, for example the frequent tactic of governments to promote sectarian tension rather than communal harmony as a governing strategy. The studies generally concur that problems and conflicts in the Gulf, which are usually ascribed to religion, in reality stem from economic, political, and security factors.

The chapters by Justin Gengler and Fanar Haddad were both drawn from outstanding recent dissertations, on Bahrain and Iraq respectively, and the results of their research are presented here for the first time. Their work provides a rich theoretical framework for understanding the subject that will be required reading for all who follow. The most critical sectarian conflict in the Persian Gulf at present is in Bahrain, which is thoroughly addressed in several chapters, notably that by Kristin Smith Diwan. Historian Laurence Louër, an expert on the role of Shi'i networks in the Gulf, here distills her research to present a comparative picture of Bahrain, Saudi Arabia, and Kuwait. Although Oman differs in many ways from states along the southern coast of the Gulf that celebrate a Najdi heritage, it shares similar political problems which have been exacerbated by the Arab Spring, as Marc Valeri explains. In this book the theme of sectarianism is not restricted to religion, and there are two chapters dealing with tribes and ethnic groups. One, by historian

John Peterson, for the first time describes the role the Baluch have played in the Gulf. Another, by anthropologist Lois Beck, distills a lifetime of study in describing Iran's ethnic, religious, and tribal minorities. It is the most comprehensive treatment ever done on that topic and will be essential background for anyone seeking to understand Iran.

I invite you to keep turning the pages and get brought up to date on one of the most important, and least understood, aspects of society and politics in the Persian Gulf.

1

UNDERSTANDING SECTARIANISM IN THE PERSIAN GULF

Justin J. Gengler

In the run-up to Bahrain's 2002 parliamentary elections, which were to be the country's first since its National Assembly was dissolved in 1976, the head of the largest Sunni political society, Shaikh Adal al-Ma'awdah, obtained an edict from religious authorities in Saudi Arabia to allow him and other Salafis to run and vote in the contest. "Entering the parliament is not a religious act," he explained, "but it becomes a must when there is a need to counter probable harm." The "probable harm" to which al-Ma'awdah referred? The prospect of allowing Bahrain's united Shi'i bloc, al-Wifaq, to seize control of the nascent legislature, despite its official announcement that it would boycott the elections out of protest against the new Bahraini constitution, promulgated unilaterally by the recently ascended King Hamad bin Isa Al Khalifa. Nonetheless, al-Ma'awdah warned, "Abandoning the stage to miscreants who would enact or pass laws incompatible with religious values would amount to a passive participation in propagating evil."[1] Thus was and remains the

[1] Quoted in Habib Toumi, "Religious Fatwas Used to Explain Poll Participation,"

electoral politics of Bahrain: while Shi'i opponents fear their participation may be tantamount to state co-option, ordinary Sunnis are concerned lest their *non*-participation permit a wholesale Shi'i—and by association Iranian—takeover.

How should one understand such a structural Sunni–Shi'i divide? Is it deep-seated religious animosity translated into modern political institutions? Or is it a mundane case of politics as usual, a group conflict over scarce resources donning the cloak of sectarianism? When, a decade later, Bahrain's Sunnis were again called upon to "counter probable harm"—this time not at the ballot box but in the streets to ward off a full-scale Shi'i-led revolt—these questions were no closer to being answered. Whereas Sunni loyalists saw Iranian hands all over the 2011 uprising, the opposition rejected the notion that its contribution to the Arab Spring was a sectarian affair. Bahrain's rulers could not decide on their interpretation. Initially painting mass protests as the product of socio-economic frustration, they announced generous social welfare packages including increased salaries and benefits, cost-of-living stipends, and plans for new subsidized housing. Neighboring Arab states in the Persian Gulf even pitched in $10 billion of their own in what was called the "Gulf Marshall Plan." When it became clear that demonstrators were not to be bought off, however, the government quickly changed its tune, joining Sunnis in decrying these "extremist elements with ties to foreign governments in the region," as King Hamad would describe them only weeks later in an op-ed in *The Washington Times*.[2]

Observers and policymakers were left to choose. Is Bahrain's political conflict at bottom a sectarian one? Or is it merely an outward manifestation of underlying societal inequality? Do Bahraini Shi'i oppose the prevailing political order on principle, because it institutionalizes rule by the rival denomination? Or rather because they tend to be poorer, are less socially mobile, and thus simply have more cause for political complaint than their Sunni counterparts? Finally, and most worryingly, is Bahrain's Sunni–Shi'i division symptomatic of a larger trend of sectarian tension spreading throughout the Persian Gulf region, or is it a unique product of local history and circumstances that precludes generalization?

Gulf News, 21 Nov. 2006, http://gulfnews.com/news/gulf/bahrain/religious-fatwas-used-to-explain-poll-participation-1.266432

[2] King Hamad bin Isa Al Khalifa, "Stability is Prerequisite for Progress," *The Washington Times*, 19 Apr. 2011.

The study of sectarianism in the current Middle East context demands a delicate, even cautious approach. Although the salience of ethnic and religious categories in shaping political outcomes across the region is clear, less well understood are the nature and functions of sectarianism as a political phenomenon, and how the processes that underlie it vary under different institutional constraints. This lack of an objective analytical framework with which to study the politicization of ascriptive group identities across country contexts has given rise to two analytical roadblocks. The first is a tendency toward description or narration of the phenomenon of sectarianism, rather than explanation. Religious and ethnic identities are said to influence politics via "entrenched hatreds," "group solidarities," and other deeply rooted emotions. Thus do King Hamad's "extremist elements" oppose the political status quo and harbor loyalties to Iran precisely because they are Shi'i, a people bound by a communal cohesion that knows no national borders.

This proclivity to explain sectarianism tautologically as a result of itself—a line of argument not restricted to self-interested Persian Gulf rulers—has encouraged on the other hand the opposite tendency: to deny the independent significance of ethnic or religious distinctions, and indeed to avoid altogether the word "sectarianism," now criticized as simplistic, derogatory, and smacking of Orientalism. As illustrated by the competing narratives of Bahrain's uprising, the upshot of this analytical polarization is that explanations that should combine aspects of both interpretations tend instead to prefer one militantly over the other. Either sectarianism stems from tensions and loyalties better suited to the field of psychology than political science, or else it is entirely epiphenomenal, the deceptive façade of some generic political conflict explicable by anyone versed in game theory or new institutional economics.

The present chapter aims to resolve these two reinforcing problems by sharpening the theoretical precision with which sectarianism is studied in the Persian Gulf context. It elaborates an analytical framework that differs from extant treatments in three crucial ways. First, in attempting to identify the actual mechanisms by which sectarianism affects political outcomes in the region, it does not appeal speciously to some description of the phenomenon itself. This way, not only does it avoid the logical error of positing that sectarianism influences politics via "tensions," "rivalries," and other ill-defined passions—that is, via sectarianism—but in helping to clarify what one means when one speaks of "sectarianism," it hopefully will serve also to rescue the concept from its current connotation as crude and outmoded. The second way this account differs, then, is that it explains how the causal processes in question are specific to the phenomenon of sectarianism, and how these differ qualitatively from non-sectarian dynamics. Finally, it emphasizes the conditional nature of the process, examining how country-level variations in history, demographics, and political institutions help explain why ethnic and religious differences become magnified in some societies but not in others.

In explaining the nature and function of sectarianism in the context of the Persian Gulf, this revised framework combines three defining features of the region: unique political and economic institutions that encourage group mobilization on the basis of ascriptive social categories, as well as the unequal distribution of state resources along these same lines; a historical legacy of religious-*cum*-political fracture followed by a deliberate but selective process of nation-building; and, lastly, a pervasive geopolitical competition for ideological and material influence involving Iran, the Arab states of the Gulf, and their respective clients and patrons. By this conceptualization, the politicization of religious and ethnic identities is understood not as a *cause* of the political experiences of the states, but rather as a systematic *effect* of their particular societal and institutional characteristics as well as the external environment.

This rethinking of sectarianism is rooted in no less than a basic theoretical revision of the prevailing understanding of the Gulf state. Challenging some four decades of received wisdom from rentier state theory, it begins by rejecting the notion of a universal rentier social contract, whereby the rulers of rent-based economies endeavor to purchase the universal political support of citizens using economic benefits. Rather than deploy limited resources inefficiently upon the whole of society, this revised account observes, most rulers of distributive states such as those of the Gulf instead seek to maximize their own share by rewarding a finite category of citizens whose support is sufficient to keep them in power, while the remaining population is disproportionately excluded from the private rentier benefits of citizenship. This incentive for targeted redistribution is especially great in countries in which a large population and/or low per capita resource revenues would limit the political utility of a more egalitarian allocation.

In the barren political landscape of the Persian Gulf states, lacking both an economic basis for mass coordination as well as institutions that might channel group interests, this process of coalition-building favors alliances based on outwardly observable, ascriptive social categories such as family and tribal descent, regional origin, and ethnic and religious affiliation. As a result, political cooperation becomes most likely among citizens of similar ethno-religious makeup, and, in distributive states with diverse and/or regionally diffuse populations, political winners and losers tend to be decided along these same ascriptive categories. Not only is there no universal rentier bargain tying all citizens to rulers of distributive states, therefore, but the lines separating those who are party to the agreement from those who are disqualified are not drawn arbitrarily.

Having elaborated this modified account of the strategic logic underlying the allocative state, the chapter proceeds in the remaining two sections to examine how the region's structural tendency toward ethnic and religious political dividing lines has been reinforced by several internal and external conditions, respectively, that have helped give rise to the contemporary phenomenon of sectarianism. The first domestic factor is political institutions that privilege and in many cases are designed to encourage political competition on the basis of latent social distinctions rather than shared issue preferences. A second internal condition is an enduring legacy of competing religious-*cum*-political narratives that has complicated the modern process of nation-building. In seeking to cultivate coherent national identities within borders determined largely by fate and by colonial regents, most of the Gulf states have been forced to invent official accounts of local history that in glorifying certain events, traditions, and ideals, inevitably privilege particular versions of citizenship and of nationhood. While no national mythology can hope to resemble perfectly the diversity of people it is meant to encompass, one community consistently and conspicuously absent from the majority of these narratives emphasizing Sunni, tribal identity is Arab Shi'i. Excluded from identities crafted in the image of ruling families, Arab Shi'i in Bahrain and Saudi Arabia have even constructed their own national folklore that draws on shared notions of political injustice and betrayal rooted in the very foundations of Islam. In this way does a millennium-old politico-religious schism continue to overlap with ongoing processes of national marginalization to reinforce societal polarization along Sunni–Shi'i lines.

A final section situates these internal dynamics in the larger regional competition for ideological and material influence being fought between

Saudi Arabia, Iran, and their respective clients and great power patrons. Initiated after the Islamic Revolution threatened to bring its brand of Shi'i populism to the Gulf, and augmented when successive regime changes in Afghanistan and Iraq made the prospect appear considerably less fanciful, this geopolitical rivalry has given further substance to the latent distinction between Sunni and Shi'i. Once mere religious deviants, now the Arab and Persian Shi'i of the Arabian Peninsula are viewed by nervous rulers and citizens as political heretics as well—indeed, as veritable fifth columns serving an expansionist Iran and united by a transnational solidarity and the common goal of Shi'i empowerment. Emboldened Shi'i populations in Iraq, Bahrain, Saudi Arabia, and Kuwait, combined with the prospect of a nuclear-armed Islamic Republic, have only amplified such existential fears, quickening plans for deeper politico-military integration among the members of the Gulf Cooperation Council (GCC). With the latter thrust into the political driver's seat by the events of the Arab Spring, the entire region is increasingly consumed by what has been termed the "new Middle East Cold War": a conflict pitting the Sunni Arab monarchies against Shi'i-led regimes in Iran, Iraq, and most recently Syria.[3]

An unlikely bargain: revisiting the foundations of the Persian Gulf state

The states of the Gulf region are, to varying degrees, distributive states dependent on directly accruing rents from the sale or use of their natural resources. As such, their primary role is the top-down allocation of these rents in such a way that guarantees their leaders' political survival while maximizing their own consumption. The standard account of how this is achieved constitutes what one may call the "rentier bargain": resource-controlling parties within rentier states can, in short, buy off their would-be domestic opponents through judicious economic policy. The form of such policy may be either positive (rent-controllers offer citizens a portion of their wealth as public and private goods) or negative (they agree not to expropriate from citizens as they otherwise would like to). In practical terms, these avenues of popular co-option correspond to two complementary mechanisms by which the region's governments are said

[3] As coined in Bill Spindle and Margaret Coker, "The New Cold War," *The Wall Street Journal*, 16 Apr. 2011. Oman—which is neither Sunni-led nor actively involved in the conflict—is an exception.

to use their positions as economic hegemon to elicit political acquiescence: first, they employ those who need employment; and, second, they agree not to levy taxes "on the basis," in Vandewalle's formulation, "of the reverse principle of no representation without taxation."[4] Together these incentives are said to foster a rent-induced consensus whereby the regime gains a political ally—at worst a self-interest-maximizing, apolitical animal—and needs forfeit only a portion of its rent proceeds to ensure continued enjoyment of the remainder.

The contemporary record of Persian Gulf politics would seem to indicate that some citizens and governments long ago reneged on their wealth-for-acquiescence agreements. In fact, one need not even reference the empirical failures of the rentier state model to understand why such an open-ended bargain never existed at all. In the first place, not all citizens will be persuaded to forfeit their political prerogative by the promise of material wealth (or, for that matter, by the promise of violence). Certainly, one can imagine myriad sources of political motivation independent of economic concerns. Moreover, and more fundamentally, even if the state could buy the unanimous support of citizens, it need not even attempt to do so, for it requires only a minimum coalition of supporters with a physical preponderance sufficient to protect it from potential challengers. Indeed, why waste limited resources chasing citizens opposed to the status quo when they might be used to reward those who already have a material stake in its preservation? The only question, then, is how the former group of political outsiders comes to be distinguished from the latter group of beneficiaries.

Group coordination in the Persian Gulf context

In principle, political elites—whether in the Gulf or in Guatemala—are indifferent as to the specific composition of their citizen coalitions, so long as these are materially sufficient to keep them in power. And, again in principle, one finds in any society a great number of underlying social cleavages that might possibly serve as bases for political coordination. In practice, however, the number and nature of the actual coalitions that

[4] Dirk Vandewalle, "Political Aspects of State Building in Rentier Economies: Algeria and Libya Compared," in Hazem Beblawi and Giacomo Luciani (eds), *The Rentier State: Nation, State and Integration in the Arab World*, vol. 2, London: Croom Helm, 1987, p. 160.

form in a given society are influenced decisively by the larger institutional context in which this coordination process takes place. In the case of the Gulf region, two features in particular privilege group formation along ascriptive social categories—tribe, region, ethnicity, religion, etc.—whose members are readily recognizable by outward markers such as dress, skin color, language and accent, names and genealogies, and so on. Neither requires vague reference to "group solidarities" or "historical animosities."

The first characteristic of society in the Persian Gulf that favors coordination along ascriptive group boundaries is a political landscape in which information about individuals' political preferences is not merely scarce but in most cases actively suppressed. The virtual absence of proper political parties, free media, autonomous civil society organizations, and other independent institutions complicates group coordination based on shared concerns for specific policy issues, since individuals cannot easily observe or infer the views of other citizens. By contrast, ascriptive social categories such as ethnicity or religion are readily communicable by outward cues that are common knowledge to both members and non-members. While they may or may not correspond to actual shared political preferences among members, such categories are both easy to observe and, as they are primarily based on descent, relatively stable over time. In short, they "combine high observability, low boundary permeability, and a common knowledge membership rule, all of which make them focal points for coordination in the absence of higher quality, more informative cues with which to work."[5]

In addition to its barren political environment, the Gulf's unique economic organization also promotes group coordination along ethnic and religious categories. "Consider," says Yates of a rentier society, "the following options for class-based politics: a declining rural-agricultural sector; a state-sponsored industrial sector; a booming service sector. Whence the revolution?"[6] Indeed, beginning with the earliest statements of the rentier thesis, theorists have held out little hope that anything resembling a traditional party system or cross-societal political movement might take root in an allocative economy. Not only, as Yates

[5] Daniel M. Corstange, "Institutions and Ethnic Politics in Lebanon and Yemen," PhD dissertation, University of Michigan, 2008, p. 22.

[6] Douglas A. Yates, *The Rentier State in Africa: Oil Rent Dependency & Neocolonialism in the Republic of Gabon*, Trenton, NJ: Africa World Press, 1996, p. 35.

laments, is there no natural social grouping like a taxpaying middle class from which such a push might originate, but moreover the patronage system itself incentivizes individual—rather than group—efforts to secure material benefits. "To the individual who feels his benefits are not enough," Luciani explains in his seminal volume on rentierism:

> the solution of manoeuvring for personal advantage within the existing setup is always superior to seeking an alliance with others in similar conditions. In the end, there is always little or no objective ground to claim that one should get more of the benefits, since his contribution is generally dispensable anyhow.[7]

Thus it is that in rentier societies the economy offers little basis for political coordination, since "the politics of allocation states leave little ground for economic interests of citizens not belonging to the elite to be represented."[8] All this leads Luciani to make in passing what two decades later can only appear a rather prescient prediction, that in rent-based societies "parties will develop only to represent cultural or ideological orientations. In practice, Islamic fundamentalism appears to be the only rallying point around which something approaching a party can form in the Arab allocation states."[9]

One sees, then, that ethno-religious categories offer the most viable focal points for mass political coordination in the Persian Gulf rentier states that otherwise, for lack of both political and economic institutions to channel citizens' interests, would be quite difficult to achieve. While identification of an individual's regional, ethnic, or religious affiliation may seem a crude substitute for knowledge of his or her precise political preferences, and while inferences gleaned from such cues are likely only to approximate the true natures of individuals, they are, first of all, very simple and cheap to obtain and, moreover, probably quite accurate given the impermeability of ethnic, and to a lesser extent religious, boundaries. Political cooperation in this way becomes most likely among individuals of similar ethno-religious makeup, who form a common bond that may be "imagined" in the sense of having a dubious basis in historical fact or in shared political interests,[10] but one that, as Horowitz

[7] Giacomo Luciani, "Allocation vs. Production States: A Theoretical Framework," in Beblawi and Luciani, *The Rentier State*, p. 74.

[8] Ibid., p. 76.

[9] Ibid.

[10] Lisa Anderson, "The State in the Middle East and North Africa," *Comparative Politics*, 20, 1 (1987), pp. 1–18.

claims, "denotes not just a certain stream of belief but a certain version of peoplehood."[11]

Capitalizing on "ethnic subsidies"

The relative ease with which these descent-based coalitions are able to form in the political and economic context of the Gulf is balanced, however, by inherent limitations stemming from their very basis in ascription. First, although group membership by descent makes it easier for members to coordinate, it also means that they are likely to vary widely among other categories—education, ideological orientation, class, profession, sex, age, and so on—that correspond in turn to fundamental differences in political preferences across a wide range of policy issues. Since, as Corstange explains, these:

> issues over which there is widespread internal disagreement … cannot serve to unify members and constitute common interests, … such issues are deemphasized in favor of interests on which the bulk of the members can agree. Yet given that so many dimensions we might consider to be "policy," "programmatic," or "ideological" are, in effect, closed off by this within-community heterogeneity, common interests default to distribution and redistribution toward the community, and hence a predisposition to patronage coalitions within which membership is marked by ethnic category.[12]

Moreover, unlike other social coalitions that individuals join and leave voluntarily, members of descent-based groups are generally members for life. While one or another individual may leave or join a community through marriage, conversion, and so on, there remains on the whole a temporal stability—often reinforced by geographical separation—that has, for example, enabled after more than a millennium the persistence of a Sunni branch of Islam, a Shi'i branch, and myriad sub-categories of each. Indeed, in Bahrain this self-imposed sectarian differentiation has been so well preserved as to allow Holes to complete a comparative study of the island's Sunni and Shi'i Arab (Baharna) dialects. On this "almost apartheid-like system of voluntary segregation"[13] he remarks:

11 Donald L. Horowitz, *Ethnic Groups in Conflict*, Berkeley: University of California Press, 1985, p. 492.

12 Corstange, "Institutions and Ethnic Politics," pp. 132ff.

13 My own 2009 mass survey of Bahrain gives some additional substance to Holes's observations. There, only 25 percent of surveyed districts were not exclusive either

One consequence of the separation of the two communities has been the preservation, over more than two centuries, and in an area no bigger than a medium-sized English county, of a major dialectical cleavage that pervades all levels of linguistic analysis: pronunciation, word structure and vocabulary.[14]

The practical inability of members to exit ascriptive social groupings means that the latter are captive constituencies to political elites of the same ethnic, religious, or sectarian affiliation. The result is what Corstange terms an "ethnic subsidy," whereby the political support of co-ethnics (or co-sectarians, etc.) can be bought more cheaply than that of non-co-ethnics.[15] Elites, who wish to target their supporters with benefits while avoiding wasting resources on non-supporters, face a difficulty in distinguishing the former type of individuals from the latter. Citizens, of course, can indicate their political support in various ways—whether by subscribing to a certain newspaper or by airbrushing an image of the king onto their rear windshield. But, as described already, under certain conditions like those that prevail in the Persian Gulf region, ascriptive categories such as ethnic or religious affiliation also communicate one's likelihood of being a supporter as opposed to being a non-supporter. As a result, it is easier for a Najdi Sunni to signal his political support for a Najdi Sunni ruling family than it is for a Persian Shi'i; and, equally, for a Persian Shi'i to signal his support for the Supreme Leader than a Sunni Baluch. "Coethnics," Corstange summarizes, "require less compensation for their political support than do non-coethnics: coethnic votes are cheap."[16]

Explaining sectarianism

The foregoing discussion provides an alternative basis for understanding a range of phenomena usually described as either resulting from, or

---

to Sunni or Shi'i respondents, and of these mixed areas one-half were confined to two urban developments. Excluding these, the survey uncovered just thirteen other ethnically mixed blocks across the remainder of the island, amounting to just 11 percent of 119 total multiple-respondent districts.

[14] Clive Holes, "Dialect and National Identity: The Cultural Politics of Self-Representation in Bahraini *Musalsalat*," in Paul Dresch and James Piscatori (eds), *Monarchies and Nations: Globalization and Identity*, London: I.B. Tauris, 2005, p. 60.

[15] Corstange, "Institutions and Ethnic Politics," pp. 132–5.

[16] Corstange, "Institutions and Ethnic Politics," p. 135. See pp. 133–6 for a game-theoretic proof.

forming a part of, "sectarianism." First, that political coalitions in the Gulf region tend to form along ethno-religious lines is not evidence of some deeply rooted complex of emotions, rivalries, and communal attachments that together form a societal condition described as "sectarianism." In fact, this tendency toward religious- and ethnic-based mobilization is a direct consequence of incentives built into the region's political and economic environment. If sectarianism is to be defined as the politicization of ethnic or religious identity, then this politicization is best understood not as a cause of this or that political malady afflicting Persian Gulf states, but rather as an effect of their particular institutional characteristics. Although they may be accentuated or muted by various means, whether deliberate or accidental, ethnic and religious categories in the Gulf context are natural foci for political coordination—they are inherently political categories.

A second phenomenon attributed to "sectarianism," or said to constitute "sectarian politics," is popular co-ethnic and co-religionist support for Gulf governments. This, combined with the reverse case—oppositions consisting disproportionately of politically disenfranchised ethnic and religious minorities (or, in the case of Bahrain, a majority)—is seen to demonstrate how Gulf rulers consistently favor their co-sectarians at the expense of those that, for reasons of doctrinal dissimilarity, moral aversion, and so on, are relegated to the status of second-class citizens and the collective political out-group. Thus the Saudi state persecutes Eastern Province Shi'i; Bahrain's ruling family discriminates against its own Shi'i; and the government of Nuri al-Maliki today neglects Iraq's Sunnis as that of Saddam Hussein previously targeted Shi'i. Yet such patterns of favoritism still emerge not because Iraq's Party of the Islamic Call (al-Da'awa) identifies at bottom with the Shi'i masses as co-sectarians, or because the Al Khalifa empathize with citizens from among *ahl al-sunna* (Sunnis), but because the political support of co-sectarians is simply cheaper to come by than that of non-sectarians.

One can observe how sectarian calculations take a back seat to pragmatic political concerns of this sort in the empirical record of alliance-building in the region. In the pre-oil era, Sunni rulers in the Gulf city-states—in Bahrain, Qatar, Kuwait, Dubai, Muscat, and elsewhere—co-opted the vital support of powerful merchant families, most of whom were of Persian, and often Persian Shi'i, origins.[17] In her influential

[17] Here one might go further to note that, with the exceptions of Iran and possibly

account of state-building in Kuwait and Qatar, Crystal recounts how these families relinquished their political claims only following the discovery of oil, when they traded roles in formal decision-making for free reign in the economic sphere and relief from onerous taxation.[18] Yet, eventually, a more economical alternative would emerge in the form of Sunni Arab tribesmen, whose demands for housing and employment in the armed forces appeared meager compared to tax breaks and trading concessions, which now corresponded to significant foregone revenue. Ruling elites did not hesitate to alter their bases of political support. When an intractable merchant class blocked legislation and constitutional reforms desired by Kuwait's royal family in the early 1980s, the latter naturalized thousands of stateless Sunni Bedouins to serve as a dependable pro-government constituency in parliament. Similarly, Bahrain's restoration of parliament in 2002 following a near-decade of Shi'i rebellion required a fundamental demographic rebalancing (along with creative electoral redistricting) to preclude the possibility of a Shi'i-controlled lower house. Once again Saudi tribesmen would fit the need, and thousands would be issued Bahraini passports in time for the November vote.

Nation-building through nation-dividing

Of course, to observe the distinct potential of ascriptive group identities as focal points for political cooperation in the region is not to suggest the inexorable emergence of sectarian conflict as a proverbial state of nature. Just as certain characteristics of the region's political and economic organization serve to augment the salience of ethnicity and religion, so too can institutions encourage the opposite. Elections, parliaments, and other consultative bodies can be used to promote intra-rather than inter-group competition. National identities need not be narrow, romanticized reflections of ruling families but may be crafted

Saudi Arabia, each of the Gulf regimes owes its existence today to an alliance with an even more dissimilar tribe: that of the Anglo-Saxon.

[18] Jill Crystal, "Patterns of State-Building in the Arabian Gulf: Kuwait and Qatar," PhD dissertation, Harvard University, 1986; *Oil and Politics in the Gulf: Rulers and Merchants in Kuwait and Qatar*, rev. edn, New York: Cambridge University Press, 1990.

around collective experiences and traditions that bind rather than differentiate citizens. In the Persian Gulf as elsewhere, conflict is not a necessary consequence of diversity.

In fact, however, the formal institutions and national narratives developed by Gulf states have, with few exceptions, been designed seemingly in service of the reverse principle, namely to enhance society's latent potential for group-based competition—not only over political and economic resources, but over the very character of the state: its history and cultural identity; the bases of citizenship; and the conditions for inclusion in public service. Electoral rules and voting districts are manipulated to foster inter-group contestation, while selective employment and naturalization policies construct tiers of citizenship ascending toward an ideal type. These single visions of peoplehood, so often glorified in official histories, neglect competing group identities and experiences, in some cases even those shared by a majority. Through these and other institutional mechanisms, governments in the Persian Gulf dictate the rules of politics, defining not only the acceptable range of political demands, but also who may make them, and by what legitimate means.

Institutionalizing group politics

The non-democratic nature of most Gulf regimes has tended to distract attention away from their respective forays into representative political institutions, and attempts at citizen involvement—elections, parliaments, and ill-defined consultative bodies—are overwhelmingly dismissed as perfunctory and inefficacious. Yet what these institutions generally lack in practical significance belies their larger analytic value, for the institutional choices of states do not materialize randomly but instead reflect deliberate strategies of structuring the forms of political competition that can emerge in a society. Electoral laws, bans or limits on political parties, and other legal regulations organize how citizens may interact with the state, but they also exert a decisive influence on how citizens cooperate and vie with each other. In the Gulf context, these institutions privilege and in many cases are designed precisely to encourage political competition on the basis of latent social distinctions—especially religious and tribal affiliations—a fact that helps explain further the region's tendency toward sectarian and other identity-based politics rather than cross-societal, issue-based coalitions.

It is notable that despite the general diversity of Persian Gulf citizen populations, fashioned by centuries of migration and shifting borders, only Iraq has attempted formal consociational arrangements to help overcome social-*cum*-political divisions born of group differences—and this only as a consequence of outside intervention. (Of course, even this deliberate effort, which includes provisions for regional autonomy, ultra-proportional representation in parliament, minority quotas, and nominal power-sharing among Sunni, Shi'i, and Kurdish elites, has met with only limited success in spurring intra-group rather than inter-group competition, and so avoiding Shi'i-dominated majoritarianism.) The remaining countries, irrespective of political orientation or regime type, have in their choices of representative institutions either passively reinforced society's underlying tendency toward ascriptive group politics, or else actively organized political competition along the bases of tribe, region, or sect. Such is true even where these institutions possess wholly symbolic significance—for example, in the United Arab Emirates, in Saudi Arabia, and in Qatar.[19] Indeed, in the Gulf monarchies especially, consciously devised rules of voting and eligibility reveal a common principle shared by elites for the structuring of contestation between citizens and between citizen and state: the pursuit of material patronage *qua* representative of a specific tribal, religious, or other constituency is acceptable; the pursuit of substantive policies *qua* member of a cross-cutting coalition of supporters is not.

In Qatar, a first-ever vote to elect two-thirds of the country's advisory Shura Council, planned for 2013, is widely expected to employ a singular method of districting: Qataris will vote in the home region or village of their father or, by some accounts, grandfather, thereby ensuring representation along family and tribal lines.[20] In the United Arab Emirates, participation in elections to choose half of the country's forty-member

[19] While not discussed here for limitations of space, the case of Oman also may be included in this list. Its Shura Council elections of Oct. 2011 were decided almost wholly on the basis of tribe, largely as a result of state design. See, for example, Sunil K. Vaidya, "Poll Outcome Shows Tribal Affinity," *Gulf News*, 17 Oct. 2011, http://gulfnews.com/news/gulf/oman/poll-outcome-shows-tribal-affinity-1.894463; and Marc Valeri, "Identity Politics and Nation-Building under Sultan Qaboos," in this volume.

[20] The recent unexpected abdication of Amir Hamad bin Khalifa Al Thani has served to delay this electoral timeline, announced in Sep. 2011.

Federal National Council—another advisory body of no practical significance—has been limited to an "electoral college" whose members are hand-selected for each of the seven emirates by undisclosed means. In the first vote in 2006, this pool of eligible voters amounted to a mere 6,689 individuals, representing less than 1 percent of Emirati nationals.[21] A second election in 2011 saw the list increase to around 130,000 citizens, or 12 percent of the national population.[22] Here, then, the invitation for ascriptive voting is even more clear than in the case of Qatar: not only is the electorate composed disproportionately of demographically and politically important tribes and families, but since candidates can only identify voters by name, they are likely to court potential supporters on the same basis. One reporter covering the 2011 vote noted that rather than waste their limited campaign budgets by appealing to Emiratis who were not even eligible to vote, some candidates "chose a more direct approach. … Instead of spending money on advertising, they went through the lists of voters and called them individually or spoke to heads of tribes."[23] These incentives are reflected in the final results. Three of the four winners in Abu Dhabi, for instance, came from the same tribe, the 'Awamir, whom Peterson describes as a longtime "pillar of support" for the emirate's ruling family,[24] while both winners in Ajman Emirate belonged to Al Shamsi.

If the UAE and Qatar have thus resorted to creative electoral rules to structure the outcomes of purely symbolic votes in societies that know no organized opposition and enjoy comparatively homogenous citizen populations—if elites here go to such lengths even under social and political conditions that are the envy of other Gulf rulers—then the electoral machinations of leaders in more diverse and divided societies, and in societies whose representative institutions wield more effective power, are perhaps no surprise. In Saudi Arabia, where municipal coun-

[21] Anna Seaman, "FNC Urges Residents to Obtain their ID Cards," *The National*, 20 Jan. 2011, http://www.thenational.ae/news/uae-news/politics/fnc-urges-residents-to-obtain-their-id-cards

[22] "FNC Election Winners Announced," *Gulf News*, 24 Sep. 2011, http://gulfnews.com/news/gulf/uae/government/fnc-election-winners-announced-1.873914

[23] Mahmoud Habboush, "UAE Nationals Ask: Why Can't All of Us Vote?" *Arab News*, 21 Sep. 2011, http://www.arabnews.com/node/391872

[24] J.E. Peterson, "Tribes and Politics in Eastern Arabia," *Middle East Journal*, 31, 3 (1977), p. 300, n. 5.

cil elections are also ceremonial but nonetheless offer a rare opportunity for sanctioned political mobilization among liberal and Shi'i opponents of the government, votes in 2005 and 2011 have involved what Kraetzschmar euphemistically terms "distinct design features that are unique by international standards."[25] To disadvantage candidates with localized bases of support, the Saudi system asks citizens to vote not only for a candidate in the district in which they reside and are registered, but also for candidates in all the other districts of their municipality. That is, voters can cast as many ballots as there are districts in their municipality, meaning that winning candidates are often able to garner several times more votes than there are voters in their district. So, for example, while Shi'i candidates can succeed in the Shi'i-dominated municipalities of the Eastern Province, they are unlikely to win Shi'i-majority districts in otherwise Sunni-dominated municipalities.[26] "[B]y putting a premium on cross-district efforts at voter mobilization," Kraetzschmar explains:

> the electoral system provided the institutional backdrop against which it was possible for Islamist candidates and their backers to coordinate successfully their campaigns and achieve impressive victories across the Kingdom. ... [It] was this level of coordination, facilitated by the electoral rules, that gave the entire [2005] campaign a distinctly ideological flavour, even though the elections were formally run on a non-partisan, individual-candidacy basis.[27]

Still, the most extreme cases of electoral engineering are found in those Gulf states with the greatest ethno-religious diversity among citizens and, not incidentally, the highest levels of popular political mobilization. In Bahrain, the government has used a combination of sectarian gerrymandering and selective naturalization to preclude its Shi'i demographic majority from realizing a legislative majority in the country's

[25] Hendrik Jan Kraetzschmar, "The First Democratic Local Elections in Saudi Arabia in 2005: Electoral Rules, the Mobilization of Voters and the Islamist Landslide," London School of Economics Public Policy Group, Working Paper, no. 6 (2011), p. 2, http://www2.lse.ac.uk/government/research/resgroups/LSEPublicPolicy/Docs/Saudi_Arabia_Democratic_Elections_Kraetzschmar.pdf

[26] And, in fact, just a day before the country's first-ever vote in 2005, Saudi authorities disqualified a popular Shi'i candidate running in a Sunni-dominated district of al-Hasa, for fear that he would be propelled to victory over his Sunni rivals by co-sectarian voters elsewhere in the municipality. See John Bradley, "Whither Saudi Arabia's Shiites?" *Front Page Magazine*, 15 Mar. 2005, http://archive.frontpagemag.com/readArticle.aspx?ARTID=9257

[27] Kraetzschmar, "Local Elections in Saudi Arabia," p. 2.

elected but largely powerless lower house of parliament. When the body was reinstated in 2002, new electoral districts were drawn almost entirely along Sunni–Shi'i lines, a process aided by the extreme geographical segregation of the two communities. The island was rearranged administratively into twelve municipalities within five governorates, producing forty gerrymandered electoral districts ranging from 500 to 17,000 registered voters.[28] In the Sunni-dominated Southern Governorate, six members of parliament would represent some 16,000 voters, while a single district in the Shi'i suburb of Jidd Hafs itself exceeded that number. Indeed, the entire Northern Governorate, a Shi'i-populated region home to around 80,000 registered voters, was allotted a mere nine seats in parliament.[29] By the time of the 2010 election, the mean Shi'i district would represent 9,533 electors, the average Sunni district 6,196—and this despite the naturalization of tens of thousands of foreign Sunnis over the intervening decade in an ongoing, deliberate process of sectarian rebalancing.[30]

Notably, then, in both Saudi Arabia and Bahrain, state efforts to prevent cross-sectarian political cooperation have the direct effect of energizing Sunni—especially Sunni Islamic—constituencies. Indeed, the entire ruling strategy hinges precisely on this ability to pit ordinary Sunnis against their fellow citizens, even those with whom they might share considerable political grievances and demands, in lieu of the government. As such, those groups and individuals who would dare to "break ranks" by collaborating with Shi'i-led opposition movements, whether in Bahrain or in the Eastern Province, are singled out for special retribution. In Bahrain, among the first opposition leaders arrested after the onset of the February 2011 uprising was Ebrahim Sharif, the head of the country's largest secular political society, whose public calls for joint action by Sunnis and Shi'is threatened to undo the narrative of an unrepresentative, sectarian-based revolt. Sharif is currently completing a five-year prison term, while the society itself was temporarily disbanded after his arrest, its headquarters raided by police and set ablaze.[31]

[28] Steven Wright, "Fixing the Kingdom: Political Evolution and Socio-Economic Challenges in Bahrain," *Occasional Paper*, no. 3, Doha: Center for International and Regional Studies, 2008.

[29] Ebrahim Sharif, interview by author, Bahrain, 11 May 2009.

[30] Justin J. Gengler, "Ethnic Conflict and Political Mobilization in Bahrain and the Arab Gulf," PhD dissertation, University of Michigan, 2011, pp. 66, 141ff.

[31] More generally, the cross-sectarian membership and following of Sharif's

Other Sunnis, including a Salafi former army officer named Muhammad Al Bu Flasa, also faced reprisal for joining demonstrators at the Pearl Roundabout. Al Bu Flasa was detained hours after delivering a speech to protesters, reemerging only several months later to issue a forced apology and retraction aired on state television.[32]

Saudi Arabia has undertaken similar precautions to help ensure that the reform demands of the kingdom's persecuted Shi'i minority do not spread to other groups structurally excluded from the political and economic benefits enjoyed by the Najdi, tribal ruling elite. When activists in the oil-rich and Shi'i-populated Eastern Province took inspiration from protests next door to begin their own mass demonstrations in February 2011, the state had merely to duplicate the successful formula piloted already in Bahrain. Protesters were met with overwhelming, deadly force, their political and spiritual leaders were arrested and imprisoned, and both groups were vilified among ordinary Sunni citizens, who were told in no uncertain terms that support for the reformists would be tantamount to surrendering the kingdom to Iran.[33] For those Sunnis still not convinced, the government possessed as in Bahrain a final remedy: targeted persecution of those who chose to transgress the sectarian political line. Three months after the onset of protests in al-Hasa and Qatif, there appeared in May a declaration signed by dozens of Sunni and Shi'i activists demanding an end to a trial of opposition figures and decrying the violent suppression of protests in the Eastern Province. The state paid little attention to the Shi'i signatories; the Sunnis, however, were soon

National Democratic Action Society (Wa'ad) made it a target of electoral manipulation throughout the 2000s. Despite its considerable popularity, the leftist-liberal society failed to capture even a single seat in the 2006 and 2010 parliamentary elections, largely as a result of the government's targeted mobilization of Sunni voters in the districts in which Wa'ad fielded candidates.

32 See Justin Gengler, "Bahrain's Sunni Awakening," Middle East Research and Information Project (MERIP), 17 Jan. 2012, http://www.merip.org/mero/mero011712; and Justin Gengler, "Bahrain: A Special Case," in Fatima Ayub (ed.), "What Does the Gulf Think about the Arab Awakening?" London: European Council on Foreign Relations, Apr. 2013, pp. 16–18, http://ecfr.eu/page/-/ECFR75_GULF_ANALYSIS_AW.pdf

33 Toby Matthiesen, "Saudi Arabia's Shiite escalation," Foreign Policy, The Mideast Channel Blog, 10 July 2012, http://mideast.foreignpolicy.com/posts/2012/07/10/sable_rattling_in_the_gulf

issued travel bans and threatened with prosecution unless they retracted their names.[34] Other Sunnis, including the co-founders of the Saudi Civil and Political Rights Association that aimed to help the families of political prisoners, were shown less leniency. Charged with a range of offenses after calling for the prosecution of the late Interior Minister Nayef bin 'Abd al-Aziz Al Sa'ud over his handling of protests in the Eastern Province, the two were sentenced to ten years in prison in May 2013.[35] For the rulers of Saudi Arabia, opposition among Shi'i is a disruptive but ultimately manageable problem; organized dissent among Sunnis is potentially destabilizing and thus intolerable.

Finally, nowhere in the Gulf have representative institutions been more decisive historically in structuring political competition—or more manipulated to this end—than in Kuwait. Initially designed to counter the rise of 1960s Arab nationalism by isolating Kuwaiti citizens from dissident expatriates,[36] the now-notorious National Assembly has since been the venue for an elaborate political balancing act involving naturalized tribes, a significant Shi'i minority, an urban commercial elite, and more recently a resurgent Salafi movement. In the two decades following independence in 1961, Kuwait granted citizenship to more than 200,000 tribesmen of the surrounding deserts,[37] first to help marginalize urban merchants and Nasserist sympathizers, and later to dilute the electoral influence of Shi'i in the wake of the Islamic Revolution. For the latter purpose, the state also took the additional step of redefining the country's electoral constituencies, expanding the number of districts from ten to twenty-five. By carefully splitting the vote, only four Shi'i candidates would gain seats in the 1981 election—compared to twenty-three tribal leaders—although they had put forward nearly a third of the candidates. Crystal explains that as a result of the state's open campaign against

[34] Ahmed Al Omran, interview by author, Kuwait, Mar. 2013. The statement and signatures are available (in Arabic) at http://menber-alionline2.info/forum.php?action=view&id=12475

[35] Mohammed Jamjoom, "Two Saudis in Human Rights Group Get 10 Years in Prison," CNN, 10 Mar. 2013, http://www.cnn.com/2013/03/09/world/meast/saudi-arabia-activists-sentenced

[36] Crystal, *Oil and Politics in the Gulf*, p. 120.

[37] Shafeeq Ghabra, "Kuwait and the Economics of Socio-Economic Change," in Barry M. Rubin (ed.), *Crises and Quandaries in the Contemporary Persian Gulf*, New York: Frank Cass Publishers, 2002, p. 112.

them, "[s]oon all four were openly pro-Khomeini," while the anti-Shi'i movement also "helped catalyze a Sunni religious identification."[38]

Despite the sectarian character of the 1981 vote and its aftermath, the primary legacy of Kuwait's calculated use of immigration and electoral redistricting was to cement an urban versus tribal cleavage reinforced by the anti-immigration sentiments of "original" Kuwaitis, who saw their shares of rentier benefits increasingly dissipated by the arrival of new citizens, the majority of whom lacked the education, skills, and motivation to find private-sector work.[39] In return for their serving as a captive pro-government constituency in parliament—as well as the backbone of the police and armed forces—the tribes would require substantial economic support from the state in the form of housing and employment. But the government's passive allies would not remain such indefinitely. Exploiting their legislative majority, tribal leaders have adopted a progressively more oppositional posture, blocking attempts at privatization and other reforms seen as jeopardizing their economic interests, and even leading parliamentary motions to grill the prime minister in 2009 and again in 2011.

In response, the state has increasingly courted the other half of the *hadhar–badu* (Bedouin-sedentary) divide, "playing on urban resentment against tribal nepotism and obstructionism toward large development projects."[40] It has also worked to undo the electoral machinations of past decades. In October 2012, after dissolving an opposition-dominated parliament for a fourth time in four years, Kuwait's amir decreed new changes to the voting system that decreased the number of electoral districts to five while lowering the number of candidates a voter may choose from four to one. This transparent attempt at taming the intransigent legislature prompted unprecedented protests and an electoral boycott by the opposition.[41] The result, ironically, was exactly the out-

[38] Crystal, *Oil and Politics in the Gulf*, p. 103.

[39] Anh Nga Longva, "Nationalism in Pre-Modern Guise: The Discourse on *Hadhar* and *Bedu* in Kuwait," *International Journal of Middle East Studies*, 38, 2 (2006), pp. 171–87.

[40] Kristin Smith Diwan, "Kuwait: Too Much Politics, or Not Enough?", The Mideast Channel Blog, *Foreign Policy*, 10 Jan. 2011, http://mideast.foreignpolicy.com/posts/2011/01/10/kuwait_too_much_politics_or_not_enough

[41] For additional background, see, for example, Abdullah Al Shayji, "A Sense of Deja Vu in Kuwait," *Gulf News*, 23 June 2013, http://gulfnews.com/opinions/columnists/a-sense-of-deja-vu-in-kuwait-1.1200884

come Kuwait had worked since the 1980s to avoid: a Shi'i-dominated parliament. Alarmed by a growing trend toward Salafism and anti-Shi'i orientations among the tribal population, much of which has strong historical connections to Saudi Arabia, Kuwaiti Shi'i indeed find themselves today among the state's closest political allies. This newfound sectarian dynamic, which has been inflamed by opposing views of Bahrain's 2011 uprising and of the regional threat posed by Iran, has added yet another dimension to the already overlapping social-turned-political cleavages institutionalized—with the active assistance of a calculating ruling family—in the Kuwaiti parliament.

The myth of a nation

Of course, the web of social divisions that contribute to what one might broadly call the sectarian politics of the Persian Gulf region—certainly the dichotomy Sunni versus Shi'i, but also interrelated distinctions such as tribal versus non-tribal, Arab versus non-Arab, and even the notion of "original" citizens versus latecomers or "foreigners"—are not institutionalized merely through convoluted laws regulating largely irrelevant legislatures and local councils. Instead, these categories are in most cases embedded into the very national fabrics of Gulf societies by their selective inclusion in, and omission from, narratives and histories meant to create coherent citizenries within physical boundaries determined mostly by accident. This process of nation-building (and, in the cases of Iraq, Iran, and Yemen, rebuilding) has required the invention of official accounts of local history that, in glorifying certain events, traditions, and ideals, have privileged particular versions of citizenship and of nationhood. While no national mythology can hope to resemble perfectly the diversity of people it is meant to encompass, one community consistently and conspicuously absent from the majority of Gulf narratives emphasizing Sunni tribal identity is the Arab Shi'i. Excluded from identities crafted in the image of ruling families, Arab Shi'i have constructed their own national folklore that draws on shared notions of political injustice and betrayal rooted in the very foundations of Islam. Thus does a millennium-old politico-religious schism continue to overlap with ongoing processes of national marginalization to reinforce societal polarization along Sunni–Shi'i lines.

Just as few Persian Gulf leaderships have taken formal institutional measures to mute the political salience of ascriptive categories, choosing instead to emphasize citizens' religious and tribal identities for their own gain, so too have only a small minority of Gulf states developed national identities that transcend or explicitly reject group-based differences among citizens. Notably, in each of these societies—Iraq, Yemen, and Kuwait—the process of identity-formation was influenced decisively by their experience of war. In the former two cases, inclusive national identities were cultivated deliberately as part of unification efforts following civil war. Yemen, where government references to *al-wahda* ("unity") are ubiquitous, goes so far as to explicitly proscribe political parties based on religion, sect, tribe, or other group affiliation. In Kuwait, by contrast, citizens share a common point of historical reference in the fabled 1920 Battle of Jahra, in which an outnumbered band of Kuwaitis (backed by British gunboats and planes) successfully repelled an attack by Ikhwan followers of Ibn Sa'ud. The latter agreed to recognize Kuwait's independence only two years later. Though the state would continue to be ruled by the Sunni, tribal Al Sabah, and while competing histories would arise as to who precisely took part in the battle, nonetheless both Sunni and Shi'i Kuwaitis would subsequently claim to have participated in the defense, indeed the very creation, of their homeland.[42]

Elsewhere in the Gulf, by contrast, the ability to identify with such nation-defining images and experiences is not spread so widely among citizens. Meant in principle to unify individuals under a single vision of peoplehood, in practice the national identities manufactured by the majority of Persian Gulf regimes—the traits and qualities promoted as defining, for example, an Omani, or an Iranian—are more likely to reflect the traditions, culture, and values of a far narrower segment of society, namely that of the ruling elites. And, since it is precisely through public expression of these national identities that citizens' support for elites is ritualized and institutionalized, those individuals whose backgrounds and group affiliations preclude their participation find themselves not only alienated from the social and political community, but also under disproportionate scrutiny for a perceived lack of patriotism and general otherness.

In Iran, for instance, official sponsorship of Shi'ism as a state religion means that Sunnis and other ethno-religious minorities are not only legally excluded—from presidential candidacy, most tellingly—but are

[42] Laurence Louër, *Transnational Shia Politics: Religious and Political Networks in the Gulf*, New York: Columbia University Press, 2008, pp. 44–55.

excluded also from the very idea of what constitutes an authentic and loyal Iranian citizen. Sunnis in particular, both as a religious grouping and as members primarily of minority ethnic communities such as the Baluch, face systematic discrimination via a policy that borders on non-acknowledgment. Whereas Iran reserves five seats in parliament for representatives of recognized minorities—two for Armenians and one each for Jews, Zoroastrians, and Assyrian and Chaldean Christians—no such provisions exist for the Sunni community, whose representatives coordinate in a united Sunni bloc. Similarly, although there are to be found in Tehran synagogues, churches, and other places of minority worship, the government, which has included but one Sunni minister since 1979, continues to prevent the construction of a single Sunni mosque, leaving followers to gather in underground prayer houses. Yet, while the latter are largely tolerated as venues for religious worship, they are not extended the same leniency on occasions when the religious overlaps with the political. In 2011, Sunni politicians and residents of the capital were compelled through written guarantees and active police coercion to join in official Eid prayer services meant to demonstrate political consensus behind the person of the supreme leader.[43] The message: if not religious, then at least *political* rites are to be performed under the auspices of Shi'ism.

In the Arab monarchies, national identity, and indeed national history itself, is tied even more intimately to the particular experiences of their respective rulers. Competing group identities and histories of non-Arab, non-Sunni, and non-tribal (and even non-Najdi) citizens are deemphasized or excluded as a matter of course, even where these correspond to a majority of nationals. Celebrations for Qatar's National Day include elaborate public performances of a traditional sword dance (*al-'arda*) by the nation's indigenous tribes, which erect tents along a kilometers-long road circuit through which the amir passes in recognition of their continued allegiance and support. To mark the fortieth anniversary of the United Arab Emirates in 2011, the crown prince of Abu Dhabi himself took part in a similar display in front of thousands of cheering spectators at a football stadium.[44] Similar sights (and state-

[43] Saeed Kamali Dehghan, "Sunni Muslims Banned from Holding Own Eid Prayers in Tehran," *The Guardian*, 31 Aug. 2011, http://www.guardian.co.uk/world/2011/aug/31/iran-forbids-sunni-eid-prayers

[44] James Langton, "The Sword Dance," *The National*, 8 Dec. 2011, http://www.thenational.ae/news/uae-news/heritage/the-sword-dance

produced television programs) glorifying a desert, tribal past—the simple but rewarding life ostensibly enjoyed by citizens' ancestors—can be seen across the region, attended by homes and vehicles adorned with public expressions of appreciation for Gulf leaders personified as patriarchs of extended national tribes.

The difficulty, of course, is that despite attempts to make it such, this heritage is not a universal one. Persians, Arab Shi'i, Saudis of the Hejaz, naturalized migrants with roots in Hadhramawt and Baluchistan—such groups find little representation in official histories and national lore written from the standpoint of Najdi tribesmen. Differing in name, dialect, custom, and even attire, they are conspicuous as the adopted children of the national family, lacking the genealogical credentials to share in traditional communal expressions of political support, and so existing in basic contrast to the prevailing mode of citizenship. What is more, these others are not simply nationless but preserve histories and traditions of their own in place of official state doctrine. Competing narratives emphasize marginalization and injustice rather than consensus and wise leadership. Nowhere is this more apparent than among the largest and most widespread political minority of the Gulf monarchies, Arab Shi'i, who over the course of decades and centuries have nurtured a national folklore that draws on shared notions of political wrong and betrayal rooted in the very foundations of Islam.

The result is a region-wide cognitive disconnect between Sunnis and Shi'is that goes far beyond superficial differences of religious doctrine. Whereas Sunnis rue a lost desert past while celebrating the modernizing visions of Gulf rulers, Arab Shi'i in Bahrain, Saudi Arabia, and elsewhere recall the time when all the Shi'i of Eastern Arabia—from Basra to the Trucial Coast—were united in a single nation called Bahrain, a country whose abundant natural resources and devout Shi'i religion were spoiled with the arrival of foreign Sunni conquerors.[45] Now, the end of this Shi'i golden age is immortalized in the continued rule and glorification in national lore of these same tribal invaders. The Al Khalifa's 1783 capture of Bahrain from the Safavid Persian Empire is institutionalized, for example, in ubiquitous popular references to "the conqueror" ("*al-fatih*") himself, Ahmad bin Muhammad Al Khalifa.[46] As pithily expressed by

[45] Louër, *Transnational Shia Politics*, pp. 23f.

[46] The choice of the Al-Fatih Grand Mosque as the base of counter-revolutionary

Bahrain's popular Shi'i cleric Shaikh Abd al-Wahhab Husain, a powerful force in the uprising of the 1990s and of February 2011 (and currently serving a life sentence for his role in the latter), the difference between Sunnis and Shi'is is the difference between "*al-fatih wa al-maftuh*": "the conqueror and the conquered."[47] "The history of Shi'ism," he continued, "is the history of opposition against Sunni powers."[48]

As the second quotation indicates, such political discourse is rendered all the more powerful because of the ready availability of a corresponding historical imagery that forms a part of collective Shi'i consciousness. Present grievances may stem from the finite actions of Gulf rulers, but these are linked inextricably with shared memories of injustice suffered by countless generations of Shi'i. Thus the pervasive political overtones and near-hysterical atmosphere of the annual festival of Ashura, which in mourning the martyrdom of the Prophet's grandson and family at the hands of the second Umayyad (Sunni) caliph in AD 680, in fact laments the political defeat of the Shi'i—*Shi'atu 'Ali*, or "the partisans of Ali" and the hereditary line of the Prophet against rival claimants to the Islamic caliphate. With the massacre at the Battle of Karbala, Yazid I assumed undisputed control of the nascent Muslim community, later cementing it through the adoption of dynastic succession. The connection of these events to the current status of Shi'i communities, still politically disenfranchised by Sunni-led, hereditary regimes, is easily made and

---

protests by pro-regime Sunnis at the height of Bahrain's crisis in Feb. and Mar. 2011 was no coincidence. Indeed, there even emerged an Al-Fatih Group for Electronic Jihad, meant to combat the international media campaign waged by protesters.

47 Moreover, while "*al-fatih*" (lit., "the opener") can mean "the conqueror" or "the victor" in the military sense, it also carries overt religious overtones that certainly are not lost on ordinary Bahrainis as they would not be on any Arabic-speaking Muslim. When seventh-century Muslim armies fought to spread their nascent religion across the Arab world and beyond, they were said to be effecting the "*fath al-islam*"—the "opening of Islam"—a euphemism for the conversion or political subjugation of non-Muslim peoples. Its use in the Bahraini context, then, implies not simply that the island was conquered militarily by Ahmad Al Khalifa and his Sunni tribal allies, but that it was "opened" for Islam—that is, for true Islam—in view of its indigenous Shi'i inhabitants and its prior status as a protectorate of Safavid Persia, which since 1501 had embraced Shi'ism as a state religion.

48 Interview by author, Bahrain, May 2009.

exploited. To be sure, it is no coincidence that an opportunistic Khomeini chose the height of Ashura to voice his first attack on the shah in June 1963,[49] and even in post-revolutionary Iran the occasion has remained a perennial flashpoint for anti-government protest. The inherent political nature of Ashura, which represents the Shiʿi counterpoint to traditional expressions of support for Gulf leaders institutionalized via ceremonies and customs from which they are largely excluded *qua* Shiʿi, is reflected in restrictions and bans on public celebrations across the Gulf monarchies.

The legacy of the "New Middle East"

Underlying the contemporary phenomenon of sectarianism in the Persian Gulf region are therefore two complementary processes operating on the country level. First, the very institutional characteristics of Gulf states—low-information political environments along with economic incentives for individual rent-seeking behavior—combine to privilege political coordination on the basis of outwardly observable social categories rather than shared policy preferences that cut across societal boundaries. Second, this latent potential for group-based competition has, with few exceptions, been enhanced inadvertently or deliberately by ruling elites, whose design of formal representative institutions and ostensibly unifying national identities reveals a common effort to institutionalize political identification and contestation along religious, tribal, and other ascriptive lines. What remains to be examined, accordingly, is how these internal dynamics are conditioned by the region's larger geopolitical setting, and why this interaction serves especially to favor the broad Sunni versus Shiʿi dichotomy that has become increasingly synonymous with the idea of sectarianism in the Persian Gulf context.

In short, the dramatic shift in the Gulf balance of power wrought by the ouster of the Baʿathist regime in Iraq (and to a far lesser extent that of the Taliban in Afghanistan) has changed the terms of debate regarding Shiʿi movements and even Shiʿi citizens as a class of political actors in Gulf Arab states.[50] Where once these were conceived by ruling fami-

[49] Louër, *Transnational Shia Politics*, p. 187, n. 32.

[50] Although it is not the focus here, one may observe the same about Sunni political movements in Iran, which face increasing suspicions of cooperation with and

lies as local political problems to be addressed in corresponding local, political frameworks, now the perceived or actual political emboldening of Shi'i communities—or indeed the mere presence of Shi'i populations—is understood foremost as a security problem, one requiring both local preventative measures as well as regional and international cooperation in defense of the common challenge posed by Iranian-backed Shi'i irredentism. The result is a vicious cycle in which exclusionary policies stemming from heightened scrutiny and suspicion of Shi'i citizens only further aggravate existing political grievances, spurring increased activism that in turn reinforces state fears and, from the latter's perspective, confirms the need for precisely the sort of preventative policies that are the source of Shi'i complaint. Beyond deepening the political and social alienation of Shi'i citizens, this near-hysterical focus on the existential threat of a meddling Iran also serves to alarm ordinary Sunnis throughout the Gulf, spreading anti-Shi'i sentiment even to places with little history of sectarian politics (for example, Yemen and Kuwait) and countries home to marginal Shi'i populations (the UAE and Qatar).

Shi'ism as a security problem

The unshackling of Iran following successive US-led regime changes in its two main regional competitors initiated a fundamental shift in the geostrategic environment of the Persian Gulf that is rivaled only by the events of 1979. Yet, while the Islamic Revolution threatened to bring *vilayat-i faqih* (Khomeini's doctrine, literally "rule of the jurisprudent") to the Gulf, the fervor of its populist rhetoric belied its ability to do so. Penned in by Sunni-dominated Iraq to the west and Afghanistan to the east, Iran's planned exportation of the revolution in fact was restricted to modest Shi'i uprisings in Bahrain and Saudi Arabia.[51] A decade-long military stalemate with Iraq would further demonstrate its material limitations. Thus was the transformation effected in 2003 so radical—and, for Gulf Sunnis, so frightening. A puritanical Sunni regime in

---

support from transnational Sunni groups such as al-Qaeda, as well as from the United States.

[51] The Bahraini government also claimed in Dec. 1981 to have thwarted a coup attempt by members of the Iranian-backed Islamic Front for the Liberation of Bahrain. See Louër, *Transnational Shia Politics*, pp. 156ff.

Afghanistan had only two years earlier been replaced with a weak government that could easily be manipulated; now, in place of a staunchly anti-Shi'i regime in Iraq, was a state run by Iraqi Shi'i. Not only did Iran enjoy a much more favorable strategic position, but Shi'i movements across the region—from al-Wifaq in Bahrain, to Hezbollah in Lebanon, to the Huthi rebels in northern Yemen—seemed to be gaining steam.

Already in 2004 Jordan's King Abdallah II would famously refer to an emerging "Shi'i crescent," a menacing band stretching from Syria and Lebanon through Iraq and Iran and into the Arab states of the Gulf. Weaving disparate events across the Islamic world into a coherent tale of coordinated Shi'i emboldening, Middle East observers wrote of a "Shi'i revival"[52] that included a new firebrand Iranian president hell-bent on erecting a military nuclear program; an Iraqi state transforming into an Iranian puppet; a confident Hezbollah in Lebanon and Hamas in Gaza armed with sophisticated hardware from Iran; and a group of Arab states in the Persian Gulf looking increasingly vulnerable to Shi'i irredentism. Whereas ruling families were occupied throughout the 1990s by the threat of Sunni radicalism, primary concern shifted now to the containment of a belligerent Iran and what one Salafi Bahraini parliamentarian described as its "octopus-like network of cells distributed throughout all of the Gulf and Arab countries."[53]

For Persian Gulf leaders, however, this need to manage domestic Shi'i populations presents a veritable catch-22, wherein the very attempt to purchase political stability in fact serves only to open the door, in the state's view, to increased instability. Specifically, the more a government would seek to cultivate the political support of Shi'i opponents using the most comprehensive tool available to it—private benefits conferred mainly through employment in the public sector—the more it exposes itself to exactly that danger meant to be relieved in the first place, by

[52] King Abdallah II is quoted in Robin Wright and Peter Baker, "Iraq, Jordan See Threat to Elections from Iran," *The Washington Post*, 8 Dec. 2004. The term comes from Vali Nasr's work, *The Shia Revival: How Conflicts within Islam Will Shape the Future*, New York: W.W. Norton, 2006.

[53] Salman al-Dawsari, "*al-Bahrain: Na'ib ra'is al-lajna al-tashri'iyya fi al-barliman yataham al-wifaq bi-'taharrukat mashbuha' ma' al-huthiin fi al-yaman*" [Bahrain: Vice-Chairman of the Legislative Committee in Parliament Accuses the al-Wifāq Opposition of "Suspicious Dealings" with the Huthis of Yemen], *al-Sharq al-Awsat*, 24 Aug. 2009, http://www.aawsat.com/print.asp?did=533078&issueno=11227

inviting those citizens deemed most dangerous to walk in, so to speak, through the front door. As a result, government agencies and services deemed politically or militarily sensitive are made off limits to those identifiable (in this case, on the basis of religious affiliation) as potential regime opponents. This begets a situation in which state employment is no longer an effective means by which to procure political loyalty, while demonstrable political loyalty—in effect, the correct family name—is a prerequisite for most forms of state employment. In practice, such sectarian screening is generally accomplished via requirements for certificates of "good history and conduct," issued by the police to verify that an individual has no prior record of arrest or detention, including for political reasons.[54] Employment itself being a political tool, those whose political allegiance is doubted are systematically disqualified from the public sector; and for every individual undeserving of service, governments reason, a dozen can be recruited from Yemen, Syria, or Baluchistan. In the end, ruling families would rather staff security services with non-national Sunnis than take a chance with Shi'i citizens subservient to their co-sectarians in Iran. While empirical evidence is scarce, a 2009 mass survey of Bahrain found, for example, that whereas 17 percent of all employed Sunni males reported being employed in the police or armed forces, not a single Shi'i among all those interviewed indicated the same.[55]

This virtual exclusion of Shi'i from the police and military in the Gulf monarchies is but another mechanism by which citizens are divided between those with a private stake in the country and those who feel not only unfairly excluded from it, but indeed unwelcome in it. Yet the issue is not merely one of discrimination. Over the decade spanning 2000 to 2009, the top eleven military spenders in the world as a proportion of GDP included five of the six GCC states: Oman (1), Saudi Arabia (2), the UAE (4), Kuwait (6), and Bahrain (11).[56] With the security sector representing such a large proportion of public spending in the Gulf,

[54] Louay Bahry, "The Socio-Economic Foundations of the Shiite Opposition in Bahrain," *Mediterranean Quarterly*, 11, 3 (2000), p. 134.

[55] Gengler, "Ethnic Conflict and Political Mobilization," pp. 79–80, 155.

[56] According to the authoritative database compiled by the Stockholm International Peace Research Institute. Data for Qatar are not reported for the years 2000, 2001, and 2009, but based on the incomplete data it would rank in 30th place. Data available at http://www.sipri.org/databases/milex

then, the targeted disqualification of citizens on the basis of sectarian affiliation further entrenches a two-tiered system of rentier benefits, wherein an entire sector of the economy—indeed, the single most dominant sector—is reserved for members of a specific social group. Just as their lack of tribal ancestry precludes them from joining in "national" expressions of political support for Gulf rulers, so too does the very condition of being Shi'i make them unsuitable candidates for various forms of public service. As Bahrain's minister of industry and commerce tellingly admitted during anti-government protests in 2007, "There is a lack of confidence between the ruled and the rulers. It is not unusual. There is a small percentage who do not have loyalty to the state. Sometimes, for good reasons, you have to be careful who you employ."[57]

Sectarianism from abroad

The reconceptualization of religious difference as a security problem rather than a political problem has also opened the door for sectarianism in Persian Gulf states with little domestic cause for or history of it. For, if the threat from Shi'ism stems not simply from an ability to mobilize followers in service of shared political aims but, more fundamentally, from the competing national loyalties of its adherents, then popular anti-Shi'i sentiment may arise even in societies where citizens do not fear Shi'i as political competitors. In Yemen, for instance, the alleged adoption of Twelver Shi'ism by (formerly Zaydi) Huthi insurgents fighting for an independent imamate in the north of the country has helped to politicize religious identity in a nation long shared by Zaydi Shi'i and Shafi'i Sunnis.[58] The Yemeni state now openly accuses Iran of arming and otherwise aiding the rebels, and one Bahraini Salafi cleric has even accused al-Wifaq of the same,[59] reflecting a popular impression that wherever one finds a Shi'i—whether in Sitra or Sa'ada—there he finds a friend of all other Shi'i, a loyal soldier ant who, when he senses that any

[57] Quoted in Bill Law, "Riots Reinforce Bahrain Rulers' Fears," *Sunday Telegraph*, 22 July 2007, http://www.telegraph.co.uk/news/worldnews/1558179/Riots-reinforce-Bahrain-rulers-fears.html

[58] In fact, for reasons that are not clear, Yemen's Zaydis do not even consider themselves "Shi'i" (a label they reserve for the Huthis), a fact that has occasioned many an argument with Yemeni friends.

[59] Cf. Salman al-Dawsari, "*al-Bahrain.*"

of his brood are in trouble, runs instinctively to their defense. As if to add to the sectarian nature of the conflict, finally, Yemen and Saudi Arabia continue to wage proxy war against the Huthis by arming local Salafi tribes keen to uproot their heretical Shi'i neighbors.

As demonstrated elsewhere in the region, however, the awakening of sectarian political identities need not even originate from some domestic cause. In the days and weeks following Bahrain's February 2011 uprising, Shi'is from Iran to northern Yemen to Lebanon to Iraq demonstrated in solidarity with their Bahraini co-religionists.[60] Indeed, the main impetus behind the heavy-handed GCC intervention to squash the Bahrain uprising was the fear that neighboring Shi'i populations—in particular those of Saudi Arabia's oil-rich Eastern Province adjacent to Bahrain—would take the cue to begin their own large-scale revolt. The United Arab Emirates openly threatened to deport any Shi'i residents speaking out publically against the GCC action in Bahrain, and was said to have expelled several hundred Lebanese expatriates.[61] But most dramatic of all was the impact in Kuwait, where the entire government fell directly as a result of a Sunni–Shi'i split in parliament over the country's response to Bahrain.

Not wanting to inflame its own Shi'i community, in late March 2011 the Kuwaiti government offered, instead of sending ground troops, to mediate talks between Bahrain's rulers and the opposition. This proposal earned the swift condemnation of other GCC members and of its own Sunni politicians, who accused Kuwait's rulers of showing more concern for Iranian-backed Shi'i terrorists than for their Sunni brothers in Bahrain. When Kuwait next tried to send a medical delegation to help treat Bahrain's wounded, it was refused entry at the Saudi–Bahrain causeway, a further public embarrassment that prompted several Salafi politicians

[60] In Iraq, not only ordinary citizens but also prominent Shi'is in government strongly criticized the GCC response in Bahrain. Al-Maliki himself warned that "the region may be drawn into a sectarian war" if the situation were allowed to fester. For such perceived one-sidedness, the GCC states forced the postponement of a Mar. 2011 Arab Summit scheduled to take place in Iraq, insisting that "the atmosphere is not right." See Serena Chaudhry and Waleed Ibrahim, "Iraq's Maliki Says Bahrain May Ignite Sectarian War," Reuters, 25 Mar. 2011, http://www.reuters.com/article/2011/03/25/us-iraq-politics-idUSTRE72O6JK20110325

[61] See, for example, "Iraq, Bahrain and the Region: Sectarian Bad Blood," *The Economist,* 31 Mar. 2011, http://www.economist.com/node/18491700

to initiate proceedings to quiz the country's prime minister for his decision to abstain from the GCC's deployment in Bahrain. At the same time, Shi'i parliamentarians moved to question two Al Sabah ministers for allowing local media to rebroadcast a program aired on Bahrain state television that insulted the prime minister and prominent Shi'i families. Under siege from all sides, Kuwait's amir opted to dissolve the government rather than allow the inquest to proceed.[62] Then—at last—shamed and bullied into participation, Kuwait dispatched a naval detachment to Bahrain. The lesson: the GCC will stand together against the shared threats of Shi'i irredentism and Iranian meddling—whether individual members like it or not.

The intimate link between domestic and regional politics in the Persian Gulf thus widens the boundaries within which the broad categories Sunni and Shi'i may become politicized. Indeed, such is the transnational political salience of sectarian identity in the post-2003 period that a reform movement in Bahrain can succeed directly in toppling the government—in Kuwait. Aided by a concerted campaign among Arab leaders in the Gulf to connect Shi'i political mobilization to Iranian interventionism (to say nothing of Saudi Arabia's active promotion of Salafism), Sunni populations across the region are increasingly distrustful of Shi'i co-nationals generally and of Shi'i political demands in particular. Shi'i citizens are no longer viewed simply as competitors in the battle to secure additional rentier benefits, but as opponents in a larger struggle over the very character of Gulf states and of the Persian Gulf region itself. And, as the Sunni-led monarchies redouble their efforts to realize the original 1981 vision of the Gulf Cooperation Council—a politico-military alliance to secure member states against Iranian-inspired Shi'i irredentism—this individual-level contest finds growing parallel at the country level. Citizens and states alike are being asked to decide between two rival factions, giving substance to a now-infamous vision attributed to Shaikh Isa Qasim, Bahrain's ranking Shi'i *marja'* ("source of religious emulation") and the spiritual force behind al-Wifaq, who is said to have observed in a sermon:

62 For a more complete version of the story, see Husayn al-Harabi, "*Muhammad al-Sabah al-sabab al-mubashir wara' istiqalat al-hakuma*" [Muhammad al-Sabah is the Direct Reason behind the Government's Resignation], *Al-Ra'i*, 1 Apr. 2011, http://www.alraimedia.com/Alrai/Article.aspx?id=266356&date=01042011

> The Battle of Karbala is still going on between the two sides in the present and in the future. It is being held within the soul, at home and in all areas of life and society. People will remain divided and they are either in the Hussain camp or in the Yazid camp. So choose your camp.[63]

Conclusion: demystifying sectarianism

Far from primordial hatreds, group solidarities, and other indecipherable passions, political competition on the basis of confessional religious distinctions—sectarianism—is in fact a particular instance of a larger category of phenomena with roots in the specific institutional context of the Persian Gulf region. A political environment in which others' policy views are not easily identifiable, combined with an economic environment that promotes individual rather than collective pursuit of material resources, works to privilege political coordination on the basis of ascriptive social groupings rather than cross-societal programmatic coalitions. Under these conditions, outward identifiers that communicate group descent—language, skin color, family name, and so on—transmit data not only about an individual's social affiliation, but moreover about one's likely political orientation as a member of a specific region, tribe, or religious or ethnic community. This allows Gulf leaders seeking to maximize their own shares of directly accruing external rents to capitalize on what Corstange terms an "ethnic subsidy": the cheap support of co-ethnics (or co-sectarians, or fellow tribesmen). Co-ethnic support is relatively inexpensive in the sense that it is more easily inferred by ruling elites, who must distinguish between political supporters and opponents so that scarce resources are employed in rewarding the former group and not dissipated on the latter. The upshot is a structural tendency toward those general political phenomena that underlie the more specific case of sectarianism, namely political coalitions based on ascriptive descent, and popular co-ethnic (or co-religionist, etc.) support for governments.

Yet, if the institutional incentives embedded in Gulf societies create a latent potential for the politicization of ethnic and religious identities in

[63] Quoted in Habib Toumi, "Bahrain's Islamist MP Calls for Removal of Sectarian Banners," *Gulf News*, 19 Feb. 2006, http://gulfnews.com/news/gulf/bahrain/bahrain-s-islamist-mp-calls-for-removal-of-sectarian-banners-1.225726. The quotation gained much publicity in 2006 when it appeared on large Ashura banners across Bahrain sponsored by the Islamic Enlightenment Society.

general—which indeed are inherently political identities—then the emergence of group competition around sectarian categories in particular, around the broad distinction of Sunni versus Shi'i, owes to other causes. A first is the inadvertent or conscious structuring of political contestation so as to enhance rather than dampen society's potential for inter-group competition. The vast majority of the Gulf states have developed formal representative institutions as well as national identities that institutionalize group difference. Rather than encourage cross-cutting citizen coalitions, electoral rules and procedures are manipulated to ensure the continued political salience of ascriptive distinctions, especially those based on tribal and confessional affiliation. Rather than unify citizens around a common vision of peoplehood with which all citizens can identify, most national identities and histories are crafted in the image of ruling elites. As a result, not only are the experiences and heritage of some citizens not represented in official state doctrine, but these citizens—whether Sunnis in Iran or Shi'i in the Gulf monarchies—lack the background necessary to share in traditional expressions of support for political elites *qua* co-religionists or *qua* leaders of an extended national tribe. In their place, excluded communities maintain competing identities and traditions, preserved in histories emphasizing injustice and marginalization that draw on Islam's centuries-old conflict over political succession and leadership.

Accompanying these domestic dynamics is a regional context in which the categories Sunni and Shi'i continue to assume a larger geopolitical significance, representing not merely a doctrinal distinction but a proxy for a wider division between the opponents and supporters of Iran and its presumed regional ambitions. The chief strategic beneficiary of the US-engineered "new Middle East," the Islamic Republic, is viewed by nervous Arab neighbors as an active promoter of Shi'i irredentism throughout the region, not to mention a veritable puppet master of the Shi'i-led government in Iraq. Accordingly, the management of Shi'i populations (and, in Iran, the Sunni population) is conceived increasingly as a security problem demanding concerted regional cooperation rather than a political issue to be solved in local political frameworks. But the resultant discriminatory policies—especially in the area of public-sector employment—only augment the frustrations of already-marginalized political minorities, feeding a vicious cycle wherein the state's very attempt to secure itself against sectarian mobilization actually serves to foment further political agitation—and not simply among members of the targeted group. By invoking the specter of an emboldened Shi'i populace operating at the behest of a belligerent Iranian regime, governments also succeed in awakening Sunni communities, who organize themselves as a counterweight to domestic Shi'aization and Iranian expansionism, in effect making their own political demands upon the state, and further polarizing society along sectarian lines.[64]

One sees, then, that the concept of sectarianism does not signify an innate complex of historical animosities, religiously inspired solidarities, or other vague sentiments to which various societal ills of Persian Gulf societies may be tautologically attributed. Neither, however, is sectarian competition a mere epiphenomenon, an outward manifestation of some generic political conflict with no particular roots in the Persian Gulf context per se. The foregoing account has endeavored to elaborate a middle ground between these two all-too-common positions, a framework for the study of sectarianism in the Persian Gulf that explains the region's institutionally induced propensity for ascriptive politics but also why sectarian conflict is not an inescapable state of nature pitting every Sunni against every Shi'i. In so doing, hopefully, it has served the additional purpose of helping to rescue the notion of sectarianism from its present connotations as crude, obsolete, and perhaps worse, in order that this central feature of the Gulf political landscape may continue to attract the scholarly inquiry it so demands.

[64] This Sunni counter-mobilization continues to play a decisive role, for example, in the trajectory of Bahrain's political crisis a year after the 2011 uprising. See Gengler, "Bahrain's Sunni Awakening."

2

SECTARIAN RELATIONS AND SUNNI IDENTITY IN POST-CIVIL WAR IRAQ

*Fanar Haddad**

Introduction

No other event—not even the Iranian Revolution of 1979—has had as momentous and detrimental an effect on sectarian relations in the Middle East as the war and occupation of Iraq in 2003.[1] In Iraq itself,

* I would like to thank the indefatigable Laith al-Yasiri and Amir al-Yasiri for their extraordinary efforts in helping me secure sources in Baghdad. Similarly my gratitude goes to Dr Hassan al-Haddad and Ameer al-Sa'adi for their help. My thanks also to Reidar Visser, Mark Farha, and to all the participants in the "Sectarian Politics in the Gulf Working Group" for their comments and input.

[1] Throughout this essay, "sectarian relations" will be used to refer to Sunni–Shi'i relations. Rather than a definitional stance, this merely reflects my research interests and the subject at hand. The term "sectarianism" appears in quotation marks throughout, the reason being that the term has no definitive meaning. Until we are able to define "sectarianism," a more coherent way of addressing the issue would be to use the term "sectarian" followed by the appropriate suffix: sectarian hate; sectarian unity; sectarian discrimination, and so forth.

internal and external forces building on events, memories, triumphs, and tragedies from the pre- and post-2003 era combined to lend sectarian identity an unprecedented degree of political relevance. In addition to thrusting sectarian identity center-stage, the removal of the Ba'ath and the subsequent political and security vacuum allowed for an explosion of previously restricted expression—from intellectuals establishing newspapers to criminals asserting their will and everything in-between.[2] As the state collapsed, the illusory veneer of relative uniformity and harmony that the Ba'ath had forcefully and violently upheld was abruptly removed, unleashing passions and identities that had been, at best, poorly understood, and at worst, completely overlooked.[3] For the first time, the Iraqi other came into full, unrestrained view to the rest of his/her compatriots. Claims and counterclaims, visions and counter-visions of what Iraq and its recent history meant were forcefully, often violently, asserted; self-proclaimed victims demanded justice from scarcely comprehending others as the depth of Iraqi division was, for the first time ever, on prominent display. Compounding this delicate situation was the security and political vacuum of the immediate post-war years and the policies and behavior of the newly empowered Iraqi political classes, the Coalition authorities, and regional actors.

The sectarian divide alluded to above is somewhat paradoxical in that, unlike Iraq's major ethnic divide, it does not entail imagining an alternative to the Iraqi nation-state. It is not a division that seeks to resurrect historic homelands; rather, the Sunni–Shi'i sectarian divide in Iraq is rooted in divergent Iraqi historical memories.[4] The story of why sectarian identity as opposed to other societal or indeed ideological cleavages attained political ascendency in 2003 is a complicated one that incorporates pre- and post-2003 social and political, Iraqi and regional factors, and cannot be adequately addressed in this chapter.[5] Likewise, an essay

[2] For a particularly vivid account of the chaotic first months of the "new Iraq," see Zuhair al-Jaza'iri, *Harb al-'Ajiz* [The Invalid's War], Beirut: Al-Saqi, 2009.

[3] Few examples are more illustrative in this regard than the Sadrist phenomenon.

[4] See Haider Saeed, *Siyasat al-Ramz: An Nihayat Thaqafat al-Dawla al-Wataniyya fi'l Iraq* [The Politics of the Symbol: On the End of the Culture of the National State in Iraq], Beirut: Al-Mu'assisa al-Arabiyya, 2009, p. 103.

[5] Unsurprisingly, given recent events, there has been an upsurge in studies dealing with this complicated and contentious subject. Some notable works, old and new, include: Marion F. Sluglett and Peter Sluglett, "Some Reflections on the Sunni/

of this length will have to be selective when discussing the working of sectarian identity and sectarian relations. As such, my purpose is to analyze the role of national and sectarian symbolism in sectarian relations and the interplay between national identity and sectarian identity in Iraq generally. Second, this essay will explore the evolution of Sunni Arab mass-group identity in post-invasion Iraq. Prior to 2003 there was scarcely such a thing as an Iraqi Sunni Arab group identity; at least not one that was consciously held and that required formulation and enunciation—a fact reflected in the literature's overwhelming focus on Shi'i identity. Since 2003 Iraqi Sunni Arabs have had to contend with an ascendant and assertive Shi'i triumphalism and have had to familiarize themselves, for the first time ever, with minority status. This chapter, in addition to discussing sectarian relations in general, will hopefully shed light on the Iraqi Sunni group-imagination and the future prospects for Sunni identity and, by extension, sectarian relations in Iraq.

Understanding sectarian relations

The negativity and passions aroused by the word "sectarianism" continue to obscure our understanding of sectarian identity in Iraq. While "sectarianism" is often understood as something that is inherently discriminatory and hence to be rejected, it should not be allowed to tar

---

Shi'i Question in Iraq," *The Bulletin of the British Society for Middle Eastern Studies*, 5 (1978), pp. 79–87; Elie Kedourie, "Anti-Shi'ism in Iraq under the Monarchy," *Middle Eastern Studies*, 24 (1988), pp. 249–53; Hassan al-Alawi, *Al-Ta'thirat al-Turkiyya fil Mashru' al-Qawmi al-Arabi fi'l Iraq* [The Turkish Impact on Arab Nationalism in Iraq], London: Dar al-Zawra'a, 1988; Hassan al-Alawi, *Al-Shi'a wa al-Dawla al-Qawmiyya fi'l Iraq 1914–1990* [The Shi'a and the National State in Iraq 1914–1990], London: self-published, 1990; Yitzhak Nakash, *The Shi'is of Iraq*, Princeton: Princeton University Press, 1996; Saleem Muttar, *Al-Dhat al-Jariha* [The Wounded Self], Beirut: Al-Mu'assisa al-Arabiyya li'l Dirasat wa al-Nashr, 1997; "The Question of Sectarian Identities in Iraq," Special issue, *International Journal of Contemporary Iraqi Studies*, 4, 2 (2010); Various authors, *Al-Ta'ifiyya fi'l Iraq* [Sectarianism in Iraq], Beirut: Al-Aref, 2008; "Al-Mas'ala al-Ta'ifiyya wa al-Ithniyya: al-Iraq Namuthaj" [The Sectarian and Ethnic Question: The Iraqi Example], Special volume, *Oriental Affairs*, 1 (2008); Hazim Saghiya (ed.), *Nawasib wa Rawafidh* [Nawasib and Rawafidh], Beirut: Dar al-Saqi, 2009. My own attempt at deciphering sectarian relations in Iraq can be found in *Sectarianism in Iraq: Antagonistic Visions of Unity*, London: Hurst, 2011.

legitimate sectarian identities and sectarian expression with the same brush of negativity. Yet, unfortunately, that is precisely what has happened. In the case of Iraq, broadly speaking, commentary on the subject can be split into alarmists (those who read a sectarian dimension into all things Iraqi) and reductionists (those who reduce the importance of Iraqi identity to irrelevance). Generally speaking, the former is more prevalent outside Iraq while the latter is a staple of Iraqi discourse—with no shortage of Western commentators dutifully following suit.[6]

Whatever the reasons behind this intellectual awkwardness regarding "sectarianism", the subject—and indeed the extreme positions taken—are inseparable from nationalism and the nation-state: the alarmist position ultimately seeks to demonstrate the Iraqi nation-state's artificiality and the tenuous foundations upon which it stands, while the reductionists are essentially doing the opposite. While both sides are able to furnish their arguments with numerous, and perfectly valid, examples from across Iraqi history,[7] an approach that insists either on a sectarian or a non-sectarian Iraq misses the point: identity, sectarian or otherwise, is ambiguous both in its meaning and its salience, hence the abundance in Iraqi history of episodes of both sectarian harmony and, less commonly, sectarian division.

The simple fact is that the political and social relevance of mass-group identities, sectarian or otherwise, are constantly shifting. Therefore, if we

[6] A relatively rare example of an alarmist Iraqi take on sectarian relations can be found in Abdul Khaliq Hussein, *Al-Ta'ifiyyah al-Siyasiyya wa Mushkilat al-Hukm fi'l Iraq* [Political Sectarianism and the Problem of Governance in Iraq], Baghdad: Mesopotamia House, 2011. For instance, on p. 7 the author states that, "If Karl Marx argued that human history is the result of class struggle then I believe that modern Iraqi history is the result of sectarian struggle more than any other."

[7] To illustrate with but a few examples, alarmists may point to medieval episodes of sectarian strife; the formation of the Iraqi state and the exclusion of the Shi'i (with an obligatory reference to Abd al-Rahman al-Gailani, Sati' al-Husri, and Feisal I's memoirs); the Ba'ath's policies towards the Shi'i; the events of 1991 and not least the sectarian civil war of 2006–7. Reductionists on the other hand may point to joint anti-British rallies in the run-up to the rebellion of 1920; the presence of Shi'is and Sunnis in many a nationalist party—indeed the early leadership of the Ba'ath were predominantly of Shi'i background; intermarriage; the consistent public desire for coexistence in an Iraqi nation-state; consistent rejection of "sectarianism" and the cross-sectarian celebration of the Iraqi nation-state even at the worst of times—the example that is most often raised is the Asia Cup celebrations of 2007.

speak of a sectarian imagination, sectarian Iraqi nationalism, or sectarian symbolism, these are only as relevant as sectarian identity is at any given time. As such what we saw in Iraq after 2003 was not the fulfillment of innate sectarian desires that had been anxiously awaiting the removal of dictatorial constraints to express themselves, nor was it the fruition of the occupation's nefarious machinations to divide and rule. Rather, it was a reflection of the sociopolitical context in which the political change took place: in short, we cannot be sure that sectarian identity would have attained the same centrality if regime change had happened in, say, 1991.

One of the reasons why understanding sectarian identity and sectarian relations in Iraq has proven so formidable a challenge relates to the aforementioned negativity associated with the term "sectarianism", alongside the positivity that is accorded to nationalism and a belief that the two are mutually exclusive. Yet a closer look reveals a more complex interplay between the national and the sectarian for those Arab Iraqis who subscribe to a sectarian identity.[8]

The mythology of sectarian nationalism

The only way to understand sectarian relations in Iraq is to view them as competing subnational mass-group identities. As such, the dynamics are in essence very similar to other competing groups, be they racial, national, ethnic, or even ideological. However, when considering these competing groups, a crucial distinction needs to be made: are they self-proclaimed members of a mutually claimed nation-state? In instances where this is the case, the nature and manifestations of group competition and perceptions of self and other are influenced by this perceptual link to the nation-state and ultimately to nationalism. To illustrate, a Lebanese Shi'i may debate with an Indonesian Sunni about the legitimacy of the Prophet's Companions and the flaws of Sunni Islam against the merits of Shi'i Islam; however, with his/her Sunni compatriots, the debate is just as likely to revolve around Lebanese demographics, history, and, generally speaking, entitlement to the national pie.

Three factors are immediately noticeable in sectarian dynamics in Iraq—and to varying degrees in other Middle Eastern contexts such as

[8] It is worth emphasizing that a degree of generalization is inescapable when speaking of sociopolitical categories as large and unwieldy as "Shi'i" and "Sunni." It bears spelling out: *nothing* can be said about *all* Shi'is or *all* Sunnis.

Lebanon, Syria, and Bahrain. First, there is a "sectarian issue" that intermittently comes to the fore due to internal, external, mass-led, or elite-led factors;[9] second, the nation-state is not in question—indeed the existence of the nation-state, its "artificiality" and so forth are irrelevant to Iraqi sectarian dynamics;[10] finally, plurality is an accepted given, meaning that no matter the level of mistrust, disdain, or even violence at any given time, there has been no desire for the total elimination of the other or any drive to divide the nation-state.[11] As long as these three factors obtain, and there is no guarantee that they always will in the future, sectarian relations have the power to alter the appearance of the nation-state, threaten its stability, or change sociopolitical dynamics within it; however, in such cases, sectarian identity does not have the power, nor is it its purpose, to threaten the nation-state itself.[12]

Paradoxically therefore, while sectarian animosities in Iraq are detrimental to national unity and the nation-state, they are nevertheless intrinsically linked to, and are a product of, the nation-state and nationalism. Put simply, the fact that competing sectarian groups are mutual adherents of a single nation-state means that their immediate competition, in terms of claims, symbols, and imaginations, is bounded by the territoriality of their nation-state, hence, and in stark contrast to Iraq's major ethnic divide, the absence of any significant sectarian secessionist movements. In other words the contest in such cases is between conflicting imaginations of, and entitlements to, the nation-state. As such, despite the religious props, it is a clash of competing visions of a singular nationalism—or to paraphrase Sami Zubaida, it is the fragments imagining the nation.[13]

This does not negate the existence of a transnational element; however, this is similarly affected by the centrality of national identity within sectarian identity, particularly in countries that have a plurality of sects. As such, Sunni–Shi'i relations are simultaneously imagined on two over-

9 As opposed to examples where outgroups do not have the numerical, political, or cultural weight to be competitive and hence create a "sectarian issue."

10 As opposed to Northern Ireland, where at one point sectarian dynamics sought to challenge the territorial status quo.

11 Hence it is difficult to draw parallels with Rwanda or the Armenian genocide.

12 Race relations in the United States form an interesting parallel in that regard.

13 Sami Zubaida, "The Fragments Imagine the Nation: The Case of Iraq," *International Journal of Middle East Studies*, 34 (2002), pp. 205–15.

lapping levels: at the level of the nation-state and at the global Islamic level; the national and the transnational—or more accurately, the national and the religious. What makes the national level more immediate is the fact that it has a more tangible impact on individual interests as opposed to the broader and more abstract religious/transnational level.

A most useful approach when discussing sectarian relations in a single country is ethnosymbolism and symbolic politics. Ethnosymbolists argue that competing groups define themselves according to their "myth–symbol complexes" as derived from the group's selective historical memory—or "ethnohistory" as Smith calls it.[14] In Kaufman's words, the myth–symbol complex is the core of group identity and is the "combination of myths, memories, values and symbols that define not only who is a member of the group but what it means to be a member."[15] In cases like Iraq, because competing sectarian groups are doing so within, and in the name of the nation-state, their myth–symbol complexes will locate Sunnis/Shi'is in the nation-state as much as they will within Islam. As such it is *Iraqi* Shi'ism and, after 2003, *Iraqi* Sunnism that are in play with all the cultural, political, economic, and national symbolism that would otherwise be absent in a spiritual Shi'ism and Sunnism.

It is within these Iraqi sectarian myth–symbol complexes that conflicting sectarian memories and visions of Iraq are contained. However, it is worth reiterating that none of the above is constant: the sectarian myth–symbol complex is only as salient as sectarian identity is at any given time. As such, rather than a perennial struggle, sectarian competition in Iraq advances and recedes according to context. The relevance of sectarian identity can be inflated by a number of factors such as state policy, external pressures, economic competition, or regional dynamics. At such times, when sectarian identity is inflamed, more people identify themselves as members of a sectarian group for the simple reason that they may perceive a threat to their sectarian identity and/or because it had gained political relevance.[16] In a climate of salient sectarian identities, the sectarian myth–symbol complex's relevance and capacity to influence

[14] Anthony Smith, *Chosen Peoples: Sacred Sources of National Identity*, Oxford: Oxford University Press, 2003, pp. 166–72.

[15] Stuart J. Kaufman, *Modern Hatreds: The Symbolic Politics of Ethnic War*, Ithaca: Cornell University Press, 2001, p. 25.

[16] For a more detailed discussion of these dynamics see Haddad, *Sectarianism in Iraq*, Chapters 2 and 3.

one's perspective will rise. However, crucially, this takes place at the national level; in other words, when the relevance of sectarian identity is inflated, the antagonisms are manifested through the prism of, and with reference to, the nation-state. Thus we may refer to forms of Iraqi sectarian nationalism that come to the fore at times of sectarian tension and which view the Iraqi nation-state through a sect-centric prism.

When sectarian nationalism is mobilized, it manifests itself most obviously in two ways. First, by seeking to satisfy the sense of entitlement that so often characterizes politicized group identities—a pertinent example of this is a group linking political rights to numerical weight: "we are the majority."[17] Second, sectarian nationalism seeks to validate the group's view of themselves and their nation-state by asserting their sect-centric imaginings of what Iraq means. Nationalism should not be viewed in rigid terms: it is rather a fickle set of emotions, myths, and symbols. As Friedland argues, "nationalism offers a form of representation ... [but] it has nothing to say about the content of representation, the identity of that collective subject, or its values."[18] Therefore, what nationalism means at any given time is subject to change and can be influenced by dominant social groups. In the simplest of terms, sectarian nationalism's aim is to furnish the props of nationalism, thereby achieving congruence between the sectarian myth–symbol complex and official nationalism, and ultimately validating the group's belief that they embody the nation-state and vice-versa—such as, for example, the Shi'is' "Iraqiness" and Iraq's "Shi'i-ness."[19] This need for validation

[17] Such a slogan, in and of itself, is a symptom of the political relevance of group identities. To link political interests and political positions to mass-group identity is the antithesis of citizenship. One of the recurring problems in Iraq, and elsewhere in the Middle East, is that the concept of democratic majority-rule is often perceived along societal identity-based lines rather than on strictly political ones. Interview, Abdul Jabbar Ahmed, dean of the College of Political Sciences, University of Baghdad, Baghdad, Jan. 2012.

[18] Roger Friedland, "Religious Nationalism and the Problem of Collective Representation," *Annual Review of Sociology*, 27 (2001), p. 138.

[19] Interestingly, in his study of "religious nationalisms," Friedland (ibid.) mentions Iraq as one of the exceptions to the rule. His argument is that religious nationalism (a state nationalism furnished with religious props of identity) is only possible in countries that are religiously near-homogenous. In Friedland's view, where this is not the case, religious nationalism will revolve around territorial separatism as in the example of the Tamils in Sri Lanka. However, I would argue that

and group prestige is particularly nourished by feelings of ontological and/or existential insecurity that in turn facilitate the mobilization of sectarian identities, a dynamic vividly illustrated in the new Iraq and the struggle to incorporate sect-centric myths and symbols into official narratives of state.

Sectarian myths and symbols, and by extension sectarian nationalisms, like the identities they embody, are not fixed. Symbols are constantly being invented and reformulated; they may lie dormant, all but forgotten, for years on end, yet they are ever-ready to be reawakened and revised to suit the needs of a future crisis.[20] A survey of modern Iraqi history indicates that, due to the perceived legitimacy of the Iraqi nation-state among Arab Iraqis and given the acceptance of the fact of plurality, the "default setting" in Iraqi sectarian relations is a banal "sectarianism" whereby sectarian identity is of little consequence to social relations.[21] This "default setting" leads sectarian myth–symbol complexes, or at least the antagonistic elements within them, to recede into irrelevance. At such times Iraqi Shi'is and Iraqi Sunnis—meaning those who actually consider themselves as such—will define themselves in much broader terms. As for their sectarian identity, it comes to be viewed through the prism of ecumenical unity by focusing on areas of overlap between sectarian myth–symbol complexes alongside a strengthened sense of "Iraqiness."

The last decade has shown sectarian relations at their worst; yet they have also illustrated the fluctuating nature of sectarian identity and sectarian relations. As one Iraqi academic reflected:

> There is a link between politics and society; one reflects the other. During times of bloodshed, violence and media incitement—particularly 2005–2007—many

---

Friedland's framework is perfectly applicable to Iraq provided we acknowledge that nationalism is not always hegemonic and that competing, even antagonistic, visions of a singular nationalism are possible.

20 For more on the selective and intermittent usage of symbols see Kaufman, *Modern Hatreds*, p. 44; Jean-Francois Bayart, *The Illusion of Cultural Identity*, trans. Steven Rendall et al., London: Hurst, 2005, p. 110.

21 Sectarian identity can be said to run along a spectrum: from banal "sectarianism" to passive "sectarianism" (the extreme of which is apologetic "sectarianism") to assertive "sectarianism" (the extreme of which is aggressive "sectarianism"). See Haddad, *Sectarianism in Iraq*, pp. 25–9.

people started dismissing the common examples of [sectarian] unity (such as intermarriage). Back in those days many people regarded such things as empty slogans. But with stability these matters wither away. And this is what happened here: we had relative stability and we had just emerged from a civil war [*harb ahliyya*][22] and these matters [sectarian animosities] waned. Sectarian coexistence has its roots and foundations [in Iraq] and the Iraqi does not dwell on these issues ... But when there is an existential threat things are different. Between 2005–2007 divorce between Sunnis and Shi'is rose and intermarriage dropped but this was reversed after 2008.[23]

Sectarian relations between aspirations and reality

None of this is unique to Iraq, and a broader view of inter-group relations may dispel the myth of perpetual sectarian hostility or the equally reductionist "we are all brothers" myth; in other words the alarmist/reductionist dichotomy. The facts of coexistence, social relations, and intermarriage are unfortunately not a bar to periodic outbreaks of inter-group hostilities. To explain this apparent paradox some scholars have used Freud's "narcissism of minor differences" theory, according to which people, both as individuals and collectives, form an exaggerated sense of their own uniqueness to differentiate themselves from others, making similarity and coexistence a fickle barrier against conflict. As anthropologist Anton Blok informs us, the Mae Enga of the western highlands of Papua New Guinea have a saying: "we marry the people we fight."[24] Or as Turkkaya Ataov put it with regards to conflict in Central

[22] Many commentators and scholars, particularly those outside Iraq, remain resistant to applying the civil war label to the sectarian violence of 2006–7. As I have argued elsewhere, whether we call those events a civil war or not is a moot point. However we label it, 2006–7 were years of acute sectarian entrenchment, horrendous sectarian violence, and a near-breakdown of sectarian relations. Among the few non-polemical works that have dealt with this subject are: Nir Rosen, *Aftermath: Following the Bloodshed of America's Wars in the Muslim World*, New York: Nation Books, 2009; International Crisis Group, "Iraq's Civil War: The Sadrists and the Surge," *Middle East Report*, no. 72, 7 Feb. 2008.

[23] Interview, Yasin al-Bakri, College of Political Science, University of Baghdad, Baghdad, Jan. 2012. It is exceedingly difficult to verify the issue of intermarriage empirically, as marriage certificates only state the school of thought according to which the marriage was performed.

[24] Anton Blok, *Honour and Violence*, Oxford: Polity Press, 2001, p. 119. Originally published in Anton Blok, "The Narcissism of Minor Differences," *European Journal of Social Theory*, 1 (1998), pp. 33–56.

Asia: "When relations are pleasant, their desirable parts come to the fore. When disagreements rise, differences get the upper hand, and minor differences are then magnified. Even if there are no minor differences, groups tend to create them."[25]

Alarmists should not take the above as confirmation of their views, nor should reductionists feel that it attacks theirs. On the contrary, the above illustrates the self-evident fact that both are partially correct but are limited by what are highly essentialized positions that place Iraqi Sunnis and Shi'is either perpetually at each other's throats or forever in each other's embrace. A more nuanced approach would begin by acknowledging the fact that "sectarianism" is viewed with profound disdain by the vast majority of Arab Iraqis. Nevertheless, at times of sectarian tension, or simply when sectarian identities are salient, a gap emerges between aspirations and reality. With hindsight we can see that even through the worst years of violence the aspiration remained constant: a unified pluralistic Iraq that rejects "sectarianism". However, despite the sincerely held aspiration, in such circumstances of violence and uncertainty, people were naturally more susceptible to identity entrenchment. More specifically they were susceptible to the effects of an activated sectarian imagination.[26]

Two points are worth making regarding the aspiration/reality gap. First, it seems to have escaped many researchers—hence the dominance of alarmists and reductionists: the former will focus on the reality of a chosen historical moment (overlooking the ephemeral qualities of this "reality"), and the latter will focus on the aspiration. It is of little value to highlight Iraqis' very obvious insistence on ecumenical unity at face value. As already mentioned, the Iraqi nation-state still commands the loyalty of Arab Iraqis who are so thoroughly socialized into accepting

[25] Quoted in Pal Kolsto, "The 'Narcissism of Minor Differences' Theory: Can it Explain Ethnic Conflict?" *Filozofija i Društvo* [*Philosophy and Society*, Belgrade], 2 (2007), p. 161. Kolsto adds to Ataov's comments by suggesting that hostilities do not stem from the minor differences themselves; rather, the conflicts are caused by something else, but "members of different groups will seize upon the minor differences in order to expand the identity gap between them and justify their mutual hostility." Ibid.

[26] This gap between societal aspirations and reality is to be found everywhere, and the ideals aspired to by a society are not necessarily adhered to at all times. One might sincerely believe in the merits of "political correctness," yet occasionally indulge in heat of the moment racial stereotypes or be amused by racist jokes.

the principle of sectarian plurality that a message of overtly aggressive sectarian hatred is unlikely to capture a broad following in Iraq. However, despite that, at times of sectarian tension the predictable refrain of "we are all brothers" means little in the face of rising sectarian entrenchment. As Rosen deftly put it:

> Their constant message [in 2003] was … "We are all Muslims." But in retrospect they were protesting too much; behind the stentorian insistence that they were all united was the fear that they were not and the knowledge of what would happen should this secret become known.[27]

Second, that a gap can at times emerge between aspiration and reality and that a sectarian imagination exists and is liable to periodic activation is not as dramatic as alarmists may lead us to believe. When we speak of salient sectarian identities we are referring to a process that, more often than not, takes place on a collective rather than an individual level. As psychologist Stephen Reicher points out, social identities are comparative in that group members make value-laden comparisons between ingroups and outgroups.[28] However, in his own words, "It is important to stress that the comparison occurs at a collective level. It is not how I, as an individual group member, compare to you, an individual member of another group. It is rather how we as a whole compare to you as a whole."[29] This may help us decipher the paradoxical nature of Iraqi sectarian relations that are undoubtedly grounded in the principles of coexistence but which are not free from antagonisms that can at times be inflamed, thereby threatening the very coexistence that is taken for granted.

Power relations, group competition, and the production of symbols

Before discussing Sunni Arab identity in today's Iraq, it is worth inquiring into the roots of Iraqi sectarian myth–symbol complexes. As will be shown, a distinctly Arab Sunni identity is evolving in Iraq today; but why did this not happen previously, as was the case with Shi'i Iraqis?

[27] Rosen, *Aftermath*, p. 36.

[28] An in/outgroup dichotomy is particularly useful when looking at sectarian relations given that numerical strength does not always translate into dominance—Bahrain being the starkest example.

[29] Stephen Reicher, "The Context of Social Identity: Domination, Resistance and Change," *Political Psychology*, 25, 6 (2004), p. 929.

The reasons relate to power relations and the functional purpose of group identities. While every group has at least a latent sense of self, not all have a coherent symbolic structure embodied in a myth–symbol complex through which to reproduce itself. For some groups a position of dominance, privilege, or ontological security derived from relative congruence between their identity and its associated norms with those of state and society safeguards the group's identity to the extent that it requires no active expression. If we frame it in terms of ingroups and outgroups, the outgroup will seek to preserve their sense of self through the production of symbols independently, and often in defiance of, the centers of political power. Whether it is the sanctification of a martyred leader or teenagers' proficiency at creating new slang, it can be argued that the purpose of such actions is to differentiate one's group from the dominant other and to assert an outgroup identity. Ingroups are not as prolific in the production of group-specific symbolism for the simple reason that their group identity is safeguarded by their position of dominance and their relation to state symbolism; hence they do not need to produce symbols as they have little need to assert their identity.

The most prominent illustration of these dynamics is to be found in the growing study of whiteness in race relations. It has been argued that white identity was previously "raceless" in that white people did not see themselves as having a race but, rather, they were "simply people." They believed that their viewpoint was not a white one but a "universally valid one—'the truth'—what everyone knows."[30] As such, white becomes the standard, the norm, so to speak, against which all others are differentiated.[31] This phenomenon is the result of relative empowerment that enables dominant groups to influence what is regarded as "the norm"; this in turn blinds them to the facts of their own empowerment and the realities of the other's marginalization. Furthermore, the reification of a dominant group as "the norm" can be internalized by outgroups who, more often than not, will seek approval and acceptance by trying to

[30] Richard Delgado and Jean Stefancic, *Critical Race Theory: An Introduction*, New York: New York University Press, 2001, p. 80.

[31] See Richard Dyer, "The Matter of Whiteness," in Les Back and John Solomos (eds), *Theories of Race and Racism: A Reader*, London: Routledge, 2000. On p. 540 Dyer gives a simple example that perfectly illustrates the point regarding identity, dominance, and discourse: "An old-style white comedian will often start a joke: 'There's this bloke walking down the street and he meets this black geezer,' never thinking to race the bloke as well as the geezer."

measure up to society's standards of acceptability as influenced by the dominant group.[32]

The dynamics of sectarian relations in Iraq, though not identical, are certainly similar. Prior to 2003, sectarian discrimination, real or perceived, was the lament of the Shi'i; they were the other who sought to raise the issue of "sectarianism" and the imbalance in sectarian representation and empowerment.[33] Given that Sunni Arabs did not perceive themselves to be victimized on the basis of their sectarian identity, there was little awareness of, or concern for, issues relating to sectarian identity among them. As a result, the highly charged and negatively perceived terminology of sect and "sectarianism" came to be associated with the Shi'i.[34] Prior to 2003, many Sunni Arabs saw themselves as "simply Iraqis" whose viewpoint, like the white one alluded to above, was not a Sunni Arab one but a universally valid one; in other words they were "sectless" in a manner similar to the "raceless" whites.[35] It is crucial to note that the empowerment that causes this is not necessarily direct material or political power—how much of either do working-class whites or Iraqis have? It is more a sense of identity-security that arises from the conviction that "we" are the *Staatsvolk* whose identity is validated in the daily reproduction of power relations.[36]

[32] Similarly Fanon argued: "When the Negro makes contact with the white world, a certain sensitizing action takes place … The black man stops behaving as an *actional* person. The goal of his behavior will be The Other (in the guise of the white man), for The Other alone can give him worth." Franz Fanon, *Black Skin, White Masks*, 2nd edn, London: Pluto Press, 2008, p. 119.

[33] An early example is the People's Pact (also known as the Najaf Pact) of 1935. See Abdul Razzaq al-Hasani, *Tarikh al-Wizarat al-Iraqiyya* [The History of Iraqi Ministries], 8 vols, 7th edn, Baghdad: Dar al-Shu'un al-Thaqafiyya al-Ama, 1988, here vol. 4, pp. 92–4.

[34] Sajjad H. Rizvi, "From Communalism to Communitarianism: Imagining Communities, Nations and their Fragments in South Asia and Beyond," paper presented at Princeton University Workshop, "Rethinking Sectarianism," 22 May 2008, pp. 2–3.

[35] This can very well be expanded and applied to sectarian identity on the transnational, religious level: for the most part, Sunni Muslims may see themselves as "simply Muslims." They are the ingroup who have no need to validate their Islamic identity and who have rarely felt the need to formulate and assert a Sunni identity. By contrast, Shi'i identity (or indeed any Islamic outgroup's identity) is far more aware of its own otherness within the Islamic world.

[36] As a result, one is far more likely to hear of a "sectarian issue" in pre-2003 Iraq

While members of a dominant group will seldom understand or even be aware of any imbalance—consider popular male attitudes towards gender—the dominated, or the outgroup, will not only have a higher awareness of the issue but will be more likely to develop the identity that they feel is the source of their plight. In short, marginalization, real or perceived, develops an awareness among the marginalized of their own otherness which in turn nourishes what they regard as an encircled mass-group identity that increasingly comes to be associated with victimhood and entitlement. In the case of the Shi'i, this process has resulted in a far more developed myth–symbol complex than is the case with their Sunni counterparts. Iraqi Shi'is can draw on both Shi'ism's and *Iraqi* Shi'ism's rich pantheons of icons and symbols to perpetuate their group identity and to define and differentiate themselves from the other.[37]

Historically, political, social, and religious dynamics meant that Sunni identity was not called upon to fulfill the functions demanded of Shi'i identity—hence the absence of a symbolic heritage similar to that found in Shi'ism. This placed Sunnis at a distinct disadvantage in the new Iraq: a triumphal Shi'i identity, with all the symbolic might at its disposal, was asserted and used to redefine Iraqi politics, society, and ultimately identity. The new Iraq was, for many Sunnis, an unrecognizable country with which it was difficult to identify.[38] The centrality of sectarian identity in post-2003 Iraq meant that, for the first time in modern Iraqi history, an explicitly Sunni Arab identity had to be formulated and

---

from a Shi'i Iraqi, just as one is far more likely to hear of a "sectarian issue" in post-2003 Iraq from a Sunni Iraqi.

[37] See Ala'a Hameed, "Al-Ayquna al-Shi'iyya: Qira'ah fi Dala'il al-Suwar al-Ramziyya li A'immat al-Shi'a" [The Shi'i Icon: Analyzing the Symbolic Images of the Shi'i Imams], *Masarat*, 15 (2011), pp. 116–20. For a fascinating examination of the iconography of Ali ibn Abi Talib see Shakir Lu'aibi, *Tasawir al-Imam Ali* [Depictions of Imam Ali], Beirut: Riad El-Rayyes Books, 2011.

[38] Early on in the post-war period, Ahmed Hashim incisively spoke of a Sunni sense of "identity disenfranchisement" as the root of Sunni opposition to the new Iraq. He elaborates: "For Sunni Arabs the downfall of the regime in April 2003 was not only or even primarily the collapse of power and privileges—indeed, many of them had little power and few, if any privileges—but of the entire edifice that has been in existence for more than eight decades and that had *identified* Iraq with them." Ahmed S. Hashim, *Insurgency and Counter-Insurgency in Iraq*, London: Hurst, 2006, pp. 68–9.

articulated to serve social and political ends—a daunting task given the head start that Shiʿi identity had in the production of symbols and the formulation of a mass-group identity.

Sectarian identity in the new Iraq

Post-2003 Iraq unfortunately offers rich terrain for researchers working on sectarian identity. The political change of that fateful year signaled a transformation of the dynamics of power in sectarian relations. In short, the roles have been reversed: Sunnis have replaced their Shiʿi compatriots as the self-perceived victims of sectarian discrimination. It goes without saying that the previous regime was not a "Sunni regime" any more than today's is a "Shiʿi regime." Nevertheless, in both cases, the political habitus that prevailed resulted in indirect, and sometimes direct, sectarian discrimination and consequently more salient sectarian identities, especially among the excluded group.[39] In today's Iraq this favoritism is much less opaque than it was in the past. For one thing, US policy and the political views and ambitions of most of the returning Iraqi political exiles ensured that ethno-sectarian identities were central in the formation of the new Iraq beginning with the Iraqi Governing Council of 2003. As a result, the assertion of sectarian identity and the very subject of "sectarianism" are much more permissible than was the case prior to 2003. Furthermore, while the symbolism used by the former regime was often compatible with the Sunni myth–symbol complex,[40] the use of Shiʿi symbolism by the state today is unrestrained and completely unambiguous.

As with much relating to post-2003 Iraq, sectarian relations have undergone several shifts since the war. Indeed, one of the difficulties of studying the new Iraq is that the political and social changes are rapid,

[39] Many instances of Shiʿi exclusion under the former regime may have been driven by tribal discrimination rather than sectarian identity. See Farouk-Sluglett and Sluglett, "Some Reflections on the Sunni/Shiʿa Question in Iraq," p. 84. As for the current regime, it is often, though not always, the case that Shiʿis are favored for party, regional, or tribal considerations rather than sectarian identity. Interview, Rafi'i al-Isawi, minister of finance, Baghdad, Jan. 2012. Nevertheless, in both cases the end result is the same: a strengthened perception of sectarian discrimination consequently nourishing the salience of sectarian identities.

[40] See Haddad, *Sectarianism in Iraq*, Chapter 3.

profound, and ongoing. We should not assume therefore that sectarian relations today are what they were in 2003, much less in 2006. Broadly speaking, sectarian relations have been through four main phases: politicization and entrenchment in 2003–5; civil war in 2006–7; retreat in 2008–9; and finally the post-civil war period since 2010. Although it might be premature to try to diagnose the nature of post-civil war sectarian relations, preliminarily it can be said that they are characterized by salience and occasional politicization, but not centrality. This may be a reflection of a growing albeit largely begrudging acceptance of the new sectarian landscape and the relative increase in the strength and stability of the state that has in turn allowed for other political issues to rise to the fore.[41] Nevertheless, despite glimmers of hope in the elections of 2009 and 2010, sectarian identity retains enough salience to be intermittently employed with success in Iraqi politics. In fact, in 2013 Iraqi sectarian relations seemed to be on the cusp of a new and more volatile phase. Initially triggered by the arrest of Minister of Finance Rafi'i al-Isawi's security detail in December 2012, a considerable protest movement emerged in Sunni majority governorates and Sunni majority areas of Baghdad. The sectarian element of the protests was spurred on by what was an intensely sectarian conflict in neighboring Syria and more generally by the climate of flux that pervaded the Middle East. Unfortunately, since at least April 2013 there was a notable rise in violence, some of which was of an unmistakably sectarian nature, raising fears of a return to civil war. Unless these trends are reversed, sectarian relations in the new Iraq may well be entering their most dangerous phase.[42]

[41] It is more than mere coincidence that KRG–Baghdad relations became more problematic after 2008 and that Sunni majority governorates have only recently resorted to constitutional measures and protections—namely federalism—to air their grievances. Furthermore, since 2008, political positions and alliances are not as neatly aligned with sectarian identity as they previously often were. I would argue that the crisis, since 2011, with Vice President Tariq al-Hashemi is not, as many insist, a sectarian issue, but one of political alliances and conveniences.

[42] It is far too early to include ongoing developments in this chapter or to speculate as to the longevity of recent trends. For an excellent analysis of the protest movements see Joel Wing, "Understanding Iraq's Protest Movements: An Interview with Kirk H. Sowell, Editor of Inside Iraqi Politics," 7 May 2013, Musings on Iraq, http://musingsoniraq.blogspot.sg/2013/05/understanding-iraqs-protest-move-

The assertion of Shi'i identity

One of the problems with sectarian relations in Iraq and beyond lies with the expression of Shi'i identity. This is rooted in two interrelated factors: first, as has been mentioned, for a variety of historical reasons Shi'ism developed a rich pageantry that serves the purposes of ritual, identity-assertion, group-definition, reproduction, and cohesion, and which had little in terms of a Sunni counterpart. Second, Sunni Arab opinion in Iraq and the broader Middle East views organized assertions of Shi'i identity, indeed any outgroup identity, with unease. The reasons for this are intimately linked to national and regional politics: from elites emphasizing the Shi'is' alien otherness to better discredit their Shi'i oppositionists, to the conflation of sectarian and ethnic identities and by extension Shi'ism and Iran. More broadly, this points to a fundamental, and unfortunately common, shortcoming on the part of the Middle Eastern nation-state in that it has failed to formulate mechanisms that would allow the legitimate assertion of outgroup identities.[43]

In Iraq, and until 2003, the absence of such a mechanism has made the assertion of sectarian identity often problematic in and of itself.[44] The other may perceive some form of hostility, or at the very least a sense of exclusion, when sectarian identity is asserted in a large and organized way even if this is done without mention of the other.[45] One of the problems

ments.html. For an equally valuable analysis of the rising levels of violence in mid-2013 see Stephen Wicken and Jessica Lewis, "From Protest Movement to Armed Resistance: 2013 Iraq Update #24," 14 June 2013, Institute for the Study of War, http://iswiraq.blogspot.sg

[43] For a brief elaboration of this point see Fanar Haddad, "The Limits of Change in the Middle East: Libya, Iraq, Bahrain and the Arab Spring," *Critical Muslim*, 3 (2012).

[44] The 1970s are an important turning point in that regard in that mass Shi'i Ashura rituals were banned by the Iraqi regime. Naturally, this nourished Shi'i identity entrenchment and accentuated Shi'i victimhood and propelled what may have been a mere religious ritual into identity politics by further intertwining sectarian identity with political rights. See Fouad Ibrahim, "Shi'at al-Iraq: Inbi'ath Hawiyya Maqmu'a wa Tahadiyyat Muraga'at al-Dhat" [The Shi'i of Iraq: The Revival of a Suppressed Identity and the Challenges of Self-Critique], *Masarat*, 15 (2011), p. 87.

[45] The most prominent example of this is the Sunni reaction to Shi'i slogans during the events of Mar. 1991.

with "sectarianism" in Iraq is that what is considered "sectarian" provocation by one group is often merely the assertion of the other group's symbols. As will be shown, this is exacerbated by the imbalance between Sunni and Shi'i symbolisms and by the existence of contradictory, sometimes offensive, elements in sectarian myth–symbol complexes.

Unfortunately for Iraq, many of the Shi'i political elites empowered in 2003 saw the fall of the Ba'ath as being the Shi'is' deliverance as much as it was Iraq's liberation. The mantra of the time was "majority rule"; however, the salience of sectarian identity was such that political majorities were formulated not according to programs, ideologies, or political positions but on ethno-religious lines, thereby furthering the politicization of communal identities and inflaming sectarian relations. Linked to this was the prominent display of Iraqi Shi'ism's myth–symbol complex, a key component of which was victimhood. Historic wrongs were to be righted, victims compensated, and transgressors punished, yet with such deep divisions in Iraqi historical memory, how was this to be accomplished without arousing Sunni fears? This is particularly so given that the victims were portrayed in ethno-religious terms, with the Kurds and the Shi'is competing for first place. Dhafir al-Ani, an Iraqiyyah-affiliated politician who has often been accused of "sectarianism", elaborates this point in his reflections on 2003:

> The fact that the parties that came [to Iraq in 2003] were backed by Iran caused serious concern among Sunnis. That they were backed by Iran meant there was a sectarian issue at work here. Secondly, when the slogans are all about Yazid and Umayya rather than Harun al-Rashid—or when Jaafar al-Mansur's statue was blown up—all of this has a sectarian coloring.[46] [As a result] I felt that this change is targeting me [as a Sunni]; it is targeting me when the Ba'ath Party is made synonymous with Sunnis; or when Al-Qaeda is pictured as Sunni or that terrorists are Sunnis, or that Sunnis previously killed Shi'is—not just the previous regime, rather it was as if the problem was with the Sunnis.[47]

[46] Yazid bin Mu'awiyya was Husain's rival for the caliphate; Bani Umayya were a Quraishi tribe that opposed the Prophet—it was also the tribe that Yazid bin Mu'awiya hailed from. They later converted to Islam and founded the Umayyad dynasty. Ja'far al-Mansur was the second Abbasid Caliph and founder of the city of Baghdad. All three, particularly the first two, are reviled in Shi'i ethnohistory. The reason for Al-Mansur's demonization is his persecution of the sixth imam, Ja'far al-Sadiq. Al-Mansur's statue was reportedly bombed in Oct. 2005.

[47] Interview, Dhafir al-Ani, Baghdad, Jan. 2012.

Al-Ani's reference to symbols is particularly interesting. Slogans about Yazid and Umayya are all but inevitable when the Shi'i myth–symbol complex is on display, yet as is clearly illustrated in Al-Ani's recollections, in certain contexts, this suffices to elicit feelings of encirclement among some Sunnis.

While the new Iraq and its political elites proclaimed their legitimacy on the basis that they had rid Iraq of the Saddam era's horrors, they did so while also proclaiming that their communal group was uniquely victimized by the previous regime. With that in mind it is unsurprising that what psychologist Qassim Hussein Salih calls the post-2003 "culture of victimhood" came at the expense of Sunnis: come the birth of the new Iraq, they had neither the power to project themselves nor the myth of unique victimhood. As argued by Ghanem Jawad, someone who is intimately familiar with many of Iraq's post-2003 political elites, Shi'i politicians fell into what he describes as a decidedly "sectarian predicament": they conflated their desire to compensate for the Shi'is' past suffering with nation-building.[48] As a result, Shi'i myths and symbols, not least the symbolism of the oppressed majority rectifying historical wrongs, were interwoven into the fabric of the new Iraq beginning with the establishment of the Iraqi Governing Council in 2003.[49]

The structural manifestations of this are in need of further research—with legislation, policymaking, educational reform, and official employment being particularly relevant. My interest here, however, is primarily in symbolic politics and expressions of sectarian identity. As already mentioned, when salient, sectarian identities in Iraq seek validation through the representation of their myths and symbols in the public sphere and in organs of state to better align "we the people" as sect with "we the people" as Iraqis. This is immediately evident in Baghdad today and often in Iraqi policymaking as well. The assertion of Shi'i identity in state and society continues to nourish the post-2003 sense of Sunni

[48] Ghanim Jawad, *Al-Shi'a wa al-Intiqal al-Dimukrati* [The Shi'i and Democratic Transition], Damascus: Dar al-Hasad, 2011, p. 236.

[49] Salih aptly sums up the problem with the IGC: "it was based on two psychological dualities: 1) victims versus oppressors and 2) outsiders [meaning exiles] versus insiders." Qassim Hussein Salih, *Al-Mujtama'a al-Iraqi: Tahlil Sikususiulugi li-ma Hadath wa Yahduth* [Iraqi Society: A Psycho-Sociological Analysis to what Happened and is Happening], Beirut: Arab Scientific Publishers, 2008, p. 13.

exclusion and victimhood and is one of the more visible drivers behind the continued efforts to formulate and assert a coherent Sunni identity.

The omnipresence of Shi'i symbols in Baghdad is difficult to exaggerate.[50] Flags—black, green, and red—are everywhere,[51] so too are portraits of the Shi'i imams and saints, pictures and murals of Shi'i religious leaders past and present, Shi'i Iraqi nationalist slogans and banners displaying Shi'i symbols both in the national and the religious sense. In the years preceding 2003 it was common to see pictures of the imams in certain areas of the capital; however, these were a relatively understated display of sectarian identity—for one thing they were a strictly private affair, such as for example inside a restaurant in a Shi'i area. Even then they were modest in size and seldom dared to compete for wall space with the near-compulsory picture of Saddam Hussein. By contrast, today's assertion of Shi'i identity is garish, loud, and unrestrained to the extent that it cannot but affect daily life in Baghdad.[52] It can be argued that this reflects a sense of insecurity and encirclement among Iraqi Shi'is. Despite the political gains made, the legacy of suppression of Shi'i identity remains a powerful part of the Shi'i historical imagination; furthermore, Shi'is are all too aware of the resentment that their empowerment has caused among many Sunni Arabs in Iraq and the broader Middle East, and as such feel that their position is under constant threat. Therefore, this assertive Shi'ism is paradoxically a sign of both empowerment and insecurity. It is perhaps this combination that lends some assertions of Shi'i identity today a confrontational, or at the very least a

[50] In a private conversation one man joked about the omnipresence of Ali ibn Abi Talib's portraits by saying that he had become the new Saddam. It is perhaps worth mentioning that he was a Shi'i—as noted earlier: *nothing* can be said about *all* Shi'is or *all* Sunnis.

[51] These are the Husseini flags and are seen in all sizes from A4 to giant cloths measuring several square meters. Black represents sorrow, green represents the House of the Prophet, and red for vengeance. The last one is, in certain contexts, viewed with alarm by Sunnis as they interpret it to be a veiled threat against themselves. See for example http://iraqirabita.org/index.php?do=article&id=17492

[52] In addition to intrusive audio and visual forms of assertion, the machinery of state all but grinds to a halt during major Shi'i events. See Ahmed al-Sa'adawi, "Utal Diniyya li Akthar min Thulth al-Sana" [Religious Holidays for More than a Third of the Year] *Niqash*, Aug. 2008, http://www.niqash.org/articles/?id=2265&lang=ar

provocative, character. As has been stressed throughout, sectarian competition is very much a competition of symbolisms which is why such an aggressive display of a sectarian myth–symbol complex is not without consequence in Iraq.[53]

It can be argued that the onus is on Sunni Arabs to learn to accept Shi'i symbolism. It is hardly the Shi'is' fault that Sunni identity lacks the iconography that Shi'i identity enjoys, and individuals should of course

From left to right: flags and banners with portrait of Hussein in the background (outskirts of Mansur); banners and portraits showing Ali ibn Abi Talib, Hussein, Abbas and Fatima (Uteifiyah); portrait of Hussein (Jadiriyah).

[53] So much so that, according to the dean of the College of Political Sciences at the University of Baghdad, a fellow dean at Mustansiriyah lost his life because of such symbols: "They killed him! He wanted to remove portraits [of the imams and Shi'i religious leaders] from university grounds in the name of creating a neutral civic space—and by the way he was a Shi'i." Interview, Abdul Jabbar Ahmed.

be free to express their identity. Indeed there is nothing outwardly provocative in the illustrations presented here and, as has been argued, Sunni Arab opinion is at times irrationally suspicious of expressions of Shi'i identity. In sum, there is certainly a need for greater acceptance among Sunnis of Shi'i symbolism. However, the situation in Iraq today is not simply one of Shi'i symbolism being unfairly resented by Sunnis. That very resentment is legitimized, exacerbated, and politicized first by the assertion of Shi'i identity in Sunni areas and second, and more importantly, by the involvement of the state. As one Sunni imam from A'adhamiyyah complained:

> Let me ask you: if there were images of Abu Bakr and Omar, would I be able to display them in Karbala? You have huge images [of the imams] in A'adhamiyah and these have foundations constructed for them [that is, they are fixed structures] and it is all happening in Sunni areas. What does that mean? They want to turn the area into a Shi'i one [*tashyee'e al-mantaqa*].[54]

Regardless of the intention behind such displays of Shi'i identity, it is scarcely surprising that they will be regarded as nothing short of provocative when seen in Sunni areas. Such actions serve as a constant reminder that the Shi'i are the Iraqi *Staatsvolk* and that Baghdad is a Shi'i-majority city. In Dhafir al-Ani's opinion:

> The Shi'i want to "Shi'ify" [*tashyee'e*] Iraq. Not just the political regime [*sulta*], not just the government; rather all facets of the state [*dawla*] whether in terms of media, faith, politics or culture … For example, take Iraqi [state-run] media: is it Shi'i media, Sunni media or neutral? It is Shi'i media! There is no enmity in what I am saying; it is just an analytical observation. I mean when you enter a state institution and you see a picture of Sistani—this is the "Shi'i-fication" of the state.

His concluding remark was interesting in that it was a rare recognition of the other's victimhood: "Sunnis today feel the same way that Shi'is felt prior to 2003: that they are second-class citizens."[55]

[54] Interview, Qasim al-Ubaidi, Baghdad, Jan. 2012. Mr Ubaidi's story is an interesting and very relevant one that illustrates the interplay between sectarian unity and division: his father is a Sunni from western Iraq and his mother is from Karbala. He himself was born in Karbala and lived there until threatened by Shi'i militants in Apr. 2003. He unhesitatingly exhibits a profound sense of Sunni victimhood and deep suspicions towards Shi'i leaders and parties; however, this does not impinge on his belief in and loyalty to a united and pluralistic Iraq.

[55] Interview, Dhafir al-Ani.

Undoubtedly the most complicating factor in the issue of competing symbolisms is the role of the state. The existence of competing myth–symbol complexes, even the existence of hostile myths, is not a problem in and of itself—nor is the fact that people will want to express their sectarian identities. However, for this to have a chance of being tolerated by the other, the state and state symbolism must be perceived as being neutral in sectarian terms. As has been explained, sectarian identities in Iraq are intrinsically linked to nationalism and hence it is the state, using a sect-neutral state nationalism, that has the potential to manage and contain the antagonisms inherent in competing sectarian identities. By first securing people's right to express their sectarian identity and second by ensuring the state is neutral with regards to sectarian symbolism, and hence inclusive in terms of sectarian identities, the state and state nationalism can depoliticize sectarian competition and ensure that a broader sense of "Iraqiness" captures popular and cross-sectarian subscription, thereby remaining above sectarian competition.[56] While this sectarian neutrality is often proclaimed by state officials, it is rarely mirrored in policy or practice.

The images above can be attributed to individual actions: a Shi'i man or woman places a banner or flag on his/her house and given that it is merely an individual's expression of their sectarian identity, the sectarian other should accept it as such. However, when such displays tax public funds or when they are seen on public buildings and institutions of state, they cease being private expression and can easily be construed as a form of state-driven cultural exclusion of the sectarian other. As the following examples show, there are now many permanent fixtures in Baghdad that exhibit Shi'i iconography.

[56] Illustrative of the impact that the state can have on sectarian symbolism were the claims by several Sunnis—and even some Shi'is—that, contrary to previous practice, they now abstain from showing any solidarity or participation in Shi'i rituals because of the state's patronage. In the words of one Sunni: "I used to cook food [to distribute to the poor] in Muharram but now things are different. Previously when a Sunni did this it was solidarity; today it is kowtowing [*tamalluq*]." Baghdad, Jan. 2012. A Shi'i businessman who was jailed under the previous regime for partaking in Shi'i rituals but who nevertheless continued to do so until 2003 claims that he no longer participates because of the political overtones that the rituals have gained. In his words: "Previously, I did it to challenge the state. Why would I do it now? The rings [characteristically worn by some Shi'is] and the turban have replaced the khaki!"

From left to right: Mohammad Sadiq al-Sadr and his son Muqtada on either side of Fatima (near Kadhimiyyah); a mural of Husain (Jadiriyyah); a metallic fixture showing Muqtada al-Sadr (Sa'adun Street); a fixture displaying messages from the Islamic Supreme Council of Iraq including images of Mohammad Baqir al-Hakim and Mohammad Baqir al-Sadr (Jadiriyyah).

As opposed to opaque symbols that emphasize an inclusive Iraqi mythology, in many instances the new Iraq has undoubtedly adopted and propagated a *Shi'i* Iraqi mythology that celebrates Shi'i symbols, heroes, and tragedies as shown in these impressive murals of Mohammad Baqir al-Sadr.

Left: This massive mural, currently under construction, is on the road to Baghdad International Airport. It shows Mohammad Baqir al-Sadr and behind him, obscured by the palm tree, is his sister Bint al-Huda. *Right*: equally impressive is this mural outside Baghdad Railway Station showing Mohammad Baqir al-Sadr and Mohammad Sadiq al-Sadr flanking the Iraqi flag in a perfect illustration of Shi'i Iraqi nationalism.

Shi'i symbolism is commonly seen in institutions of state and on state property: on ministries, ambulances, schools, police cars, museums, and so forth. This has been a cause for concern among many Sunnis including no less a figure of ecumenical harmony than Jamal al-Badri, veteran opponent of the Saddam regime and director of the Ministry of National Reconciliation:

> These displays are very provocative: what is the meaning of a military car with a picture of Hussein on its windows? This is something that is supported by the state to force Shi'i identity on the Iraqi street. Opposing this, we now have a backlash and Sunni identity is being expressed strongly for example through the Mawlid.[57]

Prior to 2003, Sunnis were often unsympathetic, if at all aware, of Shi'i suffering—real or perceived. Similarly, with the reversal of roles that began in 2003, Shi'is often do not see and cannot understand Sunni claims to victimhood today.[58] I posed the question of Shi'i symbolism

[57] Interview, Jamal al-Badri, Baghdad, Jan. 2012. The Mawlid is the celebration of the Prophet's birth and is one of the few outlets for specifically Sunni expression.

[58] Hence one hears Sunnis dismissing Shi'i claims of marginalization by pointing

and its expression through state organs and in public spaces to Abd al-Halim al-Zuhairi—a senior Da'wa Party figure and one of Prime Minister Nuri al-Maliki's chief advisors. After stating that these were individual practices that cannot be prevented by a state that is struggling to assert its authority, Zuhairi linked the issue back to Shi'i victimhood:

> The state has not reached the stage where it can forbid many things that it may not agree with. For example, the state is unable to prevent unlicensed liquor stores ... Why is this issue not raised in the way that the [Shi'i] banner on a [ministry's] window is? The issue therefore is of a feeling that this group [the Shi'i] are not allowed to take their rights because we [Sunnis] are accustomed through tens and hundreds of years to exclude this Shi'i presence. These people [the Shi'i] are not allowed to have any breathing space so when they get it the complaints revolve around these things. Otherwise [the reality is that] there are a lot of problems in the state.[59]

Zuhairi's response is far from atypical and is mirrored by Sunni views on "sectarianism" prior to 2003. In Zuhairi's case, we see an example of the link between Shi'i victimhood and Shi'i political behavior, thereby recalling Ghanem Jawad's accurate diagnosis of a "sectarian predicament" facing many Shi'i politicians. The suppression of Shi'i identity is an integral part of the Shi'is' Saddam-era marginalization. As is clear in Zuhairi's response, any suggestion that Shi'i expression should be curtailed is reminiscent of previous persecutions. Such a charged approach precludes recognition of the obvious point: that while freedom of expression should be guaranteed by the state and while the sectarian other should accept such expression, the state cannot be seen to adopt the symbols of one group to the exclusion of another's if it wishes to broaden its base.[60] Furthermore, the need for sect-neutral state symbolism is made all the more urgent by the existence of hostile myths on

---

to Saddam-era ministers who were Shi'i just as one hears Shi'is dismissing Sunni claims to current marginalization by pointing to current Sunni ministers.

[59] Interview, Abd al-Halim al-Zuhairi, Baghdad, Jan. 2012.

[60] Some have questioned whether Shi'i elites have any interest in broadening their base. This line of thinking posits that the new order projects itself as being the savior that rid Iraq of Saddam and allowed the expression of Shi'i identity, thereby silencing Shi'i opposition (but not criticism) by appealing to their desire to protect these gains. Interview, Abdul Jabbar Ahmed. Interview, Sa'ad Salloum, journalist and editor of *Masarat*, Baghdad, Jan. 2012.

both sides of the sectarian divide thereby making official adoption of sectarian symbolism potentially dangerous.[61]

Sunni identity in the new Iraq

Iraqi Sunni identity has escaped the scholarly scrutiny that its Shi'i counterpart has received for the simple reason that prior to 2003 it barely existed. There was little in the way of a differentiated sense of unique "we-ness" among Sunni Arabs in Iraq and little need to express a Sunni Iraqi identity. Since 2003, however, feelings of encirclement and exclusion based in both perception and reality have led to the formulation of a Sunni Arab identity. Perhaps one of the more discernible facets of this identity is victimhood. Today's Sunni Arab identity is a capable contestant in the narcissistic competition of victimhoods that is such a prominent feature of sectarian relations in Iraq.

As the foundation of the ethno-sectarian apportionment that Sunnis feel has disenfranchised them, demographics are a common point of reference in Sunni martyrology—to use Alfred Erich Senn's phrase. From the earliest days of the new Iraq, many Sunnis rejected the notion that they are a numerical minority.[62] Until a census is conducted—and assuming that all sides will accept its results—this issue will remain a contentious one. One could view this debate as a newly formed element of the Sunni myth–symbol complex clashing against a long-standing Shi'i symbol in yet another example of incompatible myths. For the

[61] For example, it is alleged by Dhafir al-Ani that some parliamentarians want to turn Eid al-Ghadir into an official holiday. Eid al-Ghadir commemorates what Shi'is regard as the Prophet's confirmation of Ali's succession. Regardless of whether al-Ani's allegations are true or not, this serves to illustrate the fundamental incompatibilities of certain aspects of sectarian myth–symbol complexes. As al-Ani himself pointed out, to make Eid al-Ghadir an official holiday is to exclude Sunni jurisprudence in its entirety.

[62] The argument commonly made by Sunni Arabs is that they constitute 42 percent of the Iraqi population while the Shi'i account for 41 percent; hence alongside the mostly Sunni Kurdish north, Iraq is a Sunni-majority country. I have heard this view from Sunni Arab Iraqis countless times. Public pronouncements to the same effect have been made by Sunni figures from religious leaders such as Harith al-Dhari (general secretary of the Association of Muslim Scholars) to politicians such as Khalaf al-Ulayan and Muhsin Abd al-Hamid (former head of the Iraqi Islamic Party) to extremists such as Taha al-Dulaimi to my mild-mannered interviewees such as Jamal al-Badri and Qasim al-Ubaidi.

Shi'i, their majority status is the bedrock of their sense of entitlement in Iraqi politics and a central component of the Shi'i sense of victimhood as the long-suffering majority. Sunnis on the other hand seem increasingly resistant to any notion that they are a minority, thereby nourishing their own sense of victimhood as a people who have essentially been cheated into second-class status by nothing more than a lie. As our Sunni imam from A'adhamiyah put it when the subject of demographics came up (unprompted): "Who says the Sunnis are [numerically] less than the Shi'i? Let me be frank: the Shi'i are the best media company in the world!"[63]

Identifying causality in all this is exceedingly difficult; it is, so to speak, a chicken-and-egg situation. On the one hand we can argue that the controversy surrounding demographics has little to do with sectarian relations per se and everything to do with a dysfunctional and profoundly flawed political system that equates communal identities with political interests. However, while this is undoubtedly true, the fact remains that this particular instance of political dysfunction is a product of Shi'i opinion, both popular and elite, that insisted on righting historical wrongs, one of which, as far as they were concerned, was the exclusion of the (sectarian) majority from power. Rather than accepting one argument over the other, it seems plain that the two are both relevant and indeed interrelated: we cannot assign causality strictly to the machinations of sectarian entrepreneurs independent of society, nor can we deny that an issue with a social basis can be inflated and inflamed through political engineering.

De-Ba'athification is a similar case in point. On the one hand we can identify corruption and the politicization of the judiciary, rather than "sectarianism", as the reasons why it has turned into the lament of the Sunnis. However, the divided and divisive historical memory of Arab Iraqis and the refusal to relinquish claims to exceptional sectarian victimization lend de-Ba'athification a near-inescapable sectarian dimension. To put it in plain terms: Sunnis and Shi'is, broadly speaking, held different views towards the Ba'ath and Saddam Hussein. There was no element of subnational group identity in whatever desire existed among Sunnis to be rid of Saddam and his regime; for many Shi'i, however, Saddam's demise was their deliverance as much as it was Iraq's. Therefore, as in the case of demographics, the sectarian politicization of issues

[63] Interview, Qasim al-Ubaidi. Baghdad, January 2012.

of state and governance exacerbated an *already extant* fissure that fitted, to a large extent, sectarian divisions.

Sunni Arabs have long complained that de-Ba'athification unfairly targets them and is one of the main instruments used to marginalize them in politics. Even a nuanced approach to the issue, such as that adopted by Minister of Finance Rafi'i al-Isawi, which recognizes the intrusion of party and regional discriminations into a process that is often viewed in strictly sectarian terms, nevertheless points to a highly selective and politicized implementation of de-Ba'athification.[64] There is much to indicate that de-Ba'athification is used as a political weapon to marginalize opponents and that it is used more leniently with Shi'i former-Ba'athists. Perhaps the most questionable usage of de-Ba'athification came immediately prior to, during, and after the elections of 2010. However, it should be noted that selective and politicized de-Ba'athification is not necessarily synonymous with sectarian de-Ba'athification. With regards to its manipulative use in the 2010 elections, the driver was political interest, not sectarian identity. Nevertheless, as with much that relates to sectarian relations, perceptions are more important than reality: one of the factors that entangles de-Ba'athification with sectarian identity in the perceptions of many is first its questionable implementation and second, that while de-Ba'athification has quickly become a prominent feature of Sunni claims to victimhood, it is a policy founded to a large extent on a central component of Shi'i victimhood. Indeed, many have described de-Ba'athification, especially in its earlier days, as nothing short of an act of vengeance. In one scholar's words: "De-Ba'athification was closer to a pre-Islamic [*jahili*] vendetta than a legal interpellation ..."[65]

The Sunni perception that de-Ba'athification is a tool designed to exclude Sunnis is of course not one born in a vacuum. It reflects a broader sense of marginalization and loss relating to the identity disenfranchisement that Ahmad Hashim spoke of and to more tangible disadvantages. However, identifying the line separating perception from reality in Sunni victimhood is a difficult task. What concerns us here is that, when a group is convinced that they are targeted by the other, they will perceive much of whatever detriments they face in their daily lives in terms of group discrimination. The views of Sunnis on deteriorating

[64] Interview, Rafi'i al-Isawi. Baghdad, January 2012.

[65] Qasim Husain Salih, *Al-Shakhsiyya al-Iraqiyya: Al-Madhhar wa al-Jawhar* [The Iraqi Persona: The Appearance and the Essence], Baghdad: Dhefaf, 2011, p. 161.

school examination results provide an excellent example of this. For several years, residents of A'adhamiyyah, and other Sunni-majority areas, have alleged that their children have been given poor grades due to sectarian discrimination.[66] A historian at the University of Tikrit complained that Karbala had attained the highest average passing grades in Iraq while Salah al-Din had ranked among the lowest. She indignantly asked: "Nobody in all of Salah al-Din gets good grades? All good grades are in Karbala and Najaf—Najaf is [ranked] first in all of Iraq [despite being] busy with *latmiyat*?"[67]

At face value there is a strong case to be made for sectarian discrimination impacting students' educational attainment; however, according to the deputy minister of education for scientific affairs, Nihad al-Jiburri, there is another less sensational explanation. He pointed to the fact that the state of education in Iraq as a whole, in all governorates, is such that poor educational attainment and falling standards are a national problem. To illustrate, despite nourishing a sense of sectarian discrimination among Sunnis, Karbala achieving the highest average passing grade in Iraq does not tell us what the pass rate actually is among Karbala'i students. According to Nihad al-Jiburri, it stands at a meager 28 percent—hardly a sign of favoritism.[68] The point to be made is that Shi'is no longer perceive themselves the victims of sectarian discrimination whereas Sunnis do. Hence political misfortune and the shortcomings of the state are likely to be viewed by Sunnis through the prism of sectarian identity, thereby strengthening the conviction that they are the targets of sectarian discrimination, a conviction that is the product of both perception and reality.

Sectarian discrimination in senior government employment is another common charge by Sunni Arab Iraqis, and one that is intimately related

[66] For example, demonstrations were held in A'adhamiyah and elsewhere in 2009 demanding revisions of recent examination results in which Sunnis were allegedly discriminated against. See Ra'ad Saleem, "Al-Ta'lim fi Mustanqa'a al-Ta'ifiyya fil Iraq" [Education in the Sectarian Swamp in Iraq], *Al-Hiwar*, 5 Aug. 2009, http://www.ahewar.org/debat/show.art.asp?aid=180286

[67] Interview, Shaha al-Jiburri, Baghdad, Jan. 2012. *Latmiyat* refer to Shi'i mourning rituals commemorating the death of Hussein.

[68] Interview, Nihad al-Jiburri, deputy minister of education for scientific affairs, Baghdad, Jan. 2012. Dr al-Jiburri also pointed to chronic inefficiency and corruption as the source of discrepancies between regions.

to de-Ba'athification. The evidence is anecdotal but there is scarcely any doubt that such practices take place.[69] The question is whether or not such instances are the result of institutional or individual practice. Several committees have been set up to investigate the issue but have yet to report.[70] The offices of Dhafir al-Ani have compiled a statistical report of their own that lists, by name and sectarian affiliation, all employees in the upper six grades of the Iraqi civil service.[71] If accurate, the results are damning: at the levels of heads of division, deputy director, and above, Sunni Arabs account for as little as 0 percent in the Ministry of Trade and the Ministry of Social Affairs. In defense and interior, perhaps the two most contentious ministries, Sunnis at the level of head of division, deputy director, and above account for 17 percent (30/176) in the Defense Ministry and 7.29 percent (7/96) in the Interior Ministry. A further breakdown of al-Ani's results indicates that there are no Sunni Arabs at the top two grades in either the Defense Ministry or the Interior Ministry.

The defense and interior ministries, particularly the latter, play prominent roles in the narrative of Sunni victimhood. It is alleged that Sunnis have been the victims of collective punishment in the name of combating the Ba'ath and terrorism. In fact, many of the frustrations that led governorates such as Salah al-Din to demand federal status in 2011 relate to what is regarded as punitive security measures taken by Baghdad in the governorate.[72] There is much justification to Sunni charges that they are unfairly accorded ownership of terror and/or the Ba'ath. The director of the Ministry of National Reconciliation, Jamal al-Badri, lamented that, "As a result of government and American policy, Ba'ath

[69] For example, a Sunni career policeman, at deputy director level, had his promotion continuously blocked until a Shi'i friend, also known to myself and who independently corroborated the story, vouched for the policeman with his superiors. The fact that the Shi'i friend was a civilian with no governmental role makes this incident all the more shocking.

[70] Interview, Rafi'i al-Isawi.

[71] My thanks to Dhafir al-Ani for supplying a copy. Until cross-examined with another source these statistics must be treated with caution. I have no information as to methodology and have no access to an alternate set of statistics. Nevertheless they are useful in identifying general imbalances in the various ministries, even if the exact percentages have a less than adequate margin of error.

[72] Interview, Najih al-Mizan, head of the Committee for the Formation of Federal Regions in Salah al-Din, Baghdad, Jan. 2012.

became equal to Sunni, Al-Qaeda became equal to Sunni, terrorist became equal to Sunni."[73]

The fact is that this forms part of a two-way process in which competing sides assign blame to the other, a process that is typical of divided societies, particularly ones suffering from recent internal traumas.[74] A Sunni is likely to blame Iran, the militias, and Shi'i crimes/blunders for Iraq's woes while the Shi'i is likely to blame al-Qaeda, the Ba'ath, terrorists, and Sunni intransigence. There is an emotionally charged vocabulary at play that forms part of sectarian competition today. Exacerbating this is the imbalance in power relations that strengthens feelings of Sunni encirclement. The tools of official cultural production are more prone to the influence of a Shi'i narrative than a Sunni one—alas the sect-neutral narrative of recent Iraqi history is much too marginalized at the present time. For example, many have fairly asked why Iraqi state television, namely Al Iraqiya, airs the confessions of dozens of (Sunni) terrorists but never of a (Shi'i) militia commander? For that matter, why are different terms applied to Sunni and Shi'i militant groups, namely terrorists and militias, if not to deny any moral equivalence between them? A remarkable example of double standards is how the state deals with the Mahdi Army and other Shi'i militant groups: why is it that an organization heavily involved in the civil war, and parts of which are responsible for atrocious crimes, is allowed to hold public events and rallies with state approval? And why is the extension of similar courtesies to any Sunni militants unthinkable? Such questions reinforce the conviction that the new Iraq directly or otherwise targets Sunni Arabs. The depth of Sunni feelings of encirclement is perhaps best illustrated in the claim made by some that they had personally seen banners in Baghdad on 9 April 2003 displaying the slogan "No Sunnis after today."[75]

[73] Interview, Jamal al-Badri. Likewise, alongside de-Ba'athification, opposition to counter-terrorism legislation has been a central demand of the ongoing protests.

[74] A worthy area of future research is the memory of the civil war of 2006–7, or *al ta'ifiyyah* as it is referred to in casual Iraqi conversation (for example, "*athna'a al-ta'ifiyyah*," or, "*ib ayam al-ta'ifiyyah*,"—"during the sectarianism" or "in the days of the sectarianism"). Baghdadis are rigidly divided in their memory of those events, and one hears vastly differing narratives regarding the identity of transgressors, victims, and criminals. What is obvious is that there are clearly discernible "Shi'i" and "Sunni" positions on this.

[75] "*La Sinna ba'ad al-yum*." This is a highly charged allegation not just because of

One can refer to a latent and implicit vilification of Sunni Arabs in the new Iraq. A word of caution is required here: this does not mean that every Sunni is guilty until proven innocent in Iraq today, nor that Sunnis are perpetually hounded by the state. Rather, it is an implicit negativity that is relevant perhaps to opinions towards Sunnis as a collective rather than as individuals. It is a predisposition to accepting Sunni complicity in terror and/or the Ba'ath rather than a constant charge. In that way it is similar to the often-seen public perception in the United Kingdom or the United States that associates blacks and other minorities with crime—or indeed the predisposition of Sunnis to believe a charge against Shi'is of complicity with Iran. The political parallel between associating Shi'is with Iran and Sunnis with the Ba'ath and/or terrorism is obvious: in both cases it is utilized to discredit opposition and marginalize opponents by tarring them with negative associations;[76] hence the Iraqi government's dismissal of Sunni-majority governorates' demands for federal status with the accusation of wanting to harbor Ba'athists.[77]

Competing victimhoods

I would in no way suggest that Sunni victimhood is free from exaggeration; indeed all mass-group feelings of marginalization seem to have such an element. A most useful concept in that regard is what psycho-

---

the grotesque sentiment allegedly expressed on the banner but because it paraphrases a strongly held Shi'i symbol of victimhood: the banners proclaiming "no Shi'is after today" allegedly raised by Saddam's forces as they crushed the rebellions of 1991. It is not beyond the realm of reason that both accounts are based in truth; however, more important, particularly given that I have no way of verifying either claim, is the perception that the other was callous enough to raise such banners, thereby highlighting the depth of conviction in one's own victimhood and the negativity associated with the other.

[76] Interview, Sa'ad Salloum. Salloum perceptively argues that, according to the government, they are to be thanked for getting rid of Saddam; using that, they have tried to harness Shi'i support and discredit any Sunni opposition by linking the latter to the Ba'ath and marginalizing them politically.

[77] A charge made by Prime Minister Nuri al-Maliki himself. See Laith Hammudi, "Iraq's Maliki Lashes out at Sunni Province Seeking Autonomy," *McClatchy Newspapers*, 31 Oct. 2011. It is worth noting that such a charge—equating Sunnis with the Ba'ath or Shi'is with Iran—would not be made had it not carried some degree of popular currency among a significant constituency.

analyst Vamik Volkan terms "chosen traumas." These are "the collective memory of a calamity" that befell a group; yet far more than a simple recollection, it involves a good deal of myth and sanctification, ultimately making it a representative part of the group's historical memory.[78] Post-2003 Iraq has been a highly active production mill of such chosen traumas with regards to sectarian and other identities. Shi'is and Sunnis each consider themselves to be the prime victim of the tragedies of the past decade and hence the most deserving. What is particularly noticeable in such competing victimhoods is the inability to recognize the other's suffering; on the contrary, the aim of this competition is to detract from the other's suffering while highlighting the depth of one's own and, by extension, inflating the sense of entitlement the group feels it is owed. Writing in a different context one commentator describes this dynamic of victimhood and entitlement:

> What people want to strip from the victim in order to clothe themselves in is the moral eminence, the tragic splendor it seems to enjoy ... The great superiority of unhappiness over happiness is that it provides a destiny. It alone distinguishes us, enthrones us in a new aristocracy of the outcast. An unprecedented mental register: one has to display one's own distress and if possible eclipse that of one's neighbors in order to be recognized as the most meritorious.[79]

Of course in Iraq this is exacerbated by the fact that the political DNA of the new state contains elements of this meritocracy of victimhood. As such, this rejection of the other's suffering and the inflation of one's own is a dynamic noticeable in both state and society, thereby eliminating any chance that the state can fulfill its potential to promote an inclusive state nationalism that transcends sectarian identities.

[78] Vamik Volkan, *Blood Lines: From Ethnic Pride to Ethnic Terrorism*, Boulder: Westview Press, 1998, p. 48. These chosen traumas are as ambiguous as identity itself and are subject to the same fluctuations in relevance that identity is. Volkan himself describes this point in terms particularly relevant to Iraq (p. 46): "a political leader may reignite a dormant group memory that affects collective thinking, perceptions, and actions. When such a shared mental representation of the original injury is reactivated, it may distort a large group's perceptions. New enemies involved in current conflicts may be perceived as extensions of an old enemy from a historical event."

[79] Pascal Bruckner, *The Tyranny of Guilt: An Essay on Western Masochism*, Princeton: Princeton University Press, 2010, pp. 114–15. I would only disagree with Bruckner's use of the word "unprecedented": group identity is often imagined on the basis of tragedy and/or triumph.

Shi'is today will rarely accept any notion that they are imposing an identity or that Sunnis have any grounds for complaints of "sectarianism," while Sunnis are all too likely to dismiss Shi'i claims of exceptional suffering under Saddam. To illustrate, commenting on the subject of Sunni victimhood, Parliamentary Head of the State of Law List Khaled al-Attiyah dismissed any grounds for its existence by indirectly alluding to Shi'i victimhood: "They [Sunnis] lost power but they do not express it in terms of 'we lost power after 1,400 years'; rather, they frame it as 'victimhood and marginalization.' It is a cover for their loss of power and their desire to get it back."[80]

Abd al-Halim al-Zuhairi, senior advisor to Nuri al-Maliki, commented in near identical terms:

> Since they are used to a state where the Shi'is have no presence, now that the Shi'is do have a presence it becomes [Sunni] 'marginalization'… I mean some people do not accept you taking some, not even all, just some of your rights! This whole marginalization thing is an excuse.[81]

Conversely, the comments of the leader of the Sufi Resistance (a former militant group) expressed grimly predictable and unfortunately widespread views on Shi'i victimhood: "Get me one Shi'i who tried to assassinate Saddam. They were all Sunnis! The army were mostly Shi'is—even in the high command. Most of the government was Shi'i in Saddam's day, so there is no truth to this Shi'i victimhood thing."[82]

The existence of sectarian historical memories of Iraq and the relevance they derive from the current salience of sectarian identities is one of the many hurdles facing efforts at "national reconciliation."

Where now for Sunni Arab identity in Iraq?

One of the problems Sunnis face as they formulate an identity that can compete with the assertive and triumphalist Shi'i identity described above is the fact that they lack the symbolic heritage and the iconography with which to develop coherent instruments of identity-assertion. Today, given that Sunnis regard themselves as victims of sectarian discrimination, they are in need of such symbols and, as will be shown,

[80] Interview, Khalid al-Attiyyah, Baghdad, Jan. 2012.
[81] Interview, Abd al-Halim al-Zuhairi.
[82] Interview, Adnan al-Nu'aimi, Baghdad, Jan. 2012.

there are attempts underway at the production of symbols. As argued by Yasin al-Bakri, despite countless internal divisions, the Shi'is have a symbolic heritage that they could rally around at times of sectarian tension; as for the Sunnis:

> They do not have such a symbolism, which is why they do not have a group-imagination that could lead or animate them and this is why they have failed. The Association of Muslim Scholars and Harith al-Dhari at one point briefly became such a symbol; even with Zarqawi there was an attempt to present him as a symbol. Although that one failed there was a brief point in time when Zarqawi began to take on that aura. When the Shi'i street invented Abu Diri'i as a parallel to Zarqawi, the latter indeed began to take on the role of a Sunni symbol. But this was a reaction against the other rather than something genuine from within the Sunni street.[83]

Bakri suggests that Sunni attempts to create cohesive and emotive symbols went through several phases: resistance; religion; the Ba'athist past and Saddam Hussein (particularly after Saddam's execution); and finally and most recently, federalism.

Saddam and the Ba'ath as Sunni symbols

With the post-2003 context of salient sectarian identities and sectarian confrontation in mind, two of the most readily available contenders for Sunni symbols are the Prophet Muhammad and Saddam Hussein.[84] A comparison of their symbolic potential illustrates much about the functions of group identity. It can be argued that Saddam's capacity to act as a symbol for Sunni Arabs in Iraq today is far greater than the Prophet's. The latter is not a source of sectarian contention—indeed both the Prophet and God Himself are noticeable by their near-total absence in sectarian polemics. Furthermore, the Prophet was neither a victim nor a symbol of defiance; in that sense it is difficult for the Prophet to play the symbolic role that Hussein plays for the Shi'i, namely one that nourishes the group's sense of injustice and victimhood. Saddam on the other hand can be presented as a victim; he is highly contentious and, given his near-mythical demonization in Shi'i symbolism, he is an appropriate instrument with which to respond to Shi'i assertiveness; finally, he is tangible as a recent and potentially *Iraqi* Sunni symbol.

[83] Interview, Yasin al-Bakri.

[84] My thanks to Ala'a Hamid and Sa'ad Salloum for raising this point.

The memory of Saddam has at times attained a measure of symbolic weight with which to exhibit Sunni defiance towards assertive Shi'ism. Saddam became a particularly obvious choice for Sunni expressions of defiance after his execution—an affair explicitly conducted as an act of Shi'i vengeance.[85] The manner and timing of the execution earned the former dictator the posthumous moniker of *Shahid al-Adhha'* (the martyr of the Adhha),[86] in addition to some unlikely supporters.[87] Unsurprisingly, his burial site turned into a place of pilgrimage for some—to the extent that the central government is alleged to have officially banned such practices in early 2012.[88]

However, despite the undoubted existence of this symbolization of Saddam, he has fallen short of turning into a coherent and self-defining symbol for a critical mass of Sunni Arab Iraqis. While he retains the capacity to be used as an expression of spite and rejection, his lack of genuine popularity among Sunnis prior to and after his death make it unlikely that he will ever satisfy the expressive needs of Sunni identity. In other words, the fact that he was never a Sunni Iraqi symbol makes it unlikely that he can be turned into one posthumously, particularly given his ambiguous place in the Sunni imagination.[89]

[85] One of the starkest examples of this is to be found in footage from the immediate aftermath of the execution: alongside the ambulance carrying Saddam's corpse is a jubilant crowd chanting, "*Mansura ya Shi'at Haider*" (victorious oh Haider's people—that is, the Shi'i). Among the participants is Deputy State's Attorney Munqith al-Fir'awn, who is at one point hoisted on top of the shoulders of the celebrators. See: http://www.youtube.com/watch?v=0311Vx6hmJk&oref=http%3A%2F%2F

[86] Saddam was executed on 30 Dec. 2006, which corresponds to the Muslim celebration of Eid al-Adhha in that year.

[87] Jamal al-Badri claims to have seen signs of Saddam-as-symbol in Samarra, a city with a history of friction with Tikrit and the former ruling elites.

[88] See: http://www.aljazeera.net/news/pages/0cd938d2-b5b1–47b3–9288–4d42337e4ec3. For a fascinating account of such pilgrimages and a detailed description of the "shrine" see Saad Salloum, "Ziyara ila Qabr Saddam Husain" [A Visit to Saddam Hussein's Grave], *Niqash*, Aug. 2009, http://www.niqash.org/articles/?id=2501&lang=ar

[89] It should not be forgotten that Saddam's earliest victim was the Ba'ath party itself. More pertinent is his long list of Sunni victims, which means that he will always be likely to serve as an expression of spite against Shi'i hegemony but without similarly strong feelings of love or loyalty.

Federalism as a safeguard of Iraqi Sunni identity

Federalism has been a controversial subject in the new Iraq; for the most part it remains poorly understood and confused in its implementation. The only federal region in Iraq today is the Kurdish Regional Government (KRG), currently consisting of the three northern-most governorates of Iraq; however, given that this region predates the new Iraq and its constitution, and given the exceptional circumstances surrounding its existence, the KRG is closer to a model of confederation rather than federalism. Regardless, broadly speaking, Kurdish opinion holds federalism to be an article of faith;[90] in Arab Iraq, on the other hand, the situation is less clear. To begin with, federalism was viewed with suspicion by many Arab Iraqis who feared it to be a precursor, if not a byword, for division. Despite that, there were many Arab Iraqis who championed a federal Iraq: Shi'i politicians helped enshrine federalism in the Iraqi constitution in 2005, plans for a Basra region have been unsuccessfully floated by some Basrawi politicians since 2003, and the Islamic Supreme Council of Iraq pursued a nine-governorate super-region referred to as the "region of the center and the south" that likewise failed to materialize.[91] Initially, Sunni opinion was vehemently against federalism. Whether this was due to their rejection of federalism itself or whether it was part of a broader rejection of all things associated with the new Iraq is open to debate. Either way, Sunni majority governorates voted against the constitution in the referendum of 2005, citing federalism, and a host of other issues, among their reasons for doing so.

Recently there has been a marked shift among Sunnis, or at the very least among some Sunni political leaders, towards a pro-federal stance. In the summer of 2011, for example, Osama al-Nujaifi, Speaker of the Iraqi Council of Representatives, alluded to the possibility of Sunni separatism if progress was not achieved on a number of political issues. Later that year Iraq saw three Sunni majority governorates (Salah al-Din, Anbar, and Diyala) calling for federal status, calls that were unconstitutionally blocked by the central government. More recently federalism

[90] In a recent private conversation I heard an academic complain that debating federalism in Kurdistan is like debating the Quran in Saudi Arabia!

[91] Perhaps the foremost authority on Iraqi federalism today is Reidar Visser. See http://gulfanalysis.wordpress.com/ and www.historiae.org. Also see Reidar Visser and Gareth Stansfield (eds), *An Iraq of Its Regions*, London: Hurst, 2007.

has emerged as something of a cause célèbre among some, though by no means all, sections of the ongoing demonstrations in Sunni majority governorates. What explains this shift in attitudes and what explains the federal government's refusal to allow what is after all a constitutionally guaranteed process from running its natural course?

It is undoubtedly the case that the deep frustrations with the shortcomings of the central government are at the heart of the recent calls for federal regions in Sunni majority governorates. According to Najih al-Mizan, head of the Committee for the Formation of Federal Regions in Salah al-Din, budgetary matters, services, and security issues are among the most important drivers.[92] However, it is difficult to delineate these demands that revolve around tangible issues of governance and services from perceptual issues relating to identity. As al-Mizan himself states, all governorates in Arab Iraq suffer from the center's neglect;[93] however, as was the case with southern governorates under the previous regime, there is a strong sentiment in Sunni majority governorates today that this neglect is the result of calculated sectarian discrimination. Regarding the controversies surrounding federal formations in 2011, what may have been an administrative issue relating to budgets and services (and a hint of sectarian victimhood) was lent a far stronger sectarian character by the central government's refusal to implement its own laws and constitutional procedures, opting instead to obstruct what were perfectly legal political ambitions and thereby nourishing feelings of sectarian marginalization and exclusion.

As already mentioned, sectarian relations in post-civil war Iraq are characterized by a degree of resigned acceptance of the status quo and some have ventured to suggest that the calls for federal regions in Sunni majority governorates are a product of this.[94] Commenting on the change, Yasin al-Bakri argued that federalism is the latest mechanism through

[92] Interview, Najih al-Mizan, head of the Committee for the Formation of Federal Regions in Salah al-Din, Baghdad, Jan. 2012. Minister of Finance Rafi'i al-Isawi explained the calls for federalism in identical terms.

[93] During a recent trip to Najaf I saw that, while the shrine of Ali ibn Abi Talib is clearly receiving the attention it deserves, the city itself remains in a woefully dilapidated state.

[94] It is worth reiterating that, as this volume was going to print, Iraq was witnessing major demonstrations in Sunni majority areas coupled with a rise in violence. Time will tell whether this will bring an end to the dynamics being described here and that were visible in 2010–12.

which Sunnis are trying to protect and assert their identity coupled with a conviction that political power in Baghdad will remain in Shi'i hands for the foreseeable future.[95] Therefore, one could argue that recent federal calls signal a step forward in sectarian relations in that Sunni discontent is seeking constitutional measures of redress, thereby marking a belated, albeit reluctant, acceptance of the new Iraq. In Abd al-Halim al-Zuhairi's words:

> I am not pessimistic ... despite the polarization that exists ... it is all heading towards realistic solutions. Even these calls for regions are a kind of acceptance of reality: 'let's take care of ourselves' whereas previously they [Sunnis] would say "you [the Shi'i] have no right to become [the state] in Iraq."[96]

A plausible argument made regarding Iraqi political views on federalism is that they are in some ways linked to political confidence and political security. In Yasin al-Bakri's view, Shi'i politicians' earlier support for federalism reflected their uncertainty regarding the success of the political experiment that was the new Iraq; hence, a combination of insecurity and fear led to their initial calls for federalism. This, in Bakri's view, has now turned into a position of relative strength and confidence that translates into a desire for hegemony.[97] With regards to sectarian relations, the point to derive from Bakri's argument is that the federalism controversy can be used as a reflection of the post-civil war sectarian relations of power and who the winners and losers of that conflict were.

Creation of Symbols

In contemporary Iraq there are visible indications that Sunnis are creating symbols of group-definition to help assert their identity and better

95 Interview, Yasin al-Bakri.

96 Interview, Abd al-Halim al-Zuhairi. However, at the same time, al-Zuhairi and several others charged that the reason behind attempts to form federal regions is to shelter the Ba'ath. An aide to former national security advisor, Muwaffaq al-Ruba'i, bluntly said: "The reasons behind calling for regions are not related to serving the citizen but to shelter criminals." Interview, Baghdad, Jan. 2012.

97 Interview, Yasin al-Bakri. Bakri went on to point out that this strength and confidence translating into a desire for hegemony was visible in Prime Minister Nuri al-Maliki's suggestion of a presidential order after his success in the 2009 provincial elections. Bakri's thesis is certainly an interesting one deserving of further research—not least as it is difficult to apply to Basrawi regional projects.

differentiate themselves along their own lines rather than those laid down by the other. My visit to Iraq in January 2012 ended a fortnight or so before the Mawlid—the celebrations of the Prophet's birth that are by and large a Sunni occasion—and perhaps for that reason, Sunni identity, such as it is, was on display. In Baghdad, a neighborhood's sectarian makeup was discernible by its banners: in Shi'i areas one would see the rich array of Shi'i banners, flags, slogans, and portraits. Less predictably, Sunni areas were equally discernible from the omnipresence of a newly conceived Sunni banner displaying a logo that has quickly turned into a Sunni symbol.[98] This is undoubtedly a reaction to the post-2003 salience of sectarian identities in general and to the robust assertion of Shi'i identity in particular. It seems that, despite the advantages in his favor, Saddam lost to the Prophet in the hypothetical contest mentioned earlier.

A pin-badge displaying what can be referred to as a Sunni logo. It reads: "Muhammad is our role-model."

[98] It should be noted that all photographs were taken in the fortnight separating the Arba'een from the Mawlid, which undoubtedly has a bearing on the volume of such symbols on the streets of the capital.

Entering a Sunni area in Baghdad, flags can be seen displaying the same logo (outskirts of Mansur).

"Muhammad is our role-model" emanated from a campaign by the same name that was first organized in 2010 by several Sunni Islamic organizations including the Sunni Endowments.[99] The campaign's climax is during the Mawlid and its stated aim is to familiarize the believer with the example of the Prophet Muhammad. However, in addition to the stated aims, intentionally or not, it also serves an urgent need for Sunni identity-formation and Sunni identity-expression by providing symbols and rituals of identity.[100]

The point of such symbolism—and this applies equally to Shi'i symbolism—is neither to disparage nor attack the other; rather, it is a means

[99] The campaign's website can be found on http://www.kudwatuna.com/ar/index.php. It remains for the most part an Iraqi affair and has a limited transnational echo online.

[100] It is interesting in that regard that reader comments displayed on the campaign's website repeatedly ask about where to get "Muhammad is our role-model" banners, flags, and other such paraphernalia. See http://www.kudwatuna.com/ar/index.php?option=com_content&view=article&id=74&Itemid=60

of defining the group by clarifying the boundary separating "us" from "them." Symbols in general serve as "border guards" of a group's identity; they are instruments of differentiation, cohesion, and reproduction.[101] Given that Sunni identity prior to 2003 was not salient enough to require such functions, symbols are now having to be created, borrowed, or reawakened to serve today's needs.[102]

We have yet to be able to point to a coherent set of Sunni symbols, and indeed the logo illustrated above may well prove an ephemeral phenomenon restricted to the Mawlid. Nevertheless, it is clear that the sense of Sunni victimhood is necessitating the creation of Sunni symbols. However, while victimhood is firmly in place in Iraqi Sunni Arab group-sentiment, it in itself is not a symbol; rather, it is a symbol-generator that drives the group-imagination to reach into the growing pool of symbols that can encapsulate and articulate the group's sense of "we-ness" and their victimhood.

The Mawlid is of course not a product of the post-2003 environment; however, the proportions and the manner in which the Mawlid is celebrated today differ from the pre-war era. This was surely aided by the technological opening and economic growth that 2003 eventually ushered in; yet the sudden sociopolitical relevance that Sunni Arab identity found itself burdened with in 2003, and the accompanying feelings of encirclement, undoubtedly created a need for such grand carnival-like occasions.[103] Today, Sunni Arab Iraqis, particularly in mixed cities such as Baghdad, cannot escape the Shi'i symbolism that

[101] Among countless studies into the role of symbols in group identity see Manning Nash, *The Core Elements of Ethnicity*, Chicago: Chicago University Press, 1989; Yasir Suleiman, *The Arabic Language and National Identity: A Study in Ideology*, Edinburgh: Edinburgh University Press, 2003; Anthony Smith, *Myths and Memories of the Nation*, Oxford: Oxford University Press, 1999; Kaufman, *Modern Hatreds*; Volkan, *Blood Lines*.

[102] A truly remarkable example of such borrowing came in the form of a group of adolescents walking through the streets of Yarmouk neighborhood carrying a banner with one of them beating a large drum—a *dammam*. With no Shi'i festival in sight I was confused by what at first glance looked like a distinctly Shi'i display. I was surprised to learn that it was part of the buildup to the Mawlid celebrations.

[103] Interview, Jamal al-Badri. Indeed the Mawlid is accompanied by the "A'adhamiyyah Carnival of [Islamic] Song" (*Mahrajan al-A'adhamiyyah al-Inshadi*)—now in its fifth year.

The Abu Hanifa Mosque, A'adhamiyah, Baghdad, at the 2012 Mawlid celebrations complete with "Muhammad is our role-model" banners.

surrounds them, nor can they avoid being affected by the numerous Shi'i rituals, many of which bring the city to a halt for several days. Added to the inconvenience of having someone else's rituals and symbols intrude upon one's daily life, the state's patronage turns them into a political statement that enhances the Sunnis' sense of victimhood and leaves no doubt as to who is ascendant in the sociopolitical relations of power in the new Iraq. It is in that context, I would argue, that the changes to the Mawlid celebrations should be viewed. Although one cannot be sure, the Mawlid—a venerable Sunni ritual—may attain the symbolic value to become for Sunni Arab Iraqis what Ashura and the Arba'een are to their Shi'i compatriots.

Looking to the future

None of the foregoing should be taken to mean that Iraqi politics revolve solely around sectarian identity or that Iraq today is nothing more than competing sectarian groups. I have tried to describe a specific element of Iraqi politics and society with reference to a specific timeframe. Hence the absence of other issues and other forms of identification, cooperation, and competition in this essay should not be mistaken for their non-existence. On the contrary, politics in Iraq today are far more complex and developed than they were in 2005–7 when sectarian identity played a more prominent role in driving political action.

As I have always argued, and as has hopefully been clear throughout this chapter, neither the salience nor the meaning of sectarian identity is fixed. What I have described here will inevitably change, for better or worse, along with future social, political, and economic developments in Iraq and the region. While sectarian symbols will always exist, raising a particular banner or displaying a particular image will have different meanings and purposes depending on the state of sectarian relations at any given time. Furthermore, the needs of a mass-group identity are likewise a reflection of a given context that is equally susceptible to change. Nor is Arab Iraq bereft of unifying symbols that may at some point in the future overshadow the symbolism of sectarian identity.

The challenge facing Iraqi sectarian relations lies neither in antagonistic symbolisms nor hostile myths; rather, it is the convergence of sectarian identity and political interests that politicizes and consequently inflames sectarian relations, ultimately lending such myths and symbols added salience. Most damagingly, the state today is far from a neutral observer in sectarian competition—and the more biased a state is perceived to be in sectarian terms, the less likely it is that state nationalism will be able to subsume sectarian identities. Hence despite the state's rhetoric of ecumenical harmony—rhetoric that resonates with popular opinion—it remains hollow as long as the state adopts the symbolism of one sect and excludes the other's, thereby endowing the state with a sectarian identity. What is required, in addition to an efficient state that is regarded as an equal servant to all the citizenry, is not for the state to act as a mediator between competing sects; rather, it needs to transcend sectarian identity and be regarded as neutral both in its policies and its symbolism. As the two images below illustrate, the perfectly natural competition of symbols is altered by the state's involvement. In the first image we see Sunni and Shi'i symbolism displayed side by side without rancor, which is a positive step in itself. The state's contribution to the scene is a completely sect-neutral billboard, topped with an Iraqi flag, proclaiming Baghdad to be the model of "peace and love."

Here we have an example of how sectarian identity can be given the space for expression that was so sorely lacking under the previous regime but without the state patronizing either group. In such a case, sectarian symbolism in and of itself is unlikely to inflame sectarian identity or to affect sectarian relations detrimentally. Unfortunately, the first image is the exception rather than the rule. As can be seen in the second image,

Sunni banners alongside a portrait of Mohammad Sadiq al-Sadr: Sunni and Shi'i symbols competing under a sect-neutral official billboard proclaiming: "Baghdad … the model of peace and love" (Jadiriyah).

while sectarian symbolism in post-civil war Iraq is displayed side by side without issue, the state's symbolic sectarian bias is clearly exhibited. Not only does this alter potentially healthy sectarian competition into something more divisive, it leads to the state alienating one sectarian group, thereby limiting its ability to subsume sectarian identities. In other words, expressions of sectarian identity and expressions of the state's identity should be mutually exclusive.

The image below shows an expression of Sunni identity alongside a state-sponsored expression of Shi'i identity. It is this skewed approach to sectarian symbolism that undermines ongoing attempts by the state to champion ecumenical harmony.

Given regional and Iraqi political developments, it is unlikely that sectarian identity will lose salience or political relevance in the near future—there are simply too many political actors in Iraq who are dependent on the politicization of sectarian identity and the current system of ethno-sectarian apportionment. Such actors have little incen-

A Sunni banner dwarfed by a permanent mural displaying Muhammad Baqir al-Sadr, Muhammad Sadiq al-Sadr, and the Iraqi flag (Baghdad Railway Station).

tive to try to appeal to a broad non-sectarian constituency and, given the fresh memories of the civil war, it is unlikely that any such attempt would succeed. Of more profound consequence, the divided Iraqi historical memory is such that many are simply unable to see sectarian relations from the other's point of view. As such, pictures of Muhammad Baqir al-Hakim or Muqtada al-Sadr are displayed by their adherents as Iraqi symbols, scarcely aware of the contempt with which many Sunnis hold these figures. As a result of all this, the new Iraq has failed to create and elevate new symbols with which to subsume Iraqi sectarian identities, despite having no shortage of such symbols both new and old. There is no more poignant an example of an underutilized symbol that carries immense potential for the promotion of sectarian neutrality than Uthman al-Ubaidi. He was a young Sunni from A'adhamiyyah who, in 2005, sacrificed his life to rescue Shi'i pilgrims who had fallen into the Euphrates after rumors of a suicide bomber sparked a stampede on the tightly packed Bridge of the Imams. His tragic story is perfect material with which to propagate a more Iraqi set of symbols that subsume sectarian identity without trying to negate them. However, the continuing

A modest start: a recently unveiled bust of Uthman al-Ubaidi in Baghdad's Hunting Club.

sectarian polarization and the depth of recent wounds will continue to delay the iconographic potential of the likes of Uthman al-Ubaidi from being realized.

3

THE STATE AND SECTARIAN IDENTITIES IN THE PERSIAN GULF MONARCHIES

BAHRAIN, SAUDI ARABIA, AND KUWAIT IN COMPARATIVE PERSPECTIVE

Laurence Louër

The Shi'i who live on the Arabian side of the Persian Gulf are not part of the higher strata of the social fabric. This is dominated by those who can claim an old and so-called "pure" (*asli*) Arab descent by being descended from one of the big tribal confederations originating in Central Arabia, and also by belonging to the socially dominant status group of the *hadhar*, the old settled and/or urbanized population. In all six GCC (Gulf Cooperation Council) states, the Shi'i are a demographic and/or political minority, the Bahraini Shi'i demographic majority being kept out of the most powerful institutional positions as well as sensitive sectors of the administration, which are held either by members of the Sunni ruling dynasty or Sunnis of various social and ethno-national backgrounds.

This situation, which is mainly the result of the history of state formation in the region, must not lead us to think that Shi'i everywhere in the

Gulf are subjected to various forms of sectarian-based discrimination. The mere fact that they belong to a different current of Islam than the rulers is not always the primary reason that they have less access to important institutional positions than their Sunni fellow-citizens. Saudi Arabia is the exception rather than the rule in this respect. It is the only Gulf monarchy where the identity of the state, based on a specific reading of Sunni religious orthodoxy, has led to a widespread state-sponsored policy of sectarian discrimination. When such policies exist elsewhere, they are based on motives other than religious hatred or refusal of the Other.

This chapter, based on the cases of Bahrain, Saudi Arabia, and Kuwait—the three Gulf monarchies where the Sunni/Shi'i divide has social and political relevance—aims to identify the various rationales behind state-sponsored anti-Shi'ism.

Threat perception and sectarian discrimination in Bahrain

Bahrain, with Saudi Arabia, is the most often-cited example of state-sponsored anti-Shi'ism throughout history. The historicization of this practice shows that it was motivated by different rationales. One cannot speak of "sectarianism" strictly speaking before the 1980s, in a domestic and a regional political context where Shi'i sectarian identity had become highly politicized.

Non-sectarian discrimination

The current Al Khalifa dynasty founded the modern state of Bahrain in 1783 after they had militarily defeated the previous rulers, the al-Madhkur, who governed Bahrain as vassals of the Persian Empire. The Al Khalifa had left central Arabia sometime in the seventeenth century for the coastal areas of the Persian Gulf. After settling in Kuwait, they eventually ended up in the Qatar Peninsula where they established themselves at Zubara, a prosperous port and pearling center from which they subsequently conquered Bahrain.[1] The circumstances of the conquest are a matter of dispute in contemporary Bahrain, as is history in general, which is used to substantiate political positions and, more broadly, to contest or legitimate one's position in the social stratification.[2]

[1] Ahmad Abu Hakima, *A History of Eastern Arabia, 1750–1800: The Rise and Development of Bahrain and Kuwait*, Beirut: Khayats, 1965, pp. 109–16.

[2] Nader al-Kadhem, *Isti'malat al-dhakira fi mujtama' ta'aduddi mubtala bi al-tarikh*

The official history promoted by the Al Khalifa dynasty maintains that they set Bahrain free from Persian domination, reintegrating the archipelago into the Arab nation.[3] In their eyes, the conquest amounted to a struggle for national liberation. But the Shi'i have another version of history. They insist that Bahrain had been a Shi'i-populated area ever since the quarrel over Prophet Muhammad's succession, which had led to the historic division between partisans of Ali and the partisans of the caliphs within the Muslim world. They are eager to remind any enquiring mind that, in ancient sources, the term Bahrain referred to a much broader territorial entity than the tiny contemporary Bahraini state, one that encompassed the entire Arabian side of the Persian Gulf coast from Basra to the Qatar Peninsula. They also insist that, when the Al Khalifa and their allies conquered Bahrain, all the native population professed the Shi'i creed. Bahrain's Arab Shi'i,[4] who are called Baharna (sing. Bahrani), are hence the "original inhabitants" (*sukkan asliyyin*) of Bahrain, while the Sunnis are no less than alien invaders.

This version of history has been abundantly supported by the work of Shi'i Islamic activist intellectuals who, from the 1970s onward, have published various historical accounts which have given a scientific veneer to this nativist language.[5] Because of the scarcity of sources, it remains very difficult to make a precise assessment of this version of history, and hence to distinguish between history itself and its uses in the framework of myths. The few existing academic works nonetheless suggest a more balanced picture. While there is no doubt that Bahrain is an ancient place of Shi'i settlement with a rich history of religious learning that predates the establishment of Shi'ism as the state religion

---

[Uses of Memory in a Multicultural Society Burdened with History], Manama, Bahrain: Maktaba Fakhrawi, 2008; Laurence Louër, *Transnational Shia Politics: Religious and Political Networks in the Gulf*, New York: Columbia University Press, 2008, p. 13; Thomas Brandt Fibiger, "Engaging Pasts: Historicity and Political Imagination in Bahrain," PhD dissertation, Aarhus University, Denmark, 2010.

[3] Yitzhak Nakash, *Reaching for Power: The Shi'a in the Modern Arab World*, Princeton: Princeton University Press, 2006, pp. 7–8.

[4] There is a small minority of Shi'i of Persian descent in Bahrain, who are called Ajam (sing. Ijmi). Most of them arrived between the end of the nineteenth century and the first half of the twentieth century.

[5] For examples, see Louër, *Transnational Shia Politics*, pp. 23–30.

in Iran (1501), it was probably religiously mixed throughout much of its history and was more often than not governed by Sunni rulers.[6]

The overlapping of the Sunni/Shi'i divide with the conqueror/conquered and the alien/native cleavages was reinforced by the establishment of what Fuad Khuri has described as a "feudal estate system" in the aftermath of the conquest.[7] The new rulers divided the arable lands into several fiefdoms belonging to members of the Al Khalifa clan and their allied Sunni tribes. The handful of Shi'i families who had sided with them during the conquest were able to retain their properties in exchange for a heavy land tax, but the majority of the Shi'i peasants were forced to rent their plots from the Sunni conquerors under onerous terms that amounted to debt bondage.

The conquerors also appropriated most of the other major source of Bahrain's riches, namely the pearl trade. Contrary to the Shi'i peasants who were subjected to tight control by the landlords, the Sunni pearling tribes enjoyed extensive freedom in the management of their business activities. However, the rationale behind this reshuffling of the social stratification was not "sectarianism" per se but rather the new rulers' wish to reward the conquerors and to maximize their economic benefits. Freedom was indeed the best way to ensure that the pearling tribes would not leave Bahrain for other pearling centers on the Persian Gulf coast and hence deprive the rulers of the benefits of the import and export taxes which were a major source of their income.[8]

This essentially pragmatic approach was confirmed throughout history, with the regime displaying a significant degree of tolerance towards the expression of Shi'i religiosity and at times even considering the Shi'i clerical institution an ally against its opposition. Hence upon the adoption of the country's first constitution in 1973, the ninth and tenth days of the month of Muharram were declared public holidays in respect for the Shi'i religious festival of Ashura. Moreover, the successive Al Khalifa amirs have always taken care to show their respect for Shi'ism, for example by making donations during major Shi'i festivals or by funding

[6] Juan Cole, "Rival Empires of Trade and Shi'ism in Eastern Arabia," in Juan Cole, *Sacred Space and Holy War: The Politics, Culture and History of Shi'ite Islam*, London: I.B. Tauris, 2002.

[7] Fuad I. Khuri, *Tribe and State in Bahrain: The Transformation of Social and Political Authority in an Arab State*, Chicago: University of Chicago Press, 1980, p. 35.

[8] Ibid., p. 67.

the restoration of *hussainiyya*.[9] The Shi'i have also been able to practice their rituals publicly without any restrictions. Another sign of the attention the Al Khalifa have paid to the specific needs of their Shi'i citizens is their eagerness to establish contacts with Shi'i religious authorities outside of Bahrain, most notably the *marja'iyya* in Najaf to which most of Bahraini Shi'i refer to this day.

In order to weaken the Marxist and Arab nationalist movements that emerged as the main organized opposition between the late 1930s and early 1970s, and which had a non-sectarian leadership and rank and file, the Bahraini regime even fostered the creation of Shi'i sectarian entities with the aim of countering the influence of the secular activists. This was the case in the crises of 1954–6, when Bahraini workers of the Bahrain Petroleum Company (BAPCO) and prominent Shi'i and Sunni notables coordinated to pressure the government in the hope of obtaining concessions such as the departure of the British and the establishment of an elected legislative assembly. When they created the National Union Committee in 1955—an organization meant to coordinate collective action and represent them before the regime—the rulers encouraged the creation of an alternative body, the National Convention Committee, which was a sectarian organization. Headed by a handful of Shi'i clerics, it had only Shi'is in its ranks and was divided into two branches representing the Baharna and Ajam respectively.[10] There is no better example for how the organized expression of Shi'i sectarian identity was not considered as a threat by the Al Khalifa regime, which enjoyed good overall relations with the Shi'i clergy.

Dealing with Shi'i identity politics

In the late 1960s, the emergence of Shi'i Islamic movements as the driving force of the opposition entailed a progressive shift in this pattern of the strategic use of Shi'i sectarian identity to the advantage of the

[9] Originally, a *hussainiyya* was a building where Shi'is celebrated the martyrdom of Imam Hussein during Ashura. It also serves for marriage and burial ceremonies, and has more generally become a place of social gathering.

[10] Abdulhadi Khalaf, "Contentious Politics in Bahrain: From Ethnic to National and Vice Versa," The Fourth Nordic Conference on Middle Eastern Studies, "The Middle East in a Globalizing World," Oslo, 13–16 Aug. 1998. See www.hf.uib.no/smi/pao/khalaf.html

regime. The first such movements appeared as part of two transnational politico-religious networks woven around rival centers of religious authority and political activism in Iraq: al-Da'wa (the Call) party, intimately tied to the *marja'iyya* of Najaf, and the Shirazi network, woven around the figure of Mohammed al-Shirazi (d. 2001). A leading cleric based in the city of Karbala, the latter was positioning himself as a challenger of the Najafi establishment, eager to renovate what he considered a gerontocratic institution unable to tackle the problems of the time.[11]

Al-Da'wa spread throughout the Arab Middle East through networks of students studying at the seminaries of Najaf, at the time the main learning center for the Shi'i world. In Iraq, the party aimed to combat the influence of secular ideologies and sought to replace successive Iraqi secular regimes with an Islamic state based on the Shi'i version of Islam. In the late 1960s a clandestine cell of the party was created in Bahrain by students who had recently returned to the country,[12] where it subsequently became rooted in the rural areas among the younger segments of the Shi'i clerical class and the young middle-class laymen.[13] The most well-known founder of al-Da'wa is Isa Qasem. A member of the 1972 constituent assembly and the 1973 parliament, Qasem emerged as the main politicized high-ranking Shi'i cleric in the 2000s and has held close relations with al-Wifaq (the Accord), the dominant opposition party since 2001 (although he is not a formal member). As for the Shiraziyyin, they organized around Hadi al-Mudarrisi, a nephew of Mohammad al-Shirazi who became established in Bahrain in the early 1970s after the entire al-Shirazi family had fled Iraq to escape repression and, for the most part, relocated to Kuwait. Unlike al-Da'wa, the network's first recruits in Bahrain came from the urban areas, among the pious merchant notables as well as young middle-class men. A number of them were Ajam, which also distinguished the Shiraziyyin from al-Da'wa.[14] After different incarnations, the Shiraziyyin officially announced their existence in 1976 as the Islamic Front for the Liberation of Bahrain (IFLB).[15]

[11] Louër, *Transnational Shia Politics*, pp. 88–99.

[12] Parties were banned at the time. "Political societies" have been authorized since 2001.

[13] Louër, *Transnational Shia Politics*, pp. 104–11.

[14] Ibid., pp. 126–9.

[15] Hasan Tariq Alhasan, "The Role of Iran in the Failed Coup of 1981: The IFLB in Bahrain," *The Middle East Journal*, 65, 4 (2011), p. 605.

In line with its past behavior, the regime at first viewed these new entrepreneurs of Shi'i identity as providing a good opportunity to further weaken the Marxist and Arab nationalist opposition. In fact, both al-Da'wa and the Shiraziyyin were initially more preoccupied with combating the influence of secularist movements than with tackling the regime. This was especially true of al-Da'wa, which acted mainly as a re-Islamization agent in the Shi'i communities and, contrary to its Iraqi mother organization, never seriously envisaged armed confrontation with the Bahraini regime. Prior to the creation of the IFLB, the same can also be said of the Shiraziyyin, which was largely preoccupied with consolidating the position of the network in the face of the domination of the Najafi religious establishment and its political arm, al-Da'wa. This explains, for example, why Hadi al-Mudarrisi was granted Bahraini citizenship in 1974, a few years after his arrival. He was also granted access to state-controlled television and local media. This was made possible thanks to the connection he enjoyed with a leading Shi'i merchant family, the al-Alawi, who had excellent access to the rulers. But it was also a clear sign that the regime did not consider the Shi'i re-Islamizers as a problem.

Things started to change during the first parliamentary experiment between 1972 and 1975. The Bahraini parliament, which was modeled on that of Kuwait, enjoyed legislative powers. While the amir appointed the government independently from the results of the elections, and though the government also had legislative powers, the parliament could veto the government's bills. Unsurprisingly, the Marxist and Arab nationalist movements constituted the dominant force in the 1973 assembly, organizing themselves in a parliamentary group named the Progressive Bloc. However, the members of al-Da'wa came second with a parliamentary bloc almost as important as that of the Progressives, which came to be known as the "Religious Bloc." Much to the dismay of the regime, however, the two ideologically antagonistic groups joined forces in 1974 to defeat a government-sponsored bill on state security that sought to impose severe restrictions on civil liberties (the State Security Law). As a result, the amir decided to disband the parliament, to impose a state of emergency, and to repress the Progressive activists, many of whom had to leave for exile.

While the Shi'i Islamic activists remained relatively untouched at this time, the dissolution of the parliament entailed a deep change of attitude among some of them. Indeed, it was at exactly this period that the

Shiraziyyin began to espouse a radical agenda. The announcement of the creation of the Islamic Front for the Liberation of Bahrain left no ambiguities about their program, but the members of the organization did not disclose their identity immediately, so that Hadi al-Mudarrisi, the leader of the IFLB, managed to remain in Bahrain as a Bahraini citizen until 1979. In the meantime, several members of the IFLB were undertaking training in guerrilla warfare in Lebanon, in the camps of the Palestine Liberation Organization and the Shi'i Amal militia. The members of al-Da'wa, in contrast, continued to adhere to the position of no direct confrontation with the regime, favoring re-Islamization activities over preparing for revolution.

In this context of escalating tensions between the regime and the Shi'i Islamic movements, the advent of the Iranian Revolution, and with it the principle of exporting the revolution which became one of the pillars of Iran's foreign policy, added to the anxieties of the Bahraini regime. This was all the more so since irredentist claims over Bahrain, which the shah had officially dropped in 1970, were again heard in Iran from individuals seen as being close to the ruling circles.[16] Both al-Da'wa and the Shiraziyyin enthusiastically paid homage to the new Iranian regime and espoused the principle of exporting the revolution. The Shiraziyyin—who had established good relations with Ayatollah Ruhollah Khomeini and his entourage over the course of a decade—were the most active in trying to foster a popular uprising in Bahrain. These efforts proved to be in vain, however, since such a perspective was not backed by al-Da'wa, which remained the most influential movement. Increasingly seen as a threat, Hadi al-Mudarrisi was forced out of Bahrain and deprived of his Bahraini citizenship. After relocating to Tehran he prepared a coup which he tried to implement in 1981, again in vain as the plotters were arrested in Dubai while on their way to Bahrain. The Shiraziyyin who escaped arrest and prison fled to Iran. The crackdown targeted al-Da'wa and the Shiraziyyin indiscriminately, with all the Shi'i Islamic activists becoming suspects. Most al-Da'wa members escaped prison and exile by agreeing to disband their organization and to cease their political activities.

Unsurprisingly, the 1981 coup attempt entailed a deep transformation of the regime's threat perception, and hence of its concepts of loy-

[16] Christin Marschall, *Iran's Persian Gulf Policy: From Khomeini to Khatami*, London: Routledge, 2003, p. 27.

alty and disloyalty, which increasingly came to be defined in sectarian terms. In other words, in a regional environment where Shi'i sectarian identity had become politicized and used by Iran to pursue foreign policy objectives, the Bahraini regime began to see its Shi'i citizens as intrinsically untrustworthy and liable to act as an Iranian fifth column. The eight-year-long Iran–Iraq War (1980–8), in which some of the GCC states became the main financial backers of the Iraqi war effort and were hence prime targets of Iranian retaliation, further aggravated this perception. The Shi'i question thus became first and foremost a security problem (see Gengler, this volume). It is in this context that the Bahraini regime sought to rid the security apparatus of its Shi'i elements,[17] a process that was pursued throughout the 1990s in the context of a four-year-long uprising sparked by a difficult socio-economic situation plagued by mass unemployment among Bahraini youth as well as deep frustration at the refusal of the amir to reinstate parliamentary life.

Shi'i Islamic activists were the figureheads of this movement, in particular al-Da'wa figures like Abd al-Amir al-Jamri (d.2006), but also younger activists like Ali Salman, who became the secretary-general of al-Wifaq upon its creation in 2001. In reaction to what it saw as a Shi'i revolt, the regime endeavored to activate the Sunni identity with the aim of constituting the Sunni minority as a protective buffer and also increasing its share in the national population by adopting a policy of naturalization for Sunnis only. Some additional details regarding this strategy were exposed in the 2006 Bandargate affair, which resulted from a 200-page document compiled by Saleh al-Bandar, a British citizen of Sudanese descent who worked in the Royal Court Affairs Ministry. By circulating this document among the opposition, al-Bandar was able to show how the ministry was at the heart of a secret network that sought to reinforce the Sunni population's identification with the regime while keeping the Shi'i out of key sectors.[18]

Here again, however, one cannot speak of the "securitization of the Shi'i problem in Bahrain" as a manifestation of "sectarianism" per se. Indeed, what is at stake is not the rejection or hatred of Shi'ism as a creed, but the regime's perception that Shi'ism had ceased to represent

[17] Khalaf, "Contentious Politics in Bahrain."

[18] The report can be downloaded on the BCHR's website: http://www.bahrainrights.org/node/528

mere sectarian belonging and had become a political ideology questioning the domestic and regional status quo.

State-sponsored sectarianism in Saudi Arabia

As in Bahrain, the process of Saudi state formation was based on conquest by the current ruling dynasty, a process in which the Shi'i happened to be on the side of the vanquished. For this reason, one finds similar nativist narratives among Saudi and Bahraini Shi'i when accounting for their relations with the state and the dominant elites. The Saudi case, however, is distinct in that it is probably the only example on the Arabian side of the Persian Gulf where Shi'i have been subjected to state-sponsored discrimination motivated by a sectarian rationale.

Pragmatic sectarianism

The Al Saud began to expand their power throughout the Arabian Peninsula from the second half of the eighteenth century after making themselves the armed champion of the tenets put forward by the religious reformist Mohammed bin Abd al-Wahhab. Promoting a return to "true" Islam, al-Wahhab was particularly eager to enforce strict monotheism which, in his eyes, had been distorted by associating human figures with the worship of God.

In addition to condemning the cult of saints among Sufis, Wahhabis also fought the Shi'i practice of revering the Prophet Muhammad and his family (*ahl al-bayt*). The Shi'i cult of the "Fourteen Infallibles"—Muhammad, his daughter Fatima, and the twelve imams whom the Shi'i believe had access to the hidden meaning of the Quran—was particularly abhorred. As a result, the various episodes of the Al Saud's expansion were marked by the destruction of the mausoleums of the imams. In Karbala in 1802, for example, the Saudi troops not only destroyed and ransacked the mausoleum of Imam Hussein but also slaughtered some 4,000 Shi'i inhabitants. Later, in 1925, they destroyed the sanctuaries of the imams located in the Baqi cemetery in Medina where, to this day, the Shi'i are forbidden to undertake pilgrimage and where, for this reason, there are regular clashes between Shi'i pilgrims and the Saudi religious police.

After their first two states were brought down by Ottoman governors in 1818 and 1871, the Al Saud managed to unify the major part of the

Arabian Peninsula under their rule in 1932, the official date for the creation of the contemporary Kingdom of Saudi Arabia. The new state included a sizable Shi'i population mostly living in the Eastern Province, in the two oases of Qatif and Hasa.[19] At the time of the conquest they probably represented the majority of the population there.[20] Like Bahrain, this region was a historic Shi'i population center with a tradition of high Shi'i religious learning. During its final conquest by the Al Saud army in 1913, the Shi'i inhabitants offered little resistance, the majority of their notables being convinced that the new rulers would be able to put an end to the region's endemic instability due to Bedouin exactions.[21] The Shi'i elites consequently pledged their loyalty to the Al Saud, and those who did not chose to leave rather than fight. This was particularly the case in the region of Hasa around the cities of Hufuf and Mubarraz, which many Shi'i had abandoned during the various phases of the Saudi expansion, giving birth to a Hasawi diaspora settled all around the Persian Gulf coast in the small monarchies that escaped Saudi annexation (Kuwait hosts the largest Hasawi community), in southern Iran, and southern Iraq (the region of Basra).

In exchange for their pledge of loyalty, the Shi'i notables managed to negotiate a degree of religious recognition. Hence while the public expression of their creed was banned, the Shi'i religious judges (*qadhi*) were authorized to officiate. Over the years their position was institutionalized as they became civil servants appointed by the Ministry of Interior, which recognized two Shi'i religious courts dealing with family matters, inheritance, and administration of religious endowments. Although they were left indigent in comparison with the Sunni courts, the very fact that the Shi'i courts existed indicates that, from the start, the Saudi rulers granted the Shi'i an amount of institutional recognition as a distinct sect (*madhhab*) within Islam and that the Al Saud were willing to compromise with ideology for the sake of state-building. The way the Al Saud dealt with the Shi'i population inhabiting their terri-

[19] There was also, and still is, a small Shi'i community in the city of Medina, and an Isma'ili population in the city of Najran and its vicinity.

[20] Guido Steinberg, "The Shiites in the Eastern Province of Saudi Arabia (al-Ahsa), 1913–1953," in Rainer Brunner and Werner Ende (eds), *The Twelver Shia in Modern Times: Religious Culture and Political History*, Cologne: Brill, 2001, p. 236.

[21] Ibid., pp. 244–5.

tory can also be taken as a case in point in this respect. While they no doubt viewed the Shi'i with disdain and even suspicion, they never envisaged converting them en masse to Sunni Wahhabi Islam and even resisted such projects by some Wahhabi zealots.

There is no better example of this approach than the suppression of the Ikhwan, a corps of Bedouin warriors of the faith created by the Al Saud with the aim of pacifying the nomads who were responsible for most of the anti-Shi'i persecutions during the conquest and its immediate aftermath. Their disbanding in 1930, two years before the official declaration of the Saudi state, signaled the Al Saud's willingness to initiate a phase of stabilization in which religious charisma had to be restricted in order to avoid alienating the newly conquered populations. The stability of the kingdom's eastern regions where most Shi'i lived was all the more essential because of their very dynamic economy, based on agriculture and commercial activities in the port towns. In 1938, it turned out that the Eastern Province contained the vast majority of Saudi hydrocarbon resources, making its stability even more crucial. Another sign of the Saudi regime's pragmatism toward its Shi'i citizens was the fact that it did not prohibit the employment of thousands of Shi'i in the latter, highly strategic, economic sector, as reflected in the Arabian American Oil Company (Aramco) which became a major instrument of upward social mobility for the Shi'i.

Varieties of Shi'i identity politics

Like its Bahraini neighbor, the Saudi regime had to deal with the politicization of Shi'i identity by Shi'i Islamic movements. The Al-Da'wa network did not take root in Saudi Arabia to the same extent as the Shirazi network, which, from the mid-1970s onward, ultimately became the strongest Shi'i Islamic movement on Saudi soil. The Saudi Shirazi network developed thanks to Hassan al-Saffar, who remains the most politically influential Shi'i cleric in Saudi Arabia to this day. He became a disciple of Mohammad al-Shirazi at the end of his religious education in Iraq and Iran, joining him after the latter had established his headquarters in Kuwait. Hassan al-Saffar became one of the main propagandists of Mohammad al-Shirazi's ideas in the Persian Gulf monarchies. This included Saudi Arabia, of course, but also Oman where he stayed for several years. He organized a channel to recruit young Saudi men to study at the seminary created by Mohammad al-Shirazi in Kuwait. In the aftermath of the Iranian Revolution, these men constituted the backbone of a clandestine organization known as the Organization for the Islamic Revolution in the Arabian Peninsula (OIRAP).

The activists of the OIRAP mainly came from two social milieus. On the one hand, a number of activists came from the new middle class that had emerged in the Shi'i society of the Eastern Province thanks to the development of the oil industry, with many of the young Shi'i being enrolled from the junior and middle ranks of Aramco. Yet, on the other hand, activists were also drawn from the traditional notables, both the devout merchant bourgeoisie and the clerical class, who had maintained close ties to the Iraqi centers of religious authority.

The OIRAP made itself known after the uprising of November 1979 in Qatif and its vicinity during the Ashura celebrations that followed the Iranian Revolution, when thousands of Shi'i ignored the ban to celebrate this key ritual and went out to the streets. The procession quickly turned into a political demonstration, with mourners raising portraits of Khomeini and chanting slogans that were hostile to the regime.[22] The confrontation with the police became violent, with dozens of demonstrators killed and dozens of others arrested. In a move similar to that seen in Bahrain after the 1981 coup attempt, the uprising marked a watershed in the relationship of the Shi'i with the Saudi regime, which for the first time saw the potential for the constitution of a strong radical opposition movement with wide popular support from within a previously compliant population. Here again, the fact that the event was the result of the Iranian policy of exporting the revolution made the challenge even more worrying. The Shi'i question in Saudi Arabia became a highly sensitive geostrategic issue in a regional context marked by the open rivalry of the Islamic Republic of Iran and Saudi Arabia for the leadership of the Muslim world, with the two main currents of Islam being embodied by two rival states, as it was during the sixteenth-century Ottoman–Safavid rivalry.[23]

22 Toby Craig Jones, "Rebellion on the Saudi Periphery: Modernity, Marginalization, and the Shi'a Uprising of 1979," *International Journal of Middle East Studies*, 38, 2 (2006), pp. 213–33.

23 Vali Nasr, *The Shia Revival: How Conflicts Within Islam Will Shape the Future*, New York: Norton, 2006, pp. 147–68.

As in Bahrain, the Saudi regime reacted by streamlining the ranks of sensitive sectors. Because there were basically no Shi'i in the security apparatus, the main target was the oil sector where Shi'i were overrepresented. However, in line with its previous pragmatism in dealing with its Shi'i citizens, the Saudi regime also reacted by investing money in the Shi'i areas of the Eastern Province to improve the substandard infrastructure which had earlier been a major source of discontent.[24] The regime also showed some restraint in the way it repressed the Shi'i Islamic activists, many of whom were able to travel between Iran and Saudi Arabia and hence to maintain contact with local society. Although those suspected of being members of OIRAP spent frequent spells in prison, the length of the sentences imposed were relatively short when compared to the twenty years served by several of their Bahraini counterparts. The regime reserved its most severe form of repression for another movement that appeared in the late 1980s and which, in the 1990s, resorted to terrorist violence abroad and on Saudi soil—the Hijazi Hezbollah.

A small group that never reached the influence of the OIRAP, the Hijazi Hezbollah was created directly at the initiative of the Iranian government after its relations with the Shiraziyyin had deteriorated and it felt that it needed a tool of influence among Saudi Shi'i that would be entirely under its control.[25] Several of its members were jailed after a deadly attack on American military personnel in a residential compound in the city of al-Khobar in the Eastern Province in 1996, which some Americans suspect was perpetrated on Iranian orders.[26] Some of the members of the organization were still detained at the time of writing.

Initially, OIRAP and the Hijazi Hezbollah upheld similar conceptions of Shi'i identity based on a revolutionary interpretation of popular religious rituals and clerical notions of religious and political authority. At the beginning of the 1990s, in a shifting internal Iranian political scene and a changing regional context, OIRAP undertook a radical shift

[24] Jacob Goldberg, "The Shi'i Minority in Saudi Arabia," in Juan Cole and Nikkie Keddie (eds), *Shi'ism and Social Protest*, New Haven: Yale University Press, 1986, p. 244.

[25] Louër, *Transnational Shia Politics*, pp. 211–12; Toby Matthiesen, "Hizbullah al-Hijaz: A History of The Most Radical Saudi Shi'a Opposition Group," *The Middle East Journal*, 64, 2 (2010), pp. 179–97.

[26] Joshua Teitelbaum, *Holier than Thou: Saudi Arabia's Islamic Opposition*, Washington, DC: The Washington Institute for Near East Policy, 2000, pp. 83–98.

in ideology and strategy that favored a revision of its conception of Shiʿi identity in terms fitting a strategy of national integration.[27] Faced with the pragmatic turn in Iranian foreign policy, which no longer aimed to export the revolution to the Persian Gulf monarchies in general and Saudi Arabia in particular but rather sought Iran's reintegration into the international community, the movement sought to become a legitimate interlocutor with the Saudi government in defense of the interests of the Saudi Shiʿi citizens. It changed its name to the Reform Movement, and the title of its mouthpiece from *The Islamic Revolution* to *The Arabian Peninsula*.[28] It is significant that these two new terms made no mention of religion, instead focusing on political reform and regional identity.

In a perspective already seen in Bahrain, *The Arabian Peninsula* dealt mainly with the history of Saudi Shiʿi with the aim of demonstrating their status as native inhabitants of the Arabian Peninsula. It also endeavored to reinterpret the Sunni/Shiʿi dichotomy so as to tone down the religious dimension of Shiʿi identity. The religious divide was equated with the classical opposition between *hadhara* (the settled and urbanized population) and *badu* (Bedouin desert dwellers). The Reform Movement activist intellectuals explained that the centrality of religion in Shiʿi social identity derived from their status as long-settled and urbanized people who, contrary to the Bedouins, favor religious belonging over tribal ties.[29] This permitted them to alleviate the stigma of belonging to a current of Islam which Wahhabi dogma could not but condemn by symbolically inserting the Shiʿis into the larger and socially dominant status group of the *hadhar*.

These same activist intellectuals also developed the nativist narrative seen among Baharna in Bahrain, insisting that the Shiʿi of the Eastern Province were a fully fledged part of the Bahrani people who inhabited the Arabian shore of the Persian Gulf long before the existence of the Saudi state. In this vein, a publication entitled *The Oasis* was created, entirely dedicated to academic-style articles about the customs of the

[27] Laurence Louër, "Shiʿi Identity Politics in Saudi Arabia," in Anh Nga Longva and Anne Sofie Roald (eds), *Religious Minorities in the Middle East: Domination, Self-Empowerment, Accommodation*, Leiden: Brill, 2012, pp. 232–5.

[28] Mamoun Fandy, *Saudi Arabia and the Politics of Dissent*, Basingstoke, UK: Macmillan, 1999, p. 199.

[29] Madawi Al-Rasheed, "The Shiʿa of Saudi Arabia: A Minority in Search of Cultural Authenticity," *British Journal of Middle Eastern Studies*, 25, 4 (1998): 121–38.

Shi'is of the Eastern Province. In 1993, a book in two volumes, entitled *The Shi'i in the Arab Kingdom of Saudi Arabia*, proposed an entire history of Saudi Shi'i articulated around this framework of interpretation.[30] It is probably not by coincidence that this nativist narrative, be it in Bahrain or in Saudi Arabia, echoes one of the dominant registers of political legitimacy in the modern world, where the idea is widespread that natives are entitled to more rights than latecomers in a specific territory,[31] or should be recognized as communities enjoying dispensatory statuses, as the mobilization of the so-called "indigenous peoples" in the international arena typically shows.[32]

The Saudi regime responded to this new political and symbolic strategy in a largely tolerant way. Most of the Reform Movement's leaders were authorized to return to Saudi Arabia in the course of the 1990s, at a time when the rulers, weakened by the Persian Gulf War, were willing to liberalize politically in order to better co-opt their various oppositions. But it was only after the 2003 regime change in Iraq that the Saudi regime took real steps to improve the situation of its Shi'i citizens. The Al Saud regarded the regional context as shifting in an advantageous way to Iran and the Shi'i overall, with rumors spreading of a coming grand bargain between the United States and the Shi'i which, for the Americans, would constitute a functional substitute for their old alliance with Saudi Arabia.[33]

In order to forestall any move on the part of Saudi Shi'i to embrace the supposed radical American agenda of reshaping the regional order in favor of the Shi'i, the Saudi rulers, in an unprecedented move, organized a series of conferences called a "National Dialogue" in which Shi'i clerics—Hassan al-Saffar included—were invited to express their demands. In the aftermath, the restrictions placed on the expression of

[30] Hamza al-Hasan, *Al-Shi'a fi al-mamlaka al-'arabiyya al-sa'udiyya*, vol. 1, *Al-'ahd al-turki 1871–1913*; vol. 2, *Al-'ahd al-sa'udi 1913–1991* [The Shi'i in the Arab Kingdom of Saudi Arabia. vol. 1: The Turkish Period 1871–1913 and vol. 2: The Saudi Period 1913–1991], Mu'assasat al-Baqi' li Ihya al-Turath, 1993.

[31] Jean-François Bayart and Peter Geschiere, "J'étais là avant: problématiques politiques de l'autochtonie," *Critique Internationale*, 10 (2001), pp. 126–94.

[32] Irène Bellier, "Les peuples autochtones aux Nations Unies: un nouvel acteur dans la fabrique des normes internationales," *Critique Internationale*, 54 (2012), pp. 61–80.

[33] Louër, *Transnational Shia Politics*, pp. 243–50.

the Shiʿi faith were alleviated, in particular the construction of new mosques and the public practice of rituals, showing once more the Saudi regime's capacity to compromise with Wahhabism when it deems it necessary for the sake of domestic stability.

The Shiʿi also benefitted in some respects from the acceleration of the factional struggle inside the Al Saud dynasty that characterized the second half of the 2000s. The so-called Sudayri faction, composed of the seven sons of King Abd al-Aziz (who founded the state in 1932) and Hassa bint Ahmad al-Sudayri, intensified its struggle to limit King Abdallah's room to maneuver and secure the position of crown prince for their strongman, Prince Nayef (d.2012). In the competition, the two camps tried to gain supporters outside of the royal family, both at the international and the domestic levels. While Prince Nayef was gaining a reputation as an anti-terrorist fighter and upholder of Saudi conservative moral and religious values, the king presented himself as a reformer willing to recognize the right of citizens with a specific regional, tribal, or religious background to hold a plurality of opinions. In this context, the Shiʿi were constituted into one of the king's constituencies, becoming in return the favorite target of the upsurge of religious orthodoxy from the Sudayri leaders and their allies in the Wahhabi religious establishment.[34]

The state as a shelter

Because the conditions of state formation were radically different from those of the Bahraini and the Saudi states, the situation of the Shiʿi in Kuwait has always been structurally different. While the divide between original inhabitants and latecomers is also a structuring social cleavage, it crosscuts the Sunni/Shiʿi divide, which is hence not reinforced by overlapping with other polarizing social identities. Moreover, "sectarianism" has not taken the form of state-sponsored policies but has rather emanated from various sectors of the Sunni population, pushing the Shiʿi to see the state as a shelter rather than a threat.

Diasporic Shiʿism

In contradistinction with the Bahraini and Saudi states, which were created following a process of conquest, Kuwait was born sometime in the

[34] Louër, "Shiʿi Identity Politics," pp. 239–40.

seventeenth century from the progressive assemblage of tribes and families in the small but thriving port town of present-day Kuwait city. Involved in pearling, caravan trade, and long-distance commerce to India and East Africa, the main families issued from the Bani Utub tribe, who are likely to have left Central Arabia in order to escape drought. In need of a ruler able to protect the city against Bedouin raids and to arbitrate commercial conflicts, these families designated one of them named Sabah, the eponymous ancestor of the current ruling dynasty.

While Kuwaiti common wisdom stresses that the Al Sabah were chosen as rulers because none of the richer families wanted the job, it is also very likely that the choice resulted from a "functional division of power"[35] between the Al Sabah and the merchant oligarchy. The Al Sabah were vested with political powers because they were mainly involved in caravan trade and, for this reason, had kept close ties with the nomadic tribes whose allegiance they were able to command. In contrast to the other Bani Utub traders who were involved in maritime trade and had to travel extensively, the Al Sabah remained in Kuwait on a permanent basis, which was also favorable to the exercise of political power.

What matters is that Al Sabah dynastic rule resulted from consensus among the main merchant families, who insisted on being consulted about important policy matters, including the succession. This principle was broken on the eve of the twentieth century by the amir Mubarak the Great, who killed his two rival brothers and signed an agreement with the British (1899), through which Kuwait effectively became a British protectorate, with the British guaranteeing Mubarak's power in exchange. In the aftermath of the Second World War, the Kuwaiti rulers were further emancipated from the merchant oligarchy thanks to oil.[36] The merchants, however, notably by threatening to support Iraqi irredentism over Kuwait, finally obtained the re-instatement of the principle of power-sharing in the form of a parliament that was first elected in 1963, two years after Kuwait obtained independence.

As in Bahrain and Saudi Arabia, the exact role of the Shi'i in this history is the object of controversy. There is no Shi'i family among the merchant families who claim they founded Kuwait in the eighteenth

[35] Jacqueline Ismael, *Kuwait: Social Change in Historical Perspective*, Syracuse: Syracuse University Press, 1982, p. 28.

[36] Jill Crystal, *Kuwait: The Transformation of an Oil State*, Boulder: Westview Press, 1992.

century and participated in the initial power-sharing mechanism. However, several Shi'i families contend that they settled in Kuwait after arriving from southern Iran shortly after the Bani Utub arrived. While some have Iraqi and Lebanese roots, the majority of Kuwaiti Shi'i today are organized into three major diasporic communities who maintain extensive cross-border family ties with their former place of origin: the Ajam from Iran, the Hasawiyyin from Hasa in today's Saudi Arabia, and the Baharna from today's Bahrain.

While political mobilization cuts across these ethno-regional divisions, several aspects of individuals' lives are organized according to membership in one of these categories. The largest group, the Ajam, came to Kuwait at different historical periods in the framework of a traditional pattern of border migration.[37] Many Hasawiyyin came to escape Wahhabi persecution and instability in Hasa, but also probably following pressure from the Shi'i clerical mainstream. Most of the Hasawiyyin are Shaikhi, a current of Twelver Shi'ism that follows the highly controversial teachings of Ahmad al-Ahsa'i (1753–1826) and which has one of its main centers in Kuwait, under the guidance of a line of *marja'* from the Ihqaqi family of the city of Usko in Iranian Azerbaijan. As for the Baharna, most of them settled in Kuwait to escape political instability and economic hardship in Bahrain from the seventeenth century onward.[38]

The demographic, economic, and religious domination of the Ajam among the Shi'i has for a long period made the Shi'i question in Kuwait indistinguishable from the issue of the Iranian presence in the emirate. Indeed, until the 1970s, when the Shi'i Islamic movements gained momentum and pushed to give an essentially religious content to Shi'i identity, the controversies about the presence of Shi'i in Kuwait were the result of the commitment of prominent members of the merchant oligarchy to the Arab nationalist tenets as they were put forward in Iraq, in the context of an open and harsh rivalry with Iran.[39] Nothing better

[37] Shahnaz Nadjmabadi, "Cross-border Networks: Labour Migration from Iran to the Arab Countries of the Persian Gulf," *Anthropology of the Middle East*, 5,1 (2010), pp. 18–33.

[38] Louër, *Transnational Shia Politics*, pp. 46–51.

[39] Kamal Osman Salih, "The 1938 Kuwait Legislative Council," *Middle Eastern Studies*, 28, 1 (1992), p. 70; Falah Abdallah al-Mdayris, *Al-haraka al-shi'iyya fi al-Kuwait* [The Shi'i Movement in Kuwait], Kuwait: Qurtas, 1999, pp. 13–14.

exemplifies that than the controversy about the history of the Battle of Jahra in 1920.

A founding myth of Kuwait, the Battle of Jahra saw the victory of the Kuwaiti armies over the Saudi Ikhwan in a small desert fortress 40 kilometers west of Kuwait city. When the citizenship law was enacted in 1959, it set the year 1920 as the line of distinction between the "original" (*asli*) and the "naturalized" (*mutajannis*) Kuwaitis (that is, between the Kuwaitis who resided in Kuwait before the Battle of Jahra, and hence supposedly fought at the battle, and those who arrived later on). This distinction has direct implications in terms of political rights since naturalized Kuwaitis did not have the right to vote before 1966, when an amendment to the nationality law granted them voting rights after a thirty-year period from the date of the law's promulgation. Moreover, the divide between original and naturalized Kuwaitis partly overlaps with the *badu*/*hadhar* split. In the Kuwaiti context, these identities refer to the chronology of installation in Kuwait, the *hadhar* being the Kuwaitis who were established in the country before the oil era, and the *badu* being those who came afterwards, mostly in the 1950s and 1960s.[40]

In the most commonly studied history of Kuwait in Kuwaiti classrooms (written by a member of one of the founding families of Kuwait) no mention is made of a specific role played by the Shi'i in the Battle of Jahra. There is only a brief passage in which the writer explains that the Shi'i were absent from the battlefield and how, when they believed that the Kuwaiti armies had been defeated and the Ikhwan were marching into the city, they rushed to the house of the British representative to demand protection, arguing that "they were not Arabs but Iranians."[41] From this story many Kuwaiti Sunni have reached the conclusion that the Shi'i, because of their Iranian ethnic background, are not fully committed to the Kuwaiti nation and have hence failed to fight for it at times when it was endangered.

Faced with this accusation, the Shi'i have built an alternative narrative which is based on a history of Kuwait written in the 1960s by a member of the family of Shaikh Khaz'al who, until 1924, ruled the city and vicinity of Muhammara in the present-day Iranian province of Khuzistan

[40] Anh Nga Longva, "Nationalism in Pre-Modern Guise: The Discourse on *Hadhar* and *Badu* in Kuwait," *International Journal of Middle East Studies*, 38, 2 (2006), pp. 171–87.

[41] Louër, *Transnational Shia Politics*, p. 23.

and was an ally of the Al Sabah dynasty. In this version of history, the Shi'i were not on the Jahra battlefield because the Kuwaiti amir himself feared that if the Ikhwan, who were renowned for their religious zeal, had known that Shi'i were in the Kuwaiti army, their military fierceness would have been reinforced. The amir henceforth asked the Shi'i to stay behind the wall of Kuwait city and defend it in case of siege. In another historical account written in the 2000s and focusing on the history of the Shi'i in Kuwait, the Shi'i Islamic activist Abd al-Muhsin Jamal added another story, which is widespread among his co-religionists: at a critical time when they were besieged in Jahra's Red Fort, the Shi'i supplied the Kuwaiti soldiers with water, food, and arms, hence playing a key role in the final victory.[42]

The stigmatization that the Shi'i have suffered from the Sunni merchant oligarchy has naturally led them to side with the Al Sabah each time the latter have entered into open conflict with the founding families about the old issue of power-sharing. A founding event of this objective alliance was the 1938 so-called Assembly Movement, during which the merchant oligarchy mobilized to impose on the ruler a legislative assembly of fourteen members to be elected by the heads of the leading 150 families of Kuwait. Having reluctantly accepted the project, the amir finally moved to disband the assembly after six months of existence, leading its members to take refuge in a fortified citadel. After a few days of siege, the amir obtained the capitulation of the rebels, many of whom were arrested or fled to Iraq.

The 1938 events have been classically analyzed as the result of the ruler's growing autonomy from the merchant class thanks to the beginning of oil commercialization. However, the assembly's failure was also the result of the merchants' inability to bring the Shi'i notability into their project.[43] No Shi'i was indeed among the members of the assembly, most probably because the assembly was a reflection of the oligarchy of Sunni merchant families who felt entitled to participate in decision-making and were enraged to have been sidelined. Moreover, the assembly took steps that the Shi'i saw as endangering their interests, notably by forcing the dismissal of the amir's extremely powerful secretary, Molla Salih, an Iranian Sunni who enjoyed excellent relations with the Shi'i

[42] Louër, *Transnational Shia Politics*, pp. 54–5.
[43] Crystal, *Kuwait*, p. 20.

notables and whom the Shi'i saw as the defender of their interests before the amir.[44] As a result, the Shi'i mobilized around their main religious leader, Mahdi al-Qazwini, who, after having officially protested against the assembly's policy and asking its members in vain that the Shi'i be granted sectarian institutions (notably a school and a religious court), incited the Shi'i to take to the streets to pressure for the disbanding of the assembly.

The Assembly Movement played a decisive role in framing the particular relations the Shi'i have had with the Kuwaiti regime throughout most of the modern state's history. This relationship was based on a coalition of interests in the face of a common enemy. Hence up to the 1980s, the Shi'i members of the parliament were all pro-government because they saw the Al Sabah as their best protection against the hostility of the Arab nationalists who dominated the opposition.

From unconditional loyalty to opposition and back

As in Bahrain and Saudi Arabia, the emergence of the Shi'i Islamic movements was a key factor in altering the initial model of relations between the regime and the Shi'i. These movements were also inserted into the two rival Iraqi-based transnational networks active throughout most of the Gulf monarchies. Al-Da'wa penetrated Kuwait following the installation of several of its officials in the emirate in the late 1960s. The first al-Da'wa propagandist, Ali al-Kurani, came in the framework of an old established pattern of interaction between the Najafi *marja'iyya* and Kuwaiti Shi'i society, which has always lacked an indigenous clerical class and whose notables have regularly called on Iraqi-based clerics to reside in Kuwait in order to lead Shi'i religious affairs. In the early 1970s, it was the beginning of the repression of the Shi'i Islamic activists by the Ba'th regime that led a wave of al-Da'wa members to settle in Kuwait as exiles.[45] The creation of a clandestine cell of al-Da'wa in Kuwait contributed to a transformation of the political landscape within the Shi'i communities. The movement mainly recruited among young middle-class men who aspired to challenge the old merchant notability who continued to monopolize the Shi'is' representation at the parlia-

[44] Kamal Osman Salih, "The 1938 Kuwait Legislative Council," pp. 83–6.
[45] Louër, *Transnational Shia Politics*, pp. 111–18.

ment but who, in their eyes, had not been rewarded by the regime for their loyalty.

In the beginning, the project of al-Da'wa activists was not to instigate a rupture with the regime but to readjust the internal balance within the Shi'i population with the aim of increasing Shi'i political power. This meant giving the younger Shi'i generation a better position within the sect. It also meant increasing the share of the Shi'i in the parliament, diversifying the profile of the Shi'i MPs, and negotiating more say in decision-making at the government level, for example by having a Shi'i minister. This was actually achieved after the 1975 elections, when the Shi'i increased their representation and gained their first minister, Abd al-Mutallib al-Kadhimi, who was appointed oil minister. As in Bahrain, it was the regime's decision to disband the parliament in 1976 that radicalized a part of the Shi'i Islamic activists, who came to define themselves as opponents of the regime.

This position was clearly articulated after the parliament was reinstated in 1981 and al-Da'wa activists won a resounding victory over the old notability who had refused to change the status quo of their relations with the regime despite the dissolution of the parliament.

In the following years, and especially after the 1991 Persian Gulf War which saw the onset of very tense relations between the parliament and the Kuwaiti rulers, the position of al-Da'wa MPs (who created a political entity in 1998 named the National Islamic Coalition) was of quasi-systematic opposition to the government. This was sustained by regular provocative statements about their support for the Iranian Revolution and for the pretense of Khomeini and Khamenei being the leaders of the Muslim world. Aside from their previous project of empowering the Shi'i as a distinct group in society, they also endeavored to enter into a coalition with other opposition forces and hence to tone down the religious distinctiveness in their public language and instead stress a general Islamic identity.

The positioning of al-Da'wa as the first Shi'i opposition to the regime should not overlook the fact that other Shi'i Islamic movements or independent Shi'i Islamic activists remained reliable loyalists. This was particularly the case for the Shiraziyyin, who were established in Kuwait in the early 1970s and who never shifted to a confrontational attitude towards the regime. In a logic of distinction with al-Da'wa, they reinforced their relations with the old notability after the al-Da'wa activists entered into systematic opposition to the regime and its traditional Shi'i allies. They were first and foremost preoccupied with making Kuwait a safe haven for their activities rather than confronting a regime they basically saw as benevolent towards the Shi'i and which they had no interest in antagonizing. They first obtained parliamentary representation following the 1999 election, in the person of Saleh Ashour. The latter was still an MP in 2013 and has sided with the government in each of the numerous clashes it has had with its opposition ever since, to the point of gaining a reputation for having his campaigns financially supported by the government. In the mid-2000s, Saleh Ashour and his entourage tried to set up a coalition of small pro-government Shi'i groups to fight the dominance of the National Islamic Coalition, whom they have openly accused of being a tool of Iranian influence in Kuwait. The Shi'i political landscape hence tended to be polarized between pro- and anti-government groups.

In 2008, this pattern of bipolarization was reversed to what can be described as a return to the old pattern of alliance between the Shi'i and the regime. At this period, the figureheads of the National Islamic Alliance took the controversial initiative to organize a public rally to mourn the assassination of Imad Mughniyya, one of the most notorious officials of the armed branch of the Lebanese Hezbollah. In Kuwait, Mughniyya is deemed responsible for a series of attacks most probably organized at the initiative of Iran which sought to deter Kuwait from funding the Iraqi war effort. These attacks included an attempt on the life of the amir in 1985. The eulogy was hence considered by many in Kuwait as celebrating an enemy of the state, and several senior members of the Islamic National Alliance were arrested and detained for a few days, including members of parliament and the group's general-secretary, Hussein al-Ma'tuk. They were all eventually released, but the episode seriously undermined their credibility among the Kuwaiti Shi'i. Many of them concluded that they had contributed to spreading the wrong image of the Shi'i as disloyal citizens in a particularly difficult period where anti-Shi'i feelings were rising among segments of the Sunni population. At the time many Kuwaiti Sunni were apprehensive about the misconduct of the new Shi'i-dominated Iraqi government toward their Iraqi co-religionists and the expansionist ambitions of Iran.

The result of this crisis was the total reversal of attitude of the Islamic National Alliance. In the context of the upsurge of anti-Shi'i feelings among the Sunni population, due to the Mughniyya affair but also more broadly to the shifting regional equilibrium—seen as marked by the Shi'i attempt to gain power positions everywhere they could—the Islamic National Alliance has come to see the government as a protector, hence ceasing to position itself as an opposition group. This was exemplified by their position during the long struggle between 2006 and 2011 between the parliament and the prime minister, Shaikh Naser bin Mohammed Al Sabah. Seen by many as a particularly corrupt man, Shaikh Naser, who has extensive relations with the Shi'i population as well as economic interests in Iran, was seen as benevolent by the Shi'i population. After the 2008 Mughniyya affair, the Islamic National Alliance MPs joined the other Shi'i MPs to defend the prime minister against those MPs who demanded his dismissal. After Shaikh Naser was finally dismissed in 2011, the Islamic National Alliance continued to support the government against its parliamentary opposition, in a context where several MPs from the majority (a coalition of tribal and Sunni Islamic activists) have regularly displayed anti-Shi'i attitudes. (In 2012, for example, they sided with the government to oppose a bill submitted by the parliament that would have curtailed liberties for the Shi'i. It stipulated that the death penalty would be applied to anybody cursing the Prophet Muhammad, his wives, and companions. Because the cursing of some of Muhammad wives (Aisha in particular) and companions is commonplace among the Shi'i, this law was perceived by the Shi'i as being directed against them.)

Conclusion

The comparative analysis of the Bahraini, Saudi, and Kuwaiti cases shows that the relation of the Shi'is to the state in the Persian Gulf is very heterogeneous. A key factor explaining the different situations in the three countries under scrutiny is the conditions of state formation from the seventeenth and eighteenth century onward. Bahrain and Saudi Arabia, the two states which have sponsored blatant, widespread anti-Shi'i policies, were founded following processes of conquest during which the Shi'i were on the side of the vanquished and were inserted into political systems that were initially largely organized in order to reward the conquerors at the expense of the conquered. The Sunni/Shi'i divide was reinforced by its overlapping with other polarized social identities.

The Kuwaiti case, by contrast, shows how a state formation process based on the progressive assemblage of segments of populations of various ethno-religious backgrounds has had the effect of avoiding any type of polarization between the rulers and the various Shi'i communities. The contingent history of the formation of the opposition to dynastic authoritarianism, where the Sunni founding families of Kuwait who embraced Arab nationalist tenets played a central role, is also key in understanding the old alliance between the Al Sabah ruling dynasty and the Shi'i. This was meant to protect the rulers from the encroachment of the opposition and the Shi'i from the anti-Iranian stance of the Sunni merchant oligarchy, in a situation where anti-Shi'ism came primarily from society and where the state was hence seen by the Shi'i as a shelter.

Despite their differences, the three cases have also shown that Sunni rulers, even when they have sponsored discriminatory practices towards the Shi'i, can show extreme flexibility when confronted with the necessities of government. What I have called the "pragmatic sectarianism" of the Saudi regime when dealing with its Shi'i citizens is particularly telling in this respect. In Bahrain, the strategic use of Shi'i sectarian identity to counter the influence of Marxist and Arab nationalist movements is another example that, for a long time, the Bahraini regime did not see the public expression of Shi'i difference as a problem. The same is obvious in Kuwait. The relations that King Abdallah of Saudi Arabia developed with the Shi'i in the 2000s, in the context of the contest for succession with his rivals within the ruling dynasty, is also a telling example of how Shi'i identity entrepreneurs can be seen as allies by rulers in the context of enhanced intra-dynastic factionalism.

In all three cases, the shifts in the regional geopolitical context played a key role in altering the rulers' pragmatic and sometimes benevolent attitudes. From the 1980s onward, the advent of the Iranian Revolution, after which Iran formulated a foreign policy in which Shi'i sectarian identity was used as a tool of influence, and the radicalization of some of the Shi'i Islamic movements have pushed towards the securitization of the Shi'i question. The 2003 regime change in Iraq, which permitted Shi'i Islamic movements to take power in Baghdad and reinforced the Iranian networks of influence in the Arab Middle East, further aggravated this phenomenon in which Shi'i are seen by their Sunni fellow-citizens not so much as adepts of somehow bizarre religious practices but as a fifth column of Iran.

4

ROYAL FACTIONS, RULING STRATEGIES, AND SECTARIANISM IN BAHRAIN

Kristin Smith Diwan

The February 2011 Pearl Uprising in Bahrain began as a sweeping revolt inspired by the successful protest movements in Tunisia and Egypt. When the government-imposed emergency decree was lifted on 1 June 2011, the main outcome of the political uprising was not the constitutional reform most of the protestors were seeking, but instead a harsh sectarian divide. The depth of Sunni–Shi'i animosity extended beyond the halls of government to the university, the workplace, and to personal relationships torn asunder. Views of the events break largely along sectarian lines, and the competing narratives through which Sunni and Shi'i Bahrainis view them appear irreconcilable.

This chapter proposes one framework for analyzing the conditions surrounding the rapid rise in Sunni–Shi'i polarization in Bahrain. In doing so it argues that sectarian strife is not simply the product of entrenched communal divisions; rather it is contingent upon choices made by the ruling elite. One must acknowledge, however, the structural conditions favoring the politicization of sect in Bahrain. Indeed, the oft-repeated shorthand for portraying Bahraini politics is "a Sunni monarchy ruling over a population that is majority Shi'i." Less frequently mentioned is the fact that the tribal elite came to power through conquest, and continues to be viewed by the indigenous Shi'i Arabs as foreign usurpers of their native claim to the island. Class likewise reinforces the sectarian cleavage, for while there are certainly wealthy Shi'is and poor Sunnis in Bahrain, on the whole tribal privilege and urban advantages have left the Sunnis much better off than the once rural Shi'is. Regional politics also exacerbate the sectarian divide as both major powers, Iran and Saudi Arabia, have used religion to legitimate their rule, as well as Shi'i and Sunni Islamist activists to exert their influence abroad. Thus political economy and geopolitics both seem disposed to heighten sectarian identity and condition sectarian discord in Bahrain.

Despite these difficult circumstances, Bahrain's history is not one of continuous sectarian conflict. Within the constraints imposed by history and geography, coexistence and even cross-sectarian cooperation predominate, enough so that until recently Bahrain could promote itself within the Gulf on the basis of its cosmopolitan inclusiveness. This was not the result of the liberality of the ruling family. Throughout their history, the Al Khalifas have worked assiduously to maintain their tribal privileges, to thwart democratic demands, and to sustain divisions within Bahrain's populace. Still, even within the bounds of monarchical authoritarianism notable differences have arisen in ruling strategies. These political choices—forged in factional competition, linked to economic interests, and shaped by distinctive worldviews—have a profound effect on the political salience of sectarian cleavages. Moreover, these ruling strategies extend to external alliances with the power to reshape the domestic political field.

The Pearl Uprising revealed the depth of political discontent in this small island kingdom. The state reaction to it also exposed the stark political divisions within the Al Khalifa ruling family. Analyzing these royal factions and their strategic positioning within a Bahrain that is declining in oil wealth and subject to regional rivalries is central to comprehending the distinctive new ideological and exclusionary sectarianism taking hold in the country. It is likewise essential for assessing the potential for sociopolitical reconciliation and the best channels to achieve it.

Royal factions and ruling strategies

The Al Khalifa, like many of the ruling families in the Persian Gulf, have a pre-oil history of violent internal struggles over power. The early days of their rule in the nineteenth century were characterized by leadership challenges, throwing the island into chronic instability. These disputes over rulership and their foreign entanglements were among the reasons why the British were drawn more deeply into the internal affairs of Bahrain than anywhere else in the Gulf.[1] To secure their interests and provide a more stable basis for rule, in the early twentieth century the British initiated the institutional processes of state formation and set a precedent of primogeniture in royal succession. This principle of primogeniture was later enshrined in Bahrain's constitution.

Though one might assume that this precise rule of succession would stem royal factionalism and competition in Bahrain, this is not the case: not in the setting of policies, and perhaps not even in settling future successions. One reason for this is that the rule of primogeniture supplanted the prevailing norm in the Gulf region of selection by royal consensus.[2] In most Arab monarchies there, the ruler is selected from among a group of eligible descendants on the basis of his capability and his influence as measured by his ability to assemble a supportive coalition from among his relatives. The rationale behind this approach became evident after the sudden death of the long-standing amir, Shaikh Isa, and the ascendancy of his son, Shaikh Hamad bin Isa al-Khalifa, in 1999. While this succession was uncontested, it left Amir Hamad, promoted through primogeniture, to contend with his powerful uncle, the Prime Minister Shaikh Khalifa bin Salman al-Khalifa, who had effectively governed the country under his brother's reign and held considerable influence with the country's ruling elite. Moreover, primogeniture immediately positioned an inheritor to the throne, the new amir's eldest son, Shaikh Salman bin Hamad al-Khalifa, who lacked the credible base

[1] James Onley, "The Politics of Protection in the Gulf: The Arab Rulers and the British Resident in the Nineteenth Century," in B. Pridham and J. Smart (eds), *New Arabian Studies*, Exeter: University of Exeter Press, 2004, pp. 30–92; Fuad I. Khuri, *Tribe and State in Bahrain: The Transition of Social and Political Authority in an Arab State*, Chicago: University of Chicago Press, 1980, pp. 29–34.

[2] Michael Herb has written the definitive book on the internal dynamics of dynastic monarchies, *All in the Family: Absolutism, Revolution, and Democracy in the Middle Eastern Monarchies*, Albany, NY: SUNY Press, 1999.

for power his father had established through his control of the Bahrain Defense Forces. While the new crown prince replaced his father as commander-in-chief, he faced a royal challenger from within the security forces, Defense Minister Shaikh Khalifa bin Ahmed al-Khalifa. Indeed, in 2008 Shaikh Salman relinquished the position of commander-in-chief of the Bahrain Defense Forces to Shaikh Khalifa bin Ahmed, surrendering a power base to a potential rival. Shaikh Khalifa was able to augment the power associated with this influential position through an alliance with his brother, the Royal Court Minister Shaikh Khaled bin Ahmed al-Khalifa, and his protégé Ahmed bin Atiyat-Allah al-Khalifa. The assumption of Amir Hamad to the throne thus generated at least three identifiable factions contending for pre-eminence beneath him: the prime minister, the crown prince, and the brotherly alliance known as the "Khawalid."[3]

In vying for power, royal factions assemble internal coalitions and external allies, mostly on the basis of shared interests, but often expressing a shared outlook or worldview. Together these alliances, interests, and frames of reference express a ruling strategy. For this reason fierce factional competition can produce pronounced shifts in ruling strategies, and at times significant political transformation. It was just such a tactical alliance between Shaikh Abdullah al-Salem al-Sabah and Kuwait's liberal merchants which paved the way for the establishment of Kuwait's parliament. Likewise Qatar's project of political liberalization was launched by Amir Hamad bin Khalifa al-Thani to attract international support for his rule, and to counter the resistance from conservative factions within the Al Thani backed by Saudi Arabia.[4] In Bahrain the nature of the ruling strategy—the external allies and domestic coalition assembled by competing factions—can have a profound impact on sectarian relations.

The importance of external allies is accentuated due to Bahrain's small size and geostrategic positioning. Bahrain's islands compose a mere 760 square kilometers, and its population is 1.2 million people, about half of whom are non-nationals. It is likewise relatively poor, at least within

[3] Together, Khalid bin Ahmed and Khalifa bin Ahmed are known as the "Khawalid," as they hail from a competing branch of the Al Khalifa ruling family that is traced to an ancestor named Khalid bin Ali al-Khalifa.

[4] Mehran Kamrava, "Royal Factionalism and Political Liberalization in Qatar," *The Middle East Journal*, 63, 3 (2009), pp. 401–20.

the Gulf context. While it was the first country to discover oil on the Arab side of the Gulf, it will also be the first to run out of it, holding the lowest oil reserves and consequently enjoying the smallest GDP in the Gulf. Without a large population or great wealth, Bahrain has very limited ability to restructure its international environment. At the same time, its geostrategic relevance, compared to its size, is large; in the eyes of foreign powers, then, intervention may appear to provide a big payoff for a small investment. Bahrain is therefore particularly vulnerable to the conflicts and agendas of regional and international powers. The presence of the US Naval Forces Central Command and its Fifth Fleet further augment the international relevance of the island kingdom.

The permeability of Bahrain's politics is accentuated by its diverse inhabitants. With a population of Arabs and Persians, both Sunni and Shi'i, the state and its people are keenly attuned to the dynamics of the geopolitical competition between Iran and Saudi Arabia as well as the designs of their patrons. Religious networks and tribal bonds extend from the Gulf, the Arabian heartland, and the broader Arab world to communities within the country. While these ties are primarily religious and social, they can be politicized. At times these networks have served as conduits for transnational ideologies with the ability to alter political discourse and to instigate political mobilization within Bahrain. While Arab nationalism, communism, and more recently Arab democratic revolutionaries have all left their mark on the politics of the island, religious networks and ideologies have held special significance, particularly at times of pronounced geostrategic rivalry between Iran and Saudi Arabia.

Still, Bahrain's leaders are not completely at the mercy of external forces. Decisions made by political leaders affect the appeal of transnational connections and shape their disposition toward the monarchy. The nature of the domestic coalition built by a ruler, the degree of its inclusiveness, and its mobilizing dynamics all work to accentuate particular social cleavages or to obscure them, to integrate communities within the state or to alienate them. Moreover, changes in international context are often conducive to the formulation of new ruling strategies, allowing a claimant to exploit regional trends to reshape the domestic environment. And competing royal factions may seek to instrumentalize transnational networks, directing them to their own political ends within the country.

While all of Bahrain's royal factions are intent on maintaining the privileges of monarchy, it is clear that their ruling strategies are far from the same. Different strategies have different effects on the dominant Sunni–Shi'i social cleavage, generating different types of sectarianism. And different strategies have different potential for facilitating democratic reform, even if inadvertent. The remainder of this chapter will look more closely at these dynamics by exploring the constitution of Bahrain's politics under the influence of different rulers and competing royal factions, with a special focus on their sectarian effects. It will begin by tracing the position of tribe and sect in the formation of the state and oil economy, examining the nature of traditional Al Khalifa rule as epitomized by the patronage politics of Bahrain's long-standing prime minister, Shaikh Khalifa bin Salman. It will then turn to the competing strategies utilized by the rival factions that emerged under King Hamad's rule: the inclusive reformism of Crown Prince Salman bin Hamad al-Khalifa and the exclusionary security state of the Khawalid.

From tribal rule to state

Unlike the other merchant ports of the Gulf littoral, modern Bahrain was founded through conquest and the subjugation of the indigenous people. In the late eighteenth century the Al Khalifa, a Bani Utub tribe originally from the interior of the Arabian Peninsula, seized the island from Nasr bin Madhkur, the ruler of Bushehr (thought to be of Omani origin) who was governing the island and its indigenous population of Shi'i Arabs as a dependency of the Persian Empire. After decades of infighting and instability, the Al Khalifa established a tribal government, extending tribal rule over the highly communal Shi'i peasantry.

It is true that the ruling Al Khalifa and their tribal allies were Sunni and that the subject peasantry—known locally as the Baharna—was Shi'i. However, the "right" to rule, as it were, was not based on religion, but on conquest.[5] Furthermore, the difference between the communities was deepened not only by their dominant–subordinate position, but

[5] Abdulhadi Khalaf, "Contentious Politics in Bahrain: From Ethnic to National and Vice Versa," paper presented at The Fourth Nordic Conference on Middle Eastern Studies, Oslo, 13–16 Aug. 1998. The persistence of the mentality of "settler-ruler" is vividly described by Khalaf in recalling the bicentennial celebrations of the conquest put on by the Bahraini state.

also by the profound differences in their social organization and control over resources.[6]

The economic basis of the island up until the time of oil was the cultivation of dates and the fishing of pearls. While the Al Khalifa profited from both, the socio-economy of the two was quite different. Most of the palm estates were distributed among the ruling shaikhs and run as feudal estates. Allied tribes headed the pearl diving enterprises and were granted much more independence. While the economy based on dates and pearls was superseded by the discovery of oil, the initial patterns of authority and social organization that were established at this time shaped social boundaries and cultural dispositions with surprising persistence.

Within the palm estates, which often contained a Shi'i village, the Al Khalifa "lord" was sovereign. His administration—tax collection, the subletting of land—was managed by Shi'i intermediaries, with compliance enforced by the *fidawis*, irregular forces drawn from non-tribal Sunnis, African slaves, and the Baluch, and directly accountable to the lord. As the country was run through a number of such sovereign estates, there was no uniform law to appeal to in case of abuse. Within the villages, however, society was highly regulated by Shi'i jurists and socially bound by religious ritual. The Shi'i clerics derived their authority from the community, not from the tribal rulers. In the eyes of the villagers, these clerics were the legitimate "government."

In contrast to the tight control the tribal lords kept over the feudal estates, the Al Khalifa rulers took a laissez faire approach to the pearl diving industry.[7] Pearl fleets which were dominated by non-Al Khalifa Arab tribesman and captained by Arab pilots were mobile and could leave for other ports taking their profits with them. Many of the Arab tribesmen had powerful tribal allies on the mainland who they could mobilize for war if the need arose. The power of the Arab merchants also constrained the Sunni clergy who were prevented from ruling on the usurious methods used by the pearl industry to keep their mostly Baluch, Persian, and African pullers and divers indebted to them. The authority of the Sunni clergy was restricted to matters of family law, and

[6] Khuri, *Tribe and State*, pp. 1–5. Khuri is the key source for insights into the socio-economy of tribal rule in Bahrain and this section owes much to his work.

[7] Ibid., pp. 65–9. Khuri argues that the differing treatment of Sunni tribesmen from Shi'i peasants was due to market logic, not sect.

they remained considerably less autonomous and less influential than Shi'i clerics.[8]

The British-led transition to a modern state administration in the 1920s marked a substantial departure from this tribal order. Tribal chiefs became government officials and religious jurists became state judges, all compensated with fixed salaries. *Fidawis* were transitioned into a police corps. Yet these reforms did not overturn the social base of power in the country.[9] At the apex of this new state system remained the Al Khalifa themselves, who, over time, assumed control over all of the state's "sovereign" ministries and its growing oil revenues.[10] While other tribes weakened under reforms and the onset of oil, the Al Khalifa became more exclusive, maintaining tight control over family interactions with commoners and shifting their marriage alliances off the island. These outmarriages reflected a new strategy of reliance on regional Arab monarchies in lieu of deeper integration with the people of the island.

The once independent Sunni tribes lost their autonomy. British-initiated reforms, along with the collapse of the pearl trade, drove out many tribal allies of the Al Khalifa. Those who remained moved into other businesses where they merged with the elite merchant community in Manama, made up mostly of Persians, Indians, or the Hawala, Sunnis who "returned" to the island from Iran. Others later joined the defense forces of the new state. As their tribal solidarity waned and their links to the mainland became more tenuous, the Sunni tribesmen—whether businessmen or soldiers—became a strong base of support for the ruling Al Khalifa.[11]

For the Shi'i feudal subjects, the bureaucratic intermediation the reforms offered was an improvement over the old *fidawi* enforcement of patriarchal rule. Yet Shi'i villages continued to fall behind in critical

[8] Ibid., pp. 68–9.

[9] Ibid., pp. 109–33.

[10] For more on the creation of a dynastic monarchy in Bahrain in the 1950s see Herb, *All in the Family*, pp. 127–35.

[11] For a detailed reading of this evolving relationship see Nelida Fuccaro, *Histories of City and State in the Persian Gulf: Manama since 1800*, Cambridge: Cambridge University Press, 2009; Mahmood al-Mahmood, "The Rise and Fall of Bahrain's Merchants in the pre-Oil Era," unpublished manuscript. It is noteworthy that Sunni businessmen have not played the oppositional role that one saw at times in Kuwait, which strengthened Kuwaiti civil society and gave that emirate its distinct political character.

services such as education, leaving the rural Shi'i at a disadvantage in the new oil-based economy.[12] Still, although economic transformations turned them from peasants to wage workers, their social solidarity remained high. The small size of the island meant that while some Shi'i villages were absorbed into Manama's expanding borders, and others were transformed into bedroom communities for labor in the new industries, they maintained a strong communal base. Shi'i clerics remained a potent force, often standing in opposition to the encroachment of more cosmopolitan urban values as well as to the economic inequalities these close quarters made apparent.[13] Their political clout is clearly in evidence in the 1973 parliamentary elections when these clerics orchestrated an impressive win for the "religious bloc."

This separateness of the rural Shi'is, compounded by their continued differential treatment in the new system, served as a barrier to broad-based national political mobilization on the island. Yet these conditions were not insurmountable. At key moments in the 1950s and 1970s, nationalist movements based in the more heterogeneous capital of Manama, spurred by leftist ideologies and Arab nationalism, managed to forge alliances with the village-based movements on the grounds of shared economic interests and demands for greater political accountability. Most noteworthy in this regard were the creation of the Higher Executive Committee to stem Sunni–Shi'i conflict in the 1950s and the coalition voting of the leftist People's Bloc and the Religious Bloc in the 1973 parliament, a challenge which led directly to the parliament's dissolution.[14]

To prevent such cross-sectarian coordination, the Al Khalifa developed a ruling strategy designed to maintain social divisions, rooted in the pre-state tradition of tribal tributaries and Shi'i agents. Clients were cultivated from within each corporate group, based on tribe, sect, kin-

[12] Emile A. Nakhleh, *Bahrain: Political Development in a Modernizing Society*, Lanham, MD: Lexington Books, 1976; repr. 2011, p. 19. State statistics cited by Nakhleh show that at the time of independence in 1971, 71 percent of the rural population remained illiterate, including 50 percent of school-aged children (in contrast to 22 percent of urban children).

[13] Munira Fakhro, "The Uprising in Bahrain: An Assessment," in Gary G. Sick and Lawrence G. Potter (eds), *The Persian Gulf at the Millennium: Essays in Politics, Economy, Security, and Religion*, New York: St. Martin's Press, 1997, pp. 167–88.

[14] For more on the nationalist movements of the 1950s see Fred Lawson, *Bahrain: The Modernization of Autocracy*, Boulder: Westview Press, 1989, pp. 47–71.

ship lineage, or even professional class. These intermediaries were granted privileged access and encouraged to petition on behalf of members of their communities, but only as individuals, not collectivities. As argued by Bahraini sociologist Abdulhadi Khalaf, this form of elite intermediation worked to discourage social mobilization, as the dependent elites owed their wealth and sometimes position within the community to preserving the status quo.[15]

The sharp rise in oil prices in the 1970s increased the potency of this strategy by expanding the resources of the Al Khalifa and funding an expansion of the welfare state. As head of government since the country's independence, Prime Minister Khalifa bin Salman mastered this clientelistic rule, serving as a key conduit to lucrative state contracts and access to public land for both the Sunni and Shi'i commercial elite. His partnerships within the Bahrain Chamber of Commerce and Industry provided both loyalist allies in state development and a steady stream of profits. At the same time, all citizens benefitted from the rapid expansion in social services and state employment, although not equally.

It is important to note that this ruling strategy was not narrowly sectarian. Both Sunnis and Shi'is were incorporated into the Al Khalifa clientelist network in a rather pragmatic way. Still, persistent structural inequalities and lingering tribal custom generated sectarian effects. The neglect of the rural Shi'i villages in favor of urban and exurban development left them mere appendages of the rapidly growing state.[16] Moreover, employment in public sector jobs was often found through social connections, which worked to the advantage of the already well-established Sunni and Shi'i urban communities; the Hawala held the top positions in state industries and tended to hire from within their extended families.[17]

The segmentation of the populace on ethnic, religious, and corporate grounds, augmented by persistent economic inequality, left Bahrain vulnerable to exogenous shocks from regional developments. The more

[15] Abdulhadi Khalaf, "What the Gulf Ruling Families Do When They Rule," *Orient*, 44, 4 (Dec. 2003), pp. 537–54.

[16] Fuccaro, *Histories of City and State in the Persian Gulf*, pp. 211–19. Fuccaro outlines how land policies designed to protect Al Khalifa interests failed to empower Shi'i rural society.

[17] Laurence Louër, "The Political Impact of Labor Migration in Bahrain," *City & Society*, 20, 1 (2008), p. 39.

radical transnational Shi'i ideologies that emerged at the time of the Iranian Revolution found fertile ground in the Bahrain of the 1980s. Nonetheless, efforts to import the Iranian Revolution were not initiated in the rural communities, which maintained their traditional clerical leadership and communal orientation. Instead, it was mostly urban Shi'i who followed *Hojjat al-Islam* Hadi al-Mudarrisi, a cleric from Iraq associated with the Shirazi Islamic Action Organization who was granted Bahraini citizenship in 1974.[18] It was this movement which formed the Islamic Front for the Liberation of Bahrain (IFLB), which was accused of plotting to overthrow the monarchy in 1981.

The shift toward religious-based mobilization evident throughout the region did not bypass the Sunni community in Bahrain. Activists from the Muslim Brotherhood based in the urban community of Muharraq along with Salafi groupings linked to Saudi Arabia became more engaged politically beginning in the 1980s.[19] It is noteworthy, however, that the Muslim Brotherhood in Bahrain was associated from its origins with a notable Al Khalifa shaikh, Khaled bin Muhammed al-Khalifa. The movement thus had important ties to the ruling family—ties that were deepened through the development of the Islamic banking industry in the 1990s in which Muslim Brotherhood businessmen thrived.[20] These political and economic bonds meant that the movement proved less independent and posed less of an oppositional force to the ruling family than in other Gulf states, such as Kuwait. The Sunni community, then, continued to lack a strong and consistent oppositional voice as Sunnis.[21]

[18] For more on the politics of this era see Laurence Louër, *Transnational Shia Politics: Religious and Political Networks in the Gulf*, New York: Columbia University Press, 2008, pp. 156–61; Falah al-Mdaires, "Shi'ism and Political Protest in Bahrain," *DOMES: Digest of Middle East Studies*, 11, 1 (Spring 2002); Hasan Tariq al-Hasan, "The Role of Iran in the Failed Coup of 1981: The IFLB in Bahrain," *Middle East Journal*, 65, 4 (Autumn 2011).

[19] Sunni political movements in Bahrain are discussed in Baqir Salman al-Najjar, *Al-Harakat al-Diniyyah fi al-Khalij al-Arabi* [Religious Movements in the Arab Gulf], London: Dar al Saqi Press, 2007.

[20] Based on original field research and interviews conducted within the industry, 2000–3. For more on the politics of Islamic finance see Kristin Smith, "From Petrodollars to Islamic Dollars: The Strategic Construction of Islamic Banking in the Arab Gulf," PhD dissertation, Harvard University, 2006.

[21] Statistical surveys conducted by Justin Gengler indicate that, among Sunnis, increased religiosity correlates with more pro-government positions. Justin J. Gen-

Bahrain's segmentary clientelism faced yet another challenge in the 1990s as declining oil reserves tested the limits of this ruling strategy. After the rise of Shi'i revolutionary politics in the 1980s, Shi'is were eliminated from jobs in the police and military, in addition to their traditional disproportionate exclusion from jobs in the sovereign ministries of defense, interior, foreign affairs, and justice, denying to them a significant source of employment.[22] This forced a larger percentage of Shi'is to seek employment in the private sector where they were increasingly competing with lower-wage foreigners. As economic frustrations compounded political ones, they took to the streets, feeding the village uprisings of the mid-1990s.[23] Even more threatening for the Al Khalifa was the reappearance of cross-sectarian political cooperation at this time in the form of petitions demanding the reinstatement of the parliament.[24] The use of force and the reliance on outsiders became more pronounced, as Bahrain's rulers turned increasingly to Saudi Arabia to staunch the loss of oil income and to survive the unrest. There are disputed reports that the Saudis sent National Guard troops in support of the Al Khalifa across the King Fahd causeway connecting the island to the mainland.[25] As the unrest persisted, Saudi Arabia upped the percentage of oil shared from the Abu Safaa oil field from 50 percent to 70 percent before deciding to relinquish its total production to Bahrain in

---

gler, "Ethnic Conflict and Political Mobilization in Bahrain and the Arab Gulf," PhD dissertation, University of Michigan, 2011, p. 247.

22 Khalaf, "Contentious Politics in Bahrain"; Justin J. Gengler, "The (Sectarian) Politics of Public Sector Employment in Bahrain," paper presented to the Third Gulf Research Meeting, Cambridge, 11–14 July 2012.

23 Louër, "The Political Impact of Labor Migration," pp. 32–53.

24 Fakhro, "The Uprising in Bahrain"; Human Rights Watch, "Routine Abuse, Routine Denial: Civil Rights and the Political Crisis in Bahrain," June 1997, http://www.hrw.org/legacy/reports/1997/bahrain/. Noteworthy in this regard was the series of petitions signed by intellectuals from both sects, and the plan for a rally with speeches by both the rural Shi'i cleric Abdel Amir al-Jamri and the Sunni Shariah scholar Abdel Latif al-Mahmoud.

25 In her June 2012 Chatham House report, "Bahrain: Beyond the Impasse," Jane Kinninmont makes reference to "plentiful eyewitness reports of Saudi National Guard units entering Bahrain during the 1990s uprising." However, military historian Anthony Cordesman maintains that such reports are false in his book, *Saudi Arabia Enters the Twenty-First Century: The Military and International Security Dimensions*, Westport, CT: Praeger Publishers, 2003, p. 177.

1996. By the end of the 1990s it was clear that the weaknesses in Bahrain's economic and political system were leading to chronic civil unrest, increasing political mobilization, and deepening foreign dependency.

Crown Prince Salman bin Hamad al-Khalifa and the era of reform

By the late 1990s Bahrain was beginning to look out of step with its peers as a new reformism in politics and economics made its way across the Arab states of the Gulf. The unexpected death of Shaikh Isa in 1999, and the assumption to power of his son, Amir Hamad, presented an opportunity to join in the regional transformation, an opportunity that was seized upon by the new ruler. The first political succession in decades also immediately threw into relief a contest for influence between Amir Hamad's designated successor, his son Shaikh Salman, and the long-ruling prime minister, his uncle Shaikh Khalifa bin Salman. Though primogeniture established his future succession, the young crown prince lacked the influence of Shaikh Khalifa as the long-standing head of government and patron of the business community. He thus endeavored to carve out a competing ruling strategy within the framework of his father's reformist project. Drawing inspiration from Dubai's emergence as a global city and business hub, he staked his claim as a globalizing modernizer, garnering critical support from a new international patron in the United States, and a new domestic coalition of technocratic reformers. From economic boards and through economic reform initiatives he launched his campaign to siphon influence from the prime minister. In the process, King Hamad and Crown Prince Salman would open new avenues for Shi'i cooperation with the government by extending a promise of incremental empowerment and local development—a promise that mostly failed to materialize, with damning consequences for Bahrain's stability and sovereignty.

In the aftermath of the Persian Gulf War (1990–1) a new era of experimentation prevailed in the small emirates of the Gulf littoral. The expanded military presence of the United States provided these city-states with a means to press a more independent line from Saudi Arabia, and external and internal political pressures led rulers to experiment with new, more representative, institutions.[26] In addition, a turnaround

[26] For an analysis of shifting US security arrangements and the strategic calculations

in oil prices from their nadir in 1998 presaged the start of a new era of domestic investment and international interest in Persian Gulf economies that would translate into an economic boom. By the mid-2000s the entire Gulf region had joined in the development as petrodollars seeded ambitious infrastructure projects and attracted international financial participation.[27]

The new monarch in Bahrain sought to capitalize on this altered regional environment to reorder Bahrain's domestic politics and to improve Bahrain's international appeal. With his assumption of power in 1999, Amir Hamad set a path out of Bahrain's cyclical unrest through a program of controlled liberalization.[28] Central to this strategy was a new formula for co-opting the opposition—in particular the Shi'i Islamists—into the political and economic structure of the state, without threatening the prerogatives of the ruling Al Khalifa. An amnesty which allowed the opposition to return from exile was an important step in reframing this relationship. The coming together of most of the Shi'i opposition into a unified alliance—al-Wifaq, or the Islamic National Accord—facilitated this process.[29] Achieving the "buy in" of this critical constituency and their strategic integration into the new political and economic order was essential to the success of the reforms.

---

of the small littoral states in this period see Simon Henderson, "The New Pillar: Conservative Arab Gulf States and U.S. Strategy," *Policy Paper*, 58, Washington, DC: The Washington Institute for Near East Policy, 1 Jan. 2003. Bahrain consolidated its position within the US base strategy, becoming host for the Navy's newly reconstituted Fifth Fleet in 1995.

[27] Kristin Smith Diwan and Fareed Mohammedi, "The Gulf Comes Down to Earth," *Middle East Report*, 252 (Fall 2009), pp. 6–15.

[28] The political side of these reforms has been covered in depth by Steven Wright, "Fixing the Kingdom: Political Evolution and Socio-Economic Challenges in Bahrain," *Occasional Paper*, Doha: Center for International and Regional Studies, Georgetown University School of Foreign Service in Qatar, 2008; J.E. Peterson, "Bahrain: Reform, Promise, and Reality," in Joshua Teitelbaum (ed.), *Political Liberalization in the Persian Gulf*, New York: Columbia University Press, 2009, pp. 157–85.

[29] For more on the transformation of the opposition in exile see Claire Beaugrand, "The Return of the *Bahraini Exiles* (2001–2006): The Impact of the Ostracization Experience on the Opposition's Restructuring," paper presented at The British Society for Middle Eastern Studies (BRISMES) Annual Conference, University of Leeds, 4–6 July 2008.

On the political side, Amir Hamad's National Action Charter promised the reinstatement of the parliament, addressing the popular demand for political representation. This plan was enthusiastically received by the public, which granted the reform process an important imprimatur of popular legitimacy with its overwhelming approval in a national referendum in 2001. However, subsequent actions taken by the Al Khalifa weakened the democratic impulse of the reforms and kept the opposition boxed in. In addition to declaring Bahrain a kingdom, constitutional amendments presented by the new King Hamad gave an appointed upper house legislative authority over the elected lower house. And even within the elected lower house, severely gerrymandered districts—both aggregating Shi'i populations and placing them in districts with much higher numbers of voters—ensured that the Shi'i opposition would never gain a majority in the elected Chamber of Deputies. While the opposition boycotted the first parliamentary elections in 2002 in protest, al-Wifaq and the cross-sectarian leftist opposition, the National Democratic Action Society, or Wa'ad, shifted strategies and entered the elections in 2006 in a bid to press for change from within the system. Al-Wifaq took almost all of the seats they contested and entered the Chamber of Deputies as the largest political bloc, although short of a majority and denied the leadership post.

It is within this mantle of reform that the young crown prince undertook his bid for influence.[30] Although he was the constitutionally designated successor, Crown Prince Salman bin Hamad al-Khalifa had none of the institutional advantages of his uncle. As prime minister, Shaikh Khalifa led the government and continued to preside over Bahrain's patronage economy, controlling many bids and tenders for the business community. He likewise held a long-standing relationship with the Saudi interior minister, Prince Nayef (d.2012), as well as other elites within Bahrain's key ally and benefactor. Crown Prince Salman thus designed a completely new ruling strategy resonant with the changing international context and domestic reform initiatives, championing a narrative of national development and adopting the role of technocratic modernizer. He founded new institutions where he assembled his own domestic

[30] For more on the political economy of this period see Steven Wright, "Generational Change and Elite-Driven Reforms in the Kingdom of Bahrain," *Durham Middle East Papers*, 81, Durham: University of Durham, 2006.

coalition and engaged international actors. From this new institutional base Crown Prince Salman was able to initiate significant new policies and to siphon real authority away from the prime minister.

The crown prince's economic initiatives sought to modernize the economy through the improvement of governance, economic diversification, labor market reforms, and education and training. The policy incubator for these initiatives was the Economic Development Board (EDB), a quasi-governmental body established under his chairmanship in 2002, and entrusted with the mandate of strategic economic planning for the kingdom through a royal decree issued in 2005. From this post, the crown prince directed significant reforms across many different sectors including the labor market, education, and foreign investment, burnishing the country's image of being forward-looking and open for business.[31]

This new form of economic outreach, when coupled with the improving political atmosphere on the island, enabled Bahrain to expand its international relationships beyond its primary benefactor, Saudi Arabia. The expansion of the Bahrain–US trade relationship is indicative of these changes. The signing of the Free Trade Agreement in 2004 distinguished Bahrain as the first Persian Gulf state to establish these ties with the United States. The implementation of the agreement, including environmental and labor obligations, deepened relations with American labor organizations and dovetailed nicely with the crown prince's reform agenda. But this initiative angered Saudi Arabia by undercutting the GCC customs union formed in 2003. The Al Saud indicated their displeasure, and demonstrated their economic clout, by eliminating a 50,000 b/d oil grant, and by temporarily blocking shipments of critical building supplies (sand and cement) to the island.

[31] For details on Bahrain's labor market reforms see Hasan Tariq al-Hasan, "Labor Market Politics in Bahrain," in Steffen Hertog (ed.), *National Employment, Migration, and Education in the GCC*, Berlin: Gerlach Press, 2012, pp. 117–61; Human Rights Watch, "For a Better Life: Migrant Worker Abuse in Bahrain and the Government Reform Agenda," Oct. 2012, http://www.hrw.org/sites/default/files/reports/bahrain1012ForUpload.pdf. Under the EDB and the crown prince's guidance, two new educational institutions—the Bahrain Teacher's College and Bahrain Polytechnic—were established, and the crown prince also increased the number of Bahrainis studying abroad through a meritocratic scholarship program.

Resistance to the new economic initiatives was not limited to Saudi Arabia. The labor market reforms directly challenged the prime minister's business alliance. The imposition of new restrictions and fees on businesses using foreign workers provoked opposition from the Bahrain Chamber of Commerce and Industry (BCCI), which pushed back against these policies. Government ministries likewise resisted the efforts of the EDB to reform the state bureaucracy. When the acceleration of reforms from 2006 began infringing on the authority of the prime minister, a fierce battle ensued, with the crown prince accusing his uncle of undermining reforms through surrogates, business leaders, and the bureaucracy. In 2008, this contest seemed settled as the king issued an open letter reinforcing the authority of the EDB over economic policy, and threatening any obstructive ministers with dismissal. Shortly thereafter the EDB began requiring ministers—with the exception of the sovereign ministries of interior and defense—to attend EDB meetings, essentially converting the EDB into an alternate cabinet beyond the purview of the prime minister or parliamentary questioning.

The significance of these reforms extended beyond the economy: the new initiatives and institutions of the king and crown prince opened important avenues for improving relations with the political opposition and the majority Shi'i community. While labor reforms promoted all Bahraini workers, the benefits fell disproportionately to the Shi'i due to their greater dependence on the private sector for employment and the prevalence of unemployment in their community. Moreover, the economic reforms provided new avenues for organization and representation. In 2002 Bahrain became the first Arab state in the Gulf to allow independent labor unions, and al-Wifaq activists quickly assumed positions of leadership within the newly formed General Federation of Bahrain Trade Unions (GFBTU). Opposition leaders, some newly returned from exile, were recruited to key positions, including the chairmanship of the Labor Fund Tamkeen and the Ministry of Labor, and Shi'i technocrats filled prominent positions within the new institutions.[32] There was likewise a greater willingness to allow for deeper localization, tethering the communitarianism of Shi'i villages to the broader project of national development through municipal councils and private sector–village partnerships.[33]

[32] Hassan, "Labor Market Politics," pp. 148–51.

[33] Dr Nazar Baharna, in discussion with the author, June 2012.

The integration of the Shi'is in this new national project also enhanced the potential for cross-sectarian cooperation. The crown prince's modernizing reforms drew in technocrats who were supportive of public sector reform and attracted by the promise of a more self-reliant and globally integrated Bahrain. His meritocratic international scholarship program worked to link a new generation of foreign-educated Bahrainis to the crown prince and his agenda, drawing highly educated youth into this more integrated national vision. Initially, the Council of Representatives—elected through gerrymandered districts and defined by competing Sunni and Shi'i Islamist blocs—achieved limited cross-sectarian coordination beyond religious initiatives. However, in March 2010 a parliamentary committee issued a report alleging major irregularities in an area of great sensitivity: the government management of public lands. The report outlined the leasing or outright transfer of state land to private investors who then used them for commercial enterprises. This included a shocking 94 percent of land recently reclaimed from the sea, despite the fact that sea-covered areas cannot be privately owned under Bahraini law.[34] This issue has special resonance due to the shortage of land and housing in one of the most densely populated countries in the world, and thus a call for legal action against those responsible was supported by both the Shi'i al-Wifaq and the Sunni al-Minbar, representing the Muslim Brotherhood in Bahrain. In the new constitutional order, however, the Council of Representatives did not have the political authority to impose this.

The scandal over public lands was indicative of the corruption that persisted into the reform era. Indeed, the boom economy which coincidentally followed the reforms heightened fundamental inequalities—inequalities shaped by networks of privilege linked to elements of the ruling family. At the same time as the crown prince was working to reform labor markets to the advantage of Bahraini workers, the kingdom's archipelago was being reshaped in ambitious programs of land reclamation and construction benefitting the business allies of the prime minister.[35] Capitalizing on new laws allowing foreign ownership of land,

[34] Mazen Mahdi, "Bahraini Public Lands Sold and Rented to Private Investors," *The National*, 25 Mar. 2010, http://www.thenational.ae/news/world/middle-east/bahraini-public-lands-sold-and-rented-to-private-investors

[35] Frederik Richter and Martin de Sa'Pinto, "Special Report: In Bahrain, a Symbol at the Heart of Revolt," Reuters, 16 June 2011, http://www.reuters.com/article/2011/06/16/us-bahrain-gfh-idUSTRE75F4LF20110616

commercial and residential properties, choice sections of the Bahraini coast were developed into floating islands boasting high-end hotels and apartments to attract foreign investors. Yet at the same time, villages often suffered from loss of access to coastline, or pollution associated with attendant changes in water flows. The contrast between these luxury developments built alongside the still underdeveloped Shi'i villages was stark, and provided a tangible reflection of the fundamental inequity of the Al Khalifa-led economy.

Indeed, in the boom era, Bahrain's poor fell further behind. A 2011 Economic Development Board study on income inequality shows that the share of total income for the poorest Bahrainis dropped over the period 1995–2006.[36] Moreover, statistics from the last decade show the LMRA (Labor Market Reform Authority) fighting a losing battle, as the rise in foreign labor associated with the economic boom overwhelmed the efforts at Bahrainization. The impact on the Bahrain labor market was dramatic: from 2002 to 2011 the EDB's own statistics show that the share of Bahrainis employed in the private sector almost halved, falling from 29 percent to 15 percent.[37] Despite its ambitions, the crown prince's labor reforms utterly failed to reverse the trend toward greater employment of foreign labor.

The reforms undertaken by the king and crown prince aimed to better integrate the Shi'is into national politics and markets, but they did not eliminate the differential treatment of communities, nor did they address the exclusion inherent at the heights of the "tribal" system. Much as the political reforms brought the opposition societies into the parliament without relinquishing control over the levers of power, the economic reforms worked to better integrate Bahrainis into the economy without ceding control over key resources: land and oil. The result was a growing disillusionment with the accommodative approach of al-Wifaq, and growing disputes within the opposition over fundamental tactics.

While some in the opposition thought the king's reforms did not go far enough in pressing for accountability and equity, others within the

[36] As cited by Hasan Tariq al-Hasan, "The Socioeconomic Foundations of Bahrain's Political Crisis," Open Democracy, 20 Feb. 2012, http://www.opendemocracy.net/hasan-tariq-al-hasan/socio-economic-foundations-of-bahrain%E2%80%99s-political-crisis

[37] Economic Development Board, *Bahrain Economic Quarterly*, Fourth Quarter 2011–First Quarter 2012, 31 May 2012, p. 62.

ruling family thought they had gone much too far. Over the latter half of the 2000s, a new ideological coalition would cohere around the idea that the Shi'i could not be trusted, and that integrating them into the state's political and economic institutions was courting danger. The struggle between the crown prince and the prime minister was being eclipsed by new claimants to power rooted in the security state.

The rise of the Khawalid and the security state

There is no question that the Khawalid—a ruling faction centered on Minister of Defense Khalifa bin Ahmed and his brother, the Royal Court Minister Khaled bin Ahmed—have made a significant mark on Bahraini politics.[38] Descended from an alternate branch of the family than the ruling line, the Khawalid have proven adept at assembling a coalition around a competing viewpoint: skepticism of the king's reform program, and deep suspicion of Shi'i empowerment. With a power base in both the Ministry of Defense and the Royal Court, they have demonstrated a skill for networking within Bahraini government and society to extend their influence. Through media and with the support of Sunni Islamist allies, they have promoted a conspiratorial worldview aimed at mobilizing Sunnis against the Shi'i peril.

The rise of the Khawalid was, ironically, facilitated by the era of reform and the Crown's efforts to weaken the prime minister. Khalifa bin Ahmed emerged from within the institution most identified as the power base of the king: the armed forces. He was appointed defense minister in 1988 by King Hamad's father, the previous Amir Shaikh Isa.[39] At the time of his succession, King Hamad named his son, Shaikh Salman, to replace himself as commander-in-chief of the BDF, but retained Shaikh Khalifa bin Ahmed as defense minister. In the ensuing years of factional competition, Shaikh Khalifa was viewed as being "within the King's camp,"[40] and consequently eluded the king's purges

[38] For an in-depth study of their rise and influence see Justin Gengler, "Royal Factionalism, the Khawalid, and the Securitization of 'the Shi'a Problem' in Bahrain," *Journal of Arabian Studies*, 3, 1 (June 2013), pp. 53–79.

[39] Prior to that time, the then Crown Prince Hamad, architect of the Bahrain Defense Forces (BDF), had served as both defense minister and commander-in-chief.

[40] For an analysis of the battle over ministers see Abbas Bu Safwan, "al-Malik Yakh-

which targeted the Interior Ministry, a stronghold for allies of the prime minister. However, in 2008, the king abolished the Defense Ministry in a bid to shelter the armed forces from parliamentary oversight and perhaps from interference by the head of government.[41] With the position of defense minister eliminated, he then elevated Crown Prince Salman to the newly created position of deputy supreme commander, and made Shaikh Khalifa bin Ahmed commander-in-chief of the BDF. At the time, this move was interpreted as better positioning the crown prince, especially when considered within the context of the ministerial "coup" of the EDB later that same year. Nonetheless, while his position as deputy supreme commander granted him broad authority to reform the BDF and the National Guard, the crown prince's role in the defense forces appears to have diminished.

The other member of the Khawalid, Khaled bin Ahmed al-Khalifa, heads the royal court and thus plays the important role of intermediary for the king. His nephew and ally Shaikh Ahmed bin Atiyat-Allah al-Khalifa was appointed minister of cabinet affairs in 2005, holding another key position interceding between the ruling family and the cabinet. Taken together, the two positions hold enormous potential for coordination among Bahrain power centers. In addition, observers of Bahraini politics have long noted that under Shaikh Khaled bin Ahmed's leadership the royal court has been cultivating ties within Bahrain's Sunni Islamist movements.[42] Though not well understood, the Khawalid network, then, is grounded in government influence, and bound by a shared point of view: a worldview steeped in Sunni chauvinism, amplified due to the growing Shi'i empowerment within the Persian Gulf region. The Khawalid's ascendancy within the government, fueled in part by the shifting regional context, would push Bahrain in a direction

---

nuqu Ra'is al-Wuzara' fi 'Arinihi (al-Dusturi)" [The King Throttles the Prime Minister in his (Constitutional) Lair], *Bahrain Mirror*, 16 July 2012, http://www.bahrainmirror.com/article.php?id=5068&cid=88

41 This move brought the BDF and National Guard under the king's direct authority, and while parliament has the right to question ministers, the constitution does not grant it the authority to question the king.

42 Based on personal interviews. For a journalist's perspective on this alliance see Borzou Daragahi, "Rift over Shiites is seen in Bahrain's Royal Court," *The Los Angeles Times*, 7 July 2007, http://articles.latimes.com/2007/jul/07/world/fg-bahrain7

diametrically opposed to the crown prince's reforms and its engagement with the Shi'i.

If the crown prince's strategy drew upon the regional spirit of reformism, global investment, and American influence, the crucible for the Khawalid was the Iraq War and its aftermath. For much of the 1980s and 1990s the states of the Arabian Peninsula relied upon a balance of power—and a war of attrition—between their larger and more powerful neighbors, Iraq and Iran. The balance tilted toward Iran following the first Gulf War and the punishing sanctions imposed on Iraq after Kuwait's liberation, and shifted decisively to it in 2003 with the US invasion of Iraq and the overthrow of its ruler, Saddam Hussein. Iran's more ambitious play for regional influence through the Hezbollah- and Hamas-led "resistance fronts" concerned the more conservative Persian Gulf allies of the United States. But the democratic transition in Iraq was threatening on an entirely different level. The consternation of the Bahraini ruling family and their Sunni allies in seeing a popularly elected Shi'i Islamist government take power in Iraq was considerable. A regional discourse of Sunni victimization, Shi'i savagery, and American deceit gained traction through the months of the escalating sectarian civil war in Iraq, popularized through Sunni Islamist publications and cyber media.[43] For some within the Bahraini government, concern about the growing power of Najaf, its influence with Bahraini Shi'i movements, and its links to Qom intensified their apprehensions about power-sharing with the opposition.

A window into the mindset associated with the Khawalid network and its effect on ruling strategy was opened by a British whistleblower of Sudanese origin, Dr Salah al-Bandar, who was working as an advisor to the Ministry of Cabinet Affairs. In 2006 the Gulf Center for Democratic Development released his report which purported to reveal a government-led scheme to undercut Shi'i influence within the state. Among the voluminous documents copied during his employment, and included in the al-Bandar report as evidence of the scheme, was a proposal commissioned by the Bahraini government (or elements thereof) which presumably provided the blueprint for the anti-Shi'i initiative.

[43] For more on the sectarian politics of this era see Vali Nasr, *The Shia Revival: How Conflicts within Islam will Shape the Future*, New York: W.W. Norton Press, 2006; Fanar Haddad, *Sectarianism in Iraq: Antagonistic Visions of Unity*, London: Hurst, 2011.

This plan, entitled "A Proposal to Promote the General Situation of the Sunni Sect in Bahrain" and written by an Iraqi academic, is telling in its explicit linking of Bahrain to broader regional developments in Iraq and Iran, and in its relentlessly zero-sum vision of Sunni–Shi'i relations.[44] Decrying the "marginalization of the Sunni in Bahrain" as "part of the greater regional problem faced by the Sunni of Iraq," it warns that the growing role of the Shi'i in the political system, over time, will allow them to change the political system with the aid of the transnational network of Shi'i across Iran, Iraq, the Eastern Province of Saudi Arabia, and Kuwait. In light of this danger, the proposal goes on to suggest that the government adopt a secret five-year program to take "widespread actions across various fields [political, social, economic, demographic, religious, media, education, women, regional, and international] to return balance to the political system." In short, it sketches a roadmap for unraveling the co-optation strategy of the early reform years.

The rest of the al-Bandar report provides evidence for the existence of just such a secret program. It outlines an extensive network of Sunni government officials, politicians, journalists, and other functionaries working under the direction of Shaikh Ahmed bin Atiyat-Allah al-Khalifa and run through the Cabinet Affairs and Central Informatics Organization (equivalent to Bahrain's CIA). Most of those named as part of the network were associated with the Muslim Brotherhood and other Sunni Islamist movements. Their alleged operations included measures to monitor and counter Shi'i opposition movements and their civil society groups, including funding Sunni politicians and Sunni civil society organizations; supporting Sunni groups mobilizing against Shi'is and working to convert them; and fomenting suspicion of the Shi'i opposition through the media, and in particular through the *al-Watan* newspaper which was deeply entrenched in the network. The Bandargate report also made reference to one of the more explosive issues in Bahrain: political naturalizations.[45] Over the period of reform following Amir

[44] "Tasawwur li-l-Nuhud bi-l-Wad' al-'Amm li-l-Ta'ifa al-Sunniyya fi Mamlakat al-Bahrayn" [A Proposal to Promote the General Situation of the Sunni in the Kingdom of Bahrain], published by the Bahrain Center for Human Rights as "Al-Bander Report: Demographic Engineering in Bahrain and Mechanisms of Exclusion," Manama, Bahrain: Bahrain Center for Human Rights, 2006, http://www.bahrainrights.org/node/528

[45] This issue has been covered extensively by the Bahrain Center for Human Rights

Hamad's accession, the ruling family is believed to have granted citizenship to tens of thousands of Sunnis from neighboring countries in an effort to augment the security forces and shift the sectarian demographics of the state.[46] It is noteworthy that this was done with the cooperation of the Saudi authorities and under the context of a new law passed by King Hamad allowing GCC citizens to hold dual citizenship with Bahrain.[47] The clear intent of this policy was to increase the Sunni tribal presence on the island and to shift the demographics against the Shi'i.

Thus by the end of the 2000s the ruling Al Khalifa experienced mounting factionalism which multiplied the contradictions in their rule. The existence of competing ruling strategies undermined confidence in King Hamad's reforms and weakened support for the official opposition societies advocating engagement with the regime. Increasingly, then, the divisions within the Al Khalifa were reflected in the opposition itself, particularly in the growth in popularity of the "boycott" wing of the opposition, so named because of their rejection of al-Wifaq's decision to enter the 2006 parliamentary elections. Prominent among this new opposition camp were the al-Haq [Right] movement founded by Hassan al-Mushaima and Dr Abduljalil Singace in 2005 and al-Wafa' [Loyalty] founded by Abdel Wahab al-Hussein and Shia cleric Abduljalil Maqdad in 2009.[48] These movements were much more willing to use

---

as well as by a number of scholars. On the politics of the issue see Gengler, "Ethnic Conflict and Political Mobilization," pp. 59–66.

[46] Working from official population statistics and accounting for the natural rate of growth, the opposition estimates that 60,000 individuals, overwhelmingly Sunni, were granted citizenship from 2001 to 2007. This represents an addition equal to nearly 10 percent of the population.

[47] This included the granting of citizenship to the Dawasir tribe—which left Bahrain for the Saudi mainland in 1923 during the time of the British reforms—with the electoral measure introduced in Aug. 2002. Bahrain Center for Human Rights, "Naturalization as a Mean[s] of Discriminatory Demographic Change," 4 Mar. 2005, http://www.bahrainrights.org/node/27; International Crisis Group, *Middle East Report*, 40, "Bahrain's Sectarian Challenge," 6 May 2005, pp. 7–8. It is worth noting that the Bahrain government once used its citizenship policy to naturalize Iranian workers at a time of leftist–Arab nationalist opposition in the 1950s.

[48] While these movements were largely made up of Shi'i activists, al-Haq and the BCHR did include Sunni members and al-Haq had Sunni activists in their leadership. Both Abdel Wahab al-Hussein and Hassan al-Mushaima were leaders from the mid-1990s uprising and founding members of al-Wifaq.

civil disobedience to achieve their goals.[49] They adopted a language of rights, pioneered by the Bahrain Center for Human Rights (BCHR) led by Abdelhadi al-Khawaja, to challenge the inherently discriminatory system that defied reform. The situation in Bahrain, then, was primed for acceptance of the wave of street protests that swept the Middle East region at the beginning of 2011.

The factionalism of both the regime and the opposition were in clear view during the Pearl Uprising.[50] The initial protests were called by youth activists unaffiliated with the legal political societies who seized the initiative in the wave of Arab uprisings and drew inspiration from its revolutionary promise, especially after the Bahraini government responded to their peaceful actions with lethal force. Popular anger at the "tribal privilege" at the heart of the boom economy was in full evidence in the protest sites chosen by the street opposition. While the legal opposition political societies joined the gathering in the Pearl Roundabout and sponsored marches in central Manama, the young street activists of the newly formed February 14th movement and the rejectionist front declaring a "Coalition for a Republic" pushed the protests to more confrontational and symbolically resonant sites: the Bahrain Financial Harbor, the stronghold of the merchant oligarchy, built on reclaimed land; and the royal court in al-Rifa', the tribal fortress of the ruling Al Khalifa.[51]

[49] Although Al-Haq is portrayed as more "radical" than al-Wifaq due to its tactics and more revolutionary goals, it relies less on religious legitimacy and clerical guidance. Al-Haq had several Sunnis in its leadership, although they parted with the organization before or during the events of Feb. 2011.

[50] A well-documented narrative of the Feb.–Mar. 2011 events in Bahrain can be found in the report of the Bahrain Independent Commission of Inquiry, 10 Dec. 2011, http://www.bici.org.bh/BICIreportEN.pdf. My analysis and commentary can be found in "The Failed Uprising," Middle East Policy Council, 31 Mar. 2011, http://www.mepc.org/articles-commentary/commentary/failed-revolution. For a scholarly eyewitness account of the events see Toby Matthiesen, *Sectarian Gulf: Bahrain, Saudi Arabia, and the Arab Spring that Wasn't*, Palo Alto, CA: Stanford University Press, 2013, pp. 33–50.

[51] The Coalition for a Republic included al-Haq, al-Wafa', and the Bahrain Freedom Movement, an exile group based in London. Its initial statement calling for "the downfall of the regime and the establishment of a democratic republic" can be found in "Bahraini 'Coalition for a Republic' Issues First Statement," *Jadaliyya*, 9 Mar. 2011, http://www.jadaliyya.com/pages/index/839/bahraini-coalition-for-a-republic-issues-first-statement

The al-Khalifa-led government also betrayed divisions in their shifting response to the crisis. After initially cracking down on protests and violently clearing the gathering at the Pearl Roundabout on 15 February, security forces were withdrawn from the roundabout several days later and the crown prince was given authority to negotiate with the official opposition societies. Another concession saw the removal of four ministers on 25 February, including the key Khawalid functionary Shaikh Ahmed bin Atiyat-Allah Al-Khalifa from his post as minister of cabinet affairs. The opposition exacerbated these rifts by openly calling for the sacking of the prime minister.

By March, the calculated provocations of the revolutionary opposition were met by a counter-mobilization of Sunni irregulars bearing sticks and knives in an ominous presage of civil-sectarian strife. A turning point had been reached. A day after the confrontations turned violent at the Bahrain Financial Harbor, the Gulf Cooperation Council (GCC) Peninsula Shield Forces, led by the Saudi Arabian National Guard, crossed the causeway, ending the uprising. Their arrival cut short the negotiations that the crown prince was holding with opposition political societies, eclipsing the forces of reform.

The GCC intervention changed the perception of the uprising. By the very act of intervening, it shifted the frame of reference from a domestic dispute to an international one, conveying plausibility to regime assertions of an Iranian threat. In the intervention was an implied conclusion: if the Saudi troops were needed to preserve the stability and security of the nation from a foreign threat, then those who supported the uprising must be traitors. The GCC intervention also shifted the balance of power within the ruling family decisively toward the hardliners. The uprising confirmed the darkest fears of the Sunni chauvinists, reinforcing their conviction—and convincing many others—that the Shi'i were seeking to overthrow the government. Initiatives to shut the Shi'i out of politics, the economy, and society were now brought into the open. A new sectarianism was taking hold.

The rise of a new sectarianism and the fall of the crown prince's reforms

The aftermath of the Pearl Uprising witnessed a punitive campaign notable for its expansive reach and its engagement of the broader populace. The ascendancy of hardliners, under the extreme conditions of the political crisis, created a permissive environment for anti-Shi'i rhetoric and Sunni political mobilization. Bahrain television showed video footage of protestors at the Pearl Roundabout and invited Bahrainis to inform on their fellow citizens. Government ministries, state industries, and private businesses fired those known to have been in the roundabout, and they sometimes simply fired Shi'i employees wholesale.[52] Universities—including the University of Bahrain, the site of a large clash between protestors and pro-government vigilantes—expelled students known to have been critical of the government. The crackdown was not limited to students and workers, as the Shi'i professional class of doctors, journalists, and lawyers were caught in the web of arrests and prosecutions. Sunnis who were known participants and leaders of protests were prosecuted as well. The Sunni head of the leftist Wa'ad, Ebrahim Sharif, was tried and sentenced to five years in prison despite being a known reformer who had never called for the fall of the monarchy.[53]

Loyalty pledges were instituted. Some began as "popular" campaigns of support under the patronage of Shaikh Nasser bin Hamad al-Khalifa, the younger brother of the crown prince.[54] Others were connected to places of work or study. University of Bahrain students were forced to sign a pledge of complete loyalty to the king which included a provision "not to organize or participate in any activity within the campus or outside that is irrelevant to student and academic affairs and authorized research" upon threat of expulsion.[55] Human Rights Watch issued a report which found that over 500 students were suspended or expelled and at least 100 faculty and staff dismissed between April and August 2011, in most cases for attending anti-government demonstrations or posting links on social media.[56]

[52] Based on personal interviews. The Dec. 2012 US Department of Labor report (p. iii) states that the government response to the Mar. 2011 general strike "directly engaged in discrimination on the basis of political opinion and/or religion in the public sector and failed to sanction such discriminatory practices by private sector employers."

[53] All of the leaders of the Coalition for a Republic were also tried and sentenced to life in prison.

[54] "Organizers Aim to Collect over 500,000 Signatures for Loyalty Campaign," Bahrain News Agency, 19 Apr. 2011, http://www.bna.bh/portal/en/news/453395

[55] "Mashruta bi-Tawqi' Ta'ahhud bi-l-Wala' li-l-Watan wa-l-Qiyada" [Conditioned to Sign Pledge of Loyalty to Homeland and Leadership], *Al-Wasat*, 16 May 2011, http://www.alwasatnews.com/3173/news/read/561210/1.html#.UKJmR2euXiI

[56] "Bahrain: Reinstate Ousted Students, Faculty," Human Rights Watch, 24 Sep.

These arrests and loyalty pledges served to police the moderates in the Sunni community proactively and to intimidate any potential critics of the new turn in government policy. At the same time, state-controlled media was opened to a new anti-Shi'i discourse imported from a very different context: a Saudi state where religion is used to legitimate regime policies. New terminology, echoing the Wahhabist unitarian orthodoxy against schisms, became prevalent in popular discourse, particularly in *al-Watan*, the newspaper most closely associated with the Khawalid. One example is the description of protestors as "*al-fi'a al-dāla*" or "the misguided sect"—a term of Quranic origin, previously used only in a Saudi context in reference to fundamentalists suspected of terrorism.[57] References to Shi'i as "*Safawis*" or Safavid Persians also became very widespread. And in the most direct anti-Shi'i assault, dozens of allegedly unlicensed Shi'i mosques were destroyed by the government in nighttime sweeps.

Another telling window into the new sectarianism concerns the site at the heart of the protest: the Pearl Roundabout, formally known as the GCC junction due to the sculpture at its center with arms representing the six countries of the GCC holding up a pearl and commemorating the first GCC meeting in Bahrain. After the entry of the GCC Peninsula Shield Forces, the Bahrain government ordered the iconic sculpture demolished. Bahrain's foreign minister explained that the month-long protests had divided society, and stated, "We don't want a monument to a bad memory."[58] Yet the new name for the intersection does not speak to reconciliation: the *Farooq* junction, in honor of Umar bin al-Khattab, the early Arab caliph who conquered the Persian Sasanid Empire.

The prevalence of openly sectarian discourse and the demolition of Shi'i mosques marked a signal shift in Bahrain: structural discrimination was augmented by an explicitly anti-Shi'i campaign in a religious sense. The appearance in state media of a more ideological sectarianism, steeped in religious references from a Wahhabi context, reflect transna-

2011, http://www.hrw.org/news/2011/09/24/bahrain-reinstate-ousted-students-faculty

57 Word searches for the term in the Bahraini media mark its appearance after the entry of GCC troops. The few instances it is used prior to this time show it applied exclusively to a Saudi context.

58 Ethan Bronner, "Bahrain Tears Down Monument as Protesters Seethe," *New York Times*, 19 Mar. 2011, A10.

tional influences coming from Saudi Arabia. Yet the tenor of the ever-important alliance with Saudi Arabia changed. The flow of influence was no longer restricted to the personal agreements of the tribal elite, such as were managed by Prime Minister Khalifa bin Salman. The Sunni counter-mobilization against the Pearl Uprising, nurtured by the Sunni empowerment strategy of the Khawalid, opened a broader conduit for influence through civil society. These newly empowered Sunni movements now form part of the factional battle in Bahrain and also champion the increasing transnational Sunni solidarity building in the aftermath of the Arab Spring.[59]

The factional rivalry extended into the economic sector as the prime minister and a modified business alliance grew closer to the "security" wing of the ruling family. In the midst of the security crackdown Bahrain's political economy was once again reshaped, as this new ruling coalition worked to roll back the economic policies championed by the crown prince and to weaken the institutions that served as his base of power and influence.[60] Most significantly, the lead institution for generating the new economic vision, the EDB, was reduced to an advisory body, surrendering its executive authority over economic policy back to the prime minister and his cabinet. In addition, the leadership of all of the key institutions associated with the crown prince's reform initiatives—the EDB, the Ministry of Labor, the LMRA, the labor fund Tamkeen, and the sovereign wealth fund Mumtalakat—were removed, some in sectarian-laced campaigns, and replaced by skeptics or weaker figures less able to advocate for reform.[61] Even the crown prince's new

[59] For an analysis of the new Sunni mobilization see Justin Gengler, "Bahrain's Sunni Awakening," Middle East Report Online, 17 Jan. 2012, http://www.merip.org/mero/mero011712

[60] Sources on the rollback of economic reforms in Bahrain include Hasan Tariq Al Hasan, "Bahrain Bids its Economic Reform Farewell," Open Democracy, 8 July 2012, http://www.opendemocracy.net/hasan-tariq-al-hasan/bahrain-bids-its-economic-reform-farewell; Andrew Hammond, "Bahrain Economic Reforms Take Hit as Hardliners Battle Uprising," Reuters, 13 June 2012, http://www.trust.org/alertnet/news/mideast-money-bahrain-economic-reforms-takes-hit-as-hardliners-battle-uprising. Charles Levinson, "A Palace Rift in Persian Gulf Bedevils Key U.S. Navy Base," *Wall Street Journal*, 21 Feb. 2013, quotes a source from within the royal family who speaks openly of the rise in Khawalid influence, and the growing factional rifts with the ruling family.

[61] Human Rights Watch, "For a Better Life," p. 64, addresses how several top

educational institutions, the keystone of his educational reform project, saw their leadership overturned.

These were not cosmetic changes. One by one, the policies comprising Bahrain's labor reforms were scaled back or eliminated. The government suspended the tax on foreign labor to help businesses survive the difficult environment created by the political unrest, then extended it indefinitely under pressure from the merchant class. In July 2012 the new labor minister announced that minimum quotas for hiring workers would be scrapped "to avoid placing difficult regulations on company owners," placing the entire project of Bahrainization of the labor market in question.[62] The political partnership with labor unions was also dismantled as the new regime sought to undermine a key ally of the crown prince's reforms, and to punish the opposition-controlled GFBTU for organizing a series of strikes in March during the 2011 unrest. A new labor law issued in 2011 permitted the creation of multiple labor unions per firm, in a clear effort to break the opposition hold over the union. A second amendment allowed the government to choose which union represents Bahrain's interests in international fora—a move to deprive the opposition of its contacts in international labor organizations.[63] The July 2012 launch of a new competitor labor federation, the Bahrain Labor Union Free Federation (BLUFF), siphoned off some of the membership of the GFBTU, particularly from parastatal firms which hold closer ties to the ruling family.[64]

More surprising, perhaps, has been the new policies toward Bahrain's business organization. As stated earlier, the merchant elite—both Sunni

---

LMRA officials were removed after pro-government forces singled them out as sympathizing with the opposition.

62 Suad Hamada, "Minister Hints at Plans to Scrap Bahrainisation in the Private Sector," *Khaleej Times*, 31 July 2012, http://www.khaleejtimes.com/kt-article-display-1.asp?xfile=/data/middleeast/2012/July/middleeast_July335.xml§ion=middleeast

63 The GFBTU had been working with the AFL-CIO to investigate violations of labor rights obligations under the US–Bahrain FTA which occurred following the Feb. 2011 unrest. This resulted in a formal complaint brought by the AFL-CIO in 2011, which prompted follow-up investigations and a critical report by the US Department of Labor issued on 20 Dec. 2012, http://www.dol.gov/ilab/programs/otla/20121220Bahrain.pdf

64 Bill Law, "New Bahrain Trade Federation Splits Labor Movement," BBC News, 17 Nov. 2012, http://www.bbc.co.uk/news/world-middle-east-20324436

and Shi'i—were reliable supporters of the long-standing prime minister upon whom they depended for government licenses, contracts, and tenders. As an advocacy group, then, the Bahrain Chamber of Commerce and Industry (BCCI) was less sympathetic to the crown prince, who both challenged their main patron and imposed new taxes on their businesses. However, the new sectarian policies post-uprising have threatened this pragmatic accommodation. After two Shi'i board members were stripped of their membership due to accusations of aiding protestors in the roundabout, the General Assembly of the BCCI approved their reinstatement and ordered an inquiry into the action which many suspected came at the direction of the state.[65] However, the inquiry was personally squelched by the prime minister, and in October 2012 the king issued a new law which effectively stripped the BCCI board of its independence.[66]

Other prominent Shi'i businessmen became targets of popular campaigns against them. Flyers were widely distributed in predominantly Sunni neighborhoods urging residents to boycott Shi'i-owned businesses they deemed "traitorous agents."[67] The Jawad group, a prominent Shi'i conglomerate that introduced supermarkets to Bahrain and which holds numerous international franchises, became a target of boycotts and vandalism due to reports that they provided food for the protestors in the roundabout. There were suspicions that some of these campaigns were regime-backed, a claim that gained some credence when security cameras at one Jawad convenience store filmed looters ransacking the premises under the direction of police. Political pressure thus opened a social divide in the business community, with some prominent Shi'i businessmen turning to the crown prince for protection.[68]

[65] Jamil al-Mahari, "Intiṣar Ghurfat al-Tijara wa-Hazimat al-Ta'ifiyya [Victory of the Chamber of Commerce and Defeat of Sectarianism], *Al-Wasat*, 10 Apr. 2012, http://www.alwasatnews.com/3503/news/read/654903/1.html

[66] Kingdom of Bahrain, Royal Decree Law 48 for 2012 on the Bahrain Chamber of Commerce and Industry, *Official Gazette of the Kingdom of Bahrain*, 1 Oct. 2012, http://www.legalaffairs.gov.bh/viewhtm.aspx?ID=L4812

[67] One flier placed on cars in the al-Rifa' neighborhood was posted online: http://www.3roos.com/files/ups/2011/370917/01303647955.jpg. Another flier circulated on the Internet by the "al-Fatih group for electronic jihad" helpfully provides a list of alternative, presumably Sunni-owned businesses: http://up.arab-x.com/May11/qPr17378.jpg

[68] Jassim Hussein, economist and al-Wifaq member, in discussion with the author, June 2012.

This politicization of commerce along sectarian lines was bad for business on a macro-level.[69] But from a factional perspective the continuation of the unrest had political advantages for the ideological right and the Khawalid. Popular mobilization against the Shi'i in commerce and in places of employment worked toward the goal of decreasing Shi'i ownership over strategic industries, and opened government positions for ideological kinsmen.[70] The continuation of unrest, particularly when it could be both confined to the Shi'i villages and linked to a broader Iranian threat, justified augmented defense budgets and increased the prominence of the security services and of Commander-in-Chief Khalifa bin Ahmed.[71] Even any Western sanctions floated as leverage to promote political compromise—economic sanctions, cancellation of the FTA, even the withdrawal of the US Fifth Fleet—would hold factional advantages for the Khawalid as they would harm the rival crown prince's interests more than their own due to the reliance of his strategy on international engagement and the goodwill of the United States. Indeed, it is clear that even had there not been a deliberate political purge of the crown prince's supporters, his economic vision would still be a casualty of the new security environment; the stability and openness needed to attract international businesses and visitors is nearly impossible to maintain in a climate of political unrest and rising radicalism.[72]

In the absence of diversification, Bahrain has fallen back into dependency, and into the economic embrace of Saudi Arabia. The core of Bahrain's economy—oil, banking, and tourism—has always looked

[69] Statistics from the EDB show a sharp decline in GDP in the first quarter of 2011, followed by slower growth over the next three quarters. Sectoral statistics indicate a decline in hospitality, construction, and real estate in 2011. Economic Development Board, *Bahrain Economic Quarterly*, Fourth Quarter 2011–First Quarter 2012, 31 May 2012, p. 11.

[70] It is interesting that the multifaceted plan to promote Sunni interests in Bahrain that was published as part of the Bandargate report raises concern over Shi'i control of agriculture and food distribution, areas which have been targets in post-Pearl Uprising Bahrain.

[71] Gengler, "Royal Factionalism," pp. 72–77.

[72] These challenges were on display in Bahrain's hosting of the Formula 1 Grand Prix—a pet project of the crown prince meant to bring international visibility to the island. After being canceled due to the unrest in 2011, the race took place in 2012, but under a shadow of negative publicity as protestors sought to take advantage of the presence of the international press to make their case against the government.

across the King Fahd causeway for markets. As Bahrain has suffered financial challenges in the past year of unrest, Saudi Arabia has sought to compensate: initially through a pledge from GCC states for $10 billion over a period of ten years. A telling example of the link between the evolving geopolitics and business can be found in the situation of Gulf Air, Bahrain's struggling national carrier. In 2011 the state-run airline chose to end its profitable flights to Iraq, Iran, and Lebanon, as a concrete response to its claims that Hezbollah and Iran were complicit in the uprising. To help Gulf Air overcome the losses, Saudi Arabia opened up a number of exclusive routes to its interior cities.[73] The Saudi royal family's reigning tycoon, Prince Waleed bin Talal, also made the decision to move Rotana, his news and entertainment company, from Cairo to Manama, and to base his new 24-hour news network, al-Arab, in Bahrain. And in a reversal of its policy to punish Bahrain in the wake of its signing of the FTA with the United States, Saudi Arabia exempted Bahrain from its ban on the export of cement.

With the monarchy's security and the island's economy both ensured by Saudi Arabia, it was perhaps not a leap for Saudi Arabia in the spring of 2012 to open discussions for a confederation of the two countries as a first step to a stronger political union within the GCC. This proposal was enthusiastically championed by the newly mobilized Sunni groups as a decisive means to overcome Bahrain's "Shia problem." Yet it is worth pondering how far Bahrain has turned away from the ruling strategy of the previous decade, when it was thought that the co-optation of the opposition and greater economic openness would lessen the country's traditional dependence on its larger neighbor. Yesterday the Al Khalifa looked to integrate the Shi'i in a bid to lessen dependence on Saudi Arabia; today they are willing to surrender more sovereignty to Saudi Arabia in a bid to exclude them.

Conclusion

Over the past two decades the Bahraini ruling family increasingly took on the appearance of competing factions with different strategies, alli-

[73] Jasim Ali, "Saudi–Bahraini Economic Ties Hit New High," *Gulf News*, 12 Feb. 2012, http://gulfnews.com/business/opinion/saudi-bahraini-economic-ties-hit-new-high-1.979104

ances, and worldviews. The sectarian effects of their practices differed significantly. The reform strategy, exemplified by the new economic institutions headed by the crown prince, required a blurring of sectarian divisions as it sought to prime the country for foreign investment and further diversification, to wrest economic policymaking from the prime minister, and to strengthen the country's autonomy from Saudi Arabia. To accomplish all of these things, the king and the crown prince needed the implicit support of the Shi'i community along with more progressive youth who were attracted to his modernizing vision. By contrast, the prime minister and the brotherly alliance known as the Khawalid held the support of key segments of the merchant class, the Sunni Islamist movements, and the Sunni defense forces. Over the course of the past ten years, the wing of the Khawalid linked to the royal court in particular was set on using explicitly sectarian policies to counter the perceived advantages of the Shi'i majority and the dangers these posed in a reform era with at least nominally elective politics. The shift towards Shi'i empowerment in post-invasion Iraq, and the rising influence of Iran in that country, loomed large.

These shifting views and polices toward sect created new divisions in the (mostly) Shi'i opposition who lost much of their unity over the course of the decade as well. The decision of al-Wifaq to end their boycott of elections and to adopt a strategy of accommodation split the movement. The growing leverage of the Khawalid and their policies in the following years then did much to legitimate the strategy of street protests and civil disobedience favored by the boycott wing led by al-Haq, especially among the youth. The failure of the political uprising to advance the objectives of political reform further weakened the accommodationists. And the heavy hand of the security state further radicalized the street protestors. By controlling the cities and confining the Shi'i unrest in their villages, the government has reinforced the "sectarian" nature of the uprising. This strategy is self-fulfilling: caged in by police forces, protests in the Shi'i villages have become more sectarian, adopting religious imagery and language in addition to the more predominant rights-based language.[74]

At the same time, the post-uprising order has offered a much more permissive environment for sectarian rhetoric and Sunni mobilization.

[74] One recent example is the formation of irregular proto-militia forces commemorating the martyrdom of a protestor in the village of Bilad al-Qadim.

Billboards and newspapers as well as visual media were open to a new anti-Shi'i language infused with terms and religious references betraying Saudi origins. The need to counter the popular mobilization of the uprising also resulted in much broader space for Sunni organization and political mobilization. At times these new groups have been instrumentalized by ruling factions to counter Shi'i movements, but also to pressure rivals in key decisions regarding domestic political compromise and international alliances.[75] The broad mobilization of both Sunni and Shi'i movements thus makes political compromise more difficult and civil strife more likely. This chronic instability itself acts as a justification for the security state favored by the Khawalid faction of the ruling family. It also undermines the conditions for an open economy on which the reform faction's ruling strategy was based.

All of these conditions point to greater reliance by Bahrain on Saudi Arabia. Yet it appears that, as sectarian violence deepens in the Arab region in 2013, fed by a complex civil struggle and proxy war in Syria and escalating unrest in Iraq, debates exist within the Saudi royal family over the best way to secure stability in the Gulf states. Deeper involvement with Bahrain offers Saudi Arabia more control over the affairs of the island, but it may also encourage deeper identification and sympathy between the Shi'i of Bahrain and those of Saudi's Eastern Province, who share a common heritage and similar grievances. The potential mobilization of both Shia and Sunni transnational movements could threaten social cohesion across the Gulf in ways difficult for Gulf governments to contain, potentially creating inroads for Iranian encroachment.

As the stakes have risen, then, a small door has been opened for de-escalation in Bahrain. In February 2013 the Bahraini government initiated a national dialogue between government and civil society representatives and the legal opposition. Then in March the crown prince was provided a first step toward rehabilitation in being appointed deputy prime minister by the king. Both moves were thought to be blessed by, and perhaps even encouraged by, Saudi Arabia. Still, in the context of broad sectarian mobilization, social forces operating across the borders of a more closely allied confederation may yet escape the control of the Saudi state and Bahrain's divided monarchy.

[75] Rallies by a new Fatih youth movement have protested any moves to provide amnesty for opposition leaders, and have decried any political intermediation by the United States.

5

IDENTITY POLITICS AND NATION-BUILDING UNDER SULTAN QABOOS

Marc Valeri[1]

Sultan Qaboos has ruled Oman since overthrowing his father, with British support, in July 1970. The new ruler's room for maneuver with regard to the British was reduced to a minimum, however, as was his legitimacy vis-à-vis the Omani population. In this context, the building of a nation lay at the heart of the political project established by Sultan Qaboos as a means of asserting his authority over the whole of Oman. This nation-building policy was based on one major objective: to establish himself as the "natural" sovereign, the only individual able to draw together all the religious and ethno-linguistic groups located within Omani territory. However, sectarian politics, understood as the process of sociopolitical instrumentalization of subnational (ethno-linguistic, religious, etc.) identities, either by the regime or by non-state political

[1] This research was supported by the UK Economic and Social Research Council [grant number ES/J012696/1].

actors, has always been a key dimension of Omani politics. If sectarian identifications have rarely been openly politicized under Qaboos, debates over each group's loyalty to the Omani nation have never stopped.

In this chapter, after a brief presentation of the ethnic and religious diversity of the Omani population, I analyze how, far from erasing subnational allegiances, the advent of a nation-state in Oman centered on the personality of the new ruler engaged with subnational identities in order to maintain the old social order while depriving these identities of any potential for political harm to the new regime. This regime's policy of manipulating sectarian affiliations has long blocked the possibilities of sociopolitical mobilization on criteria other than these identities: by channeling claims and demands according to these identifications, the ruler prevented the emergence of "transversal" mobilizations, such as social class or ideology. As a result, it allowed Qaboos to be the only individual able to claim to embody the whole political community. The chapter then argues that this "sectarian game," which supported the regime's stability, has now shown its limits. First, it proved unsuccessful in resolving social tensions in 2011 and 2012, and notably failed to prevent the emergence of dissonant voices. More broadly, if the public expression of these sectarian identities represents a threat, it is now a threat to the political system itself, to the rules imposed by the regime—a monarchy in the hands of a single man, without counterbalance and without any possibility of alternative expression—and not to the firmly established framework in which it is held: the nation.

The tribal, ethno-linguistic, and religious diversity of the Omani population

In building a national identity and a stable political authority, Sultan Qaboos has had to work with Oman's rich but complicated social and historical legacy, starting with the various local identities present on Omani territory. The first of these *'asabiyyat*[2] is the tribe, headed by a

[2] Introduced by Ibn Khaldun, the notion of *'asabiyya*, usually translated as "group feeling," is understood as populations linked by blood ties or behavior, acting as a group or defining themselves as such, and most of the time—but not always—organized to achieve common goals (like taking positions of power). See Ibn Khaldun, *The Muqaddimah: An Introduction to History*, trans. F. Rosenthal, Princeton, NJ: Princeton University Press, 1980, Chapter 2.

shaikh, usually conveyed in Oman by the term *qabila*. The group's cohesion is supposed to rely on a common genealogy (*nasab*); at lower levels, the tribe is organized in branches or sections (*fakhdh*), each one having its *shaikh rashid*. The shaikhs of the most powerful tribes of the noble branches are given the title of *shaikh tamima*. Kinship with the Prophet is a minor sociopolitical factor in Oman, as no tribe, except some Dhofari groups and a few Shi'i personalities in Muscat, invokes his lineage.

On the religious side, estimates of allegiance among the Omani population are not based on official figures, as the authorities have never published any data. There have been various estimates by foreign observers, however. Dale Eickelman considers that "roughly 50–55 percent of [the] citizen population is Sunni, 40–45 percent is Ibadi and less than 2 percent is Shi'i."[3] John Peterson gives estimates of 45 percent Ibadi, 50 percent Sunni, and probably less than 5 percent Shi'i and Hindu.[4] According to my calculations, based on the results of the 2003 census, Ibadi Omanis appear to number from 48 to 53 percent of the population, Sunnis 45 to 49 percent, and Shi'i 3 to 4 percent.

The contemporary diversity of Omani society also results from its origin in waves of migration across the Persian Gulf and Indian Ocean for many centuries. This has been especially true since the nineteenth century, when Sa'id bin Sultan (r.1806–56), who gave his name to the current royal family, extended Oman's possessions overseas and made Zanzibar his capital in 1832. On Sa'id's death, the formal sovereignty of the Omani Empire covered the whole northwestern edge of the Indian Ocean, from Mozambique to Baluchistan. As part of his imperial conquest, Sa'id bin Sultan encouraged the settlement of Omani people on the eastern African coast, a process which did not cease until the mid-twentieth century. The "return"[5] of their descendants started after the

[3] Dale F. Eickelman, "Kings and People: Information and Authority in Oman, Qatar and the Persian Gulf," in Joseph A. Kechichian (ed.), *Iran, Iraq, and the Arab Gulf States*, New York: Palgrave, 2001, p. 202.

[4] John E. Peterson, "Oman's Diverse Society: Northern Oman," *Middle East Journal*, 58, 1 (2004), p. 32.

[5] In the usage of actors themselves, the term "return" is used of the resettlement in Oman, from the 1960s until now, of individuals and families who claim Omani ancestry and who previously lived in East Africa. Talk of "return to the native country" is only partially accurate, as most of them had personally never set foot in Oman before their "return." But here this explicit vocabulary is retained, and attests both to their will to appear distinct from the African societies (especially

1964 revolution in Zanzibar which had led to the end of the local al-Busa'idi dynasty.

A second wave of returnees came following a call made in 1970 by Sultan Qaboos inviting the Omani elite abroad to contribute to the "awakening" of the country. As many of the returnees spoke English fluently and had been trained in technical fields in Europe or in other Persian Gulf countries, the Omanis from Africa provided a valuable workforce for the ruler's planned modernization. Today the "back-from-Africa" Omanis, who are known as "Swahilis" (referring to their vernacular language) or "Zanzibaris," are thought to number more than 100,000. Most of the tribes and ethno-linguistic groups contain within them so-called "Swahili" individuals or clans, including the royal tribe, the Shi'i communities, and the Omani groups native to Baluchistan. The "Swahilis" are thus a highly heterogeneous group, which cannot be defined solely according to genealogical criteria. Families, or even individuals, descended from the same clan can be considered "Swahili" (or not) whether they have ties (or not) to Africa. Finally, a strict and well-known distinction is established between the back-from-Africa Omanis who can lay claim to a patriarchal genealogy in southeast Arabia and the Omani citizens who are descended from slaves brought forcibly from Africa (*khadim*) and who are not considered to be of Arab blood.

There are also an estimated 200,000 nationals of Baluchi descent in Oman, equally spread between the capital and the Batina region. Their origin can be explained by the need for the Omani rulers, since the seventeenth century, to raise mercenary armies independent of internal tribal forces. Family connections with Baluchistan vary; many people who hold dual nationality still possess lands in Pakistani Baluchistan and go back for major events.[6]

The Omani population of Indian origin has historically been concentrated in Muscat and Muttrah, owing to their long involvement in maritime trade. They are divided into two major groups, the Shi'i Lawatiyya (sing. Lawati) and the Banyans, who belong to the Hindu faith and number an estimated 1,000 in Oman. The Banyans live in Muscat, Muttrah, Salalah, and on the Batina coast. Most families have been

---

their former slaves) among which they lived for decades and to the complexity of their symbolic ties with Oman since their re-settlement in that country.

[6] For more details, see John Peterson's contribution in this volume.

established in Oman for six or seven generations. They nevertheless retain profound links (especially matrimonial ones) with the town of Mandvi in Gujarat (India), where many Banyans of Muscat have their roots, and Mumbai.

While their origins are still the subject of divergent interpretations, most of the Lawatiyya families appear to have settled in Oman in several migration waves from Sind between 1780 and 1850.[7] Initially disciples of the Aga Khan (and therefore Isma'ili Shi'i), the Lawatiyya were excommunicated after a quarrel over the legitimacy of the succession in 1862 and became Twelver Shi'i. The Lawatiyya were for long separated from the rest of Omani society as they lived in a closed district on the seashore of Muttrah, the *sur al-lawatiyya* (Lawatiyya's enclosure). They are currently estimated to number between 20,000 and 30,000 and live in the capital and in the Batina. Because of their economic and political position under the rule of Qaboos, inherited both from their mercantile tradition and from their commitment to the rulers of Muscat in twentieth-century history, they are major actors in the contemporary political game. The integration of Lawatiyya into Shi'i transnational networks (except for family ones) is very loose and by no means comparable to what happens with Shi'i communities in Bahrain and Saudi Arabia. This weak integration, combined with their proximity to Oman's decision-makers before and after 1970, helps explain why the Lawatiyya have never organized themselves for any collective political action.[8]

Two other Omani Twelver Shi'i groups must also be mentioned. The Ajam are said to originate from various regions of southern Iran[9] and today live in the Batina, where they represent the largest Shi'i group, and in the capital. Established in Oman for centuries, thanks to the relations between the two shores of the Gulf of Oman since time immemorial, they are thought to number approximately 20,000 in total. The Ajam,

[7] Calvin H. Allen Jr, "Sayyids, Shets and Sultans: Politics and Trade in Masqat under the Al Bu Sa'id, 1785–1914," PhD dissertation, University of Washington, 1978, pp. 118ff.

[8] For more details on the Lawatiyya, see Marc Valeri, "High Visibility, Low Profile: The Shi'a in Oman under Sultan Qaboos," *International Journal of Middle East Studies*, 42 (2010), pp. 251–68.

[9] Fredrik Barth, *Sohar: Culture and Society in an Omani Town*, Baltimore: Johns Hopkins University Press, 1983, p. 212. The Ajam came mainly from Khuzistan, the Persian Gulf coast east of Bandar Abbas, and the Lar area.

who only rarely speak Persian, are over-represented in the police and the army. The Baharina (sing. Bahrani) are even fewer, with their numbers thought to range between 1,000 and 2,000. Related to various Arab Shi'i communities of the northern Persian Gulf area (Bahrain, Kuwait, southern Iraq), with whom they maintain sustained contact, they have been settled in Muscat for at least a century. The majority of Omani Shi'i follow the *marja'iyya* of Najaf and thus Ayatollah Ali Sistani, but among Lawatiyya his influence was widely challenged by the Lebanese Ayatollah Muhammad Husayn Fadlallah (d.2010).

When dealing with Omani ethno-linguistic diversity it is important to mention the most southerly province of the country, Dhofar, whose population is Sunni. Several south-Arabic Semitic dialects, such as Mahri, Jabbali, and Shahri, are widely spoken in today's Dhofar. The area came under the rule of the sultans of Muscat in 1879. This political subjection increased with the special relationship that Qaboos's father, Sa'id (r.1932–70), established with the province after 1958. Dhofar was the site of a nationalist uprising in 1962, which morphed into the Marxist–Leninist Popular Front for the Liberation of the Occupied Arabian Gulf after 1968. In June 1970, when two-thirds of the province was out of control of the central power and the rebellion was about to spread to northern Oman, the British forced Sultan Sa'id to abdicate in favor of his son. This decision enjoyed the support of the other Persian Gulf amirs as well as the shah of Iran, all worried by potential revolutionary contagion. The official end of the war was proclaimed in December 1975.

The naturalization of Sultan Qaboos's rule through the building of a nation

When Qaboos bin Sa'id overthrew his father, he inherited a territory without a state. He thus immediately faced the need to assert the legitimacy of his accession to the throne by defining a "new order" for which he alone would hold the keys. The main element of the new regime's strategy of legitimization rests on the nation-building process implemented since 1970. This links the country's economic and social development to the modernizing state (as the administrator of the oil rent) on the one hand, and to the person of the sultan, who embodies the state and has become the subject of a personality cult, on the other. Qaboos's idea has been to break with a model in which the temporal sultanistic legitimacy was only perceived as one among other legitimacies (tribal, religious, etc.), and to instead impose it as the legitimacy above all others, acknowledged as the arbiter of all.

Qaboos financed his nation-building endeavors with Oman's oil rent, a godsend that enabled him to create a public sphere offering an inexhaustible pool of jobs open to skilled and non-skilled individuals alike. These new civil servants, employed in the national army, the police, the intelligence service, the ministries, and governmental services, were extremely unlikely to turn against the regime because they depended on it for their survival. Thanks to new asphalted roads, and to schools and health centers which were built in the smallest villages, the state became a pervasive presence, both materially and symbolically, throughout all of Oman, while simultaneously assuming the role of interlocutor for every administrative action and becoming the point of reference in the strategies adopted by all social and political actors. Ethnic and tribal communities, unable to compete with the process of promoting the nation, lost their prior legitimacy and role in protecting members of their groups, and gradually lost their control over them.

Concomitantly, the ruler has endeavored to promote an original Omani national identity for which he himself has constituted the keystone. Exploitation of the oil rent has made it possible to implement an ambitious policy of national unification, which has become the pivot of the regime's ideology. By the double assimilation of all Oman to the state, as "master craftsman" of the economic and social development, and then of the state to the person of Qaboos himself, the sultan has sought to provide a strong basis for his hegemony in the country. The contemporary Omani nation is built on the negation of the country's pre-1970 history, any reference to which remains taboo. Referred to as the "dark period," these times are evoked only as an antonym to the glorious national awakening of 23 July 1970—the date of Qaboos's accession to the throne, later renamed Renaissance Day (*'id al-nahda*). The selectivity of Oman's national memory is well illustrated by the way Omani history is taught in public schools. Twentieth-century Oman is only skimmed over, leaving a black hole between the nineteenth century and the 1970 "Renaissance." References to major events in Omani history, such as the conflict that arose in the Jabal Akhdar in the 1950s between the Ibadi Imamate, controlling both sides of the Hajar mountain range, and the sultan, backed by Britain, are nowhere to be found.[10]

[10] The shaikhs of Inner Oman elected an Ibadi Imam in Nizwa in June 1913. Jihad

The selective reading of Oman's history does not stop at religion. While Oman's territory has been strongly influenced by Ibadism,[11] Qaboos's regime soon began to promote a consensual and generic Islam[12] that is peculiar to Oman and neglects both Oman's controversial past and the role of foreign influence. This enables the authorities to maintain a feeling of repulsion among the population against what they call "political interpretations foreign to peaceful Omani Islam" and to justify the recurring arrests of "Islamic militants" and other "extremists." By establishing standard Friday sermons for the guidance of preachers since 1982, in which differences of schools (*madhhab*) are never mentioned, the Ministry of Religious Affairs seeks to dilute the differences between the Ibadi and Sunni schools of Islam. In most important towns, the older Ibadi mosques are supplanted by new "Sultan Qaboos mosques" in order to promote a somewhat sanitized official Islam in line with the sultan's policies. The creation of this "national Islam" goes with the endeavor at an early stage to "bureaucratize" men of religion by integrating them into the state apparatus. This does not mean that all Muslim schools are on an equal footing, as Ibadism still has a more than symbolic pre-eminence: both of the muftis who have been appointed since 1970 are Ibadi, as are the ministers of justice and religious affairs and most of the leading

---

was immediately proclaimed against Sultan Faisal of Muscat (r.1888–1913) and his British allies. Following the Seeb agreement, signed under British supervision on 25 Sep. 1920 by Sultan Taimur (r.1913–32) and the Ibadi shaikhs, the tribes were left to enjoy effective control over Inner Oman, and Sultan Taimur's full sovereignty was restricted to the northern coast and Salalah. In Oct. 1955, when the British were convinced that there was no alternative to reunifying Oman, the Muscat and Oman Field Force (MOFF) launched a head-on attack on the Imamate, leading to its collapse. After a temporary rebirth of the Imamate in Inner Oman in June 1957, Sultan Sa'id's forces, with the support of the British Royal Air Force, gained control of the whole territory during the summer.

[11] From the eighth century, Ibadism became the cement of an emerging Omani identity, strengthened in the building of a political and geographical entity identifiable from abroad, *al-misr al-'umaniyya* ("the Omani country"). This notion of an Ibadi heartland, centered on the Hajar mountain range and the towns of Nizwa and Rustaq (Inner Oman), supposedly repository of the original Omani features, has lived on until now.

[12] Dale F. Eickelman, "Identité nationale et discours religieux en Oman," in Gilles Kepel and Yann Richard (eds), *Intellectuels et militants de l'Islam contemporain*, Paris: Le Seuil, 1990, p. 117.

personalities and imams in both of those institutions. Also, the *nahda* ideology is an implicit—but obvious—reference to the Ibadi tradition and to the Imamate's recurring renaissance.[13] As Franck Mermier explains, the Ibadi heritage is "both covered up and glorified";[14] on the one hand covered up to be merged into the consensual "national Islam" promoted under Qaboos, but, on the other, at the forefront of national symbols in order to support the legitimacy of the regime.

By recreating a national identity within the framework of an omnipresent state and by unifying cultural and religious references, the triptych encompassing Oman's renaissance, the state apparatus, and its supreme figure, the sultan, cannot be touched without putting into question the entire nation-building project. In fact, the state apparatus is personified by the ruler who has become the subject of a genuine personality cult. All major contemporary urban achievements bear the sultan's name: the capital's main highway that connects the city's quarters in a metaphoric hyphen, the main towns' hospitals, the most modern mosques, the wealthier areas of the capital where occidental expatriates and the local high bourgeoisie reside, and so on. This omnipresence of the ruler is completed by his effigy on banknotes, his glorification in the national anthem and on National Day—the sultan's birthday.

The "encapsulation"[15] of subnational references into the modern state

Although the omnipresent official discourse since the 1980s has constantly emphasized the feeling of national unity which lay behind the ruler's authority, this process of substituting identity allegiances, with the local giving way to the national, was not to lead to the destruction of subnational identities. One of the regime's strategies of legitimization has clearly been the "encapsulation" of traditional local allegiances into the new state. The regime's permanent political strategy has been the

[13] A reference popularized in modern Ibadi intellectual circles by Muhammad al-Salimi's book, *Nahda al-A'yan bi-Hurriya 'Uman* [The Notables' Renaissance in the Liberation of Oman], Cairo: Matabi' Dar al-Kitab al-'Arabi bi-Misr, 1961.

[14] Franck Mermier, "De l'invention du patrimoine omanais," in Marc Lavergne and Brigitte Dumortier (eds), *L'Oman contemporain: État, territoire, identité*, Paris: Karthala, 2003, p. 255.

[15] Frederick G. Bailey, *Stratagems and Spoils: A Social Anthropology of Politics*, Oxford: Blackwell, 1969, Chapter 8.

integration of the traditional elites into the state, thereby reaping the benefits of their legitimacy while bringing them under control.

In the 1960s Clifford Geertz argued that "what the new States—or their leaders—must somehow contrive to do as far as primordial attachments are concerned, is not, as they have so often tried to do, wish them out of existence by denying their reality, but instead domesticate them. They must reconcile them with the unfolding civil order by divesting them of their legitimizing force with respect to governmental authority."[16] For several decades, far from working for the destruction of sub-national identities, one of the guidelines of the sultan's strategy of legitimization has been to "de-autonomize" local solidarities (tribes, ethno-linguistic groups, etc.) with the aim of neutralizing their impact by subordinating them to the state and making them more and more dependent on a game which the regime controls. This has taken the form of a determined co-optation policy toward the most prominent tribes and noble families as well as the integration of the smaller local elite into the state apparatus.

No national debate on the role of tribes in building the modern nation-state has been started in Oman. In the promotion of a national identity, the official historiography has done its utmost to present the state or the sultan himself as the Omani citizens' only interlocutor. The question of the role of local groups in the state is strictly taboo, as is shown by the fury of a Sultan Qaboos University professor when the word "*qabila*" was pronounced in his office: "Do not try to make tribes and communities grow artificially in Oman like plants … There have been no more tribes and communities since 1970 … What did the English do in Oman before 1970? Nothing for the development of this country, no school, no hospital … nothing! They did everything to divide us!"[17] Here the mentioning of tribes evokes without ambiguity the division of the nation and historical regression, characteristic of the pre-1970 period, through the presupposed idea that the individual cannot claim several collective allegiances at the same time, one necessarily excluding the other.

[16] Clifford Geertz, "The Integrative Revolution: Primordial Sentiments and Civil Politics in the New States," in Clifford Geertz (ed.), *Old Societies and New States: The Quest for Modernity in Asia and Africa*, London: Free Press of Glencoe, 1963, p. 128.

[17] Personal interview, Muscat, 26 May 2003.

Despite this official discourse, the tribal issue has remained a major concern of the authorities since the 1970s. The regime has worked hard to co-opt the most powerful tribes, and the leading clans and families of the Imamate were soon offered a general amnesty to rally to the new regime. The most obvious example of such a co-optation is the noble branch of the Khalili family, heir to a prestigious lineage of Ibadi imams. The nephew of the last imam, Sa'ud al-Khalili, owns the powerful business group Al Taher that he founded in 1973, which is active in contracting (Caterpillar), food and drink (Sprite, Coke), and the distribution of Shell products in Oman. One of his nephews, Abd Al-Malik bin Abd Allah, formerly the executive chairman of the Royal Court Pension Fund, the chairman of the most important Omani banking group, Bank Muscat, and the minister of tourism, is currently the minister of justice. Another illustration of this "deal" with the authorities is provided by the descendants of Abd Allah al-Salimi, one of the principal instigators of the Imamate's renaissance at the beginning of the twentieth century. While his son Muhammad had a leading role within the Imamate's political authorities in exile and opponents to Qaboos's father, his grandson Abd Allah has been minister for religious affairs since 1997.

This identity politics has also been active when dealing with cabinet positions. John Peterson noted the prevalence in post-1970 cabinets of personalities from the very populated northwestern areas of Dhahira and West Batina.[18] Originating from tribes who had established ties with Riyadh in the 1950s, they were said to receive preferential treatment aimed at diverting them from the enticements of the late Shaikh Zayed of Abu Dhabi since the 1970s. This extreme caution in composing cabinets and balancing the regional and tribal origins of its members was illustrated once again in March 2011, when the sultan restructured the Council of Ministers a few days after the start of protests in Sohar: three of the newly appointed ministers were natives of the Batina region, raising the total contingent of cabinet members from Batina to six (out of a total of twenty-nine ministers).

The post-1970 state also hastened to integrate the small notability into the bureaucratic hierarchy. The tribal hierarchy was not destroyed

[18] John E. Peterson, "The Emergence of Post-Traditional Oman," *Durham Middle East Papers*, 78 (2004), p. 10.

but rather subsumed within the state apparatus. The Diwan has regularly granted gifts in cash and in kind (cars, houses, etc.) to the most influential tribal leaders, the ones most likely to challenge the established order, especially in Inner Oman and Dhofar, so as to ensure their loyalty. Moreover, the *shaikh*s *rashid*, remunerated as state employees, act as intermediaries between individuals and the public administration. They perform multiple daily acts aiming at facilitating relations between individuals and the state apparatus, such as certifying a person's lineage in order to obtain a passport, and in the solution of minor disputes.

Moreover, in 1980 the Omani authorities decided to establish *shaikh*s *qabila* for the Baharina and Lawatiyya communities of Muscat, comparable to those of the Inner Oman tribes. While this process was not unanimously approved, the government sought, immediately after the Iranian Revolution, to emphasize the anchoring of Oman's Shi'i to the nation by "tribalizing" non-Ibadi groups. Another illustration of the way the former order's references have been encapsulated into the modern state is the official decision, in 1981, to give every citizen a patronym referring to his native tribe. This decision focused on the groups which cannot claim Arab tribal descent, like the Lawatiyya, the Baharina, and Baluch-native Omanis. For these last three groups, it was decided to give them the patronyms of "al-Lawati," "al-Bahrani," and "al-Balushi."

The existence of tribes within the state and the social status of their shaikhs have even been recognized in practice by the Directorate of Tribal Affairs of the Ministry of Interior, which lays down an exhaustive list of tribes, as well as their respective shaikhs. This determines the individuals officially allowed to hold the title of shaikh. The Ministry of Interior has thus taken over the symbolic system of traditional local leaders to consolidate its own local anchoring. No social recognition remains beside that granted by the state, which has absorbed the traditional social structures by depriving them of any autonomous symbolic meaning.

Last but not least, in the 1980s and 1990s, a semi-official, but universally recognized, distribution of employment in various economic sectors and government departments operated on tribal and ethnic bases. Several phenomena must be distinguished, the first being the consolidation of the old hegemonic positions. For instance, the high proportion of Baluch-native Omanis in the security forces, like that of the tribes historically allied to the sultan (Hawasina, Ma'amari, Bani Kalban, etc.), has never been in doubt. Besides, senior office-holders have tacitly been allowed to reconstitute their client networks by recruiting individuals from the same group or the same area for positions in the sectors they control. For instance, the Dhofar-native Shanfari tribe was over-represented in the Ministry of Oil and Gas, and the minister for fifteen years was Shaikh Sa'id al-Shanfari; Ibadis still hold the majority of positions in the ministries of the interior, of religious affairs, of national heritage, and of justice. This has worked to strengthen individuals' primordial identification. In social interaction within the new Omani state, it is not possible for citizens to escape from their name, their geographical origin, or their ethno-linguistic group.

Another very efficient tool used by Sultan Qaboos to play the identity card and to integrate subnational groups in the state has been the Council of Oman, which is composed of two chambers: the Majlis al-Shura (Consultative Council), elected since 2003 by universal suffrage, and the Majlis al-Dawla (State Council), appointed by royal decree a few days after the Consultative Council elections. The regime has consistently worked to depoliticize the Consultative Council elections and reduce them to local community issues. In the 2003 and 2007 elections it was forbidden to discuss any general topic (like the role of religion in society, or that of the assembly in the division of powers) or to make public promises or campaign together with a candidate from another wilaya. These limits prevented the elaboration of political strategies. If public gatherings were allowed in 2011 for the first time, campaigning took place mostly in the *majlis* of the tribal shaikhs, but also through door-to-door and personal networks. Since 2003, voters residing in the capital have also been strongly encouraged to vote in their native wilayas through indirect measures, like the organization of the voting on a working day, and the granting of an additional holiday without loss of pay the next day on presentation of a stamped voter's card. Thus it is not very surprising that the criteria of choice most commonly used by electors have related to primordial solidarities, especially in rural areas where choice mainly follows lines of tribal belonging. This tendency was reinforced by the format in which the candidates' names were given: first name, father's first name, grandfather's first name, great grandfather's first name, tribe's name. Clientelism (*mahsubiyya*) and personal relations (*ma'arif shakhsiyya*), as well as the shaikh's support for a certain candidate, have thus been the most important determinants of choice.

The State Council formalizes even more clearly the integration of subnational identities into the state apparatus. It offers a second chance for groups whose members have been defeated in the Consultative Council elections. In Muttrah, for instance, the candidature of two Lawatiyya notables led to a split in the community's vote in 2003, which meant that there were no Lawati as Consultative Council members. After the sultan appointed two Lawatiyya to the State Council in the days that followed, they remembered the lesson a few years later. The Lawatiyya organized "primary" elections within the community in 2007 (and drew lots in 2011) in order to present only one candidate to attract the entire community's electorate. A strong representation of the Imamate's historically influential families in the State Council is also noted, in particular the presence of the last imam of Oman's son, al-Khattab al-Hina'i, and, since 2003, of Zahra al-Nabhani, daughter of one of the Imamate's most powerful personalities. The de-politicization process reaches its climax here, with the co-optation of traditional elites. If a local notable or shaikh wins a seat in the Consultative Council, his prestige is theoretically strengthened—but to the benefit of the central state as this notability becomes an intermediary between state and society. If he is defeated, his fate lies in the hands of the sultan, whose paternal benevolence can grant him a seat in the State Council, which will allow him to retain a degree of social visibility. Thus dependence upon royal goodwill is total. The social prestige of the tribal shaikhs consists merely of that which the state agrees to confer on them, a phenomenon of which a growing part of the population has become aware.

Through this identity politics, the ruler has been freed from the constraints imposed by notables and traditional authorities and has prevented the latter from freeing themselves from the state's influence. He avoids any sociopolitical polarization on criteria other than that of local allegiances (tribal or ethno-linguistic bonds): by tacitly recognizing the role of traditional subnational legitimacies in the state architecture, and channeling claims according to this identification, the ruler has prevented the emergence of non-sectarian identifications, such as social class or ideology, which have broader capacities to gather support and challenge the current order. Lastly, the instrumentalization of tribal and ethnic discourse gives credit to the perception that the system follows a principle of truly Omani authentic democratic redistribution, as "the sultan has given positions to each group so that everybody is happy."[19]

[19] Personal interview, Muscat, 8 Feb. 2003.

The exacerbation of socio-economic frustrations leading to identity re-polarization

Until the mid-1990s, an abundance of material resources, public sector jobs, and other benefits arising out of oil rents, combined with the subtle moves of the authorities to integrate and co-opt actors into the modern state, helped to moderate claims based on local or ethno-linguistic identities. However, for more than ten years, Oman has faced a series of social and economic challenges which are calling into question the order established in the 1970s. The Omani population is one of the youngest in the world: 33 percent of nationals are less than fifteen years old and 45 percent are less than twenty.[20] As these young educated people arrive on the labor market, the economy remains extremely dependent on oil-derived revenue. At the same time, the limited results of the Omanization policy for private sector jobs cannot hide the slow pace which has characterized the process of diversifying sources of revenue.

These economic difficulties have produced growing frustrations which have been made sharper by the multiple dividing lines of Omani identity. Due to the authorities' intransigence about sharing any part of the political decision-making process and the absence of any legitimate safety valve to release these tensions (independent trade unions, lobbies, or political parties are banned), the only available channel to express frustrations has been the "identity" rhetoric. In this context, the individual is labeled by the rest of the society as belonging to a group, with or without that person's agreement and even if the wish to be above ethnic identities and communities is affirmed. As Olivier Roy notes, "One of the perverse effects of the *asabiyya* game is the presupposition of belonging which is charged to any actor … even if he affirms his will to be above *asabiyya* and communities … Individual strategies of promotion can happen through the support of the group only, since there is no recognized general and impartial framework of social promotion."[21] Thus the encapsulation of subnational identities into the state, the monopolization of identity registers to the state's benefit, in a word the voluntary—but not politicized—perpetuation of local particularisms by Sultan Qaboos's

[20] *Statistical Year Book 2012*, Muscat: National Center for Statistics and Information, 2013, http://www.ncsi.gov.om/book/SYB2012/2-population.pdf

[21] Olivier Roy, "Groupes de solidarité au Moyen-Orient et en Asie Centrale: États, territoires et réseaux," *Cahiers du CERI*, 16 (1996), p. 43.

regime, have contributed to the resurgence of "visible differences" at exactly the same time as the socio-economic situation began to deteriorate. This is particularly true when dealing with religious affiliations.

Until the early 1990s, "for most of the Omanis … it was practice which defined the belonging to Islam, purely and simply."[22] If some were aware of differences of interpretation or practice, they were not criteria for hostile polarization. Despite the official teaching of religion which aims at promoting a "generic" Islam, the general spread of access to school and basic knowledge, and migrations within the national territory, have led to a growing awareness of mutual religious differences. This has led to a polarization over places of worship according to confession (Sunni or Ibadi). Moreover, while the Omani authorities always endeavored to place the religious issue in a timeless framework, they were not able to prevent the intrusion of political issues, or the awareness of differences between Islamic schools, into the mosques. The Omani authorities' tolerance of this religious development was originally based on the idea that someone occupied with religious matters would not question the political regime. But nowadays religious charity associations' aid to the underprivileged and newcomers, the widespread idea that the gap is continually widening between those who have access to the levers of power and others, and finally the lack of public means of expression all give support to the spread of conservative practices in the name of Islam.

The waves of arrests in 2005 involving personnel of the Education and Islamic Studies colleges of Sultan Qaboos University as well as senior military and civil officials, such as the son-in-law of the mufti, which led to judicial sentences for more than seventy people, can only be understood in the context of these debates on Oman's national identity. All those arrested belonged to the Ibadi school. The public prosecution accused them of having been members of a banned secret organization that was attempting to overthrow the regime by force in order to establish an Ibadi imamate. Presumably, a very small minority of the individuals arrested had political objectives. Most of them were certainly not involved in politics but were instead motivated by identity goals. As a consequence of the authorities' determination since 1970 to reduce the possibility of political rallying behind the memory of the Imamate, Ibad-

[22] Eickelman, *Identité nationale*, p. 114.

ism, as a historical criterion of "Omanity," has lost its pre-eminence, to the profit of the country's Muslim and Arab identities. From this perspective, most of the individuals arrested claimed to be acting in "defence of the Ibadi doctrine"[23] in a context where many Ibadis perceive the promotion of a consensual Omani Islam to be a threat to the Ibadi identity of Oman. No connection with networks abroad or with international organizations was presented during the trial.

Thus, for the first time since the Imamate fell in the 1950s, Ibadism seemed to have arisen as a rallying cry for political mobilization, which could openly contradict the legitimacy of the nation-state built by and around Sultan Qaboos since 1970. The strong reaction on the part of the regime is therefore not surprising. Within the government itself differences of interpretation were perceptible, between the officials who believed that a harsh response was necessary against individuals threatening the stability of the country, and those pushing for more tolerance and benevolence. The latter argued that the people arrested were first and foremost "sons of Oman," and had been animated by laudable intentions, even if the means they employed were condemnable.

If sectarian polarization based on religion is deepening, mutual prejudices are also related to ethno-linguistic identities, involving in particular Shi'i groups (especially the Lawatiyya), Swahili-speaking Omanis, and Baluch-origin Omanis. These groups, which do not have any genealogical, linguistic, or geographical homogeneity, have a point in common which makes them more vulnerable to stigmatization: they are external to the Ibadi and Arabic-language heart of Oman, so that they permanently need to justify their belonging to the nation.

This atmosphere affects young Omanis of Baluchi origin, and particularly those who live in outlying districts of Muscat; they are the subject of many fantastic ideas, because of the difficulty a great number of them have in speaking Arabic, the language of administration and hence of integration. For many Omanis, Baluch of Muscat are identified with forms of illicit behavior, like drug trafficking or clandestine immigration from the north of the Gulf of Oman. In this climate of frustration, the following episode in August 2004 is not surprising. While I was waiting for a taxi, a car stopped and made a sign for me to get in. Many Omanis working in the public sector augment their incomes by becoming taxi

[23] *al-Hayat* (London), 19 Apr. 2005.

drivers in the evening with their own vehicles. But this occasional taxi driver was a fifty-year-old soldier, who used his brigade's pick-up. During the conversation, his "broken Arabic" speech led me to ask him his town and family name. His answer—"No tribe, I am Baluch"—was the beginning of a diatribe about changes which had occurred in Muscat, where he had lived all his life:

> Before, these tribes did not exist. I am the son of my father, and himself the son of his father, and that is all. In Muscat, everyone lived together; one did not know his neighbor's tribal name. The Omanis [from Inner Oman], the Arabs, are those who made distinctions when arriving in Muscat. As they make distinctions between themselves, then they wanted to create some between us to create divisions. They completely destroyed Muscat. Arabs all are devils! (*kul 'arab, kul shaytan*).[24]

Competitive bidding of "Omanity"

While the wealth creation opportunities that the state can offer are dwindling, leading to a revival of frustration and mutual prejudices, everyone seeks to consolidate their anchoring into the Omani nation by asserting a greater acknowledgment of their belonging to the "Oman" entity. This strategy aims to strengthen the political or economic positions of power within the state apparatus and then to benefit from the material and symbolic dividends (administrative posts, financial advantages, public contracts, etc.) these positions entitle them to. This polarization has now taken place through competitive bidding in declarations of "Omanity," questioning of loyalty to the nation of other groups, and claiming oneself to be more Omani than the others. Thus everyone must devise social and political strategies aimed at calming suspicions about their loyalty and even overplay their assurances of belonging fully to the Omani nation.

The strongest religious grievances are directed against the Shi'i of the coast, who are seen as a homogeneous group, usually identified with the Lawatiyya. The Lawatiyya's visibility in society, because of their political and economic weight, combined with their religious affiliation which inevitably leads to them being suspected of sympathy towards Iran, explains why they are necessarily more liable to find themselves at the

[24] Personal interview, Muscat, 24 Aug. 2004

heart of the others' frustrations. With reference to their cohesion and their economic successes, they are frequently accused of having pushed for a Lawati lobby in the state's top positions. Influenced by collective memories of the pre-1970 period—when Muttrah traders, who were mostly Lawatiyya, had the monopoly of sugar and rice imports—many individuals from Inner Oman are still convinced that the Lawatiyya are able to press their interests through threatening trade stoppages. This mistrust only increased after the 1979 Iranian Revolution. In 1997 rumors proliferated because of the regime's silence about the arrests of Shi'i accused of transmitting documents to Iran. The Lawatiyya were depicted by others as a "fifth column" working for Tehran, as (it was implied) they had done for the British until the mid-twentieth century. In addition, such arrests reinforced popular attitudes and are an effective way of playing on many Ibadi and Sunni Omanis' distrust of the Lawatiyya. On their part, the Lawatiyya often complain about their isolation and their frustration at not being considered "real" Omanis.

In order to overcome political suspicions, the Lawatiyya overbid in declarations of loyalty to the sultan. As a Lawati imam explains, "The Shi'i have traditionally defended the sultan's interests against attacks from other tribes … In many towns, Shi'i districts are close to the forts, which means that they have their roots here."[25] But in the current context, ostentatious shows of loyalty are no longer sufficient. It is not uncommon to hear the term "Indian Shi'i" to describe the Lawatiyya, as opposed to "Arab Shi'i"—the Baharina. Thus if they do not want the Other to impose the criteria of their identity, the Lawatiyya have been forced to build a genealogy which connects them to the Arabian Peninsula and establishes their Arab origin. Currently, several historical interpretations exist among the Lawatiyya regarding their origin, all attaching great importance to their Arab-Muslim roots. One of them asserts that the Lawatiyya are related to an Arab tribe from the Hijaz. According to the Lawati author Jawad al-Khaburi,[26] the Ahl Lawatiyya settled in Oman during the pre-Islamic migrations; later they participated, among people from Oman, in conquests by Muslim armies in the Indian sub-

[25] Personal interview, Muscat, 15 Feb. 2006.

[26] Jawad al-Khaburi, *Al-Adwar al-'Umaniyya fi al-Qara al-Hindiyya: Dur Bani Sama bin Lu'ay—Ahl Lawatiyya* [The Omani Role on the Indian Continent: Role of the Bani Sama bin Lu'ay—The Lawatiyya], Beirut: Dar al-Nubala', 2001, pp. 47ff.

continent around the year 15 after the Hijra, and then settled in Sind and Punjab provinces.

Thus, by a historiographic shift of the major argument which underlies their stigmatization in contemporary Oman, their ancient presence in the Indian subcontinent finds its justification in their pure Arab genealogy and their early devotion to the expansion of Islam. These conceptual reinterpretations of their own history are clearly intended to tally with the requirements of contemporary official historiography, in which Arabness and Islamic observance are identified as key elements of the identity of the post-1970 sultanate. In this context, the Lawatiyya have constantly proclaimed their wish to be recognized as fully Omani by the other groups and to receive the same legitimacy as the Ibadis in appropriating the country's historical legacy and taking positions of responsibility in serving the sultan and the state.

Like the Lawatiyya, Omanis of Baluchi origin have been called on constantly to reassert their attachment to the national community. To stress the loyalty of Baluch-native Omanis, notables of the community explain with pride that they have "become like Omanis," understood as "real Omanis" from Inner Oman. Thanks to documents of Yemeni authorities and Ibadi Omani scholars attesting the "Arabness" of Baluch, they are regarded as a "tribe descending from Qahtan" sent (it is suggested) to what is now Baluchistan to propagate Islam. Thus they consider that they can legitimately reclaim the terms traditionally used by Inner Oman inhabitants, describing their group as a "tribe, the largest tribe in Oman."[27] The Baluch of Oman consider themselves properly Omanis of Baluchi origin: their political strategies use the Omani categories of identity and sociopolitical positioning, and are consciously within the framework of the contemporary Sultanate of Oman.

If the Lawatiyya and the Baluch are examples of the repositioning of some sectarian identities "whose existence and mode of operation precede the setting up of a State society [but] use it to their own advantage,"[28] the Swahili identity in Oman is an instance of a new collective identity which has its *raison d'être* within the framework of the modern

[27] Personal interview, Muscat, 22 Mar. 2003.

[28] Olivier Roy, "Patronage and Solidarity Groups: Survival or Reformation?" in Ghassan Salamé (ed.), *Democracy without Democrats? The Renewal of Politics in the Muslim World*, London: I.B. Tauris, 1994, p. 270.

Omani state, and can only be explained by the necessity for the back-from-Africa Omanis to find their place in it.

The "Swahilis" in Oman constitute a highly heterogeneous group, with many marks of division according, for example, to the date a person came back to Oman, their native tribe, and even the place of residence in Africa. Before arriving in Oman, the returnees had no real group feeling. Thus the gathering together of these different Omani populations, who only shared the fact of having lived in East Africa and having brought Swahili cultural referents back with them, was certainly not voluntary or spontaneous, but a consequence of the post-1970 Omani context. This led to the creation of a new *esprit de corps*, the criteria for which were established by others, the "home" Omanis. An old woman who came to Oman from inland Tanzania in 1972 bewailed the way they were all lumped together: "We were all called 'Zanzibari' [with a contemptuous motion of the hand] and could not do anything about it. It is difficult to accept but the Omanis say that we are all Black people, so … What can we do?"[29]

It is thus as a consequence of their—peaceful—confrontation with the other Omani people that a particular group feeling emerged among those who were collectively called, in the common discourse, "Zanzibaris" or "Swahilis." Since 1970, this new identity group has adopted strategies which are comparable to those used by other Omani *'asabiyyat*. From a social point of view, the Swahili-speaking Omanis consolidated their positions through nepotism. Through their client networks, people in charge of an administrative department have been inclined to favor the recruitment of relations from their group. Marriages between Swahili-speaking Omanis of low or middle social class and other Omanis remain uncommon. Many young Swahili-speaking Omanis, whose "creolized" way of life was a consequence of the time that their families spent abroad, have experienced difficulty in complying with the strict rules governing relations between the sexes observed in Oman. On the other hand, Omanis who did not live in Africa will rarely agree to allow a son to marry a young woman who is perceived to be "independent" in her lifestyle and less "well behaved" from a religious point of view. "Swahili" weddings are also occasions for the assertion of a Swahili cultural particularism regarding music and festivities. The ceremonies, mixing

[29] Personal interview, Muscat, 2 June 2003.

families from various social classes, are entertained by musical groups invited from Tanzania or the Congo especially for the occasion. The Swahili-speaking Omani community illustrates, then, the formation of an identity group independent of genealogy, relying instead on a criterion which is easily mobilized at a national level: the practice of a vernacular language.[30]

An (almost) undisputed Omani nation

The sultanate is crossed by multiple identity and social dividing lines, made sharper by the economic difficulties which have restricted room for maneuver for the regime and for the oil rent's redistribution. One intellectual was well aware of the political choices imposed by the official historiography:

> The problem is this—what is Oman? If I put the sultan aside, what remains as national "cement"? The country looks like an archipelago. And I wonder how a dialogue can be established between all these groups. Asking how the country will fare after Sultan Qaboos and how we will do without him is forbidden. But the people want to know, I think![31]

These words reveal a growing feeling of anxiety affecting all sectors of society. People have become aware of the symbolic centrality of the person of Qaboos, who has been a reassuring paternal figure for more than forty years. At the same time, they are aware that sooner or later the sultanate will have to find its own way without its protector.

However, the Omani nation, such as it was built after 1970, certainly exists in 2013. One of Qaboos's major achievements is the inculcation of the idea of an Omani nation as the horizon of all social and political actors' strategies. Neither the Omanis of Baluchi origin, nor the Swahili-speaking Omanis, nor even the Ibadis, express the will to dissociate themselves from the Omani nation or to reject the validity of this framework of references—on the contrary. Each group asserts a greater acknowledgment of its belonging to the "Oman" entity[32] and hopes that

[30] For more details see Marc Valeri, "Nation-Building and Communities in Oman since 1970: The Swahili-Speaking Omani in Search of Identity," *African Affairs*, 106, 424 (2007), pp. 479–96.

[31] Personal interview, Muscat, 1 May 2004.

[32] The major exception concerns Dhofar. Dhofari particularism is based on the

will reinforce its own position in the heart of the state. Accordingly there is competitive bidding of declarations of loyalty to the nation, each group making objections to the Other relating to its history, its past, or some social attitude in order to denigrate or downgrade that Other's "Omanity," while claiming itself to be more "Omani" than the others. However, as the 2011 events that shook the country illustrate, we can wonder if what is threatened here are the political rules established by the regime.

Identity politics in light of the 2011 Omani Spring

In 2011 and 2012, the sultanate experienced its widest popular protests since the end of the Dhofar War in the 1970s. The depth of the social malaise in the country was illustrated in particular by a series of two month-long peaceful sit-ins between February and mid-May 2011 (at Sohar's Globe Roundabout, on the Muscat–Dubai motorway, in front of the governor's office in Salalah, and in front of the Consultative Council in Muscat) as well as by sustained mobilizations after Friday prayers calling for political reforms. In an initial attempt to appease the protests, arbitrary gestures of goodwill (for example, an increase of the minimum salary by 43 percent in mid-February 2011, Sultan Qaboos's orders to establish a monthly allowance for individuals registered as job-seekers, and the creation of 50,000 new public sector jobs in late February) preceded two reshuffles of the cabinet in early March and the removal of long-serving ministers widely perceived as embodying corruption and as being obstacles to reform. The sultan also announced his intention to grant the bicameral Council of Oman greater legislative and regulatory powers. Even if positively received, these measures had little impact on dulling the protesters' resoluteness.

---

shared perception of a central state-led "internal colonialism" process—the regime being accused of siphoning off wealth extracted from under the soil of the south. While many Dhofaris are proud to be "represented" at the top level—through the sultan's mother, who is of Dhofari origin—and hold core decisional positions in the state and the national economy, these elements have never been able to mask the peripheral character of this region. Much more than the rest of the country, for Dhofar the succession to Qaboos will represent a major test of people's adhesion to the country's post-oil development and the role they wish to play in it.

After the entry of Saudi and UAE forces into Bahrain on 14 March 2011, it became clear that the ruler, like his GCC counterparts, did not intend to break the absolute taboo on discussing key political issues. Spring 2011 showed that repression remained an active strategy to choke off dissenting voices. Two protesters died in clashes with the police in the northern town of Sohar in February and April; several hundred protesters were arrested all around the country; repeated arrests of journalists and human rights activists occurred; and Internet discussion forums were closed. Also the sentence to jail terms of more than 100 individuals (on charges of "possessing material with the intention of making explosives to spread terror" or "sabotaging and destroying public and private properties") was evidence of the dignitaries' incapacity to accept the legitimacy of the expression of alternative opinions (without accusing them of breaching public order). A new crackdown on civil society started in May 2012, when human rights activists and lawyers were arrested while they tried to interview striking oil workers. In June, peaceful protesters and bloggers documenting the strikes and the lack of substantial reforms since 2011 were arrested too. Between July 2012 and January 2013, more than forty writers, human rights activists, lawyers, and bloggers were sentenced to jail terms (from six to eighteen months) on various charges related to "illegal gathering," "violation of information crimes law," and "defamation of the sultan."[33]

It is important to stress first that the protests experienced in Oman in 2011 and 2012 stem less from sectarian dynamics than from social and economic variables. The key demands of the strikes and demonstrations that mushroomed all over the country—from Ibri in the west to Ja'alan Bani Bu Ali and Sur in the east, and from Shinas in the north to Salalah in the south, with the notable exception of the Interior province—revolved around better wages, job opportunities, and proactive measures to curb rising prices and inequalities. They also called on the sultan personally to intervene to fight corruption among top officials and to prosecute them. From this perspective, the fact that demonstrations began in the town of Sohar, with its rich trade history going back thousands of years, is highly symbolic.

Neglected for years by the post-1970 centralized modernization process (like other regional centers), Sohar viewed the establishment of an

[33] In March and July 2013, the ruler issued two royal pardons for all activists jailed for defaming the ruler or taking part in protests since 2011.

industrial port, in service since 2002, as a godsend. For a total investment of US$12 billion, the whole Sohar industrial site, conceived by the regime as an international showcase of the economic diversification of the country, was officially scheduled to generate more than 8,000 stable jobs and 30,000 other jobs indirectly in the region. Yet the transition of Sohar within a few years from a small, sleepy provincial town into the industrial capital of the country led to the disintegration of the social fabric. This badly digested economic boom benefitted above all a handful of local notables and foreign GCC nationals, as well as the top Omani business groups (OMZEST, National Trading Co., Zubayr, WJ Towell, Bahwan, etc. in partnership with foreign investors) already embedded in the heart of the political-economic decision process, who had taken advantage of the dramatic rise in land prices. At the same time, the majority of the local population had no access to the economic benefits of the development, and experienced stagnation or a diminution of their living standards due to the increase of all costs.

This general climate of frustration sparked the crisis in February 2011 in the Sohar branch of the Ministry of Manpower. Young unskilled people native to neighboring cities, convened for the umpteenth time by the administration to be told that no job offers were available for them, decided to start a sit-in inside the branch. Promptly evacuated by the police, they were arrested and taken to the central prison. When the news became known in town, skirmishes developed around the Sohar police station and one protester was shot dead. From that moment on, Sohar's main roundabout, on the Muscat–Dubai road, became the gathering place of the protesters, who were mainly young, unskilled, or low-skilled and native from all over the Batina region, demanding work and better salaries as well as measures to end the reign of *wasta* (social intermediation) and corruption in the public sector.

Through a well-proven technique, the government described the protesters as being under foreign influence in order to discredit them and their demands. Rumors spread by security-circulated text messages and tweets flourished about supposed Emirati involvement in the organization of the Sohar protests. Similarly, the protesters in Ja'alan and Dhofar were said to be supported by Saudis, because of the local population's Sunni affiliation. These unfounded allegations did not attract much attention, though. Interestingly, the Ministry of Interior also tried to involve tribal shaikhs in Sohar and Salalah to appease the protesters on several occasions. This mediation was blatantly rejected by the protesters, with insults and obscene gestures,[34] as a clear illustration of the actual level of prestige and authority enjoyed by the tribal leaders in these towns after decades of Qaboos's encapsulation and co-optation policy.

If the protests were primarily motivated by social and economic issues, two noticeable sectarian dimensions of the mobilization should be highlighted. First, if it is clear that mobilizations were not organized on a sectarian (ethno-linguistic, regional, or religious) basis or along sectarian-oriented demands (claiming rights for a particular community or group), it cannot be denied that the visibility of Islamists quickly grew among the protesters and that the latter played a crucial role in channeling discontent. The influence of underground Muslim Brotherhood cells and networks kept expanding in the Sur, Salalah, and Sohar protests, while the Salafis were very much present in all Batina protests, Sohar and Shinas in particular.[35] Interestingly, Ibadis and all components of Sunni Islamists, along with a significant number of young secular intellectuals, have temporarily managed to suspend their disagreements and made a united stand in these movements, especially in Muscat (with an effective entente between Ibadi Islamists and Muslim Brothers) and in Sohar (where the Muslim Brotherhood and Salafis coordinated very efficiently).

The second dimension which is particularly interesting is that the Interior province (around Nizwa), where absolute poverty is probably as common as it is in Batina and Dhofar, remained untouched by the "Omani Spring." More than an Ibadi particularism, this immunity can probably be explained by a combination of different factors. One has to do with twentieth-century history. As explained by an Internet activist native to the Interior province:

> The memory of the Jabal Akhdar war in the 1950s, when the Sultan's Armed Forces and the British destroyed the Imamate, is still alive. People in Inner Oman remember how bad the al-Busa'idis were and know they are all alike. In Dhofar, they have this same memory of the war against the sultan, but it is different because this memory is a good one: they won the war and pushed out Qaboos's father.[36]

[34] Personal interview, Muscat, 12 Oct. 2011.

[35] In Liwa (Batina region), Taleb al-Ma'amari, a Salafi activist who took a leading part in the Sohar protests, was elected in the Majlis al-Shura elections in Oct. 2011.

[36] Personal interview, Muscat, 10 Oct. 2011.

Due to this historical legacy, Qaboos has always been very careful not to alienate Ibadi Inner Oman, with tribal and religious leaders of this region being granted prominent positions in the new state. For example, Omanis from Inner Oman (together with Baluch-native Omanis) are over-represented in all security forces, but also in the ministries of justice, national heritage and culture, and the interior, as well as at Sultan Qaboos University. In this perspective, the feeling of abandonment by the central state experienced in other regions and among other communities since 1970 has been less pronounced in the Interior province. This, combined with the memory of the 2005 wave of arrests among Ibadi activists, helps to explain the absence of protests in the Interior province.

Moreover, contrary to Batina and Dhofar, where social structures have not resisted the tremendous changes instigated by a badly digested modernization, the "traditional" social organization in Inner Oman remains very solid and has served to palliate growing inequalities and frustrations. Both the mufti of Oman and the Ibadi religious establishment in Nizwa retain a high degree of prestige, and their statements since 1970, unfailingly in favor of the preservation of the social and political order, are still greatly respected. Thus despite the failures in Batina and Dhofar of the encapsulation policy implemented by the sultan for several decades to keep all prominent actors under his control, the Interior province served in 2011 as a successful counter-example.

Conclusion

Since the mid-1970s Sultan Qaboos's personal legitimacy has relied on the building of both an Omani state and an Omani nation. With the remarkable achievements in technical, economic, and social development, there has been a rewriting of identity frames of reference around the person of Qaboos, identified in the new historiography with the contemporary welfare state and consequently with Oman itself. This political reworking of history has aimed at "naturalizing" his rule and at preventing the emergence of any alternative to the established order, in the name of the requirement of national unity behind the ruler and the threat of *fitna* (division). However, far from destroying subnational identities, the ruler has hastened to turn them to his own profit by integrating them into the new political order and using them to consolidate his authority. In Oman, this sectarian politics has sought to "de-autonomize" subnational allegiances from the state, rendering them fully dependent on a political game that the regime controls and whose rules the regime establishes. In this way, the ruler has been freed from the constraints imposed by community leaders and alone can claim to be an arbiter above all lesser allegiances.

There can be no doubt that one of Sultan Qaboos's major achievements has been the imposition of the idea of an Omani nation as the horizon of all social and political actors' strategies, as well as a collective framework of belonging. With the exception of Dhofar, where particularism remains, there is currently no questioning of Omani national unity. Even re-polarization based on sectarian identities (ethno-linguistic groups, regionalism, religious sects, etc.), observed in the past fifteen years, is not opposed to that of the nation, but is complementary to it. It represents a new means of positioning at the core of the Omani political system. While the opportunities for wealth that the state can offer are dwindling, everyone seeks to consolidate their anchoring into the Omani nation in order to show that they are more Omani than the other. Such strategies have been carried out in the name of the Omani nation and within the framework defined by it. They are the proof that both national feeling and the Omani state are fully applicable as references of thought.

However, the "Omani Spring" has shown how this long-term encapsulation policy, intended to prevent any social claim or the emergence of alternative discourses, has reached its limits. If this sectarian policy can explain why the Interior province was immune to protests in 2011, there is no doubt that growing sectors of society, particularly among the younger generations, are reluctant to guarantee the perpetuation of a system in which they feel excluded from political and economic decisions that engage the country for a new era. It has certainly proved unable to prevent the emergence of politicized transversal identifications, based on social class (unskilled and unemployed workers) or religious ideology (Muslim Brotherhood, Salafism, Ibadi Islamism), that are directly calling into question the old "divide and rule" order.

6

YEMEN

SECTARIANISM AND THE POLITICS OF REGIME SURVIVAL

Khaled Fattah

Violent sectarianism is unusual in Yemeni society, where local ties of tribalism and regionalism have traditionally been more powerful than those of ethnicity and religious affiliation. This chapter illustrates that the roots of Yemen's recent sectarian violence lie not in the age-old Sunni–Shi'i theological discord, but rather in the dynamic interactions of a politics of regime survival in a self-cancelling state, regional rivalry between Riyadh and Tehran, and the international and global geopolitical climate after September 11, 2001.

Yemen is a unique entity in the sociopolitical aquarium of the Arabian Peninsula. In addition to being a poor republic in a vast neighborhood of wealthy monarchies, Yemen is distinguished by having a significant and proud pre-Islamic history that stretches back over 3,000 years. Along with the Nile Valley and Mesopotamia, Yemen represents one of the core ancient civilizations around which the modern Middle East has been built. Ancient Greek geographers were so impressed with Yemen's civilization, agricultural techniques, and abundance of natural resources that they named it Eudaimon Arabia (fortunate Arabia). Later, the Romans divided Arabia into three main regions: Arabia Felix, Arabia Petra, and Arabia Deserta. Yemen, according to these ancient geographers, occupies the felix (happy) part of Arabia. The celebrated tenth-century BC kingdom of Saba and other sophisticated Yemeni "caravan kingdoms" of Qataban, Awsan, and Hadramawt were wealthy entities that controlled the frankincense and myrrh trade in the ancient world and developed extensive cultural contacts and commercial networks with South and Southeast Asia, East Africa, and the Eastern Mediterranean. Thus, for the people of Yemen, the Arabian Peninsula's concept of pre-Islamic ignorance (*jahiliyya*) is unacceptable.[1] The historic pride of the people of Yemen extends so far that Yemeni folklore considers the capital city, Sanaa, as one of the earliest sites of major human settlement on earth, founded by Noah's son, Shem.

In sharp contrast to the recent history of the names of Arab countries in the Persian Gulf region, the term "Yemen" is millennia old. Repeated invocations of the term *Yaman* are found in the Hadith. The Prophet of Islam is quoted as saying, "The people of Yemen have come to you, and they are more gentle and soft-hearted. Belief is Yemenite and wisdom is Yemenite, while pride and haughtiness are the qualities of the owners of camels (i.e. Bedouins). Calmness and solemnity are the characters of the owners of sheep."[2] Centuries-old local literature and practice, such as music, clothing, and crafts, are said to be explicitly "Yemeni."[3]

Contextualization of Sect and State in Yemen

Yemen's sectarian map is distinguished by its unique interaction with geographical features, topographical factors, and patterns of habitation. For instance, Yemen's Shi'i Zaydis, who comprise approximately 35–45 percent of the Yemeni nation, have traditionally been concentrated in the rugged mountainous northern areas and in the drier flatter eastern sections of the country. In such an ecological context, pastoralism rather

[1] Fred Halliday, "The Formation of Yemeni Nationalism: Initial Reflections," in James Jankowski and Israel Gershoni (eds), *Rethinking Nationalism in the Arab Middle East*, New York: Columbia University Press, 1997.

[2] Saheeh Al Bukhaari, *Book of Military Expeditions*, Hadeeth No. 4070.

[3] Paul Dresch, *A History of Modern Yemen*, Cambridge: Cambridge University Press, 2000.

than farming dominated socio-economic life. As a result, Zaydis have generally been organized along tribal patterns. For more than a thousand years, Zaydi tribes in the northern mountainous terrain constituted the military backbone of a string of successive Zaydi imams. The harsh topography of the Zaydi northern highlands of Yemen has also prevented centralized penetration and control by any Yemeni or non-Yemeni political authority.

The Sunni Shafi'is, who constitute the major religious sect in Yemen, dominate the southern highlands and coastal areas which receive abundant monsoon rainfall, known collectively as Lower Yemen. Such geographical locations led the socio-economic life of the Sunni Shafi'is to become characterized by sedentary farming, seafaring, and commercial activities. Throughout the history of Yemen, most cultural contacts and trading activities with the outside world were channeled through Shafi'i cities and towns. As a result, the Sunni Shafi'is of Yemen were more outward-looking and had a higher rate of emigration than the Shi'i Zaydis. Recently, literature on the Yemeni Sunni diaspora, with a focus on the Hadrami community, has grown steadily.[4] One motivation for this growing interest is the "notorious biography" of one migrant among their offspring: Osama bin Laden's father, who migrated to Saudi Arabia and established himself as a wealthy and influential businessman.[5] Influential money changers and bankers in Saudi Arabia, particularly in the Hejaz region, have usually been of Hadrami origin. In addition to their notable economic power in Java and south Sumatra in Indonesia, the Hadrami Shafi'i diaspora played an active role in shaping the economic, religious, and intellectual lives of the Malay Muslim community in Singapore. Interestingly, the Hadrami community of Singapore emigrated from Indonesia, not from Yemen. In India, on the other hand, the Hadrami community established a good presence and extensive commercial activities in the states of Kerala and Hyderabad.[6]

[4] An example of recent research on Yemen's Hadrami Sunni diaspora in Southeast Asia, from an anthropological point of view, is Engseng Ho, *The Graves of Tarim: Genealogy and Mobility across the Indian Ocean*, Berkeley: University of California Press, 2006. Another example, through the prism of political history, is Ulrike Freitag, *Indian Ocean Migrants and State Formation in Hadhramaut*, Leiden: Brill, 2003.

[5] Andre Gingrich, "Review of Leif Manger, *The Hadrami Diaspora: Community-Building on the Indian Ocean Rim*," *Social Anthropology*, 2 (2012), pp. 113–15.

[6] Major General Sayyid Ali Aidroos, the commander-in-chief of the Hyderabad State Army in 1948, is of Hadrami descent.

This sectarian and mode-of-production division among the Zaydi and Shafiʻi offshoots of Islam has created, over time, two different histories of Yemen.[7] Today, the Republic of Yemen, created in May 1990, is a fragile and deeply unstable Arab entity that occupies a peripheral position in the political and economic order of the Middle East. In addition to recurrent political instability and acute scarcity of natural resources (including water and oil), Yemen's human-development indicators are among the worst in the world.[8] Since its entry through the gate of modern political history, the Yemeni state has been continuously locked in a poverty–conflict trap, overloaded by societal demands and restricted by severe institutional weakness and limited capacity to provide public services and establish security and authority. As a result, the Yemeni state often cancels itself out in order to protect the survival of a chronically weak central authority.

Throughout its modern history, the central authority in Sanaa has seen its power limited by its military weakness, in comparison to the armed strength of the fiercely independent tribal confederations in the vast northern and eastern parts of the country. As a consequence of the deep tribal penetration of Yemen's military at the lower and upper levels, attempts at strengthening the military so that it can protect and enforce the will of the central authority carry with it the risk of turning the heavily tribalized military into a threat to the weak polity. The inability and/or unwillingness of the central authority to monopolize the use of coercion renders the Yemeni state irrelevant in many tribal areas of the country.

This condition of state self-cancellation creates a national politics that is exclusively guided by regime survival, even if survival means frequent radical shifts in policy and posture. It also allows Yemen's armed non-

[7] For a summary of the various schools of thought and offshoots in Yemen's history of Islam, see Wilfried Madelung, "Islam in Yemen," in Werner Daum (ed.), *Yemen: 3000 Years of Art and Civilizations in Arabia Felix*, Frankfurt: Umschau-Verlag, 1989. See also Daniel Varisco, "Making 'Medieval' Islam Meaningful," *Medieval Encounter*, 13 (2007), pp. 385–412. For a detailed retrospective view of Islam in Yemen in the seventh and eighth centuries, see Abd al-Muhsin Mad'aj, *The Yemen in Early Islam*, London: Ithaca Press, 1988.

[8] According to the UNDP Human Development Ranking (HDR) for the year 2011, Yemen is ranked 154 out of 176 countries. Development indicators for Yemen share similarities with those of the least developed sub-Saharan African countries.

state actors to flourish and expand in the many spaces of disorder in the northern, eastern, and southern provinces of the country. The spectrum of these actors ranges from militant jihadists and sectarian rebels to secessionist groups and tribal militias. In the context of state self-cancellation, these actors created parallel power centers, alternative ad hoc institutions, and their own transnational networks. Lisa Wedeen demonstrates how national solidarities and the notions of citizenship and nationalism in fragile Yemen were not developed through the institutions of the state but through what she calls the performative politics of people in everyday life.[9] (She refers, for example, to the regular daily gatherings to chew qat, which often lead to engagement in wide-ranging discussions of political and socio-economic issues.)

During the last decade, the fragility of the Yemeni state has catapulted to the top tier of the national security concerns of the United States. Following the suicide attacks against the Navy destroyer *USS Cole* in October 2000, while it was harbored for refueling in the Yemeni port of Aden, and against the French oil tanker, *MV Limburg*, in October 2002, off the Ash Shihr oil terminal near the Yemeni port of al-Mukalla, the US government placed Yemen in the arc of suspected breeding sites of terrorism that stretches from the Sahel and the Horn of Africa into the Middle East and Southeast Asia. According to strategic and security reports after September 11, 2001, Yemen has provided sanctuary for fleeing transnational militant jihadists from Pakistan, Iraq, and Saudi Arabia, and has enabled them to shelter and reorganize in the "dark spots" of the impoverished country. The foiling of some high-profile terror plots emanating from Yemen, such as the underwear and printer-ink bomb plots, highlighted the claim that the country has turned into a safe haven for terror cells to plan, organize, train, and prepare for operations against American targets.

Terrorism experts go further to assert that Yemen's al-Qaeda in the Arabian Peninsula (AQAP, *al-Qaida fi Jazirat al-Arab*), formed in January 2009, is a serious international security threat, rivaling that of its al-Qaeda parent organization. This group resulted from a merger between al-Qaeda's Yemeni and Saudi branches. Saudi Arabia's successful counter-terrorism campaign in the mid-2000s pushed many of the

[9] Lisa Wedeen, *Peripheral Visions: Publics, Power, and Performance in Yemen*, Chicago: University of Chicago Press, 2008.

Saudi operatives to flee to Yemen. Another cause for concern is the possibly dangerous connections between al-Qaeda-linked militants in the country and al-Shabab militant jihadists in Somalia. The Yemeni coastline stretches for 2,000 kilometers from the Red Sea town of Midi in the northwest to Hof in the southwest corner of the Bab al-Mandab (Gate of Tears), and from there it is only a 25-kilometer sail across the strait to the coast of Djibouti. If Yemen falls apart, it would mean collapsed states on both sides of the intersection of the Red Sea and the Indian Ocean, and the resulting chaos would likely exacerbate and extend the turbulence already generated by Somalia's collapse. The scenario of a collapsed state on the doorstep of oil-rich Saudi Arabia and along the northern shore of the strategic Gulf of Aden, through which more than 22,000 merchant vessels pass each year, generates waves of alarm through Western capitals. Europe in particular is heavily dependent on the cargoes that transit this vital maritime trade route, with nearly a trillion dollars (US) of trade to and from Europe traveling through the Gulf of Aden each year.

For the regime of the former president, Ali Abdullah Saleh, the man who ruled the difficult-to-rule Yemen for more than three decades (1978–2012) through a delicate balance of patronage networks and "dancing on the heads of snakes" (as Saleh often put it), al-Qaeda was not Yemen's main security nightmare. Saleh's regime did not perceive terrorism and militant jihadism as an existential threat on a par with the threat posed by the revivalist Houthi Zaydi militant rebellion, which had erupted in 2004 in the mountainous northern parts of the country along the porous border with Saudi Arabia. Saleh described the Houthi Zaydi rebels in 2008 as a "racist" group who "try to exploit people" by claiming that "the state is fighting all Zaydis." According to Saleh the rebels believe that:

> Power should be given to the Hashemite family, the so-called Ahl al-Beit [those who claim lineal descent from the Prophet Muhammad]. Some Hashemites are nationalists and patriots who believe in democracy and the multi-party system. The others believe in a racist vision, the restoration of the role of the Imam.[10]

Houthi grievances include the dilution of the ancient Zaydi sect and culture; the underdevelopment of Sa'dah province, including sociocultural, economic, and political marginalization; the close alignment of

[10] Interview with President Ali Abdullah Saleh, *The New York Times*, 28 June 2008.

the government in Sanaa with Washington in the War on Terror; and the excessive Wahhabi and Salafi influence on state institutions, media outlets, mosques, and schools.[11]

Since the Yemeni government's first anti-Houthi military campaign in mid-2004, the authorities in Sanaa have mounted an extensive media war against the group, sometimes accusing its members of claiming prophethood for their leader, while at other times accusing them of being Iranian agents carrying orders from Tehran to destabilize security in the southwestern corner of Arabia. Between 2004 and 2010, the conflict between Yemen's military and Houthi rebels was characterized by periodic low-level fighting which escalated into six major violent bouts. These confrontations resulted in thousands of casualties and tens of thousands of displaced civilians. From mid-2009 until the ceasefire in February 2010, over 300,000 people were internally displaced, most of whom remained in protracted displacement at the end of 2011.[12] Yemen's central authority expanded its political and military confrontations with the Houthi movement to the ideological sphere. Many Zaydi theological schools were shut down, a number of Zaydi mosques were confiscated, and Zaydi religious preachers were replaced by imported Egyptian preachers to lead Friday sermons in Zaydi mosques in the capital city.

The conflict took a serious regional turn in November 2009 when the Saudi military launched an anti-Houthi offensive. Hundreds of Houthi rebels and Saudi troops were killed in the fighting. Riyadh was alarmed by the prospect of an Iranian-backed Houthi autonomous region springing up along its border, not only because of the ramifications of such a prospect for the Saudi–Iran balance of power in the Persian Gulf region, but also because of its direct implications for the kingdom's stability. The restive Yemeni northern province of Sa'dah, the power base of the Houthi rebellion, is close to the Saudi province of Najran, where a Zaydi minority and a majority of 1 million followers of the Shi'i Ismaili sect reside. The rise of Houthi rebels along the porous Saudi–Yemeni border added an extra national security threat for Riyadh. Saudi authorities

[11] For details on Houthi grievances, see B. Salmoni, B. Loidolt, and W. Wells, *Regime and Periphery in Northern Yemen: The Houthi Phenomenon*, Santa Monica, CA: Rand National Defense Research Institute, 2010.

[12] UNHCR, "Internal Displacement Grows in Yemen," 9 Mar. 2012, http://www.unhcr.org/4f59e9009.html

were confronted with serious security challenges along their 1,500-kilometer shared border with Yemen, including movements of terror cells and militant jihadists, smuggling of weapons and drugs, human trafficking, and the illegal entry of migrants.

A few months after the winds of the Arab Spring reached the squares of Yemeni cities in early 2011, vicious sectarian violence in the eastern and northern provinces of the country erupted between Houthi Zaydi rebels and Salafi militant activists. Relatively new to Yemen, the hyper-orthodox Salafi strand of Sunni Islam emerged during the 1980s, having found wide appeal among the thousands of Yemeni jihadists who fought against the Soviet Union in Afghanistan, as well as among Yemeni migrant workers in Saudi Arabia. The Salafist wing of the Islah political party, the most influential and best-mobilized opposition party in Yemeni politics, spearheads the wing politically. Less than ten months after the initial uprisings that forced Ali Abdullah Saleh to step down as president, hundreds of Salafi and Houthi fighters had been killed, thousands injured, and many homes, hospitals, schools, markets, and even mosques attacked. Because this sectarian violence took place in the context of preexisting tribal feuds and revenge conflicts, it has resulted in an alarming escalation of collective violence and instability that is aggravating Yemen's constellation of radicalization and militancy.

Zaydiyya in Brief: History, Theology, and Politics

Zaydism is one of Yemen's three branches of Shi'ism, together with Twelver Shi'ism and the Ismailis. It is distinguished from the two other branches by being confined to Yemen, and it is closer to Sunni Islam than the other strands of Shi'ism. Zaydism is so close to the Sunni strand that some Shi'i groups refer to it as the fifth school of Sunni jurisprudence. The founder of the Zaydi *madhhab* (Islamic doctrine) is Imam Zayed bin Ali bin Zein al-Abdin bin al-Hussein bin Ali bin Abi Talib (695–740), an uncle of Jafar al-Sadiq, who was killed in Kufa while leading an unsuccessful revolt against the tenth Umayyad caliph, Hisham bin Abd al-Malik. Unlike most Shi'is who regard Zayed's half brother, Muhammad al-Baqir, as the fifth imam, Zaydis recognize Zayed as the rightful fifth imam.

Zaydism's emphasis on the philosophy of free will and rationalism rather than on textual literalism is related to the similarities of its theological foundations with those of the Mutazili school of speculative theology, which flourished during the eighth through tenth centuries in Basra and Baghdad.[13] Zaydism adopted both the principal tenets of Mutazilism and the Shi'i belief in an imamate vested in descendants of the Prophet Muhammad. Zaydism differs from Twelver Shi'ism regarding those who are qualified to rule as imam and the nature of his imamate. Unlike the Twelvers, the Zaydi religious heritage maintains that the imam needs not be an infallible and sinless man (*ma'sum*) with supernatural powers, but should be a learned scholar who is required to lead armed uprisings against tyrants. Zaydism rejects the concept of a Hidden Imam and stresses that the imams who had been designated by God and His Prophet are restricted to Ali and his two sons, al-Hassan and al-Husayn.[14] Moreover, Zaydism accepts the possibility of having more than one imam at a time and acknowledges that an imam is a temporal and spiritual leader who can be disposed and replaced by another. This philosophy of Zaydi governance encouraged numerous armed conflicts between Zaydi rulers and imamate-ambitious persons. Also, the Zaydi *madhhab* is pragmatic to the extent that it accepts "the rule of the less preferred [but still qualified] over the rule of the preferred [but unavailable]."[15] This distinguishing feature of Zaydism is known in the circles of Islamic religious scholars as "*taqdim al-mafdul ala al-fadil.*" Many fundamental bases of the Zaydi doctrine were intellectually challenged in the nineteenth century by the distinguished Yemeni religious scholar Muhammad al-Shawkani,[16] who led the shift from traditional Shi'ism to Sunni reformism.[17]

[13] The founder of this group is believed to be Wasil ibn Ata (d. 748). Scholarship on the group has increased following the discovery in Yemen in the 1950s of the eleventh-century texts of Abd al-Jabbar al-Qadi. For a study of the theological foundations of the Mutazili, see J.R. Peters, *God's Created Speech: A Study in the Speculative Theology of the Mutazili Qad-i-Quddt abu al-Hasan Abd al-Jabbar ibn Ahmed al-Hamadani*, Leiden: Brill, 1976.

[14] Etan Kohlberg, "Some Zaydi Views on the Companions of the Prophet," *Bulletin of the School of Oriental and African Studies*, 39 (1976), pp. 91–8.

[15] Shelagh Weir, *A Tribal Order: Politics and Law in the Mountains of Yemen*, Austin: University of Texas Press, 2007, p. 231.

[16] Najam Haider, "Zaydism: A Theological and Political Survey," *Religion Compass*, 4 (2010), pp. 436–42.

[17] For an intellectual biography of al-Shawkani, see Bernard Haykel, *Revival and Reform in Islam: The Legacy of Muhammad al-Shawkani*, Cambridge: Cambridge University Press, 2003.

As a political project, Zaydism had been implemented in the ninth century in the form of two main Zaydi states in two distant locations. The first was established by Hasan ibn Zayed in 864 in historical Tabaristan, south of the Caspian Sea, but its political and ideological impact was marginal. This Zaydi state only lasted until 928. Four decades later, it was revived in Gilan along the Caspian Sea and survived until 1126. By the fifteenth century, the majority of Zaydi communities in the Caspian region had converted to Twelver Shi'ism.[18]

The second Zaydi state was established in 897 in the northern highlands of Yemen. It was initiated by Yahya bin al-Husayn bin al-Qasim al-Rasi bin Ismael bin Ibrahim bin al-Hassan bin Ali bin Abu-Talib (d. 911), who resided in Sa'dah and became the political leader of a Zaydi imamate state that continued until the middle of the twentieth century, when a military coup in 1962, supported by Nasser of Egypt, deposed the last Zaydi imam, Mohammad al-Badr. Yahya had arrived in Sa'dah from his hometown in al-Ras in Hijaz, invited by a Yemeni tribal delegation from Khawlan to mediate in bringing an end to years-long violence and fighting between the tribes of Bani Sa'ad and al-Roubayah in the Sa'dah region.[19] Once he succeeded in ending these tribal fights, Yahya began to establish his imamate and adopted the title al-Hadi ila-Haqq (Guide to the Truth).[20] Territories under his control were in constant expansion and contraction. By the time of his death, the Zaydi state was confined to Sa'dah, where he and eleven of his successor imams are buried at the ninth-century al-Hadi Mosque (which was enlarged in the thirteenth century).[21] Although al-Hadi ila-Haqq did not succeed in consolidating his political and spiritual authority in all of Yemen, his descendants continued to be Yemen's religious aristocracy for almost ten centuries after his death.

[18] Moojan Momen, *An Introduction to Shi'i Islam*, New Haven: Yale University Press, 1987.

[19] For details on the arrival of al-Hadi in Sa'dah, see Hassan Ahmed, *Qiyam al-dawla al-Zaydiyya fi al-Yaman* [The Rise of the Zaydi State in Yemen], Cairo: Madbouli Bookstore, 1996.

[20] Two coins are in the Museum of Islamic Art in Cairo, issued in Sa'dah in 289 Hijri, with the inscription "al-Hadi ila-Haqq Amir al-Mu'minin bin Rasoul Al-lah" (inventory numbers 12817/2 and 21817/2).

[21] Tawfeek al-Shara'abi, "Al-Hadi Mosque: Unique Islamic Architecture," 2001, Arch Net Digital Library, https://archnet.org/library/places/one-place.jsp?place_id=8601&order_by=title&showdescription=1

In running state affairs, the Zaydi imams relied on two main social groups, the Sayyids[22] and Qadis.

The Sayyids (or Sadah) consist of a group of notables who are believed to descend from the Prophet Muhammad through his daughter Fatima and his son-in-law Ali and his grandsons al-Hassan and al-Husayn. Ten million sayyids live in the Muslim world today. Their number and social status vary from country to country, but wherever they are found, they are associated with a sense of authority and honor. In Yemen, the Sayyids acquired special significance. All Zaydi imams of Yemen were recruited from within their ranks.[23]

At a social level, the Sayyid families served as a religious reference in case of a dispute between tribes and religious scholars. Although the northern region of Sa'dah used to be the main center of the Sayyids, they were also important farther south in Hadramout, where a migrant from Iraq named Ahmad Isa established their presence in AD 952. The Sayyids were scarcely a class in the modern sense.[24] Some of them were poor but were able, despite their poverty, to claim social status with wealthy and powerful shaikhs by virtue of being descendants of the Prophet. Following the toppling of the imamate system in 1962, all members of the Hamid al-Din family, the last ruling imamate family, and from whose ranks Imam Yahya and Imam Ahmed came, were banned from living in Yemen. Many Sayyids were killed during the civil war (1962–70), and their properties were confiscated. A few Sayyid families today continue to play a political role in Yemen. For example, the al-Mutawakkil, al-Mu'ayyad, and al-Jafri families were recruited under the former North Yemen and South Yemen to fill ministerial and diplomatic posts. During the civil war, these families sided with the republican forces. The Sayyids of south Yemen were well represented in the Hadrami diaspora in Southeast Asia. One member of a Hadrami Sayyid family in Indonesia, the al-Attas, served as Indonesia's foreign minister.

[22] Gabriele Vom Bruck writes on the Sayyid families in *Islam, Memory, and Morality in Yemen*, Basingstoke: Palgrave Macmillan, 2005; and Vom Bruck, "Evacuating Memory in Post-Revolutionary Yemen," in M. Al-Rasheed and R. Vitalis (eds), *Counter-Narratives: History, Contemporary Society, and Politics in Saudi Arabia and Yemen*, New York: Palgrave Macmillan, 2004.

[23] Paul Dresch, *Tribes, Government, and History in Yemen*, Oxford: Oxford University Press, 1989, p. 161.

[24] Dresch, *History of Modern Yemen.*

The Qadis (or *Quda'h*) (judges) were a socially privileged educated group of non-Sayyid origin that filled governmental posts that were not occupied by the Sayyids, and they acted as the right hand of the Sayyids in managing state affairs. Thus they were close to the core elite of the imamate system. Although in theory any Yemeni at the time of the imam can become a Qadi through the study of Islamic law, in practice this privileged status was hereditary.[25] Most Qadis were drawn from urban families that had no particular tribal allegiance, and most of them were Zaydis, but a few Sunni Shafi'i Qadis were appointed as well. In public, the Qadis wore a distinctive sheath in a belt and carried their daggers obliquely to the right. In some cases, the status of Qadi was an honorary title given by the imam, regardless of nationality. For example, in the 1930s, a Turkish official, Muhammad Raghib, who remained in Yemen after the withdrawal of Ottoman forces, was given the title, and he eventually became Imam Yahya's foreign minster.[26] In the 1950s, there were 108 Qadi houses. Four prominent old Qadi families (al-Iryani, al-Arshi, al-Amry, and al-Ansi) continue to provide the Yemeni state with technocrats for senior governmental and diplomatic positions.

Governance style of Yemen's Imams

The following reply of Imam Yahya to a mission of religious scholars from Mecca sent by the Ottomans in 1906–7 illustrates the nature of the imamate's rule:

> The land of Yemen was in the hands of our ancestors, the most noble family [that is, the Prophet's kin], from the third century [of Islam] to the present, and never has there not been a claimant to that right, whether ruling all Yemen or part of it, as is known from the chronicles of Yemen. There were constant battles between our ancestors and those who opposed them, thus opposing the wish of the people (*ahl*) of Yemen to be ruled by their lords and the sons of their Prophet, may God be pleased with them … They have no desire save to order the right and extirpate what is loathsome and reprehensible, to establish the *Shari'ah*, set straight he who strays, and advise the ignorant …[27]

[25] Dresch, *Tribes, Government.*

[26] Leigh Douglas, *The Free Yemeni Movement 1935–1962*, Beirut: The American University of Beirut, 1987.

[27] Cited in Dresch, *History of Modern Yemen*, p. 6.

Another letter by Imam Yahya, to the imam's emissary in Cairo in 1928, reflects his ambitions to extend his spiritual authority beyond Yemen:

> Further it is recognized and well-known that the Mohammedans, in accordance with the provisions of God's book, are all brethren [*sic*], and therefore it is of importance to us here to be able to know everything about the welfare of our brethren the Mohammedans in distant countries and we therefore order you to carry out the exhortations above referred to, and in addition to appeal to them to contribute what is due from them to the descendants of the Prophet, prayers be upon him, as a duty and as a sign of their loyalty and devotion to us owing to our lineage—such an assistance to us from the Mohammedans has been ordained by God himself, who prescribed the "*Zakat*" from the income of all *Moslems*.[28]

The imamates of Yahya (r. 1918–48) and his son Ahmad (r. 1948–62) sought to combine their spiritual authority with an Ottoman style of management mixed with traditional forms of legitimation.[29] For example, the imam used to receive complaints (*shakwa*) from people as he walked through the city streets, and an official apparatus with offices of grievances (*mazalim*) processed petitions and selected serious complaints to pass on to the appropriate notables.[30] All governors appointed by the imam were required to walk every day through the main market and collect petitions. For instance, one governor during Imam Yahya's rule placed "a barrel with a slot for hand-submitted complaints to be posted" to the imam.[31] Leigh Douglas discusses the state of law and order in Imam Yahya's system and documents the observations of visitors about the punishment meted out to governmental officials or others who committed misdemeanors and were not deserving of Shari'a punishment. Leg irons and chains were attached to guilty officials for as many hours or days as the offense warranted.[32]

28 John Willis, "Leaving Only Question Marks: Geographies of Rule in Modern Yemen," in *Counter-Narratives*, p. 51.

29 For a study on attempts to adopt governance techniques in Yemen's modern history, see John Peterson, *Yemen, The Search for a Modern State*, London: Croom Helm, 1982.

30 S. Zubaida, *Law and Power in the Islamic World*, London: I.B. Tauris, 2005.

31 Brinkley Messick, *The Calligraphic State: Textual Domination and History in a Muslim Society*, Berkeley: University of California Press, 1993.

32 Douglas, *Free Yemeni Movement*.

The tribal factor

More than 185 tribes are found in Yemen, the majority located in the northern and eastern parts of the country. These tribes vary in size and influence. For security, political, and economic reasons, many of these tribes have been united under the umbrella of confederations. The three main tribal confederations currently in Yemen are Hashid, Bakil, and Medhej. Although Hashid is smaller than the other two, it is the most influential in Yemen's political arena. The demographic size of Yemen's tribal population in the northern and eastern tribal areas of Yemen is far smaller than that of the non-tribal population in the rest of the country. For example, the number of electoral constituencies in al-Hodeidah governorate along the Tihama coastal plain is thirty-three, which is more than the combined number of constituencies in the four tribal governorates of Marib, al-Jawaf, Amran, and Sa'dah. Yet tribes make up the central nervous system of politics, and tribal shaikhs are the most influential pressure group in the political arena. Yemen is the strongest remaining bastion of tribal power in today's Middle East, mainly because of the severe weakness of the state's institutions.

As a result of the historical absence of strong central authority and the failure of the political socialization of Yemenis as citizens, the state often behaves like a tribe, and each tribe behaves like the state. Yemen is to Saudi Arabia what Mexico is to the United States: a source of concern. The founding father of Saudi Arabia, King Abd al-Aziz ibn Saud (1876–1953), is famously quoted as saying, "The good or evil for us will come from Yemen." To prevent or at least reduce the threats emerging from its backyard, the Saudi kingdom cultivated a vast network of patronage with tens of influential shaikhly families in Yemen. The most prominent of these are Bayt al-Ahmar of the Humran section of the al-Usaymat tribe of the powerful Hashid confederation, Bayat Abu Ras of Dhu Muhammad, and Bayt al-Shayef of Dhu Husayn of the large Bakil tribal confederation. Geographically, Hashid and Bakil dominate the northern and eastern areas around Sanaa and encircle the capital like a bracelet around a wrist.

The northern tribes of Yemen are armed to the teeth and possess an arsenal of medium and heavy weaponry. In some tribal areas, the presence of national security forces or military units is perceived as a foreign intrusion. The increasing inability of state institutions to meet the basic needs of the population, and the failure of the central government to mediate important societal interests, such as security and stability, have enabled the government to isolate itself from society. The Yemeni state is an anemic political community of law and order, unable to push its agenda in the vast tribal areas outside the capital. To compensate for its weakness, the state relies on tribal leaders as bridges between state and society. In the pursuit of regime survival, all the modernizing agents—namely state institutions, political parties, and the military—have been tribalized.

The rise of the Houthis: from a social movement to a rebellion

The Houthi rebellion has its ideological roots in the activities of a revivalist Zaydi group that called itself al-Shabab al-Mu'men (Believing or Faithful Youth). The establishment and organization of the group passed through two evolutionary phases: collective action and militant response. The collective action phase started in 1990, as an outcome of party pluralism and the lifting of restrictions on association and expression, which were the cornerstones of Yemen's north–south unification project. The reason behind the choice of the province of Sa'dah, 240 kilometers north of the capital Sanaa, as the power base of the group is obvious. Sa'dah is the ancient learning and political seat of the Zaydi school of thought and the center par excellence of Zaydism. During the collective action phase, the group concentrated its activities in summer centers, where religious lectures, debates, theater performances, and sport events were held on a daily basis. In the absence of job opportunities and the lack of governmental facilities for the youth during the summer holidays, these centers became popular destinations for students not only from Sa'dah but also from other governorates and towns that are historically known to have a traditional sense of Zaydi belonging (for example, Hajah and Amran).

Within a few years, twenty-four of these centers were established in Sa'dah and forty-three in nine other governorates. These centers drew between 15,000 and 18,000 students in Sa'dah province alone. They were administered by a board of management comprised of six members. The success of al-Shabab al-Mu'men in the collective action phase is attributed to the zealous reaction of Zaydi youth to the ideological and identity challenge posed by the Salafist movement in Sa'dah—the heart and mind of Zaydism. Such a challenge was crystallized since the establishment of the so-called Dammaj center for conventional Salafis.

The Salafi center was under the management of Shaikh Moqbil Hadi al-Wade'i, the founder of Salafism in Yemen. The late shaikh (d. 2001) was a strong critic of all shades of Shi'i doctrine. In his sermons, books, and cassettes, he often accused the Shi'is of being heretics who propagated non-Islamic superstitious beliefs and practices. In the early 1990s, the Zaydi–Salafi ideological clash in Sa'dah reached a dramatic level when Salafis attempted to take over the mosque of Razih—the major mosque of al-Shabab al-Mu'men. Salafi–Zaydi confrontations intensified and were described as "the clash of fundamentalisms."[33] In the collective action phase, the Zaydi movement in northern Yemen took the form of a defensive social movement, which had the Salafists as the challenging group and Sa'dah province as its constituency. Despite its massive success, the movement did not grow into a powerful grassroots Islamic organization such as Hezbollah in Lebanon and Hamas in the Palestinian territories.

In 1999 the Zaydi summer religious centers began to be classified as moderate and conservative ones. The latter were headed by Hussein Badraddin al-Houthi, who was the founder of the radical Houthi group, the son of an influential Zaydi cleric, and a former member of the Yemeni parliament from 1993 to 1997. In some cases, the moderate–conservative typology took place even inside a single center. A formal split of the centers occurred in 2000, and the board of management was no longer capable of administering them. The split highlighted the division within the Zaydi Shi'i elite in Yemen. Armed with his rebellious and charismatic personality, and inspired by the revolutionary ideas of Ayatollah Ruhollah Khomeini and the organizational strategies of Hezbollah's Hassan Nasrallah, al-Houthi began to radicalize a growing number of Zaydi youth.

Yemen's central authority was alarmed in 2003 by Houthi activities when al-Houthi's followers began to shout "Death to America" inside and outside the capital city's grand mosque after Friday prayers. In Sa'dah, al-Houthi's followers wrote their anti-US slogan on the walls of buildings, including governmental offices, and distributed leaflets containing accusations directed against the governor of Sa'dah for being a CIA agent and against the government of Sanaa for being an ally of the United States in the War on Terror against the Muslim world. President Saleh was placed in a quandary after the attacks on September 11, 2001,

[33] Shelagh Weir, "A Clash of Fundamentalisms: Wahhabism in Yemen," *Middle East Report*, 204 (1997), pp. 22–3, 26.

by Washington's categorizing of the world's countries and leaders as being either "for or against" the United States and by the Pentagon's perception of Yemen as a failed state like Afghanistan that might have to be invaded. To save his country and regime, Saleh had to offer his cooperation, despite the widespread anti-US sentiment that has intensified in Yemen since the launch of the War on Terror. In the capital city and the Sa'dah governorate, authorities began arresting hundreds of al-Houthi's anti-US slogan chanters.

According to Hassan Zaid, secretary-general of the Zaydi opposition party (al-Haq), Yemen's security agencies suspected that if today the followers of al-Houthi chanted "Death to America," tomorrow they could be chanting "Death to the president of Yemen." After Sa'dah, al-Houthi began to mobilize the northern population with the objective of delegitimizing the central authority. In speeches, he encouraged people to stop paying any kind of taxes to the central authority. Saleh's government attempted many times, through the use of peaceful mediation techniques, to diffuse the tension. But its attempts were unsuccessful. Al-Houthi's defiance against Sanaa escalated; his followers blocked the vital highway to the capital city, occupied local governmental offices, took over strategic positions on several mountain tops, and started to adopt guerrilla and militia tactics. Sanaa had to react.

Clashes between Houthi militia forces and the Yemeni army ensued on 18 June 2004. However, the military operation against the rebels did not go as quickly as expected. The few hundred rebels showed fierce resistance, and tens of troops were reported dead. Although governmental troops succeeded in killing Hussein al-Houthi, the violent insurgency did not end. Houthi grievances include the dilution of the ancient Zaydi sect and culture; the underdevelopment of Sa'dah province, including social and political marginalization; the close alignment of the government in Sanaa with Washington; and the excessive Wahhabi and Salafi influence on state institutions, media outlets, mosques, and schools.

Since the first round of confrontations, five fierce armed clashes have occurred with an increasing number of Houthi recruits, led by Abdel Malik, the younger brother of the deceased Hussein al-Houthi. With every new round of confrontation, clashes increased in intensity, scope, and repercussions, causing new grievances to be provoked, and thereby multiplying the points of conflict.[34]

[34] The dates of the six military confrontations between Yemen's government forces

The puzzling Houthi slogan

Slogans are headlines crowded with meaning. The more correctly the slogan expresses the dissatisfaction and suffering of the people, the more effective it may be in mobilizing latent emotions. Observers of the Houthi rebellion have been puzzled by the centrality of the anti-US slogan in the hearts and minds of the rebels. Some reports describe how Houthi prisoners refuse to pledge to the authorities to stop chanting the slogan in return for their release. The history of this stubborn insistence dates back to 17 January 2002, when the later-slain Hussein al-Houthi began chanting it in a sermon in al-Imam al-Hadi school in Ma'ran, Sa'dah province. He appealed to the people to respond to what he called "the massive American arrogance."

"For how long should we keep doing nothing in response to the American arrogance?" al-Houthi asked his followers. In answering the question, he made a statement that ignited his supporters. "I say to you, my brothers, shout! Don't you have the ability to shout, 'God is the Greatest … Death to America and Israel …Victory for Islam and Muslims'? Don't you think that it is possible for every one of you to make this shout? This shout is a great honor for us to have, right here in this school." "By making this shout now, we will be the first who made the shout, which certainly will be made not only in this hall but also in other places. With God's will, you shall find those who will make the shout with you in other places. Make this shout with me, 'Death to America and Israel.'" Since this sermon, the anti-US shout has turned into a holy slogan for al-Houthi followers and has become an integral part of their educational and religious ceremonies, including at Friday prayers.[35]

Sectarian violence in Yemen's Arab Spring

Yemen's massive uprisings, inspired by the toppling of Bin Ali of Tunisia and Mubarak of Egypt, were not merely a "rebellion of the belly."

---

and the Houthi Zaydi Shi'ite rebels are as follows: 1st Round (20 June–10 Sep. 2004); 2nd Round (19 Mar.–12 Apr. 2005); 3rd Round (12 July–28 Feb. 2006); 4th Round (27 Jan.–1 Feb. 2008); 5th Round (15 May–17 July 2008); and 6th Round (11 Aug.–11 Feb. 2010).

[35] Khaled Fattah, "Yemen: A Slogan and Six Wars," *Conflicts Forum*, 28 October 2009, http://www.conflictsforum.org/2009/yemen-a-slogan-and-six-wars/

Instead, they were expressions of an overlapping set of factors, including acute sociopolitical frustrations among the youth, a power struggle among the elite, broader disenfranchisement among the citizenry, and unresolved security grievances. The uprisings reignited all of Yemen's existing tribal, ideological, and political conflicts. One of these in particular, the Houthi rebellion, has taken a worrisome turn.

During the insurgency between Houthi rebels and Yemen's central government (2004–10), thousands of Salafi fighters engaged alongside the government's troops. The power vacuum created by the Arab Spring encouraged both sects to settle their accounts with one another. Under the cover of the growing anarchy and the nationwide security vacuum, both sects have been expanding geographically into the spaces of disorder. Since the start of Yemen's Arab Spring, for instance, Houthi rebels have seized control over the entire province of Sa'dah as well as many districts in Amran and Hajjah provinces along the porous border with Saudi Arabia. One of their current strategic objectives is to gain access to the small Red Sea port of Midi, which would permit logistical support and a maritime supply chain for weapons from Iran. The battle lines cut across sect. During the multiple rounds of military confrontations, some Zaydi tribes and clans fought alongside governmental forces, and many governmental and senior military figures were even of Zaydi origin, even though they no longer explicitly referred to that identity. A more accurate analysis of the conflict should recognize the overlapping Zaydi–Shafi'i distinctions with tribal cleavages at the center of Yemeni politics.

The sectarian distinction is simultaneously also a geographical one. The overlapping of sectarian differences with tribal and regional identities means that sectarian notions can always become a factor in rebel recruitment. Saleh's regime understood this fact and for decades had practiced "management through conflict" as the most essential tool of governance in the northern provinces. For people there, the Yemeni state is no more than a "checkpoint state" (which appears along the highway in the form of a few soldiers standing next to an empty oil drum) or a "garrison state" (which occasionally patrols the road that links the main provincial districts). Critics of Saleh's regime accused it of manipulating sectarianism among the tribes to receive financial and military aid from Riyadh, for which an autonomous Zaydi zone along its border has always been a nightmare scenario. Thus the tangled roots of politicized sectarianism lie in the Saudi–Iran rivalry in the region and Saleh's politics of manipulation for survival. After the Arab Spring, the conflict has also taken greater sectarian overtones.

Recently, Houthi rebels and militant Salafists began attacking and occupying each other's mosques, which sent shock waves through Houthi stronghold areas and the loose and non-hierarchical coalition of Salafi networks dispersed across the country. Salafi activism in Yemen does not have a single power base but is instead organized around teaching centers, charity organizations, and mosques. Confrontations reached dramatic levels when Houthi rebels laid siege to the town of Dammaj in Sa'dah in mid-October 2011 and launched attacks on its famous Salafi-run Dar al-Hadith religious institute. Dozens of students at the institute, including some foreign nationals, were killed. An estimated 7,000 students of Salafism in Dar al-Hadith, including Arab, Asian, and European nationals, and about 2,500 families of these students live in the vicinity of the institute. According to the Houthi rebels, Dar al-Hadith is a Saudi-funded Salafi learning center that has turned into a magnet for young transnational jihadists, and a storehouse of medium and heavy weapons.

Houthis have capitalized on the withdrawal of Yemen's army to Sanaa (to strengthen the position of the embattled regime in the capital) by expanding their operations. The prolonged unrest of Yemen's Arab Spring allowed the Houthis to expand far beyond their traditional power base in Sa'dah. Their unprecedented and ambitious geographical reach in the northern and eastern provinces of Yemen is alarming for Yemen's Islah party and the Saudi authorities. Along the main roads that link these provinces with the capital, Sanaa, Houthi rebels have increased the number of their armed checkpoints. Recently, the Houthi movement has even reached the capital city. When riots erupted over a disgusting anti-Islam film in September 2012, posters, banners, and graffiti with Houthi slogans covered the walls in the historic old part of Sanaa. Some inflammatory posters borrowed directly from the lexicon of the Iranian Revolution of 1978–9, such as "US is the Great Satan" and "American Global Arrogance."

In an attempt to change its public image, the Houthi rebels have recently renamed themselves Ansar-Allah, and agreed to take part in a National Dialogue Conference which was launched on 18 March 2013. The conference includes 565 delegates representing Yemen's multitude of political, ideological, and geographical factions, as well as independents representing youth, women, and civil society.

Concluding remarks

Yemen is a deeply unstable political entity resting on a knife's edge. By the time the Arab Spring reached Yemen in February 2011, the country was already a fractured political entity governed by a self-cancelling state that, while avoiding collapse, remained stubbornly resistant to stabilization. Such a condition permits autonomists, secessionists, terrorists, insurgents, rebels, and irredentists to flourish and fill a political and security vacuum. The roots of Yemen's sectarian violence lie in such an environment of severe domestic socio-economic grievances and a security vacuum in Yemen's northern spaces of disorder. The violence has been further exacerbated by many factors: the geographical proximity to the Saudi border; the Saudi–Iran rivalry, which has stimulated Riyadh and Tehran to intervene directly and indirectly in the conflict; the US invasion of Iraq, which provided leaders of the Houthi rebellion the opportunity to mobilize anti-US sentiment among local populations; and the Saleh regime's politics of manipulation, which added fuel to the fire of violence on both sides.

Yemen lacks the sharp sectarian divides and hostilities found in Iraq, Saudi Arabia, and Bahrain. Former president Ali Abdullah Saleh is a Shi'i Zaydi, and Zaydis are well represented at all levels across state institutions, including the security apparatus and the military. Also, some Shi'i Zaydi tribes and clans have been fighting alongside governmental forces against the Zaydi Houthi northern rebels. Yemen's escalating sectarian violence should also be examined through the broader prism of the turbulent political and security climate that was created by the US-led War on Terror. In many parts of the Arab Middle East, particularly in countries with pro-Washington regimes, the consequences of the War on Terror resulted in further delegitimization of the ruling elites, further radicalization of opposition groups, and the surfacing of decades-old accumulated feelings of frustration and anger. These feelings are byproducts of political disempowerment, sociocultural alienation, economic marginalization, and a deep-seated collective sense of subordination and humiliation at the hands of the Western world.

Sectarian conflicts generate junctures from which we can learn. The complex and multilayered conflict in the northern governorates of Yemen teaches us how anti-US and anti-Israeli sentiments in the region are serving as a cover for voicing local demands and as a catalyst for mobilizing local communities against their own central governments.

The conflict also teaches us that the actions of the United States after September 2001 have contributed significantly to mobilizing insurgencies, and not only in Iraq. Although Houthis are fierce opponents of radical and militant Sunni jihadist groups such as al-Qaeda, they both share a fierce hostility to US policies in the Middle East. Visitors to remote areas in Yemen are regularly quizzed by average tribesmen about US and Israeli actions in Iraq, Lebanon, and Palestine. In the twenty-first century, Arab satellite television brought to the tribespeople of Yemen images of tortured and sexually abused Iraqi prisoners, the brutal destruction of south Lebanon, and besieged Palestinian families sitting in front of their bombarded or bulldozed homes. The restructuring of the current international and regional order in the Middle East has become essential for diffusing sectarian conflicts, even if such conflicts are taking place in a remote tribal area of mountainous northern Yemen. The dynamic interactions of local, national, regional, and international politics has made sectarian conflict in Yemen less localized and increasingly internationalized.

7

THE BALUCH PRESENCE IN THE PERSIAN GULF

J.E. Peterson

Contrary to popular perception, the Persian Gulf—including the Arab littoral—exhibits a variegated mélange of sectarian, ethnic, and communal groups. Some are of recent addition to the mix, while many others can boast of an ancient presence and contribution to society. The Baluch form one of the communities most integral to society in the Gulf, with representation in all six states of the Gulf Cooperation Council (GCC) and a presence that, in at least some of these countries, dates back innumerable centuries. As long-time residents and as Sunnis, the Baluch tend not to stand out or to be noticed in any obvious way. Nevertheless, they maintain a clear identity shaped by linguistic and cultural factors that makes them distinct on closer inspection. Consequently, an examination of their role provides an important insight into one aspect of the multicultural mosaic of the Persian Gulf. This chapter furnishes as extensive a look at the Baluch of the Arab littoral as is possible given the extent of available information.

The term Baluch refers to a major ethnic group primarily located in Pakistan's southwestern province of Baluchistan (Balochistan) and across the border in neighboring Iran.[1] The Pakistani province extends from the Makran Coast along the Gulf of Oman to the northern frontier of Pakistan with Afghanistan; there are consequently some Baluch across the border in Afghanistan as well. Baluchi tradition claims that the Baluch and the Kurds share a common ancestry originating in Aleppo. It is more certain that the Baluch lived along the Caspian Sea before migrating into present-day Iranian and Pakistani Baluchistan in the early centuries of Islam. A political identity was forged in the eighteenth century when the rulers of Kalat in northern Baluchistan created an independent state that lasted until the arrival of the British. The Baluch resisted incorporation into both Reza Shah's Iran in 1928 and into Pakistan in 1947, and sometimes violent Baluchi opposition has persisted in both countries.[2]

It is estimated that between 70 percent and 80 percent of the Baluch live in Pakistan, with most of the remainder in the Iranian province of Sistan and Baluchistan and in Afghanistan.[3] There are also Baluch in the

[1] These introductory paragraphs draw from Selig S. Harrison, *In Afghanistan's Shadow: Baluch Nationalism and Soviet Temptations*, New York: Carnegie Endowment for International Peace, 1981; Selig S. Harrison, "Ethnic Conflict in Pakistan: The Baluch, the Pashtuns, and Sindhis," in Joseph V. Montville (ed.), *Conflict and Peacemaking in Multiethnic Societies*, Lexington, MA: Lexington Books, 1990, pp. 301–25; Selig S. Harrison, "Ethnicity and Politics in Pakistan: The Baluch Case," in John Hutchinson and Anthony D. Smith (eds), *Ethnicity*, Oxford: Oxford University Press, 1996, pp. 294–301; Peter R. Blood, *Pakistan: A Country Study*, 6th edn, Washington, DC: Library of Congress, Federal Research Division, 1995; Carina Jahani, Agnes Korn, and Paul Titus (eds), *The Baloch and Others: Linguistic, Historical and Socio-Political Perspectives on Pluralism in Balochistan*, Wiesbaden: Reichart Verlag, 2008; Muhammad Sardar Khan Baluch, *History of Baluch Race and Baluchistan*, Quetta, privately printed, ca. 1958; M. Paul Lewis (ed.), *Ethnologue: Languages of the World*, 16th edn, Dallas, TX: SIL International, 2009, www.ethnologue.com

[2] There have been periodic attempts by some Baluch, particularly those living in Arab countries, to claim that the Baluch actually are of Arab descent. Therefore, they should be treated as other Arabs and some would even argue that the Arab world should support the movement for the independence of Baluchistan. This contention seems to be rejected by most Baluchis, however. (Harrison, *In Afghanistan's Shadow*, pp. 120–6; interviews in Oman, various years.) Valeri also mentions this point in this book, p. 198.

[3] The Pakistani province of Baluchistan was created in 1970 by merging Kalat and Quetta districts. Robert G. Wirsing, "South Asia: The Baluch Frontier Tribes of Pakistan," in Robert G. Wirsing (ed.), *Protection of Ethnic Minorities: Comparative*

Sind and Punjab provinces in Pakistan. Population figures are vague, with Baluchi nationalists claiming more than 16 million while the government of Pakistan put the total at 3.2 million in the late 1980s. One seasoned observer estimates a total of about 5 million with 4 million in Pakistan and 1 million in Iran; the same observer put the literacy rate at 6 percent to 9 percent.[4] The 1996–7 census in Iran counted 1.7 million inhabitants of Sistan and Baluchistan province, although this includes many Persian speakers.[5]

The Baluch are mostly Sunni Muslims of the Hanafi school (although some are Zikri, a sect that believes in a prophet superseding Muhammad) and speak their own language (subdivided into distinct dialects or, as is sometimes contended, languages). Their language is from the Iranian group of Indo-European languages. The Baluchi language was unwritten until the nineteenth century and is now written in Arabic script. The dialect that is most relevant vis-à-vis the Gulf is Southern Baluch. The Baluch are divided into a number of tribes, some of which are replicated, at least in name, in Oman and perhaps elsewhere. The picture is complicated by the existence of many Jadgal living among the Baluch in both Pakistan and Iran. Although close to the Baluch in many ways, their origins are a matter of dispute and they speak the distinctive language of Jadgali.

It can be conjectured that the migration of Baluch to the Arab countries of the Gulf was prompted by three motivations. The first, and perhaps the most primal, factor seems to have been the general tendency for ethnic or sectarian communities to spread into neighboring lands. This has been particularly true up and down the Gulf with Arab groups settled on the Iranian coast and inland from it for many centuries, and with Persian groups, first as merchants and then as laborers, settling in Arab littoral towns from Kuwait to Dubai. Over the longer term this type of migration exhibits a pattern of movement from areas along the Iranian littoral to the nearest points on the Arab littoral. Thus Behbeha-

Perspectives, New York: Pergamon Press, 1982, p. 281. There also exists a pocket of Baluch in Soviet Turkmenistan. Ibid.

4 Harrison, "Ethnic Conflict in Pakistan," p. 304. Lewis, *Ethnologue*, gives a total Baluch population of 3,405,000 with 2,770,000 in Pakistan and 405,000 in Iran.

5 Abdolhossein Yadegari, "Pluralism and Change in Iranian Balochistan," in Jahani et al., *Baloch and Others*, p. 247.

nis are predominant in Kuwait, Bushehris in Bahrain, and Bastakis in Dubai. Under this reasoning, it is not surprising that a sizeable proportion of the population of Oman's Batinah Coast on the Gulf of Oman should be Baluch.

The second factor in the settlement of Baluch in the Gulf is related to the Baluchi martial reputation. Baluch mercenaries have served as soldiers and armed retainers in the service of more than one Gulf ruler, but especially the rulers of Oman, where their presence has been recorded with the Ya'rubi imams in the sixteenth and seventeenth centuries.[6] Recruitment directly from Baluchistan continued well into the twentieth century in Oman and Bahrain. A factor in this process unique to Oman was the sultanate's ownership for more than a century and a half of the enclave of Gwadar on the coast of Baluchistan.

The third factor is part of a general migration of labor to the Persian Gulf during the oil era. While the Baluch have not been as numerous in this respect as other Pakistanis, not to mention Indians, Bangladeshis, Sri Lankans, and other Asian nationalities, Baluchi workers can be found in all the Gulf states. "Here the Baluch found work as unskilled laborers, policemen, or fishermen. Other Baluch joined the military. Still others labored in the oil fields and on the farms of the wealthy Gulf states. Although the Baluch work extremely hard, they are much better off than they were in Baluchistan, one of the poorest areas of the world."[7]

Oman

Oman is the one country in the Gulf where Baluch live in profusion and have done so for a long but indeterminate period of time. This is undoubtedly due to the proximity of Makran to the Batinah. Early European travelers to Oman in the sixteenth and seventeenth centuries mentioned the Baluch, and it can reasonably be assumed that Baluch have resided in the country for centuries before that.

[6] S.B. Miles, *The Countries and Tribes of the Persian Gulf*, London: Harrison and Sons, 1919, 2nd edn, reprinted in one vol., London: Frank Cass, 1966, pp. 201–64; Willem Floor, *The Persian Gulf: A Political and Economic History of Five Port Cities, 1500–1730*, Washington, DC: Mage, 2006, pp. 347–51.

[7] Beatrice Nicolini, "The Baluch Role in the Persian Gulf during the Nineteenth and Twentieth Centuries," *Comparative Studies of South Asia, Africa and the Middle East*, 27, 2 (2007), p. 385.

Omani Baluch form a large proportion of the population in all the towns of al-Batinah Coast (stretching from Muscat to the UAE border in the west), as well as in the Muscat capital region. As the Sultanate of Oman census does not break down the population by ethnicity or religion, there can be no accurate figure of the Baluch population but a reasonable estimate would reckon between 205,000 and 245,000, or around 10–13 percent of the total Omani population.[8]

There are smaller communities of Baluch elsewhere in Oman, notably in al-Dhahirah region (on the inland side of the Hajar Mountains opposite al-Batinah and close to Abu Dhabi). At some forgotten point in time, a group of Baluch settled in this area where they adopted the organization of an Arab tribe as well as the Arabic language. By their own explanation, the enclave was created when earlier rulers of Oman sent Baluch to the region as soldiers and guards for officials.[9] Although they dressed as Arabs and spoke Arabic, they were regarded as being on poor terms with all the neighboring Arab tribes. Because they were threatened by the Ibadi imam in the early 1950s, they allied themselves

[8] J.E. Peterson, "Oman's Diverse Society: Northern Oman," *Middle East Journal*, 58, 1 (Winter 2004), p. 36; Sultanate of Oman, Supreme Council for Planning, National Center for Statistics and Information, *Statistical Yearbook 2011*, Muscat, 2011, http://www.ncsi.gov.om/book/SYB2011/contents.htm. These very rough estimates were calculated on the basis that one-third of the Omani population of al-Batinah is Baluch. The 2010 Omani census enumerates 773,000 residents of al-Batinah, of whom about 80 percent were Omani, with 1,957,000 Omanis in total. It is possible that the Baluch form a lesser proportion of al-Batinah's population but, on the other hand, the numerous Baluch of the capital region were not included in this estimate. The Joshua Project, an online website proclaiming to be "a research initiative seeking to highlight the ethnic people groups of the world with the fewest followers of Christ," puts the total of Baluch in Oman at 434,000, http://www.joshuaproject.net/people-profile.php. However, there is no indication of date, sources of information, or methodology. Earlier estimates of the Baluch population of Oman were much lower. A compendium of information on Omani tribes and groups in the early 1950s put the total at between 15,000 and 16,000. Of these, it was estimated that 5,000–6,000 were settled in Muscat and the remainder along the Batinah. Only about 500 were in al-Dhahirah and the numbers that J.G. Lorimer had found in the Ja'lan of the east and the Western and Eastern Hajar Mountains were considered insignificant. United Kingdom, National Archives, Kew Gardens, Foreign Office (later Foreign and Commonwealth Office), FO/1016/3 (1949–51), "Notes on Certain of the Tribes of the Sultanate of Muscat and Oman."

[9] Interviews in Oman, various years.

with the Saudis.[10] Local tradition in Manah, a town of the central, interior, Omani heartland, holds that Baluch have been among the earliest inhabitants.[11]

The *Gazetteer of the Persian Gulf, 'Omân, and Central Arabia*, compiled by J.G. Lorimer for the Government of India at the beginning of the twentieth century and in some respects still the most exhaustive source of information today, noted that the Baluch in Muscat and Matrah constituted half or more of the population and served as soldiers, sailors, porters, servants, and petty traders.[12] Both towns possess a Harat al-Balush, or Baluch Quarter, although most of Muscat's population outside the walls seemed to be Baluch.[13] The Baluch may still predominate in Muscat and Matrah today, in part because they tend to fall within lower income groups and because many other Muscat and Matrah families have abandoned the towns for newer residences in the suburbs. While many Omani Baluch preserve tribal names, such as Ra'isi or Sangur, there does not seem to be any interaction with tribes in Makran.

The second factor in Baluch immigration to the Arab side of the Gulf, that of mercenary or soldier, applies squarely to Oman. Ahmad bin Sa'id Al Bu Sa'idi, who had unified Oman to drive out the invading forces of Nadir Shah of Persia and subsequently served as imam, died in 1783 and was succeeded by his son Sa'id. Sa'id abdicated after a year in favor of his son Hamad, but other sons of Ahmad bin Sa'id contested his leadership. When one of them, Sultan bin Ahmad, was forced to flee Oman, he was given refuge in the Makrani coastal fishing village of Gwadar by the khan of Kalat, who had assumed power in the Makran when Nadir Shah's forces retreated. Sultan bin Ahmad continued to contest the leadership of Oman and he never surrendered his claim to

[10] FO/1016/3 (1949–51), "Notes on Certain of the Tribes of the Sultanate of Muscat and Oman"; FO/371/156820, BC1821/1, "Tribes of Oman"; compendium updated and maintained by GSO 2 Int., HQ LFPG, Bahrain (n.d. but 1961).

[11] Soumyen Bandyopadhyay, "Manh: the Architecture, Archaeology and Social History of a Deserted Omani Settlement," PhD thesis, University of Liverpool, School of Architecture and Building Engineering, n.d., Chapter 3 (unpaginated).

[12] J.G. Lorimer, comp., *Gazetteer of the Persian Gulf, 'Omân, and Central Arabia*, Calcutta: Superintendent, Government Printing, vol. I (1915); vol. II (1908); reprinted by various publishers in 1970, 1989, and 1998. Here see vol. II, pp. 1185 and 1200.

[13] J.E. Peterson, *Historical Muscat: An Illustrated Guide and Gazetteer*, Leiden: Brill, 2007; interview in Oman, 1989.

Gwadar, apparently using the small port to launch attacks on the Omani coast. After his nephew Hamad's death in 1792, Sultan succeeded in besting the other members of his family and took control of Muscat. He then sent a governor to administer Gwadar and build a fort there.[14]

A visit by the British political resident in the Persian Gulf and the consul-general in Muscat to Gwadar in 1952 revealed that the economic situation was satisfactory and that the opposition Baluch Reform Association—which had agitated for the return of Gwadar to Pakistan—had become defunct. A new school was planned—in addition to the existing school for Agha Khanis—and a dispensary received considerable use. The sultan's administrator was British, and Britain maintained an agent of Indian origin who apparently looked after the British subjects who were Hindus.[15] The population of Gwadar was estimated to be around 20,000 in the early 1950s.[16] Gwadar remained a dependency of Oman until 1958 when Sultan Sa'id bin Taymur was pressured to sell it to Pakistan for £3 million. Omani sovereignty over Gwadar undoubtedly facilitated Baluchi movement to Oman in search of work and settlement. This continued after the enclave's return to Pakistan, as a 1962 report noted the interception of a number of boatloads of Baluch seeking to enter the sultanate illegally, possibly seeking to travel overland to the oilfields of Abu Dhabi.[17]

More importantly, however, Baluch have long served as soldiers throughout the Gulf and the western Indian Ocean, including Oman. The use of Baluch as *'askaris*, armed retainers and guards, began long before Omani acquisition of Gwadar and dates at least to the early eighteenth century under the last Ya'rubi imam. They were employed alongside Najdis, Yemenis, and black Africans, as well as men from Arab tribes allied to the ruler. Imam Ahmad bin Sa'id Al Bu Sa'idi was reported to have relied occasionally on Baluch mercenaries, in addition to a garrison of African slaves used for the defense of his capital at al-Rustaq and a mounted force of Arabs for mobile use around the country. A bit later, it was said that Sayyid Sultan bin Ahmad employed

[14] Lorimer, *Gazetteer*, vol. I, pp. 418–22 and 601–3.

[15] FO/371/98329, EA1018/3, W.R. Hay, Political Resident in the Persian Gulf, to Anthony Eden, Secretary of State for Foreign Affairs, 19 May 1952.

[16] FO/1016/3 (1949–51), "Notes on Certain of the Tribes of the Sultanate of Muscat and Oman."

[17] FO/371/162842, BC1013/6, Muscat Monthly Diary, 1–31 May 1962.

about 300 armed slaves and 1,700 Sindi, Baluchi, and Arab mercenaries. The garrisons of the two forts commanding Muscat's heights were described in the early twentieth century as being manned by some 200 Baluch and Arabs. Baluch *'askaris* also assisted Indian Army troops during their 1915 battle defending Muscat from Omani tribes.[18]

The first modern organized army unit in Oman was entirely Baluch in composition. The Muscat Levy Corps was formed when the British brought the redundant Sistan Levy Corps from Iran to Muscat in April 1921.[19] Never more than several hundred in strength, the force, later named the Muscat Infantry, provided the nucleus of the subsequently created Sultan's Armed Forces (SAF). However, the 250 Sistani soldiers were badly affected by malaria and many were discharged in the initial year. They were replaced mostly by Makrani Baluch recruited from Gwadar. A few Omani Baluch and a handful of Arabs and Africans previously in the sultan's service also joined, as did one member of the ruling family.[20] The Muscat Infantry also served as a model and source of recruits for the Bahrain Levy Corps (which later transitioned into the Bahrain Police Force—more details below).[21]

By 1939, the barely effective force of about 150 men consisted of half Makrani Baluch from Gwadar and the other half Omani Baluch, with a few Arabs.[22] Because of the preponderance of Baluch, the language of command was Urdu and remained so until the unit was absorbed into the SAF in 1958. Baluch soldiers figured heavily in the Jabal al-Akhdar War of the mid- to late 1950s. In 1964, the SAF consisted of 779 Arabs, 170 Omani Baluch, and 1,081 Gwadar Baluch.[23] The heavy reliance on

[18] J.E. Peterson, *Oman's Insurgencies: The Sultanate's Struggle for Supremacy*, London: Saqi, 2007, pp. 38, 40, and 43.

[19] For an account of the force's activities in 1916, see the *London Gazette*, Supplement, Issue 30360 (31 Oct. 1917), p. 112170. The Sistan Force was formed by order of the Indian Army at the onset of World War I as the East Persia Cordon to protect British interests in Persia from German activities and it was last utilized in 1920. "Seistan Force," Wikipedia <http://en.wikipedia.org/w/index.php?title'Seistan_Force&oldid'457722286>

[20] Peterson, *Oman's Insurgencies*, p. 48.

[21] J.E. Peterson, *Oman in the Twentieth Century*, London: Croom Helm, 1978, p. 92.

[22] Peterson, *Oman's Insurgencies*, p. 49.

[23] Ibid., p. 150. Recruitment for the Sultan's Armed Forces over the years was regulated to prevent reliance on any one region or social stratum of Baluchistan.

Makrani Baluch could be explained partly by the age-old reliance of rulers in the region on foreign mercenaries (who could be supposed to be more loyal and trustworthy) and a marked reluctance of local Arab tribesmen to join the British-officered armed forces—indeed, Sultan Sa'id bin Taymur (r.1932–70) forbade recruitment in most areas of Oman. Nevertheless, the Baluch soldiers did not get along well with the local population.

At the same time, Sultan Sa'id bin Taymur's eagerness to create a unit in Dhufar entirely separate from the SAF led to the creation of Dhufar Force, composed entirely of Baluch at the beginning, although it later included *jabbalis* (mountain tribesmen) and palace slaves.[24] The subsequent outbreak of full-scale insurgency in Dhufar required a rapid build-up of SAF capabilities and forced Oman to recruit even more heavily from Gwadar. Some of the Baluch received full training and status as members of the SAF, while others served as *'askaris* (irregulars) to hold small forts and picket posts.[25] After 1970 the old Dhufar Force was incorporated into the SAF as a separate unit and transformed into an all-Baluch unit, while Arab recruiting was stepped up as the size of the SAF mushroomed. This led to some easily contained animosity between the Arabs and the Baluch. By the end of the war in the mid-1970s, the Baluch in the SAF were largely grouped into three all-Baluch battalions.

After the fighting stopped, the heavily Makrani Baluch majority of SAF personnel was reversed in favor of Omanis and the recruitment of Makrani Baluch ceased in the 1980s. A number of the soldiers chose to settle in Oman rather than return home. Omani Baluch remain well represented in the SAF and the first Omani officers in the armed forces

---

"The greater number of recruits are from the Kech area, but many come from the coast, especially from Gwadar, and from Panjgur. Soldiers of other areas are sometimes recruited; a few Iranian Baluch are found, some from Karachi and some Brahuis from the east of the province. Even the odd Pathan manages to be recruited. The majority of recruits are from the middle-ranking social strata, but some are from more wealthy and influential hakim families and a good many from the lower hizmatkar classes of fishermen, artisans and ex-slaves." N.A. Collett, "Baluch Service in the Forces of Oman: A Reflection of Makrani Society and an Impetus for Change," *Newsletter of Baluchistan Studies*, 2 (1985), p. 9.

[24] Peterson, *Oman's Insurgencies*, pp. 187–8.

[25] A position to which only a small detachment of men is posted.

were Omani Baluch from Matrah. By 1968, there were thirty-one Omani officers in the SAF, all of them Baluch.[26]

Most Omanis of Baluchi background are Omani nationals by birth, although some of the soldiers recruited from Gwadar who chose to remain in Oman were naturalized. There is no official distinction between various ethnic communities in the sultanate. However, Omani Baluch are often regarded with some disdain by Omani Arabs, and their socio-economic status tends to be lower. Some Baluch are less proficient in Arabic, although the extension of universal education in Oman over the past few decades has had considerable effect in ameliorating this.

Because of perceptions of discrimination, some younger Baluch exhibit signs of alienation and, interestingly, sometimes identify with "black power" expressions similar to African Americans and the Caribbean populations of the United Kingdom. This was evident in the numbers of young Baluch who some years ago frequented a CD shop in Muscat in search of a particular song by Bob Marley and the Wailers that seemed to encapsulate the self-perception of their identity.[27]

Discrimination against the Baluch, for the most part, appears to be relatively subtle and has no legal basis. Indeed, there have been several Baluchi ministers in government, such as Muhammad Zubayr (Baluchi father), Ahmad Suwaydan al-Balushi (the former minister of Posts, Telegraphs, and Telephones), and Ali Muhammad al-Musa (former minister of health). Some of the most prominent merchants are Baluchi, including Yahya Muhammad Nasib and Musa Abd al-Rahman Hasan. Baluchis have also risen in the ranks of security forces, including a former commander of the air force, Talib Miran Ra'isi. In mid-2012, it was reported that Oman had appointed its first ambassador to Pakistan of Baluchi origin.[28]

Although most Omanis of Baluchi background trace their origins to what is now Pakistani Baluchistan and identify, even if weakly, with Makrani Baluch tribes, there is an element of Iranian Baluch in Oman

[26] FCO/8/589, D.C. Carden, Consul-General, Muscat, to Sir Stewart Crawford, Political Resident in the Persian Gulf, 27 June 1968, "Report for 2nd Quarter of 1968."

[27] Personal observation in Oman, 1990s. See also the brief discussion of the Baluchi role in Omani society in Marc Valeri, *Oman: Politics and Society in the Qaboos State*, London: Hurst, 2009, pp. 232–4.

[28] *The News* (Karachi), 23 Aug. 2012.

as well. The dates of their arrival in Oman appear to be later, a result at least in part of the shah of Iran's attempts to extend his authority to the Iranian Makran in the 1950s and 1960s. Some of these immigrants were used by the present sultan's father as a sort of paramilitary force, in similar fashion to his use of the Bani Umar and al-Hawasinah Arab tribes. These Iranian Baluch settled in both Kalbah in Sharjah and Shinas in Oman. For many years until the mid-1990s, Oman paid salaries to them but the practice was stopped when a new minister responsible for defense affairs took over.[29] Notice should also be made of the existence in Oman of the closely related community of Zadjalis, the local variation of the name Jadgal employed in Pakistan and Iran. Some live in the UAE where they may also be known as Ziyalis.[30]

Bahrain

The Baluch community in Bahrain seems to be of far more recent arrival than the Baluch community in Oman. However, one young Baluch (who spoke Arabic and no Baluchi), interviewed in Bahrain in 1980, claimed to be head of a Baluchi tribe of "Hoots" with 28,000 members in Bahrain. These he claimed had come to Bahrain in 1782 with the Al Khalifah. He also claimed an aunt was married to Shaykh Isa bin Salman, the ruler of Bahrain.[31] Traditionally, Baluch were among the *fidawis* (armed retainers) in the estates of the ruling Al Khalifah family up to 1920 and were regarded as part of the *bani khudayr*, the "green stock" who had no clear tribal origin, along with "Omanis, 'stray' Arabs who had lost tribal affiliation, and people of African origin."[32] In addition, Baluch were said to serve in the pearling industry as divers and pullers, along with south Persians and people of African origin, although this has been disputed.[33]

[29] Interviews in Oman, 1990 and 2012.

[30] Peterson, "Oman's Diverse Society: Northern Oman," p. 37; Behrooz Barjasteh Delforooz, "A Sociolinguistic Survey Amongst the Jadgal in Iranian Balochistan," in Jahani et al., *Baloch and Others*, p. 25.

[31] Harrison, *In Afghanistan's Shadow*, pp. 121–2. The Baluch speaker also claimed that there were 350,000 Baluch living in the Arab Gulf states. Ibid.

[32] Fuad I. Khuri, *Tribe and State in Bahrain: The Transformation of Social and Political Authority in an Arab State*, Chicago: University of Chicago Press, 1980, pp. 47 and 51.

[33] Ibid., pp. 59–66; interview in Bahrain, 2012.

As in Oman, the second factor in Baluch immigration was prompted by the community's reputation for martial service. As part of the nascent efforts to modernize the government in Bahrain, recruitment began in Muscat in February 1924 of 150 men, many of them Baluch, for service in Bahrain. Most of them were recruited from the Muscat Infantry, who were originally from the Sistan Levy Corps. In July 1924, 107 of these soldiers arrived in Bahrain as the nucleus of the new Bahrain Levy Corps (BLC). While nearly all of the force's composition in 1925 was Baluch, they were broken down into forty-six British subjects, twenty-three Persian, thirty-nine Muscat (from Gwadar), plus one Yemeni.

The BLC was not a success, however, particularly after several non-commissioned Indian officers were shot by their men. In addition, an attempt was made to murder the head of the existing police force (apparently this was the municipal police of al-Manamah founded in 1920 and composed mainly of Persians) and the British political agent was wounded. As a consequence, the BLC was disbanded and 186 Baluch of the BLC and the old police were deported that same year. A new Bahrain Police Force recruited from the Punjab was hastily created that year to provide defense against al-Dawasir attackers from al-Dammam that the BLC was unable to do.[34]

The Punjabis proved to be unsuitable, and so the government began to bring in local recruits. However, many Bahrainis were unwilling to join because of the association of paramilitary activities with socially inferior minorities, so the force was comprised mainly of African stock with some Baluch, Yemenis, Omanis, Pakistanis, and Iraqis. It was not until after Bahrain's independence in 1971 that Bahrainis, mainly Sunni Arabs from urban lower-income groups, came to predominate. In contrast, the Bahrain Defense Force (BDF), created in 1968, found its personnel among Sunni tribal groupings.[35] In later years, the Bahrain Police came increasingly to rely upon non-Bahraini personnel, including Jordanians, Pakistanis, and Yemenis. Many of these, all Sunnis, were said to have been given Bahraini citizenship in a deliberate attempt, according

[34] United Kingdom, British Library, Oriental and India Office Collections, Government of India, Political (External) Files & Collections, L/P&S/12/3719, "Administration Report of the Persian Gulf for the Year 1926"; Political Residency in the Persian Gulf Records, R/15/1/437, "Bahrain Levy Corps," various correspondence.

[35] Khuri, *Tribe and State in Bahrain*, pp. 114–15.

to the Bahraini political opposition, to redress the sectarian imbalance. Certainly, many of these have been Baluch. Recent reports have spoken of the government's efforts to hire "hundreds" of retired Pakistani Baluch soldiers and police to join the Bahrain National Guard and the BDF.[36]

The Baluch community in Bahrain remains small. In Manamah, it is centered on a mosque on Palace Road, originally built by a wealthy merchant in the 1920s and later taken over by the Baluch. The Baluch Welfare Society was founded in 1973, although it was banned shortly afterwards due to fears that it would become involved in politics. It was followed by the Baluch Club, established later in 1973 as a cultural and sports club.[37] As of 2013, one member of the Bahraini Council of Ministers carried the name of al-Balushi.

The Other GCC States

There is considerably less information available on the Baluch in the other Gulf states, although small communities exist in each of the GCC countries. The Joshua Project lists a population of 14,000 Baluch in Saudi Arabia, 37,000 in Qatar, and 565,000 in the UAE, but these numbers are unverifiable.[38]

It cannot be determined how old the Baluch community in the UAE is, but it is logical to assume that it predates the oil era that spurred the massive immigration of expatriates. At least two distinct older communities of Baluch can be discerned. One resides in al-'Ayn, the inland second city of Abu Dhabi, and presumably is related to the al-Balush tribe of Oman's al-Dhahirah region.[39]

[36] Bruce Riedel in the *National Interest*, 2 Aug. 2011.

[37] http://www.balochclub.org; interview with Ali Akbar Bushehri in Bahrain, 2012. Bushehri believes that the Baluch in Bahrain are of recent arrival and the earliest document he has found referring to them dates only from 1930. He also contends that they were not known to be involved in pearling. Furthermore, the British agency and the government of Bahrain in the early twentieth century relied upon Minawis (Persians from Minab, near Bandar Abbas) for security duties and not Baluch. Lorimer's *Gazetteer* (vol. II, p. 258) makes note of "an appreciable part of the population" from Minab district. Nelida Fuccaro, *Histories of City and State in the Gulf: Manama Since 1800*, Cambridge: Cambridge University Press, 2009, p. 93, asserts that Baluch, along with fellow "dispossessed" Persians and former slaves, provided casual labor for the harbor and pearling industries.

[38] See comment on The Joshua Project in note 8.

[39] Interview in the UAE, 2012.

The other community in Kalbah, on Sharjah's Gulf of Oman coast, is comprised of Iranian Baluch who left Iran to escape claimed oppression by Muhammad Reza Shah Pahlavi, who was apparently seeking to "modernize" the Baluch by abolishing old customs such as the veiling of women. Some of this group settled in Shinas in Oman and both settlements served the Sultanate of Oman as paramilitary groups, as explained earlier. Presumably in this connection, British intelligence reported in the late 1960s that a cell of the Free Baluch Movement, allegedly supported by Iraq in order to embarrass the Iranians, was in operation in Dubai, as well as Abu Dhabi and Muscat.[40] Other communities of more recently arrived Baluch presumably came as menial and semi-skilled laborers during the oil boom years.

One effect of the emergence of Dubai as a transnational, cosmopolitan metropolis has been its attraction as a place of exile or second home for politicians from various parts of the Middle East and Asia. For example, Pakistan's Benazir Bhutto spent most of her time in Dubai during her years in exile and her children were also educated there. Pakistani politics in Baluchistan has produced another connection. One observer contends that "The State [of Baluchistan] is being increasingly administered not from Quetta, but from Karachi or Dubai. The members of the Baloch State Government are being increasingly seen by the people as quislings of Islamabad and are afraid of staying in Quetta. They spend more time in Karachi or Dubai than in Quetta. Government files go to them for orders there."[41]

The size of the Baluch community in Kuwait is unknown. There is a feeling that Baluch have been there for a long time, as they have in Oman, but there is no available evidence one way or the other. Because they are Sunni, they assimilate rather easily—contrary to the Shi'i for

[40] FCO/8/1256, Abu Dhabi Intelligence Reports, Record of Abu Dhabi Local Intelligence Committee Meeting of 12 Nov. 1969.

[41] B. Raman, "Weakening Pakistani hold in Balochistan," South Asian Analysis Group, paper no. 3958, 30 July 2010, http://www.southasiaanalysis.org/%5Cpapers40%5Cpaper3958.html. Raman quotes the *The News* (Karachi) of 25 July 2010 as charging that "While half of the province [of Balochistan] is inundated because of floods, killing scores of people, Chief Minister Aslam Raisani is languishing in Dubai. His staff said he was in Dubai for many days and they could not confirm when he would return. In any case, he is known to be a part-time CM as he lives in Dubai or Islamabad nearly 15 days a month and is never available, intelligibly that is ..."

example. Many are indistinguishable from other Kuwaitis, even in name (except for those few who call themselves al-Balushi). Interestingly, however, there has been a small revival of social or ethnic *diwaniyahs* (a casual social or political gathering of family, friends, or constituents), among them al-Awadi and Baluch. Yet these *diwaniyahs* have been established more for political than ethnic reasons. The meetings allow them to host candidates for parliament and to promise votes. In return, a successful candidate does not hesitate to listen to their grievances. The utility of this approach does not depend on the concentration of Baluch in specific constituencies but rather represents a countrywide voice.[42]

Conclusion

This chapter has introduced and analyzed the limited amount of detail available about the presence and roles of the Baluch residents of the Arab side of the Gulf. Certainly the biggest contribution to Gulf society has been in Oman where the Baluch are not only numerous but exceedingly long settled.

It is widely held that Baluch have been well represented in the creation of modern armies and police forces in various states of the Arabian littoral, not just Oman and Bahrain, although details are unavailable. In addition, Baluch from Pakistani Baluchistan and presumably the Baluch areas of Iran as well have been attracted to jobs in the Gulf over the last several decades. Again, detailed information is lacking, although it can be surmised that in general the poverty and low levels of education in Baluchistan means that most of these Baluch are employed as unskilled or semi-skilled workers. Similar to other expatriate communities, these workers play no role in local politics and, because of their extreme vulnerability to arrest and deportation, tend to eschew political activities related to their homelands. Still, this has not prevented all political activities. Baluch opposition groups in Pakistan opposed the emigration of better-educated Baluch to service in Oman in the 1970s and 1980s and prominent figures called for an end to it.[43]

The Baluch residents on the Arab side of the Gulf, and particularly those who hold citizenship in the GCC states, are among the least

[42] Interview in Kuwait, 2012.

[43] Collett, "Baluch Service in the Forces of Oman," p. 9.

noticeable and least contentious minorities. Those of long residence have fit well into local society and have contributed significantly to their countries' military forces, civilian governments, and large and small businesses. Their presence adds to the richness of Gulf society and politics without creating significant challenges.

8

IRAN'S ETHNIC, RELIGIOUS, AND TRIBAL MINORITIES

Lois Beck

In this chapter I investigate identity and politics in contemporary Iran as they relate to the languages, religions, ethnicities, national minorities, and tribes there. Writers on Iran often blend or confuse these terms or intermix them with others. Additional factors relevant to a discussion of Iran's people and related to the five entities include the geographical region, level of economic development there, placement (center or periphery, urban or rural), livelihood, socio-economic standing, and integration and assimilation in the nation-state. If authors consider societal complexity, they sometimes include people such as the Kurds or Armenians but without discussing what these labels mean or how such groups have changed over time.[1]

[1] I thank Mehran Kamrava and the Center for International and Regional Studies at Georgetown University's School of Foreign Service in Qatar for organizing and hosting this productive working group. Lawrence Potter, Mehran Kamrava, Julia Huang, Shahla Haeri, Mary Martin, Christian Bromberger, and the work-

The identity of a Kurdish man living in Iran in the early twenty-first century, for example, involves a language (one or more regional variants of Kurdish), a religion (Sunni or Shi'i and perhaps Sufi Islam), ethnic and other cultural features, national minority awareness, and possibly tribal affiliation. He calls a specific underdeveloped region of northwestern Iran home, he is an urban or a rural dweller, and his socio-economic status relates to his family and its livelihood. He is more or less integrated and assimilated in the nation-state of Iran, depending on his background, place of residence, level of formal education, occupation, inclination, and degree of orientation toward the Kurdish people. He emphasizes his Kurdish linguistic, religious, ethnic, and tribal identities according to the intensity of these affiliations for him. Likewise, he relates to an Iranian national identity based on his experiences. Each of these traits is fluid and reflects his stage in life and the particular context at the time. His politicization as a Kurd (and any of its associated identities, such as membership in a Sufi order) also pertains to his background. If he is a Sunni Muslim, he may feel alienated from the Shi'i-dominant Islamic Republic of Iran. Even if he is a Shi'i Muslim, the Sufi orientation of his sect may antagonize the government. Iranian state agents might have attacked or harassed him or his family members, leaving him further estranged. After a kinsman, conscripted by force by the Iranian army, was killed in the Iraq–Iran War, he might have intensified his negative sentiments against the two nation-states. If he lives close to the Iraqi border, he interacts periodically with relatives and tribesmates in Iraq, an association that heightens his sectarian sentiments rather than his loyalties to Iran. Perhaps he supports a Kurdish political party, participates in other civil society non-governmental organizations, and is attracted to regional Islamist movements. His access to the Internet and

shop participants offered helpful comments on this chapter, and Khaled Fattah, Ziba Mir-Hosseini, Shahnaz Nadjmabadi, Georg Stober, and Gernot Windfuhr provided useful information. Julia Huang assisted me with the final draft when I visited her in 2013 in her anthropological research site in rural Bangladesh. I base this chapter on periodic residence and research in Iran over a five-decade period and on research among Iranians in the diaspora in the Middle East, Europe, and the United States. My cultural-anthropological research in Iran has focused on the Turkish-speaking, tribally organized, nomadic, pastoral Qashqa'i, who are one of Iran's many ethnolinguistic minorities.

his growing reliance on the related technologies and media link him further with other Kurds in the region and the world. The political autonomy of Iraqi Kurdistan intrigues him. The Turkish military's continuing oppression of Kurds in Turkey appalls him. And the civil war in Syria with its debilitating effects on the large Kurdish community there horrifies him.

This example illustrates the complexities of identity formation, its multiple bases, the interrelationship of its components, and the ways identity can be politicized. It also demonstrates the importance of history and geography and how these complexities change through time and according to location. Labels of different sorts—such as "Sufi," tribal names, and even "Kurd"—are political constructions to be employed for specific purposes. A person's identity is unlike that of any other person because of its multiple, interlinking features, its historical and geographical specificities, and the ways its components alter in importance for the person during his life. Identity is fluid and malleable for the individual and changes over a lifetime and according to context. Certain aspects of identity rise in importance and expression over time while others recede.

Most writers on Iran focus, often implicitly, on the Persian elements of society and culture and ignore the other half of society. Many of them equate the terms "Persian" and "Iranian," thus negating the self-identities, even the very existence, of all citizens who are not Persians. They may comment on recent political unrest in Baluchistan or Khuzistan (two of Iran's border provinces) but without examining the circumstances or the participants, and they may regard the disturbances as threatening to Iran's territorial and political integrity regardless of any legitimate reasons for protest. Any discussion needs to acknowledge and take into consideration the diversity of Iranian society, which includes Persians and an equivalent number of many other peoples.

Here I focus on the political dimensions of identity in contemporary Iran, after the revolution in 1978–9 against Mohammad Reza Shah Pahlavi and the declaration of the Islamic Republic of Iran. Iran is an especially intriguing country given the suddenness with which political activists and a popular mobilization forced the transition from a seemingly well-established, modernizing, westernizing, and secularizing regime to a regime that aimed to stop and reverse these trends through the consolidation of power and authority by a newly reemerging politico-religious elite.

This abrupt transition had an impact on all dimensions of Iranian society, including its languages, religions, ethnicities, national minorities, and tribes. Iranians use these categories to identify themselves and others, and outsiders find them useful. Other issues also pertain to identity, such as regional, socio-economic, and educational factors, which I address. Geography especially corresponds with and affects each category. Here I outline the five entities, and in separate sections below I discuss how they each relate to the diverse peoples of contemporary Iran.

As a foundation of Iranian society, language is fundamental to constructions of identity. It forms part of a social and cultural matrix, each feature influencing the others. Language can become politicized within this larger context. The major language groups in Iran are Indo-Iranian, Altaic, and Semitic, with variations in each family, and other languages are represented as well. Language is a major identifying characteristic of each of the four other categories.

Religion, the second category, has saliency for every Iranian. As another foundation of society, it has social, cultural, and political dimensions for its adherents. In 1979 the Islamic Republic proclaimed a particular version of Twelver Shi'i Islam as the heart of the state and society. Iranians who are Muslims but not Shi'is, who are part of Shi'i sects that the state does not condone, or who are not Muslims, have experienced this development in profound, often negative, ways. These other Iranians include Sunni Muslims, Bahais, Christians of different sects, Jews, Zoroastrians, and Mandaeans. Iranians advocating the implementation of secular ideals, regardless of their religious backgrounds, oppose the official, legitimized, and sometimes mandated intersection of religion, government, politics, and society in Iran.

Third, ethnicity also affects every Iranian. Ethnic identity for Iran's Persians—the dominating half of society—is more amorphous and less explicit than the ethnic identities of other Iranians, for reasons this chapter explains. Most Iranians in Iran are influenced to different degrees by Persians, the Persian language, and the Persian attributes of Iran's national identity, while Persians are not necessarily affected by Iran's other languages and ethnicities. In asking some urban Persian Iranians about cultural diversity in Iran, I found that many did not understand the question. Some of them seemed disinclined to consider themselves a "group" that could be equivalent to any of Iran's minority groups, and some resisted the notion. Some elevated their identity as

Persians above those of Iran's other ethnicities, about whom they offered often disparaging remarks regarding their backwardness and lack of sophistication. I examine the impact of these asymmetries.

The fourth category is national minority status. Unlike language, religion, and ethnicity, this factor is explicitly relevant for only certain segments of Iranian society. Only some Iranians have a politicized sense of "nation" that differs from that of the Iranian nation. Over time, national minority identities emerge, develop, and perhaps recede, similar to and yet different from the ongoing changes in the identities formed by language, religion, and ethnicity. The Iranian state, neighboring nation-states, and outside powers view Iran's national minorities as threats to the territorial and political integrity of Iran, the security of its neighbors, and the stability of the region. Language, religion, and ethnicity impact the lives of all Iranians, but these traits are politicized to a higher degree among the national minorities. A focus on the minorities requires a parallel discussion of Iranian nationalism and its relation to the history, geography, languages, religions, societies, and cultures of Iran. Many people, particularly the Persian-speaking majority in Iran, equate Iranian and Persian nationalism. Those who are not Persians find this notion objectionable, if not offensive, and are motivated to reassess their place in Iran and to highlight their own minority nationalisms.

Fifth, tribal affiliations are also relevant for only certain sectors of Iranian society, and they are politicized in ways similar to those of the national minorities. They also have linguistic, religious, and ethnic characteristics, which strengthen these cultural systems and the polities of which they are a part. Tribal people are organized politically by means of certain structures and ideologies, which differentiates them from Iran's non-tribal peoples. As groups, they have the ability to defend their interests and repel incursions by activating these structures, organizations, and ideologies. Tribal structures are alternative systems to state structures, and states often regard these polities as threats and try to subjugate, relocate, or eliminate them. States also exploit tribal systems for their own benefit, such as sending tribesmen to fight enemies or invaders, and tribal people participate in some state institutions without necessarily distancing themselves from their own polities.

These linguistic, religious, ethnic, national minority, and tribal factors in Iran interrelate in people's constructions of their identities. Sometimes individuals and groups stress one factor over others; sometimes another factor takes precedence. People invoke these identities according to specific times, situations, and contexts.

Baluch nationalists in Iran, for example, stress their religious sect (Sunni Islam) to differentiate themselves from the Shi'i Muslims who control state power, while Baluch nationalists in neighboring Pakistan emphasize their language (Baluchi) and their uniquely Baluch religion (the Zikri sect of Islam). The Baluch in Pakistan share Sunni Islam with most citizens there, while their language contrasts with the state's official ones (Urdu and English) and provides a distinctive, unifying symbolic system for them.

As another example, if some Baluch in the Iranian city of Zahedan meet to negotiate a marriage alliance, they focus on their lineage and tribal affiliations. They hold certain linguistic, religious, ethnic, and regional factors in common and would not need to mention them in their discussions. Other issues such as kinship ties and residential locations would figure more prominently when these Baluch decide whose daughter will marry whose son and what consequences their families and kinship groups may experience. If the same Baluch meet with kinsmen who have just returned on furlough from their wage-labor jobs in Doha, they are apt to talk about the Baluch community in Qatar; its origins in Pakistan, Iran, and Afghanistan; and its overlapping linguistic, religious, ethnic, and tribal characteristics compared with those of other foreign migrant workers in the Persian Gulf states.

After commenting on the Persian Gulf region and on theoretical and methodological issues, I investigate the ways the five categories relate to Iranian society and politics during the post-revolutionary era. In the conclusion, I outline overarching and underlying topics relating to sectarianism (as broadly defined) in Iran.

Geographical Context

The focus of this volume on the region of the Persian Gulf invites comparisons between and among the Gulf's nation-states and other nearby countries.[2]

[2] For unifying factors that have led historically to the region's distinctiveness, see Lawrence G. Potter, "Introduction," in Lawrence G. Potter (ed.), *The Persian Gulf in History*, New York: Palgrave Macmillan, 2009.

The political role that Iran plays in the Persian Gulf region affects each country there and its own diverse citizenry. Expatriate Iranians are long-term residents as well as more recent immigrants, migrant workers, and visitors in these countries.[3] The Islamic regime in Tehran attempts to influence the Shi'i Muslims in the Gulf region, including expatriate Shi'i Iranians.[4] Rulers in the Persian Gulf aim to protect themselves from Iran's expanding reach and regard Iran's efforts to develop its nuclear industry as a threat. International sanctions against Iran, because of the nuclear issue and other provocations, increase the pressure on its leaders to respond and could result in yet another military action in the region, especially if Iran's military restricts access to the narrow Strait of Hormuz, through which the oil that other countries depend on passes.[5] The US military expands its presence and vigilance in the Persian Gulf region because of Iran's postures, and any escalation would affect the other Gulf states and the extent of their cooperation with the United States. Rulers in the region who intensify their military and political ties

[3] Iranian residents include those born in Iran and those of Iranian ancestry: Kuwait (80,000), Saudi Arabia (few), Bahrain (172,000), Qatar (270,000), and the United Arab Emirates (500,000). I comment in the next section on the use of population figures and percentages in this chapter. The term "Ajam" or "Ajami" refers to Persians (as compared to Arabs) in some parts of the Persian Gulf region. In other parts it means Shi'i Muslims or Iranians, especially people from Iran's south (the Gulf littoral). On this topic and others, the literature does not often distinguish between "Persians" and "Iranians," and the actual identities of the people to whom writers refer are unclear or unknown. Iran's coastal Sunni Arabs currently use the term "Ajam" for inland people, to denote their Shi'i affiliation; see Shahnaz Nadjmabadi, "The Arab Presence on the Iranian Coast of the Persian Gulf," in *The Persian Gulf in History*, p. 140. Early on, Arabs had used the term for Iranians who converted to Islam but did not speak Arabic. They often deployed the label pejoratively. Later the term also became a generic linguistic, ethnic, geographical, and/or national designation.

[4] Shi'is in the Persian Gulf states, as a percentage of each country's Muslim population, include: Iraq (62–70 percent), Kuwait (20–35 percent), Saudi Arabia (10–25 percent), Bahrain (58–74 percent), Qatar (10–19 percent), United Arab Emirates (9–10 percent), Oman (3–10 percent), and Yemen (Shi'i Zaydis (Fivers), 34–45 percent). For a map, see: http://gulf2000.columbia.edu/images/maps/GulfReligionGeneral_lg.jpg

[5] Recent hostilities include the Iraq–Iran War (1980–8), the Persian Gulf War in response to Saddam Hussein's invasion of Kuwait (1990–1), and the US invasion and occupation of Iraq (2003–11).

with the United States face growing opposition among some citizens, especially those who support Islamist movements.

Iran's major ethnic minorities (including Arabs, Kurds, Armenians, Azeri Turks, Turkmans, and Baluch) are located along the borders of the respective neighboring states of Iraq, Turkey, Armenia, Azerbaijan, Turkmenistan, Afghanistan, and Pakistan. Ethnic majorities and other large ethnic concentrations similar to Iran's citizens are found in these states. Iran's relationships with its neighbors are often influenced by their common, sometimes potentially opposing, ethnic and religious components.

Other authors in this volume consider the Persian Gulf countries of Iraq, Kuwait, Saudi Arabia, Bahrain, Qatar, the United Arab Emirates, Oman, and neighboring Yemen. The rulers of these states consider the religious and ethnic diversity there problematic for regime stability. Vast numbers of temporary and semi-permanent migrant workers who originate in many countries complicate the issue of population dynamics.

The Persian Gulf country sharing an international land border with Iran is Iraq, and the linguistic, religious, ethnic, national minority, and tribal identities of their two populations are similar.[6] Some groups are found in both countries, and some overlap the border. The autonomous northern Kurdish region of Iraq worries Iran (and neighboring Turkey and Syria).[7] Shi'i-Sunni distinctions in Iraq's state and society are more pronounced and politicized than in Iran, partly because the two groups are more equivalent in size in Iraq. Major Shi'i shrines and seminaries are located in Iraq and bring millions of pilgrims and students every year, especially from Iran. Iran has assisted by political, military, and financial means the rise of Shi'i political influence in Iraq since Saddam Hussein's overthrow in 2003, an issue that unsettles other components

[6] For Iraq's ethnic breakdown, see: http://gulf2000.columbia.edu/images/maps/Iraq_Ethnic_lg.jpg. Some sources on Iraq list its Shi'i Muslim population as 55 percent (and not 62–70 percent), perhaps referring only to Shi'i Arabs and not also to Shi'i Kurds, Shi'i Turkmans, and other Shi'is who are not Arabs. Some Sunnis in Iraq say that Sunnis comprise 42 percent of the country and Shi'is 41 percent (Fanar Haddad, "Sectarian Relations and Sunni Identity in Post-Civil War Iraq", this volume). Houchang Chehabi discusses historical connections; "Iran and Iraq," in Abbas Amanat and Farzin Vejdani (eds), *Iran Facing Others: Identity Boundaries in a Historical Perspective*, New York: Palgrave Macmillan, 2012.

[7] Kurds comprise 15–21 percent of Iraq's population; 3 million Kurds are located in the three northern governorates.

of Iraqi society, especially Sunnis, who had formerly predominated in the government.[8] The US military occupation of Iraq (2003–11) and its continuing presence there in 2013 have led to the death, injury, and displacement of millions of citizens; destroyed institutions, industries, and infrastructure; reoriented and accentuated sectarian conflicts; disrupted the restoration of government and civil society; and made Iraq more vulnerable to outside influences (especially Iran, Turkey, Syria, and regional and global Islamist groups including al-Qaeda).

Iran's internal and foreign policies also affect the nearby countries of Turkey, Afghanistan, and Pakistan. As with Iraq, comparisons between Iran and its other immediate neighbors demonstrate their similarities (and differences) and counter the efforts of other writers to portray Iran as an isolated, anomalous state.

Turkey has a large population of Kurds, as does Iran, but the Turkish government finds the issue more problematic than Iran's does.[9] In seeking to expand and reinforce the concept of Turkish citizenship and identity, the government used to label its Kurdish inhabitants as "mountain Turks" and more recently has called them "Turks of Kurdish background." Its military has tried to suppress them; they have resisted, sometimes violently, and have supported political parties that demand greater rights, autonomy, or independence, such as the Kurdish Workers' Party (PKK). Being a Kurd in Turkey is politically charged in ways that the Kurds in Iran do not experience as intensely. Turkey is not as diverse as Iran in the languages, religions, ethnicities, national minorities, and tribes found there, but these entities and topics are still present and continue to have resonance, due in part to the legacy of the vast Ottoman Empire and its inclusion of disparate peoples. Turkey's proclaimed secularism since 1923 has raised issues for members of all its religious communities, Sunni Muslims being the vast majority.[10] Iran and Turkey share a border, and emigrating Iranians (via legal or other

[8] Sunni Muslims in Iraq include some of the Arabs, Kurds, and Turkmans.

[9] The 14–19 million Kurds in Turkey comprise 18–25 percent of the national population (2011).

[10] Turkey's population is 97 percent Muslim, with Sunnis being 85–90 percent of all Muslims. Many of Turkey's Shi'i Muslims (Alevis) are Kurds, an affiliation prejudicing the Turkish government and military against both peoples. Richard Tapper and Nancy Tapper discuss contradictory elements in Turkey's secularism in "'Thank God We're Secular!'" in Lionel Caplan (ed.), *Aspects of Religious Fundamentalism*, London: Macmillan, 1987.

channels) find Turkey hospitable; the government does not require Iranian visitors to obtain visas. Turkey is a gateway to Europe for many Iranians, whose population in Turkey has soared since 1979.[11]

Afghanistan is similar to Iran in societal composition and diversity, but it lacks the state institutional structures and organizations that are essential to the centralization of power in Iran. Afghanistan has suffered foreign occupations and civil war in ways never experienced by Iran. The continuing presence of oppositional Taliban and al-Qaeda forces there, and the US and NATO military occupation since 2001, affect neighboring Iran and its foreign policies. Sunni Muslims dominate politics in Afghanistan, unlike in Iran and Iraq (after 2003).[12] Afghanistan's leaders and power brokers (including the Taliban) have often been Pashtuns, a powerful tribally organized ethno-linguistic group.[13] The long, open border between Afghanistan and Iran creates security issues and allows relatively free passage, in both directions, for refugees and emigrants.

Like Iran, Pakistan has a diverse population and a centralizing government, but it relies more heavily on its military and intelligence services to control the citizenry. Pakistan's leaders are predominantly Sunni Muslims.[14] Iran and Pakistan also share a border. Pakistan is a US ally in the fight against al-Qaeda and the Taliban, despite sectors of Pakistan's government, military, and security services aiding and abetting these non-state actors. US ties with Pakistan add to US–Iran tensions. The US military presence throughout the Persian Gulf region furthers Iran's agitation about being encircled.[15]

Incoming refugees have complicated Iran's relationships with its neighbors. Civil war in Afghanistan, Taliban oppression, and the US and NATO bombings and occupation since 2001 have driven many

[11] Turkey hosted hundreds of thousands, perhaps a million, Iranian asylum seekers, refugees, immigrants, and long-term visitors in 2013, more than any other country in the world.

[12] Muslims in Afghanistan are 85–90 percent Sunni and 10–15 percent Shi'i.

[13] Pashtuns, Afghanistan's largest ethnic group, are about 40 percent of the national population. Thomas Barfield discusses the country's ethnic matrix in "Afghanistan's Ethnic Puzzle," *Foreign Affairs*, 90 (2011), pp. 54–65. For a tribal map of Afghanistan, color-coded by ethnic affiliations, see: http://gulf2000.columbia.edu/images/maps/Afghanistan_Tribes_lg.jpg

[14] Muslims in Pakistan are 85–94 percent Sunni and 6–15 percent Shi'i.

[15] The caption for a map of Iran reads, "Iran Wants War. Look How Close They Put Their Country to Our Military Bases"; https://www.facebook.com/MisesvsKeynes

refugees westward into Iran. Three recent wars involving Iraq (1980–8, 1990–1, 2003–11) forced refugees across Iraq's eastern border and into Iran. Religious and ethnic factors meshed with politics when Shi'is and Sunnis of varying ethnicities (especially Kurds) fled from Saddam Hussein's persecutions before, during, and after the Iraq–Iran War. Refugees strained economic and social services in Iran and intensified linguistic, religious, ethnic, national minority, and tribal sentiments there. Iran has tried to expel the Afghans; many refugees from Afghanistan and Iraq have returned home on their own.

Refugees and other emigrants from Iran are also part of this discussion. Iran's minority peoples, especially those targeted since 1979 by violence and discrimination, have left the country in larger proportions than have members of the dominating Shi'i and Persian majorities. Still, most emigrants from Iran have been Persians, primarily Shi'is but also the non-Muslim religious minorities, and are often from the well-educated and professional middle and upper classes. Their residence abroad, likely to be permanent for most of them, has changed the society remaining behind, especially given the loss of people with the expertise and specialized skills of modern professions. Many countries host large diaspora communities of Iranians.[16] Potential emigrants are more likely to leave Iran if they have social networks (including family and group members) in foreign countries. New technologies and the Internet have facilitated these interconnections. People's online discussions about identity in Iran, the diaspora, and the host countries demonstrate the new dynamics. Websites appealing to specific groups, such as Zoroastrians, connect people to Iran, integrate them in larger global communities, and intensify and further politicize people's ethnic and related identities.

Theoretical and Methodological Considerations

Iran's sectarian, infra-national, "competing subnational mass-group identities" are this chapter's focus.[17] Non-sectarian, transversal, cross-societal

[16] Including millions of people in 2013, the Iranian diaspora consists of Iranians born in Iran but living outside Iran (the first generation) with their children and grandchildren (born abroad, the second and third generations). The diaspora differs from other Iranian peoples who have historically lived outside of Iran, such as in Afghanistan, Tajikistan, and the Caucasus.

[17] Haddad, this volume.

mobilizations in society—based on socio-economic class, religious ideology (such as fundamentalism in general, without stressing sectarian attributes), and other ideologies (such as democracy, secular nationalism, socialism, and communism)—underlie and overlap with sectarian identities.[18] Studies of Iran's urban poor, Islamic reformists, and leftists, for example, demonstrate the ways that non-sectarian and sectarian factors intersect. Leftists may regard their Tudeh or Mojahedin affiliation as the most profound aspect of their personal, social, and political identities, but their sectarian associations help to explain their educational trajectories, political choices, and dedication to certain ideologies.

Sectarian identities emerge in dynamic fashion, are politically motivated, and are contingent, relational, and shifting. Despite their flexibility, they also have elements of stability. Once born into a specific subnational group (however defined), individuals have difficulty joining another group in the same category. Group borders are relatively impermeable in this regard. Especially in face-to-face communities, religious conversion is difficult, as is trying to "pass" (dissimulate) as a member of a group that is not one's own.[19] Some people are part of multiple sectarian groups (such as the Sunni Kurds in Iran); each identity relates to the other and yet has its own compelling character. As contexts change, so do the relative valuations.[20] People in dominant groups have fewer incentives to emphasize their sectarian identities than those in subordinate groups. When the balance of power between them shifts, so do their self-identities.[21] The Pahlavi shahs (1925–79) had advocated notions of secular nationalism for Iran, while the Islamic regime has favored a form of national unity created by Twelver

[18] Marc Valeri, "Identity Politics and Nation-Building under Sultan Qaboos," this volume; Justin Gengler, "Understanding Sectarianism in the Persian Gulf," this volume.

[19] Jews in Iran who converted to Islam were still called "new converts" 100 years later and were still discriminated against, and some "converts" were actually crypto-Jews (those who were still Jews, secretly); see Daniel Tsadik, "Identity among the Jews of Iran," in *Iran Facing Others*.

[20] The Pahlavi regimes denigrated ethnic Kurds while the Islamic Republic was hostile toward Sunnis and Sufis, whether or not they were also Kurds.

[21] Haddad (this volume) discusses the changing balance between Sunnis and Shi'is in Iraq since 2003. The Sunni–Shi'i divide in Bahrain intensified during the Pearl Uprising and Saudi Arabia's military intervention in 2011 (Kristin Diwan, this volume).

Shi'i affiliation. Ethnic identities change more slowly than national loyalties. People internalize ethnic notions, thus giving these constructs greater durability.

Modern notions of nationalism emerged in Iran only in the early twentieth century and cannot be applied to previous eras.[22] Iranians shaped their national identity by appropriating and misappropriating features from Iran's cultural past.[23] Before the modern nation-state, people defined their relationships to extra-local polities (such as tribal confederacies, khanates, ruling dynasties, and empires) by acts of loyalty to local, mediating rulers. Sectarian identities, however related to earlier affiliations, took new forms when a modernizing nation-state emerged in Iran, and they posed challenges to and vied with the national identity as it developed. Sectarianism and nationalism interrelate, each forming and enhancing the other.

This chapter requires specific, detailed, numerical information about the diverse peoples of contemporary Iran. Yet reliable and accurate statistics do not exist, and the figures and percentages included in the text, notes, and tables come from hundreds of sources, are often averages or ranges (10–20 percent), and are approximations.[24] Iranian census data for the past and present do not exist for the five categories considered here.[25]

Iran's population in 2013 was approximately 79 million. Any figures for the country's component peoples are not current, and writers do not usually provide even approximate years for the numbers they include.[26] Except for Persian-speakers and the non-Muslim religious minorities, the estimated percentages found in the literature for each of Iran's diverse peoples in the country's total population were probably still relevant for 2013. The percentage of Persian-speakers has increased over recent decades because of Iran's expanding educational system, continuing rural-to-urban migration, and rising rates of bilingualism, but the

[22] Some scholars extend modern notions of national identity back through time, such as to the Achaemenians or Sasanians. Afshin Matin-asgari examines recent debates in "The Academic Debate on Iranian Identity," in *Iran Facing Others*.

[23] Abbas Amanat, "Iranian Identity Boundaries," in *Iran Facing Others*.

[24] Limitations of space prevent me from citing most of these sources.

[25] Bernard Hourcade et al. demonstrate the categories used in censuses and other surveys in Iran, such as urban and rural distributions; see *Atlas d'Iran*, Paris: Reclus, 1998.

[26] All numbers should have a corresponding year so that annual population increases and decreases can be calculated.

percentages of speakers of other languages have probably remained about the same.[27] The primary identities of most speakers of other languages are still linked to their linguistic, religious, ethnic, national minority, and tribal groups and not necessarily to Persian society and culture or the nation-state of Iran, regardless of how fluent in Persian they become. Many Iranians who are not Muslims have emigrated since 1978–9, and their percentages in Iran's total population have decreased.

The characteristics of each of the five categories in Iran have different degrees of visibility. How do Iranians and outsiders classify the citizens of Iran, and on what bases? What traits distinguish one social group from another? Some traits are objective, in the sense that we can accurately describe, count, or measure them, such as demographic patterns (Gilakis inhabiting the Caspian Sea coast, for example), specific clothing (fringed headdresses), and particular kinds of dwellings (felt yurts). Other traits are subjective and more difficult to assess. Members of an ethnic group may claim that they are more hospitable to guests than are members of another group, but an outsider would have difficulty verifying this assertion. How could a general, even abstract, concept, such as hospitality, honor, or women's modesty, be measured and compared between and among communities?[28] Many defining traits connected with identity have both objective and subjective features, as in their outer appearances and inner meanings. A man shopping in the Shiraz bazaar for a horse saddle wears a beige felt hat with two upstanding flaps. What does the hat mean to this man and to others who see him? His accompanying kinsman left his hat at home when he traveled to Shiraz. What are his reasons (practical and otherwise) for doing so?

In anthropology, when we consider cultural systems such as ethnicity or tribal identity, we rely on notions of ascription and self-ascription (or self-identity) in concert.[29] Is a particular person regarded by others as a

[27] The increased incidence of bilingualism explains the imbalance in these two percentages. Speakers of other languages retain them even though they may also adopt (some) Persian.

[28] Notions such as hospitality are more complex than just their physical expressions, for example, the number of glasses of tea that a host offers a guest. Subjective notions such as honor may be more significant to people and their identities than any objective traits.

[29] Anthropologists also compare ascribed (given, acquired) and achieved (earned) identities. Even where people increasingly value achievement, as under modernizing conditions, the ascribed elements of identity often remain strong.

member of their group, and does she or he also self-identify as a member? If a person self-identifies and others in the group agree, the juxtaposition provides the necessary connection for us. We rely on this process when we consider the more subjective aspects of identity, and we trust people with whom we talk to tell us about their concepts. If a native speaker of Tati does not identify himself as a member of the Tati ethnic group, we would ask him how he compares himself with those who do.

The multiple names and terms associated with Iran's diverse peoples complicate the discussion in this chapter. People have their own, often multiple, names for themselves and their groups and subgroups. They also name their languages, religious sects, tribes, regions, and places of residence by using variations of these names and others. Their neighbors apply yet other terms to them and their groups. Outsiders, some of whom may be hostile toward them, have still additional names, some pejorative.

The identities of men and of women in Iran often have different dynamics. Men and women most commonly trace descent from their fathers and other patrilineal kin, and their linguistic, religious, ethnic, and tribal identities are usually the same as those connected with this kin group.[30] Yet women sometimes marry men whose identities differ from theirs.[31] They join the household of their husband, and they spend

[30] Iranians sometimes say that other characteristics, such as temperament, derive from a person's mother and her family. "Look at a boy's mother's brother, and you will see what kind of a man he will become." Such an observation could be intended as a positive or a negative reference. Members of patrilineal groups often malign the attributes of the mother's side if she is not part of their group. Some middle-class, urban, Persian Iranians stress bilateral affiliations, the identities they receive from their mother's and their father's sides. On marriage, some middle-class couples establish new residences rather than live with the man's family, as had been customary in the past; separate residences contribute to the activation of bilateral ties.

[31] The predominant marriage pattern for many women in Iran is to marry within their groups, especially with close paternal kin. ("Groups," as in in-group marriage, are defined by kinship, place of residence, language, religion, ethnicity, tribe, and/or socio-economic class.) In these cases, wives and husbands share kin-group, locational, linguistic, religious, ethnic, tribal, and/or socio-economic identities, as do their daughters and sons. People who marry outside their groups experience both negative and positive social and political consequences. Men have more flexibility than women in marrying someone who is perceived to be "below" them in category or class, but they are discouraged from marrying wom-

the rest of their lives with his group and the manifestations of its various identities.[32] Their children's identities stem from their father's.[33] Thus these women identify with their natal group, but after marriage they live with their husband's group and are influenced by the identities there. For these reasons, issues of identity may be more clear-cut and continuous for men than for some women, and women who have dual, sequential associations (first their natal ones and then those of their husband and children) may have mixed sentiments.[34] Issues of identity become more complex when we consider both genders and the dynamics of kinship, marriage, and the family.

The literature mentioning or describing Iran's population sometimes includes statements about the proportion of Persians (ethnic Persians, native speakers of the Persian language) to others in Iran. Many writers and others use the terms "Persian" and "Iranian" synonymously—and confusingly.[35] They do not ordinarily define who Persians are, nor do

---

en "above" them (the women's family and group usually prohibiting it). Women can marry men "above" but not "below" them.

[32] Spatial and sociocultural factors help to explain the extent of a married woman's continuing contacts with her natal group.

[33] A member of our working group in Qatar notes that he and his wife come from different sects. When they married, they agreed that their sons would follow their father's sect (Sunni Islam) and their daughters would follow their mother's (Ibadi Islam).

[34] Women may pass some traits of their natal group to their children, who grow up attuned to the identities of both sides of their family. A multigenerational stance demonstrates the richness of these cultural details. The possibly diverse backgrounds of a man's grandmothers, mother, wife, and daughters-in-law contribute to the ways he identifies himself. Julia Huang provides accounts of women who marry within their tribal groups, and women who do not, and explains some consequences in *Tribeswomen of Iran: Weaving Memories among Qashqa'i Nomads*, London: I.B. Tauris, 2009. Naheed Dareshuri and Lois Beck show how multigenerational ties among women relate to textile production; see "Bands, Ropes, Braids, and Tassels among the Qashqa'i," in Fred Mushkat (ed.), *Warp-Faced Bands and Related Weavings*, unpublished book manuscript. Women of the Qashqa'i tribal elite created women-centered kinship links that run parallel to the otherwise dominating patriarchal, patrilineal, patrilocal system.

[35] The restrictive editorial mandate of the monumental *Encyclopædia Iranica*, since its founding and first solicitation of entries in the 1970s, has been to require all contributors at all times to use the term "Persia" for Iran and to consider all residents of "Persia" to be "Persians," regardless of their languages, cultures, and

they define any people who are not Persians, and accurate figures do not exist. Yet many writers continue to assert that Persians comprise 51 (or more) percent—that is, the majority—of Iran's population. Persians tend to overestimate the number of ethnic Persians in Iran and to stress the increasing integration of others, a process by which some non-Persians supposedly become Persians over time.[36] Iranians who are not Persians are aware of the difficulties of being a minority in Iran. As a strategy to strengthen their positions, they assert distinctive traits and affirm their internal cohesion. Persians tend to ignore or disregard the disadvantageous economic and political standing of many non-Persians, thus perpetuating (intentionally and unintentionally) these inequalities. If they do acknowledge unfavorable conditions, they do not necessarily explain the factors that created them: primarily, discrimination against these minorities by Persians and by a Persian-dominated state.[37]

As a term, "Persian" lacks the specificity of other terms such as "Assyrian." As one of Iran's many diverse peoples, Persians should have the same kinds of defining characteristics that each of the minority peoples

---

self-identities. Such a (ludicrous) practice is inaccurate, misleads readers, and furthers notions of Persian supremacy. Many other works demonstrate the same usage. Abbas Milani labels as "Persians" the 150 prominent people highlighted in his book, regardless of their actual identities; see *Eminent Persians: The Men and Women Who Made Modern Iran, 1941–1979*, 2 vols, Syracuse: Syracuse University Press, 2008. Only recently have a few Iranian scholars objected publicly to this policy (Matin-asgari, "Academic Debate").

[36] Some Persians view ambivalently people of non-Persian origins who have become Persianized. They applaud this recognition of Persian identity, but explicitly and implicitly they still remind these people of their earlier identities and the traits they have not (yet) eradicated. (Members of Iran's upper class under the shahs held the same kinds of attitudes toward the nouveau riche.) People having Persian ancestors do not usually consider nouveau Persians as "Persians" for the first and perhaps second generations; for the duration, they tell these individuals that they are still Lurs or Kurds, for example. Even one ancestor, such as an Arab grandmother, seems enough to label (and even taint) a grandson as an Arab (and not a Persian). These entrenched attitudes further polarize society and perpetuate inequality.

[37] If being or identifying as a Persian in Iran confers significant advantages, why would people who are not Persians continue to assert their identities, even to the point of suffering discrimination and persecution? This question has implications for other times and peoples, well beyond contemporary Iran.

have. Yet the dominant sectors of any society (including Iran) tend not to stress their social and cultural identities, which often appear self-evident to them. Already holding superior status (along with its accompanying political and economic benefits), they do not need to make additional efforts to demonstrate their distinctiveness.

When I ask (self-defined) Persians in Iran about the components of their identity, many of them do not emphasize any. Some mention Persian when I inquire about the language they speak. When I ask further, some note Ferdowsi's *Shahnameh* (Iran's epic poem) but without explaining how this millennium-old literary work relates to their identity. Others refer to the Persian Empire but again without explaining the relevance. Some say they visited the ruins of Persepolis. A few cite poets, such as Hafez, Sa'di, or Rumi.[38] Others point to New Year (No Ruz) celebrations. In general, many Persians in Iran seem not to be self-conscious about their linguistic, ethnic, and other cultural identities, especially in all-Persian or Persian-majority contexts.

By contrast, many people in Iran who are not Persians are more self-conscious and definitive about their identities and emphasize them in many contexts and situations. Of course, their identity is not that of a "non-Persian" but rather one of Iran's many specific groups. Thus the terms "Persian" and "non-Persian" (especially with the negative prefix) are problematic in any discussion of Iran. Authors have little difficulty writing about "Kurds" or "Arabs." Why, then, is the "Persian" label so troublesome? Why do so few authors investigate its meaning, especially if they acknowledge social and cultural diversity in Iran?

Some scholars try to find common elements that have laid the foundation for national identity and unity in Iran: a political heritage, a cultural heritage, and the influence of religion.[39] How do these three complexes create specific identities for Persians? If, as some authors state, these complexes are the unifying factors in Iran's national identity and also apply to people who are not Persians, what features differentiate

[38] The Persian poet Ferdowsi wrote the *Book of Kings*, the most significant work in Persian literature, in AD 977–1010. He recounts the mythical and historical past of greater Iran before the arrival of Islam in the mid-seventh century. The ceremonial capital of the Achaemenian (Persian) Empire (550–330 BC) is Persepolis in southwestern Iran. Hafez (1315–90) is Iran's most beloved poet, and Sa'di (1184–1283) and Rumi (1207–73) are also popular.

[39] Hamid Ahmadi, "Unity within Diversity," *Critique*, 14 (2005), pp. 127–47.

Persians from others? Do those who are not Persians simply have "fewer" of these characteristics than Persians? How do they factor in their own political, cultural, and religious heritages, especially when Persians have already claimed their own as the country's foundation?

Being "Iranian" means "being from Iran" or "coming from Iran" (the country, the modern nation-state). Where does being "Persian" fit in this notion, and what does the term "Iranian" imply about those who are not Persians? Many Persians outside of Iran are self-conscious about being Iranian. People in other countries often associate Persians and/or Iranians (perhaps not distinguishing between them) with Iran's recent history (at least what they recall about it)—a despotic and vainglorious king, an Islamic revolution, turbaned ayatollahs in power, hostage-taking, children used as minesweepers in war, "axis of evil," rising oil prices throughout the world, nuclear threats, and hostility toward Israel. Against this backdrop, their views are usually negative. How do such perceptions affect Persians and other Iranians while they consider and evaluate their identities?

Iranians who are not Persians carry their identities with them when they travel outside of Iran. They are minorities abroad, just as they had been in Iran. Unlike the situation for Persians abroad, this experience is not new, and they seem to adjust more smoothly to new settings. Just as Persians abroad do, they are likely to reject stereotyped notions about Iran when they encounter them. Yet they also identify less with Iran and are not as disturbed by others' negative views. Depending on their personal experiences in Iran, they may even agree with some of these outside valuations.

Traveling or living abroad, particularly in Europe and North America, presents problems for some Persians, especially if they have an elevated sense of themselves as a people in Iran, compared with others there. Suddenly they are a minority abroad and may not be welcomed. Citizens of the countries they visit are probably not aware of the privileged position of Persians in Iran, and they harbor suspicions about Iranians in general regardless of their ethnic and other identities. Many are apprehensive that Iranians are probably Muslims, and they confuse Iranians with Arabs and Turks (about whom they also hold stereotyped notions).[40] Persians abroad find these experiences sobering if not shocking.

[40] These perceptions vary according to the countries that Iranians visit and the dominant notions there about "the other."

Socio-economic factors are essential in any discussion of Iran's peoples. Underprivileged sectors of society experience debilitating living conditions, discrimination, and prejudice, seemingly without reference to other dimensions of people's identities. Yet these sectors often correspond with the poorest members of Iran's linguistic, religious (especially Sunni Muslims), ethnic, national minority, and tribal groups. Such people are doubly disadvantaged and have fewer opportunities than do Iran's other poor people, who at least share linguistic, religious, and ethnic traits with Iran's ruling Shi'i and Persian majorities and gain some privileges because of these commonalities.

No one has ever conducted any comprehensive anthropological studies of most groups considered in this chapter, and sufficient information on the diverse languages, religions, ethnicities, national minorities, and tribes of Iran is lacking. Even when anthropological studies do exist, their investigators do not always provide adequate details. I offer five examples here, if only to demonstrate the difficulties in finding adequate material on Iran's societal and cultural complexities.

For four decades, Reinhold Loeffler and Erika Friedl have studied Boir Ahmad Lurs living in a village in southwestern Iran. (They do not always identify the villagers as Boir Ahmad Lurs, which are labels that the people themselves use for their tribal and ethnic affiliations and identities. Friedl created the pseudonym of Deh Koh for the village name, Sisakht.) Despite their longitudinal investigations, the two anthropologists often fail to mention in their publications the people's native language (their mother tongue), ethnicity, minority standing, tribal affiliations, and specific location.[41] Readers, lacking crucial information about the villagers, cannot adequately comprehend their circumstances or

[41] Reinhold Loeffler, *Islam in Practice: Religious Beliefs in a Persian* [sic] *Village*, Albany: State University of New York Press, 1988; and Erika Friedl, *Women of Deh Koh: Lives in an Iranian Village*, Washington, DC: Smithsonian, 1989. In the two works, they do not explain their reasons for omitting these details, which should have played crucial roles in their descriptions and analyses. Loeffler mentions "Persian and Luri words" in a footnote on transliteration (ibid., p. 1). Only recently, he states a few facts in the first paragraph (the village's correct name, the province of "Boir Ahmad and Kuhgiluyeh"—the two names should be reversed—and the "Luri dialect"); "The Ethos of Progress in a Village in Iran," *Anthropology of the Middle East*, 6 (2011), pp. 1–13. He still does not mention the villagers' ethnicity, minority status, or tribal associations.

compare them with villagers elsewhere in Iran. Loeffler refers to the "Persian" village, even in the title of his book, yet the inhabitants are not Persians. The authors do indicate that the villagers are Shi'i Muslims, which would be the case for most of Iran's villages (despite the many variations in religious belief and practice from one village to another).

Patty Jo Watson encountered other issues. Having conducted ethno-archaeological research in a village in western Iran, she notes that the linguistic, ethnic, and even religious identities of the residents remained unclear to her throughout the study.[42] Was she uncertain about the questions to ask or the observations to make in order to elicit this information, or were these identities complex and intermixed even for the inhabitants? Grace Goodell undertook an anthropological study in a village in southwestern Iran but does not clearly state the linguistic and ethnic identities of the inhabitants.[43] They did celebrate Shi'i rituals. Jacob Black-Michaud is more explicit in his descriptions of tribally organized Lurs in western Iran. They spoke Luri, Laki, and Kurdish, and they described themselves as Lurs and separated themselves culturally from Arabs (to the west) and Persians (to the east). These Lurs are Shi'is, although the author barely mentions religion.[44]

Most anthropological studies on Iran concern ethnic minorities; few researchers have turned their attention to Persians. In one exception (and the fifth example here), Mary Hegland focuses on Persians in the Persian village of Guyum (for which she uses the pseudonym Aliabad), just north of Shiraz. Yet, similar to some other researchers, she does not identify the villagers in terms of any linguistic, ethnic, or cultural char-

[42] The villagers referred to themselves as Kurds and to their language as Kurdish, but their language seemed instead to be Laki and closely related to Luri. Watson was even uncertain about their religious identity, and later she heard that the people could have been Ahl-e Haqq, a Shi'i sect; Patty Jo Watson, *Archaeological Ethnography in Western Iran*, Tucson: University of Arizona Press, 1979, pp. 24–5, 28.

[43] Three "tribal or ethnic" groups commingled in the Dezful region of Khuzistan: Bakhtiyaris to the east, Lurs to the west and north, and Arabs to the south and southwest. Several villagers spoke Arabic at home but also the "regional Dezful dialect" (a dialect of Persian, presumably). Several other villagers referred to their Bakhtiyari or Lur tribal backgrounds. Grace Goodell is not specific beyond these remarks, despite the depth of information on other dimensions of the villagers' lives; see *The Elementary Structures of Political Life: Rural Development in Pahlavi Iran*, New York: Oxford University Press, 1986, pp. 20, 36.

[44] Jacob Black-Michaud, *Sheep and Land: The Economics of Power in a Tribal Society*, Cambridge: Cambridge University Press, 1986, pp. 22, 131–2.

acteristics. She does not say that they are Persians. Perhaps she (and others) regard being Persian as the default identity; some writers presume that Iran's majority does not need an ethnic label. The villagers are Shi'i Muslims.[45]

Other anthropological works are also specific to a certain time, place, and local community, which may limit readers in understanding larger groups and their broader characteristics. My studies focus on the Qashqa'i tribal confederacy but I have spent most of my time living with members of a specific Qashqa'i subtribe who might or might not always represent the larger Qashqa'i community.[46]

For Iran, from the mid-twentieth century to the present, perhaps only one researcher, Christian Bromberger, offers wide-ranging, explicit information about the societies and cultures of a specific region of Iran and the identities associated with them.[47] His long-term studies of Gilan (an area along Iran's Caspian Sea coast) and its ethnic groups cover many dimensions of life there. We lack recent, comparable, detailed information for practically all other regions and groups in Iran.[48]

[45] Mary Hegland, "Aliabad of Shiraz," *Anthropology of the Middle East*, 6 (2011), pp. 21–37. A survey of Hegland's other publications may reveal more information, as may also be the case for the authors mentioned just above. Yet in this section I refer to each author's major published study, which should include these vital details but does not.

[46] Lois Beck, *Nomad: A Year in the Life of a Qashqa'i Tribesman in Iran*, Berkeley: University of California Press, 1991.

[47] Christian Bromberger, *Habitat, Architecture and Rural Society in the Gilan Plain*, Bonn: Ferdinand Dümmlers, 1989; Christian Bromberger, "Eating Habits and Cultural Boundaries in Northern Iran," in Sami Zubaida and Richard Tapper (eds), *Culinary Cultures of the Middle East*, London: I.B. Tauris, 1993; and Christian Bromberger, *Un autre Iran: Un ethnologue au Gilan*, Paris: Armand Colin, 2013. Bromberger's entries in the *Encyclopædia Iranica* on Gilan and its peoples offer examples of his range of studies.

[48] Other anthropological monographs on the pre-1979 period exist; their authors sometimes restrict their coverage to a few facets of a society or culture. The 1978–9 revolution ended practically all anthropological research in Iran conducted by foreigners. Since then, a few Iranian anthropologists who reside abroad have worked in Iran. Iranian anthropologists living in Iran have experienced difficulties, and, in addition, they rarely publish in English or other European languages and hence lack an external audience. See Shahnaz Nadjmabadi (ed.), *Conceptualizing Iranian Anthropology: Past and Present Perspectives*, New York: Berghahn, 2009.

Each of the five categories considered in this chapter poses its own challenges for research and analysis, and I examine them in turn.

Languages

The spoken languages of contemporary Iran include many Indo-Iranian and Altaic ones, some Semitic ones, a few Caucasian ones, a Dravidian one, and some others (for Indo-Iranian ones, Table 8.1; for others, Table 8.2).[49] Language does not stand alone but relates to other cultural systems, such as religion and ethnicity, when people form and assert their identities. If a person speaks Persian as a first language, is she necessarily an ethnic Persian? Other than language, what factors determine Persian identity? When is religion more prominent in identity formation than language? Many Jews in Iran speak Persian (and not Hebrew) as their first language, but their primary identity is based on their faith, the cultural system accompanying it, and the strategies they devise as a minority community to cope with discrimination. For all Iranians, how do these kinds of circumstances change through time and from one regime to the next?

I focus here on spoken languages, but written forms are also relevant to the discussion. Iran's people use varying alphabets (some being unintelligible to others), writing has risen in importance, rates of literacy have increased, and new technologies and professions requiring literacy have emerged. Iran's governments in the twentieth and early twenty-first centuries have spread the country's official language—oral and written Persian—throughout Iran, their policy (with practical implications) for politically integrating the dispersed citizenry.[50]

Iran's national minorities want to study their native languages in school, disseminate them to the next generations, augment their cultural heritages, and enhance intra-group communications. Not all of these

[49] I participated in an academic course at Christian Albrechts University in Kiel, Germany, in 2007 on documenting endangered Iranian languages, which contributed to my knowledge of this topic. For color-coded maps on the linguistic composition of Iran, see: http://gulf2000.columbia.edu/images/maps/Iran_Languages_lg.jpg, and http://gulf2000.columbia.edu/images/maps/GulfLanguage-General_lg.jpg

[50] Many people in the world speak and/or use official state languages, and Iran is similar to others in having policies to advance this process.

Table 8.1: Indo-Iranian Languages in Iran[51]

Group	1. NORTHWEST IRANIAN									
Sub-groups	**1.1 Zazaki (Dimli, Dimili)**	**1.2 Kurdish (Kurdi, Kordi)**	**1.3 Gorani (Gurani)**	**1.4 Tati (Azari) (in Azerbaijan)**	**1.5 Talyshi (Taleshi)**	**1.6 Central (Plateau)**	**1.7 Baluchi (Balochi)**	**1.8 Caspian dialects**	**1.9 Semnani**	**1.10 Sangesari**
	1.1.i Northern	1.2.i Kurmanji (Kurmanci) (Northern) (*in north Kurdistan, Iran; in Khorasan*)	1.3.i Auromani (Hawramani, Awramani, Hawrani, Uromanat) (*in Kermanshah area*)	1.4.i Northern	1.5.i Northern	1.6.i Northwestern	1.7.i Western (Rakhshani)	1.8.1 Galeshi (*in Alborz Mountains*)	1.9.i Semnani	
	1.1.ii Southwestern	1.2.i.a Behdini/Bahdini	1.3.ii Bajalani (Bajelani) (*in Mosul area of Iraq*)	1.4.i.a Harzani	1.5.ii Central	1.6.ii Northeastern	1.7.i.a Sistani [not the Persian dialect]	1.8.ii Gilaki	1.9.ii Sorkhei	
	1.1.iii Southeastern	1.2.ii Sorani (Central)	1.3.iii Shabaki	1.4.i.b Karangani	1.5.iii Southern	1.6.iii Southwestern	1.7.i.b Sarhaddi	1.8.ii.a Western	1.9.iii Lasgerdi	
		1.2.ii.a Sorani (*in central Kurdistan, Iran; in northern Iraq*)		1.4.ii Western		1.6.iv Southeastern	1.7.ii Southern	1.8.ii.b Eastern	1.9.iv Aftari	
		1.2.ii.b Mukri (*in Iranian Kurdistan, Caspian provinces, Khorasan*)		1.4.ii.a Khoini (*in Zanjan*)		1.6.v Sivandi	1.7.ii.a Lashari	1.8.ii.c Taleqani-Tonkaboni		
		1.2.iii Southern and South-eastern		1.4.iii Southeastern		1.6.vi Kaviri	1.7.ii.b Makrani	1.8.ii.d Rashti		
		1.2.iii.a Laki (close to Luri) (*in Pish-e Kuh*)		1.4.iii.a Khalkhali		1.6.vii Eastern	1.7.ii.c Bampuri	1.8.iii Mazandarani		
		1.2.iii.b Kermanshahi		1.4.iii.b Taromi (*in Zanjan*)		1.6.vii.a Khuri (Kurdish features) (*in Kavir*)	1.7.ii.d Sarbazi			
		1.2.iii.b.(a)Kalhori		1.4.iii.c Rudbari (transitional to Gilaki)		1.6.viii Transitional languages/dialects (*in Tafresh region*)	1.7.ii.e Kechi (*in Pakistant*)			
		1.2.iv Yazidi		1.4.iv Eastern		1.6.viii.a Vafsi	1.7.ii.f Karachi Baluchi (*in the southeast, influenced by Urdu*)			
				1.4.iv.a Southern Tati (*in Qazvin*)		1.6.viii.b Ashtiyani	1.7.iii Transitional between Western and Southern			
				1.4.iv.b Eshtehardi (*in Karaj*)		1.6.viii.c Alviri-Vidari	1.7.iii.a Sarawani (*in Iran*)			
							1.7.iii.b Panjguri (*in Pakistan*)			

[51] The organization of languages in this table comes primarily from Gernot Windfuhr, "Dialectology and Topics," in Gernot Windfuhr (ed.), *The Iranian Languages*, London: Routledge, 2009, pp. 9–15.

							1.7.iv Eastern (*mostly in Pakistan; dialects often known by tribal names*)					
							1.7.iv.a Marri					
							1.7.iv.b Bugti					
							1.7.v Northern					
							1.7.v.a Turkmenistani Baluchi (*in Turkmenistan*)					
							1.7.vi Bandari (close to Persian)					
							1.7.vii Koroshi					
Group	2. SOUTHWEST IRANIAN											
Sub-groups	**2.1 Persian (Farsi)**	**2.2 Farsi (dialect of Persian) (from Persian Gulf to western and central Fars)**	**2.3 Luri (Lori)**	**2.4 Laki (close to Luri and Kurdi)**	**2.5 Lari (Laristani) (several dialects, with Tati features)**	**2.6 Judeo-Persian (Judeo-Shirazi)**	**2.7 Tat Persian (in southeast Caucasus)**	**2.8 Dari (Afghans in Iran; Afghan Persian)**	**2.9 Herati**	**2.10 Aimaqi**	**2.11 Hazaragi (Hazaras)**	**2.12 Tajiki (Afghans)**
	2.1.i Khuzistani		2.3.i Luri proper				2.7.i Judeo-Tat (Juhari) *(in Azerbaijan and Dagestan)*	2.8.i Zartoshi (Dari of Zoroastrians)				
	2.1.ii Shushtari		2.3.ii Northern				2.7.ii Muslim-Tat					
	2.1.iii Dezfuli		2.3.ii.a Luristani				2.7.iii Christian-Tat (Christian Armeno-Tat) *(in Armenia)*					
	2.1.iv Khuzi		2.3.iii Central									
	2.1.v Sistani		2.3.iii.a Bakhtiyari									
	2.1.vi Kohistani		2.3.iv Southern									
	2.1.vii Khorasani		2.3.iv.a Mamassani (Kuhgiluyeh)									
	2.1.viii Sivandi		2.3.iv.b Boir Ahmadi (Kuhgiluyeh)									
	2.1.ix Davani		2.3.v Laki (close to Kurdi)									
	2.1.x Afghan Farsiwani											
	2.1.xi Persian Gulf group											
	2.1.xi.a Bandari (close to Baluchi)											
	2.1.xi.b Minabi (*in south Iran, near Strait of Hormoz*)											
	2.1.xi.c Bashkardi											
	2.1.xi.d Kumzari (*in Oman peninsula*)											

Group	3. EAST IRANIAN
Sub-groups	**3.1 Pashto (Pashtu)**
	3.1.i Pashto (proper)
	3.1.ii Western (*in Kandahar, southwest Afghanistan, Baluchistan*)
	3.1.iii Central (*in Kabul*)
	3.1.iv Eastern (Nangarhar) *(in northeast Afghanistan, North West Frontier Province in Pakistan)*
	3.1.v Northwestern
	3.1.vi Northeastern
	3.1.vii Southwestern
	3.1.viii Southeastern
Group	4. NORTH IRANIAN
Sub-groups	**4.1 Ossetic (in central Caucasus)**

Table 8.2: Altaic, Semitic, and Other Non-Iranian Languages in Iran[52]

Group	1. ALTAIC	2. AFRO-ASIATIC SEMITIC		3. INDO-EUROPEAN		4. SOUTH CAUCASIAN (KARTVELIAN)	5. DRAVIDIAN	6. AFRICAN		
Sub-groups	**1.1 Turkic**	**2.1 Arabic**	**2.2 Neo-Aramaic**	**3.1 Armenian (independent branch of Indo-European languages)**	**3.2 Indic**	**4.1 Georgian (in villages west of Isfahan)**	**5.1 Brahui (in Baluchistan)**	**6.1 Bantu**	**6.2 Somali**	**6.3 Swahili**
	1.1.i Southwest Turkic 1.1.i.a Oghuz Turkic 1.1.i.a (a) Azeri (Azerbaijani) 1.1.i.a (a)i Tabrizi 1.1.i.a (a) ii Urumia'i 1.1.i.a (a) iii Ardabili 1.1.i.a (a) iv Zanjani 1.1.i.a (a) v Galugahi (*in southeast of Caspian*) 1.1.i.a (a) vi Daragazi (*in north Khorasan*) 1.1.i.a (b) Central (transitional) 1.1.i.a (b) i Qazvini 1.1.i.a (b) ii Khalajestani (*in north of*) 1.1.i.a (c) Sonqori (*in south Kurdistan; isolated enclave*) 1.1.i.a (d) South 1.1.i.a (d) i Qashqa'i 1.1.i.a (d) i.i Aynallu'i 1.1.i.a (d) ii Afshari 1.1.i.a (e) Khorasani 1.1.i.a (e) i Quchani 1.1.i.a (e) ii 5 more dialects 1.1.i.a (f) Turkmani 1.1.i.a Khalaj (independent; not Oghuz Turkic) (*in Central province, north of Arak*) 1.1.ii Northwest Turkic 1.1.ii.a Kazakh	2.1.i Khuzistani (similar to Mesopotamian in Iraq) (*in Khuzistan*) 2.1.ii Mesopotamian (*in Khuzistan and Iraq*) 2.1.iii Khaliji (gulf Arabic) (*along the Persian Gulf coast*) 2.1.iv Khamseh (close to Khaliji) 2.1.v Khorasani	2.2.i Western (*in Syria*) 2.2.ii Northern (*in south Turkey*) 2.2.iii Neo-Mandaic (*among Mandaeans in Khuzistan and south Iraq*) 2.2.iv Northeastern (*in Kurdistan and Azerbaijan—Iran, Iraq, Turkey*) 2.2.iv a Assyrian 2.2.iv b Chaldean 2.2.v dialects among some Christians and Jews (*in Azerbaijan and Kurdistan*)		3.2.i Domari ("Middle Eastern" Romani; gypsies) 3.2.i a Ghorbati (*in west Iran*) 3.2.i b Luti (*in west Iran*) 3.2.i c Karachi (Garachi) (*in north Iran and Caucasus*) 3.2.ii Romani ("European" Romani; *other speakers in Europe, Balkans, Middle East; gypsies*) 3.2.ii a Zargari (*in Zargar region of Qazvin province, in Khorasan near Quchan, in Afghanistan and Pakistan*) 3.2.iii Sindhi 3.2.iv Urdu 3.2.v Punjabi 3.2.vi Hindi 3.2.vii Gujarati					

52 The organization of languages in this table comes primarily from Gernot Windfuhr, "Iran. vii. Non-Iranian Languages," *Encyclopædia Iranica*, 13, 4 (2006), pp. 377–410.

languages have their own scripts. Since the emergence of Iran as a modernizing nation-state, its regimes have opposed the efforts of the country's minorities to develop and expand their languages, especially literary forms. They have viewed these languages as threats to the hegemony of the Persian language and the dominance of native Persian-speakers. They worried that minority languages would serve as vehicles for intensifying communications within minority communities and territories and across international borders, with negative consequences for Iran's unity, solidarity, and political control.

Many of Iran's spoken languages lack alphabets of their own. When writing is necessary, people use and adapt other alphabets, usually the Persian one.[53] Persian (an Indo-Iranian language) is depicted by a modified Arabic script (Arabic being a Semitic language). Qashqa'i Turkish (an Altaic language) is not written, and writers imperfectly transliterate the sounds of Qashqa'i Turkish by means of the Perso-Arabic script (thus intertwining three distinct language families—Altaic, Semitic, and Indo-Iranian). State policies of Persianization (which go well beyond the dissemination of written and spoken Persian) also disrupt other aspects of the lives of the Qashqa'i and diminish the Turkish elements they value as central to their society and culture.[54] Unlike the Qashqa'i, Persians have had centuries to adapt the Arabic script to their spoken language.

Oral traditions, especially in societies lacking their own literary languages, are essential means for disseminating historical, religious, and cultural information through the generations. They serve to pass on myths of origin, local histories, details about prominent people, and symbolic systems. Children learn what it means to be an Afshar or a Lak, for example, when they hear these legends, tales, and songs. The Ahl-e Haqq relied on oral traditions, especially poems in the Luri, Gurani, and Azeri-Turkic languages, to transmit information to people about their esoteric religion and its inner and outer aspects.

[53] Iran's literary languages include Persian, Arabic, Azeri Turkish, Armenian, Assyrian, Mandaic, Kurdish, and Baluchi. People along Iran's borders use other literary languages, including Georgian and Pashto, and some Georgians and Pashtuns also live in Iran.

[54] Some Qashqa'i in 2012 experimented with other alphabets, to avoid using the Perso-Arabic one, partly for political reasons. They preferred a modified Latin alphabet and added some features found in modern standard Turkish (adopted by Kemal Ataturk in 1928 as part of his modernizing and secularizing policies to distance the new Republic of Turkey from Islam and Arabic).

Linguists determine the identity of the languages spoken in Iran and the language families to which they belong. Generally, these judgments are objective and based on the established field of linguistics. Still, linguists disagree on some controversial points such as differentiating languages, dialects, and accents, a significant issue for this chapter because personal and group identity in Iran often hinges on such distinctions. Scholars who stress the preeminence of Persian-speakers in Iran tend to include the speakers of other Indo-Iranian languages and dialects. They often list Luri, for example, as a dialect of Persian. Others consider Luri a language of its own. Luri is an Indo-Iranian tongue, as is Persian, but is Luri a variation of Persian or a separate language? Linguists who study Kurdish, Luri, or Baluchi encounter many regional variants, to which they often apply the term "dialect continuum" (used in cases where a common standard language exists). Linguists often describe Kurdish, for example, as multiple languages rather than multiple dialects. Each of the Kurdish languages also has its own dialects, thus complicating the analysis.

Linguists regard the Persian language in its varieties—including Persian in Iran, Dari in Afghanistan, and Tajiki in Tajikistan and the region—as a dialect continuum. The official and written forms across this broad area are similar, but the spoken Tajiki of Uzbekistan is virtually incomprehensible to a Persian-speaker on a Persian Gulf island. Western dialects of Persian demonstrate influence from Arabic and Oghuz Turkish, while eastern dialects such as Dari and Tajiki preserve many classical features of Persian in their grammar and vocabulary.

Based on research in Luristan, Black-Michaud notes that the tribal people there identified themselves as Lurs and spoke Luri, Laki, and Kurdish (which were not written languages in the region). They also used a large vocabulary of borrowed Persian words "which they so deform in pronouncing them that the non-Luri listener is often tempted to classify them as belonging to the realm of dialect."[55] Black-Michaud could not distinguish between "pure" dialect and "garbled" Persian, and Persian-speakers found the Luri spoken by the tribal people to be incomprehensible.[56] Such complexity within this small community of Lurs demonstrates in microcosm how these kinds of linguistic (and

[55] Black-Michaud, *Sheep and Land*, p. xiv.

[56] Ibid., pp. xiii–xiv, 22.

broader cultural) attributes must also be present in hundreds of thousands of other communities in Iran.

Speakers of different languages in Iran have varying degrees of mutual intelligibility. Researchers associated with *Ethnologue* asked native Persian-speakers to assess Iran's spoken languages. For Armenian, Assyrian, and Georgian, a Persian lacks any comprehension. For Sorani Kurdish, a Persian comprehends 5 percent. For Azeri Turkish the figure is 10 percent, and for southern Luri 80 percent.[57] These patterns demonstrate the degree of social interaction likely to have occurred between Persians and speakers of other languages.[58]

Bilingualism and multilingualism are often found among Iran's non-native Persian-speakers. Some of them have needed to learn Persian in addition to their "mother tongue" (or "first" or "native" language). Some speakers of Persian dialects (such as Dezfuli or Sistani) learned standard Persian when they traveled elsewhere in Iran to attend institutions of higher education or to take up professional employment. Many rural migrants speaking Persian dialects or other languages learned standard Persian so they could succeed in their new settings and jobs. Men and boys are more apt than women and girls to adapt linguistically in these ways, due to their greater contact with the wider Persian-dominating society and their more extensive participation in paid labor outside their homes and local communities.

Relatively few native speakers of standard Persian in Iran are bilingual or multilingual (excluding consideration of English, other languages foreign to Iran, and Arabic).[59] Most Persians lack reasons to learn any of the languages of Iran's other peoples, a fact contributing to the polarization of society (Persians and non-Persians) and the supremacy of the Persian language. When Persian-speakers and non-Persian-speakers

[57] *Ethnologue* is an encyclopedic reference work cataloging the world's known living languages. M. Lewis, *Ethnologue*, 16th edn, Dallas: SIL, 2009, http://www.ethnologue.com

[58] For any nation-state, an official or common language (such as Persian) helps to bridge these communication difficulties and furthers the political integration of citizens.

[59] Iran's theological students and religious scholars and judges studied formal, Quranic Arabic, but their understanding of spoken Arabic varied. Those who lived in Iraq or other Arabic-speaking areas (such as Khuzistan) became familiar with some conversational Arabic.

interact, the responsibility to adjust linguistically usually rests with the latter and reflects the balance of power between them.

People in Iran who are not native Persian-speakers speak the language(s) of their family, local community, region, and/or ethnic group, and some may also learn the official, dominating language of Iran. For some scholars, anyone in Iran who speaks Persian competently is a Persian-speaker, a term they use simultaneously (and sometimes erroneously) to convey an ethnic identity. Yet they do not often note that many Iranians are bilingual or multilingual, with one or several first languages, one or several secondary ones, and perhaps also Persian.

Regional and ethnic factors also relate to patterns of bilingualism and multilingualism among Iranians who are not native speakers of Persian. Kurdish, Luri, and Laki, for example, are shared languages among some people in western Iran. Brahui-speakers in Baluchistan may also know Baluchi, a lingua franca in the region. Talysh-speakers along the Caspian Sea often speak Gilaki (a dominant language there) and/or Azeri Turkish (predominant just to the north and northwest). Thus the issue of language use in Iran is more complicated than simply listing Persian and other languages.

Certain questions have implications for determining people's (multiple) linguistic identities, on which other identities are partly based. A person's socio-economic status, gender, degree of literacy, occupation, extent of travel, and access to the modern media affect the answers. Are people fluent in one language and acquainted with but not fluent in others? Do they speak one language at home and another outside? Do they live in a community that speaks one or more languages and use another or other languages when they leave it? Do children of mixed marriages learn the languages of both of their parents or only one, and when and where do they use these respective languages? How do speakers of multiple languages value each one and under what circumstances?[60]

Persian, the official language of Iran, impacts most citizens via schools, governmental and para-statal agencies, the military, the media,

[60] A young man who studied aeronautical engineering in Tehran at the undergraduate and graduate levels never let anyone there know that he was a Qashqa'i Turk and a native speaker of Turkish. Only when his cousin was elected to Iran's parliament in 1996 and did not publicly hesitate to identify himself in linguistic, ethnic, tribal, and regional terms, did the engineer also make his own identities known. Within his natal group, he was proud of these affiliations. Only outside, when he feared others' scorn, did he conceal them.

the marketplace, and public discourse. Many Persian words enter the speech of other-language speakers in Iran.[61] For political and religious purposes, the Islamic Republic has formally and informally introduced to the Iranian public many Arabic words, phrases, and concepts which have increasingly become part of spoken and written Persian and applicable to Persian and non-Persian Iranians. Even before 1979, half of the words used by Persian-speakers were Arabic in origin.[62] Modernization and globalization are expressed in the Iranian people's attraction to Western culture (via its dress, personal adornment, consumer goods, modern technology, cuisine, music, television programs, and films), increased foreign travel, and expanded use of the Internet. These ongoing, dynamic processes have added English words and others to the vocabulary of Iranians.[63]

Scholars and others note that the number of Persian-speakers in Iran is mounting. They are not necessarily referring to population growth in Iran (in which Persians increase every year through biological reproduction) but rather to the rising percentage of Iranians who speak Persian. Throughout the country, rates of literacy in Persian are growing, access to the national media is spreading, governmental agencies and parastatal foundations (all of which are often headed and run by Persians) are expanding, and rural-to-urban migration is continuing. (Cities have

[61] Linguists could determine the percentage of Persian words in the speech of non-Persian-speakers, evidence that would demonstrate the extent of contact between non-Persians and Persians. Qashqa'i schoolchildren, whose first language is Turkish, increasingly used Persian words as they progressed through the grades, in response to their all-Persian textbooks, instructions, and examinations.

[62] My daughter's first-year Arabic teachers at Yale University were surprised that she already understood many Arabic words. For her, these words were part of the Persian language that she already knew. The Oscar-winning Iranian film, *A Separation* (2011), depicts a father insisting that his daughter use a Persian word, instead of an Arabic one, when she prepares for an examination. She says she will fail that question if she does not write down the Arabic word. He replies, "It doesn't matter if you do." Similar to many Persian Iranians, this fictional character opposes the Arabization of the Persian language, a process accelerating under the Islamic Republic. Such resistance is paradoxical. Many Persian-speakers assert their right to impose the Persian language (at the expense of Iran's other languages) on those who have other linguistic identities.

[63] Some Iranians in the United States, especially in southern California, speak a mixture of Persian and English, a "language" they call "Feranglish" ("foreigners' English").

many Persian-speakers, and jobs there often demand some familiarity with Persian.) Governmental institutions (especially the bureaucracy, judicial system, and formal education), the state-controlled media, and the dominant Persian-speaking population (with which non-Persians have growing contact) direct and implement these policies of Persianization. Yet the rising number of Persian-speakers does not necessarily mean that they have also become Persians and have lost their prior ethno-linguistic identities. Iranians who are subjected to Persianizing policies often become more attached to their own ethno-linguistic backgrounds. As pressures on them to Persianize escalate, they may intensify their ties with the communities of their primary affiliations. People who regard their languages as indigenous and as essential parts of their cultures often strive to retain them, an effort that is part of broader processes and relates to the ways that minorities are politicized. Even when some members of linguistic minorities learn Persian as a first language, they may still embrace their minority identities. Some of Iran's Azeri Turks in northwestern Iran are examples of this process. The spread of Persian there has accelerated but many people still retain their primary identities as Azeri Turks.

Language and culture intersect. If a person in Iran learns Persian as a second language, we do not know the extent to which he or she also becomes familiar with or adopts other elements of Persian culture. People base their ethnic identity on cultural traits that often include their primary language, and the non-linguistic cultural elements also figure prominently. The scholarly literature on diversity in Iran often considers only language as the basis of identity, which is too narrow a framework.

Religions

The religions of Iran include Islam, the Bahai faith, Christianity, Judaism, Zoroastrianism, and the Mandaean faith (Table 8.3).[64]

Iran's 1979 constitution (amended in 1989) states that the official religion is Twelver Shi'i Islam—also called Ithna Ashari ("Twelver" in Arabic), Imami, and Ja'fari Shi'i Islam. "Twelver" refers to the twelve

[64] For a map of Iran's religions, see: http://gulf2000.columbia.edu/images/maps/Iran_Religions_lg.jpg

Table 8.3: Religious Groups in Iran[65]

Group	*Percentage in Iran*	*Population Figure*
Muslims	98–99	
Shi'is	89–91	
Twelvers (Ithna Ashari)		vast majority
Seveners (Ismailis)		100,000
Fivers (Zaydis)		few
Ahl-e Haqq (Yaresan, Yarsan, Ali-Ilahis)		100,000s–1 million
Alevis		
Yazidis (in Iraq mostly)		
Shaikhis[66]		few
Sunnis[67]	9–11	
Baluch		
Turkmans		
Pashtuns		
Kurds (majority, 75%)		
Arabs (minority, 20%)		
Talysh (some)		
Aimaq (incl. Timuris)		
Persians (minority)		
Sufis (Shi'i and Sunni)[68]		2–5 million
Zikris (Baluchistan)		
Non-Muslims	1–2	
Bahais		300,000–350,000
Christians	1	300,000
Armenians (Apostolic)		170,000–200,000–250,000
Assyrians (Nestorians)		10,000–20,000

[65] For Tables 8.3–8.7, reliable statistics on Iran's diverse peoples and their languages, religions, ethnicities, national minorities, and tribes do not exist. Current (2000+) figures are especially difficult to find. The figures and percentages listed in Tables 8.3–8.7 (and in the text and notes) come from hundreds of sources and are approximations. I have often averaged them or shown them as ranges (such as 10–20 percent). Sources rarely add a year to figures, thus not making it possible to calculate annual population increases and decreases.

[66] Most Shaikhis merged with other Shi'i groups or became Bahais.

[67] Half of Iran's Sunni Muslims are of the Shafi'i legal school, half are Hanafis, and a small minority is Hanbali.

[68] Shi'i Sufi orders in Iran include Nimatullahi (the largest one). Sunni Sufi orders include Naqshbandiyya and Qadiriyya (mostly among Kurds).

Chaldeans (Roman Catholics)	7,000
Protestants (various)	7,000–15,000
Jews	80,000 before 1979, 11,000–25,000–40,000 after 1979
Zoroastrians	60,000
Mandaeans (Sabeans)	5,000–7,600–20,000
Hindus	68,000
Sikhs	12,000–14,000
Animists (of African origins)	unknown

Shi'i imams beginning with Ali (the Prophet Muhammad's cousin and son-in-law) and ending with the Mahdi (who disappeared and will return in the future to restore justice to the world).

Muslims comprise 98–99 percent of the population, and the other religious communities are 1–2 percent. Of the Muslims, 89–91 percent are Shi'i, and 9–11 percent are Sunni. These percentages are not as controversial as those for Iran's ethno-linguistic groups (particularly Persians and non-Persians). Some Shi'is and Sunnis are also Sufis. Sufism represents the inner, mystical, esoteric dimensions of Islam and has many kinds of popular expressions.[69]

The Shi'i Islamic government in Iran supports Shi'i Muslims over Sunni Muslims, which complicates its relationships with Kurds and Arabs (some being Shi'i, others Sunni). It discriminates against Sunnis on doctrinal grounds but also because most of them are located along Iran's international borders, where they are less Persianized, more alienated from the central government and less compliant with it, and more susceptible to external influences.[70] The Islamic regime and its predeces-

[69] Sufis include members of Sufi orders and Sufi-related Shi'i sects; also, these and other Iranians use Sufi beliefs and practices to express their individual spirituality. Interest in Sufism has grown in Iran since 1979 in response to the ways Iran's ruling clergy has drawn Islam into politics and has defined and narrowed what constitutes acceptable Islamic belief and practice. Some Sufis say they are returning religious faith to its essence, a personal connection with God without needing to rely on mediating institutions and personnel (such as those essential to the Islamic Republic).

[70] For a map of ethno-religious groups in Iran, see: http://upload.wikimedia.org/wikipedia/commons/d/de/Iran_ethnoreligious_distribution_2004.jpg

sors have not been interested in developing these areas and expending funds there, unless their supporters could profit substantially. The regime also disapproves of or condemns some beliefs and practices of Sufi Muslims, members of Ahl-e Haqq, and Zikris.[71]

Many characteristics of each of Iran's numerous religious groups are relatively straightforward and objective, especially for those that are not Muslim. Shi'i Muslims in Iran—as members of the majority faith, having vast numbers, and dispersed throughout the country—have a wider range of beliefs and practices than do each of the other religious groups. Over the centuries, they have influenced some expressions of Sunni Islam in Iran, which have come to resemble Shi'i ones or serve to differentiate the two sects. Some heterodox Shi'i and Sufi sects, especially those emphasizing esoteric traits, are also less straightforward (for outsiders) than the other religions.

Each religion in Iran has specific traits, including a documented history, ancient religious texts, a written language (perhaps with a distinctive alphabet), priesthood, places set aside for worship and pilgrimage, liturgy, rituals, symbols, and a religious calendar setting off special days (including a weekly Sabbath). Members of religious communities are often co-resident or in close proximity. Each faith has special attire for its adherents (such as men's and women's head-coverings) and for its community leaders, and each has food restrictions and taboos, rites of passage, social practices, and rules about gender, women's roles, marriage, and the family. These and other aspects of each faith in Iran are often visible to and recognizable by practitioners of other religions there. They mark these faiths in general terms and also demonstrate regional-specific forms. More community uniformity exists for these religious groups than for many ethnic groups in general; their beliefs and practices have specificity and documented historical depth. For these faiths

[71] Ahl-e Haqq (Followers of Truth; also known as Ali Ilahi, deifiers of Ali) and similar groups have traits dating from pre-Islamic times; many have eventually been considered as Shi'i sects. Ziba Mir-Hosseini provides an anthropological account in "Redefining the Truth: Ahl-e Haqq and the Islamic Republic of Iran," *British Journal of Middle Eastern Studies*, 21 (1995), pp. 211–28. Zikris have a prophet who supersedes Muhammad, and they adhere to a Mahdi who has already reappeared (unlike the Mahdi for the Twelver Shi'is). Their practices deviate from the regime's Shi'i Islam. See Sabir Badalkhan, "Zikri Dilemmas," in Carina Jahani et al. (eds), *The Baloch and Others: Linguistic, Historical and Socio-Political Perspectives on Pluralism in Balochistan*, Wiesbaden: Reichert, 2008.

to persist over time, especially under regimes that asserted the primacy of other religions and engaged in persecution, some forms of unifying commonality have been essential.

The Islamic regime and its supporters draw attention to and highlight each non-Shi'i-Muslim faith and its community of believers. The state imposes restrictions on where people can gather and worship, if they can establish schools and media outlets, where they can bury their dead, and if they can produce and consume certain foods (such as pork and alcoholic beverages).

The Islamic Republic offers or denies formal recognition and certain legal rights to the religious minorities. The 1979 constitution gives Sunni Muslims higher status than the other minorities and "fully respects" the four legal schools of Sunni Islam (two of them, Shafi'i and Hanafi, are represented by many citizens in Iran). The state considers some religious communities as People of the Book (those having prophets and God's revealed scripture).[72] Armenians, Assyrians and Chaldeans (together), Jews, and Zoroastrians can elect their parliamentary deputies; Bahais cannot.[73] Sunni Muslims lack allocated seats in parliament, but they can be, and are, chosen in general elections (unlike Bahais).[74]

Pious dissimulation (*taqiyya*)—the practice of obscuring one's religion or pretending to be a practitioner of one faith while actually adhering to

72 The Qur'an lists—as People of the Book (*ahl-e ketab, ahl al-ketab*)—Jews, Christians, and Sabeans (Mandaeans), who represent monotheisms older than Islam. Ayatollah Khomeini, as Iran's supreme leader from 1979 to 1989, denied the Mandaeans in Iran the status of a legally protected religion. His successor in that role (1989–), Ali Khamenei, overturned the ruling. Zoroastrianism also preceded Islam but has more than one deity, according to some Sunni Muslim scholars. Whether or not Zoroastrians are People of the Book has been controversial since the origin of Islam and to the present day.

73 Iran's 1979 constitution confers these rights, just as the 1906 constitution and its amendments had done. Under the Islamic Republic, five parliamentary seats (in total) out of 290 (270 before 2000) belong to three Christians, one Jew, and one Zoroastrian.

74 Writers note the "discriminatory" policies that deny Iran's Sunni Muslims a parliamentary quota, as if a designated seat (or seats) would benefit them. Yet, without a quota, they achieve more Sunni deputies, who are better integrated in parliament and potentially more influential than are the three Christians, one Jew, and one Zoroastrian who hold allocated seats. Twelve Sunni deputies, part of the Sunni Faction in parliament, wrote to the supreme leader in 2012 expressing concern about the rights of Sunnis in Iran.

another—is part of Iran's history and complicates a discussion of contemporary times. Some Iranians who were not Muslims or who belonged to some Shi'i sects (such as Ahl-e Haqq) have hidden their actual or ancestral religions so they could avoid discrimination, abuse, and even execution.[75] For their protection, some converts to Shi'i Islam have eradicated signs of their former religions. Later generations might not be aware of their ancestors' conversions and would not be dissimulating.[76]

The large diaspora of each of the non-Muslim religious minorities draws attention to them.[77] The communities outside enhance the social and symbolic boundaries of the groups within Iran. Sometimes the Islamic government distrusts or punishes the minorities for these associations.

Iran's Sunni Muslims are located primarily along international borders and the Persian Gulf coast, and the Islamic regime further peripheralizes them by deploying economic, political, and religious sanctions against them. They include the Baluch, Turkmans, a majority of Kurds, a minority of Arabs, Aimaq (including Timuris), some Talysh, and some Persians. These Sunnis are also members of ethnic and ethno-linguistic groups, national minorities, and sometimes tribes, and these identities often appear to be more significant to them than their religion alone. Yet the fact that they are Sunnis in a Shi'i-led state has a negative impact on them and highlights their non-Shi'i affiliations. Iran's government does

[75] Some members of religious groups in Iran having pre-Islamic origins or traits have dissimulated as Shi'is.

[76] Constance Cronin (personal communication), an anthropologist who studied the Qajar ruling elite and its descendants in Iran, occasionally uncovered the Jewish background of some Muslims when she examined family collections of ancestral materials and found Jewish ritual paraphernalia there. Some people told her that they had not known that any ancestors had been Jews who converted to Islam. (Jews in Iran and the diaspora know that some Iranian Jews in the past had adopted Islam or the Bahai faith.)

[77] The worldwide community of Bahais is 5 million; the religion originated in Iran. Three million Armenians live in the Republic of Armenia; 3 million more are found in other countries. The global Assyrian population is 4.5 million. Iranian Jews in Israel number 134,000 (2007), those born in Iran and those born in Israel of Iranian-born fathers. The worldwide population of Zoroastrians is 145,000–210,000. The larger branch of two communities of Zoroastrians in India, the Parsis, totals 69,000 (2001). Sunni Muslims have no diaspora per se, unless we also consider their ethno-linguistic identities. Kurds (many of whom are Sunnis) do have a large diaspora, for example.

not allow Sunnis to have mosques in Tehran, and journalists sometimes claim that Sunnis elsewhere in Iran suffer a similar restriction. Many Sunnis outside Tehran (and especially where they are the majority sect) do have their own mosques, Friday prayer leaders, religious schools (madrasas), seminaries, and public rituals.[78]

Citizens of Iran who are not Muslims experience varying degrees of toleration, discrimination, hostility, and violence.[79]

The Islamic regime and some ardent supporters (hezbollahis and *basij* militiamen in particular) treat the largest non-Muslim group, the Bahais, the worst.[80] Global human rights organizations publicize their plight. Bahais recognize prophets who succeeded Muhammad, which violates Islamic doctrine. (Muslims regard Muhammad as the seal of the prophets, the last one.) Also, since the origin of the Bahai faith (and its predecessor, the Babi movement), most followers were converts from Islam, which Islamic tenets regard as apostasy and a punishable act.[81]

Iran's government and society treat Armenian, Assyrian, and Chaldean Christians more tolerantly, but they oppose any proselytizing

[78] Despite the Shi'i regime often tolerating these formal institutions (and abiding by Iran's constitution), the state's vigilantes have attacked Sunnis because of their sect and have destroyed Sunni mosques; see A. William Samii, "The Nation and Its Minorities," *Comparative Studies of South Asia, Africa and the Middle East*, 20 (2000), pp. 128–42. Shi'i Friday prayer leaders (*imam jomeh*) in their respective cities and towns throughout Iran are representatives of the country's supreme leader and are often more powerful than the provincial governors-general (*ostandar*) who had dominated under the shahs. Sunni Friday prayer leaders do not play this kind of role in national politics but do influence local and regional events. The regime assigns Shi'i ayatollahs to Sunni-majority areas, to conduct surveillance and supervise political and religious activities.

[79] Eliz Sanasarian, *Religious Minorities in Iran*, Cambridge: Cambridge University Press, 2000.

[80] The Islamic Republic did not allow Bahai children to enter or to continue at primary and secondary schools from the early 1980s until the 1990s. It did not permit Bahai students to enroll in Iran's universities, a ban that continued through 2012. A few exceptions occurred, although most admitted students were reportedly later expelled.

[81] All people are born Muslim, according to Islamic teachings. Those who intentionally choose other faiths, especially if they were raised as Muslims, violate this principle. Other Bahai converts were Jews and Zoroastrians. Mehrdad Amanat discusses Jews, Bahais, and Shi'i Muslims in nineteenth-century Iran in *Jewish Identities in Iran: Resistance and Conversion to Islam and the Baha'i Faith*, London: I.B. Tauris, 2011.

groups (such as evangelicals). Christian churches have not experienced the kinds of violence that Bahai holy sites and community centers have suffered. The regime regards Christians and Jews as People of the Book. Along with Iran's other religious minorities, Christians and Jews have experienced a reawakening of religious identity since 1979. Despite denials by Iran's government, the current regime considers Jews as Zionists and spies for Israel, where many Iranian Jews have emigrated. Iran has the largest Jewish community in the Middle East, outside of Israel.

Zoroastrians represent the dominant faith in Iran before the arrival of Islam in the mid-seventh century.[82] Shi'i (but not most Sunni) theologians identify Zoroastrians as People of the Book and Zoroastrianism as a legally protected religion, a status recognized by Iran's 1979 constitution. The Pahlavi shahs (1925–79), and especially Mohammad Reza Shah, drew attention to Zoroastrian kingship, society, and culture as the heart of their newly constructed notions of secular Iranian nationalism.[83] Iranians in Iran and abroad still celebrate pre-Islamic Zoroastrian rituals, especially those of the New Year (No Ruz, beginning on the first day of spring).

The non-Muslim religious minorities are not as territorially concentrated as the Sunni ethno-linguistic ones. Bahais, Christians, Jews, and Zoroastrians are found primarily in urban areas, intermixed with people of other religions, and their livelihoods often center on commerce. They have engaged in formal education to a higher degree than many Shi'i Iranians have done (based on a proportion of their respective populations), and many have achieved professional and social mobility.[84] Some of these minorities (but usually not Jews) are also located in rural areas and engage in agriculture. Small communities of Christian and Jewish

[82] The Islamic expansion into Iran (637–651 CE) led to the end of the Sasanian Empire and the eventual decline of Zoroastrianism. Most Iranians were Muslim, at least nominally, by the late eleventh century. In the early sixteenth century, the Safavid dynasty made Shi'i Islam the official state religion, and by the mid-seventeenth century most people had become Shi'is. Since that time, Shi'i Islam and "Persian" culture were increasingly intertwined. Mary Boyce describes the lives of Zoroastrians in a village near Yazd in *A Persian Stronghold of Zoroastrianism*, Oxford: Oxford University Press, 1977.

[83] Monica Ringer, "Iranian Nationalism and Zoroastrian Identity," in *Iran Facing Others*.

[84] The Islamic regime has restricted the access of Bahais to all levels of formal education since 1979 and has intentionally limited their occupational opportunities.

Kurds are found in western Iran.[85] Bahais are more dispersed in Iran than the other non-Muslim minorities.[86] These minorities do not have the political presence and potentiality of the ethno-linguistic and tribal ones (including Sunnis).

The primary identities of the non-Muslim minorities are based on their religion, but some have their own languages (and perhaps alphabets), and all have distinguishing cultures. Some of them are distinct ethnic groups and are seen as such by other Iranians. Armenians, for example, have a sociocultural system extending beyond their language (Armenian) and religion (Armenian Orthodox Christianity).

The formation of a conservative, fundamentalist Islamic regime in 1979 focused attention on religion, especially when the state and its fervent supporters turned violent against Bahais and Jews. Iranians in general became more aware of the non-Muslim minorities after 1979. They often said that Iranians of different religions had once lived together in relative harmony and had engaged in commerce and education regardless of their religious traditions.[87] The religious practices of the minorities had been private, family, and local community events and did not infringe on the lives of other Iranians. Once the Islamic regime took power, people said, its agents regarded any signs that citizens were not Shi'i Muslims as a provocation and subjected them to restrictions and punishments. Wary of conditions worsening and fearing for their children, many members of these minorities emigrated.

The Islamic Republic's formation has also led to the increased penetration of Iranian society by the ruling clergy's interpretations of Twelver

[85] Some Iranians (such as Kurds who are also Christians or Jews) have multiple bases for their minority status and are often doubly disadvantaged.

[86] Ten Bahai families resided in a small village near Qashqa'i summer pastures, where some Qashqa'i nomads were building houses for winter residences. They kept a low profile and did not engage in village politics.

[87] Some Shi'i Muslims attended Iran's first modern, secular schools, which foreign powers and West-based religious institutions had founded for the non-Muslim religious minorities in the nineteenth and early twentieth centuries. When Iran's government introduced its own modern, secular schools in the early twentieth century, religious minorities enrolled alongside Shi'i Muslims. As a university student in Shiraz in the early 1960s, I lived in a culturally diverse, lower-middle-class neighborhood. My neighbors would often say that they did not know the religious affiliations of one another until each family celebrated religious rituals. Another indicator of religion is the day of the week that merchants routinely close their shops and businesses.

Shi'i ideologies and practices. Each state agency, regardless of its intended focus (such as agricultural irrigation), contained overseeing clergymen and sections devoted to religious dissemination and the staff's compliance with approved religious practices. These agencies, along with religious functionaries such as theological students, distributed information and instruction to all parts of Iran.[88] The regime wanted to polarize society according to religion (Shi'i Muslims versus others) and to systematize and homogenize the beliefs and practices of Shi'is. To that end, it attempted to eradicate or supplant some popular expressions of Shi'i Islam that many Iranians (even those of other religions) had once enjoyed but that now incurred the clergy's displeasure.

Fortune-telling using the Qur'an, invoking the names of Islamic figures for mundane purposes, and revering deceased local Sufi shaikhs are examples of the regime's prohibited or discouraged acts.[89] The regime's newly introduced or elaborated customs include household and street-side alms boxes, glorification of the revolution's and the war's martyrs, refurbished or new local shrines (*imamzadehs*), and veneration of Fatemeh, Abbas, and the absent Twelfth Imam (the Mahdi).[90] To remind

[88] Friedl describes in *Women of Deh Koh* the black-clad "Islamic sisters" (my term) arriving in a Boir Ahmad Lur village to inculcate proper behavior and religious practice.

[89] Clergymen saw that pious Shi'is still wanted a rich array of rituals, despite the apparent austerity of the new Islamic regime, and they restored some of them or at least stopped forbidding them. They especially needed the support of women, who avidly practiced rituals that extended beyond the basic rites of the faith. Women were, after all, the ones who socialized the next generation. See Zahra Kamalkhani, *Women's Islam: Religious Practice among Women in Today's Iran*, London: Kegan Paul, 1998; and Kamran Aghaie (ed.), *The Women of Karbala: Ritual Performance and Symbolic Discourses in Modern Shi'i Islam*, Austin: University of Texas Press, 2005.

[90] New signs along Iran's paved highways direct travelers to shrines, where visitors are encouraged to perform prayers and make donations. Fatemeh, the "exemplary Muslim woman," is the Prophet Muhammad's daughter, Imam Ali's wife, and Imam Hosain's mother. Abbas (Abu al-Fazl) is Imam Hosain's half-brother. The Mahdi, the twelfth and "hidden" Imam, went into occultation in a supernatural, subterranean realm in 874 CE and will return to restore justice to the world and then lead his followers to heaven on Judgment Day (according to devout Shi'is). Some Iranians criticize the cult-like fascination with the Mahdi. Iranians flock to Jamkaran mosque (near the city of Qom) and its well, where some people say the Mahdi disappeared (or where he will return) and where supplicants leave writ-

Shi'is of the tragedy of Kerbala, the government constructed in Tehran a bronze replica of the goatskin water bag that Abbas (Abu al-Fazl) had wanted to deliver to the embattled Imam Hosain and his family members and followers (just before their brutal deaths in AD 680).[91] Through these new, altered, and expanded rituals and practices, the regime has aimed to enhance and unify Shi'i sentiments, draw distinctions with other religions and sects, attract people's loyalty, and solidify its control.

Some Iranians have used the practices and symbols of the non-Muslim minorities to demonstrate their independent thinking, their opposition to the Islamic Republic and the ruling Muslim clergy, and/or their solidarity with and empathy for these minorities. They have drawn on the signifiers of Zoroastrianism to connect with Iran's pre-Islamic cultural heritage (and Iran's national identity). Attendance at Christian churches in Iran has risen dramatically, not necessarily because Muslims were converting to the faith but because these places of worship provided alternatives for those who resisted the ways the Muslim clergy tried to control religious expression. They said they revered the same God as before, just in a different setting. Some Iranian women noted that they found churches more comfortable than mosques, where men did not always allocate space for them, and the codes of modest dress were less severe in churches.

Some Iranians wore publicly or privately the symbols of Christianity and Zoroastrianism (the *farvahar* image).[92] Many Iranians assert that the original religion of Iran is Zoroastrianism and that much of Persian-Iranian culture (and Iran's national identity) has its source there. Festive celebrations of the pre-Islamic rites of the New Year (No Ruz) are the highlight of practically every Iranian's social life.[93] Muslim cler-

---

ten requests for him. Caretakers had to narrow the well's opening so that people could no longer drop meat kebabs for the Mahdi to enjoy. President Mahmud Ahmadinejad (2005–13) said that he believed in the Mahdi's power and made state decisions accordingly.

[91] Visitors collect water issuing from the new sculpture (erected in 2011) to use in healing. Khamenei, Iran's supreme leader, tells the emotional story of Abbas and his sacrifice to a sobbing audience in 2008. See: http://www.youtube.com/watch?v=j_OaZDvudPO

[92] *Farvahar* (*faravahar*) is a Zoroastrian symbol that has also become a national symbol, and the Islamic Republic has not banned its use.

[93] By comparison, many somber rituals of Shi'i Islam commemorate the deaths of imams and their family members.

gymen have attempted to prohibit some features of these rites but have failed. The practice of leaping over fires during Wednesday's Celebration (*chahar shanbeh suri*), just before the New Year, has especially drawn their ire.[94]

Sufi rituals and affiliations with Sufi orders have also increased since the Islamic regime took power, and the Muslim clergy has tried, unsuccessfully, to control these actions as well. Sufi poets and poetry, another long-standing part of Persian-Iranian culture, have gained in popularity throughout Iranian society. Many people, especially the youth, attended the tombs of Iran's famous poets. The clergy has not welcomed these trends; it opposed the improper, even forbidden, behaviors associated with mysticism, especially traits it regarded as esoteric or hedonistic. Sufi practices performed in groups were not always sex-segregated, and women there did not necessarily observe state regulations for modest dress.

Many Iranians in Iran and abroad have said that the current regime has ruined Islam for them. Some abandoned the practice of Islam, and some sought alternative religious expressions.[95] People proclaimed that no concerted effort to destroy Islam in Iran could have been as successful as the Islamic regime has been.[96]

[94] For a photograph, see Massoume Price, *Iran's Diverse Peoples*, Santa Barbara: ABC-CLIO, 2005, p. 317. Used in this way, fire represents the Zoroastrian faith for the Muslim clergy, who object to its continuing symbolic centrality.

[95] Growing numbers of Shi'is in Iran and especially in the diaspora are not observing central religious rites—including daily prayers, fasting during the month of Ramadan, alms-giving via the clergy, pilgrimage to Mecca, attending Friday prayers in mosques, and mourning during the month of Moharram. Angry about or rejecting the ways the Islamic regime has politicized and manipulated the religion for non-religious purposes, they have turned away from Islam (or toward Sufism) or toward other religions. Many were explicitly defying the regime in Iran, even those who now lived far away. Some outsiders presume that only the modern upper-middle and upper classes are rejecting Islam, but people throughout Iran in rural and urban locales and in all socio-economic classes have also made these choices. Well before 1979, some Shi'is, especially in the West-oriented, urban, middle and upper classes, had not participated in most religious rites. Their behavior did not change after 1979, when they reasserted their disinterest. Regardless of people's non-observance of other religious practices, the Islamic rites of death, burial, and mourning still appear to be strong for most Shi'is in Iran. At times of sadness and despair, and lacking alternative expressions, people (re)turn to traditional ones.

[96] People in the Persian Gulf region and elsewhere who express anti-Shi'i sentiments

Secular Iranians were now the new "religious" minority in Iran. Increasing numbers of citizens have rejected the restrictive politico-religious orientation of the ruling clergy and its regime and have urged a separation of religion from state and government.[97] The government's policies and actions have elicited or reinforced people's secular notions. In some ways these individuals were as suppressed, because of their secular views, as some other religious minorities. They could not enroll in state universities, receive financial or other benefits from Iran's powerful para-statal foundations (*bonyads*), hold major governmental jobs, or run for elected office. All of these opportunities (and others) were available only to those Iranians who could convincingly proclaim and demonstrate their support for the supreme leader (*rahbar*), the institution of the jurist's guardianship (*vilayat-i faqih*), and the Islamic Republic and its politico-religious ideologies. In response, some Iranians have adopted new patterns of pious dissimulation. They performed Islamic rituals publicly and dressed and behaved conservatively, thus hiding their opposition to the regime in order to obtain these privileges. Men grew facial hair to a certain (and identifiable) length and kept strands of beads handy (for occasional twirling).[98] Women took care to dress modestly and to behave circumspectly in public (for example, by not laughing out loud).

Ethnicities

Ethnicity is the third category examined here. Iran has many different kinds of ethnic, ethno-linguistic, and ethno-religious groups (for Muslims, Table 8.4; for non-Muslims, Table 8.5).[99]

---

connect these trends (of Muslims moving away from Islam) with actions by Shi'is that have "destroyed Islam from within" ever since the founding of the religion. Sunnis still often use the pejorative term "Rafidi" (Repudiators) for them.

[97] Cultural expressions having specific symbols and meanings (such as men's neckties and clean-shaven faces and women's flimsy headscarves and tight overgarments) often accompany these secular (and anti-regime) attitudes and create an identity visible to other people, including those who enforce the regime's edicts on attire and appearance.

[98] In Iran, these strands (*tasbih*) are not ordinarily "prayer beads" (used to keep track of prayer chanting). Rather, men casually handle them, an act conveying their religious and socio-economic statuses. Strands sometimes contain ninety-nine beads, to represent each of God's names.

[99] For a map that includes Iran, see: http://gulf2000.columbia.edu/images/maps.Mid_East_Ethnic_lg.jp. For a map on ethno-religious groups in Iran, see: http://

Table 8.4: Ethnic Groups in Iran (Muslims)

Group[100]	*Percentage in Iran*	*Population Figure*
Persians	36–49–51[101]	27.1–39 million
Azeris Turks (Turkic)[102]	13–16–25–41	11.2–19.4 million
Kurds	7–10	5–7.5–10 million
Lurs[103]	2–6	2.6–4.7 million
Gilakis	3–4	3–4 million
Mazandaranis	3–4	3–4 million
Arabs	2–3–3.2	1.3–1.6–2.1 million
Qashqa'i (Turkic)	1.6–2	1.5–1.8 million
Baluch	2.2–2.5–3	1.2–1.6 million
Turkmans (Turkic)	1.4–2	1–2–2.4 million
Bakhtiyaris (Lurs)	2	1–2 million
Laks		1–1.1 million
Other Turks	1	
Tajiks (Afghans)		357,000
Daris		350,000
Tatis		307,200
Hazaras		283,000–355,000
Afshars (Turkic)		200,000–342,000
Khorasani Turks		200,000–854,000
Aimaq (incl. Timuris)		170,000–213,000
Shahsevan (Turkic)		130,000–310,000
Pashtuns		50,000–113,000
Talysh (Talesh)		430,000
Domaris (gypsies)		100,000–1.3 million
Romanis (gypsies)		
Laristanis		100,000–108,000
Parsis (Parsi Daris)		90,000–376,000
Tajiks (Tajikistan)		81,000
Georgians		60,000

upload.wikimedia.org/wikipedia/commons/d/de/Iran_ethnoreligious_distribution_2004.jpg

100 Groups are listed according to approximate population figures.

101 Native speakers of Persian are 36–49–51 percent; native speakers of all Indo-Iranian languages are 65 percent.

102 Some sources erroneously include all of Iran's Turkic peoples under the label "Azeri."

103 Bakhtiyaris (below) are also Lurs; their numbers may or may not be included here.

Qaraqalpaqs	49,000
Sangesaris	38,000
Gujaratis	32,000
Punjabis	32,000
Khalaj (Turkic)	20,000–48,000
Brahuis	20,000–21,000
Vafsis	20,000
Kazakhs (Turkic)	3,000–5,700
Bandaris (related to the Baluch)	
Qaragozlus (Turkic)	

Table 8.5: Ethnic Groups in Iran (non-Muslims)

Group	*Population Figure*
Bahais	300,000–350,000
Christians	300,000
Armenians	170,000–200,000–250,000
Assyrians	10,000–20,000–80,000
Chaldeans (Catholics)	7,000
Protestants (various)	7,000–15,000
Jews	80,000 before 1979
	11,000–25,000–40,000 after 1979
Zoroastrians	60,000
Hindus	68,000
Sikhs	12,000–14,000
Mandaeans	5,000–7,600–20,000

An ethnic group has distinctive cultural characteristics, as seen by its members and by outsiders. The extent of distinctiveness is sometimes a subjective assessment and can be nuanced in its expression.[104]

An ethno-linguistic group adds language as a primary or a major trait. The range of languages spoken in Iran (Tables 8.1, 8.2) means that a

[104] The tribal peoples in the southern Zagros Mountains have different languages and ethnicities but similar kinds of music, dance, sports, and attire. Each group asserts its unique identity and the special qualities of its customs, even though some features are similar to those of other groups in the region. Sometimes the differences among these groups seem minor (to outsiders), such as the length of a woman's gathered skirt (to the ankle or just below it).

range of ethno-linguistic groups could also exist. Yet not all languages necessarily have their own social groups. Speakers of "languages" are more likely than speakers of "dialects" (however defined) to have distinct social groups.

An ethno-religious group uses religion as a primary or a major characteristic. In Iran, these groups are the religious minorities, including Sunni Muslims, but they also include some Shi'i Muslims. Where Shi'is are in the minority (as in much of Baluchistan), they often demonstrate distinctive traits, as do the adepts of some heterodox syncretistic Shi'i sects.

Language and religion are important components of people's notions about cultural identity in Iran, their own and others. Some of Iran's ethnic groups are also national minorities, and some are tribally organized. The factor of ethnicity for many Iranians brings together the four other categories discussed in this chapter.

Iran's Persians (ethnic Persians, native speakers of Persian) with their vast numbers (half the population) and geographical dispersion could not have the uniformity of traits that smaller, often more localized, groups have. (The same situation pertains to Iran's Shi'i Muslims, the other dispersed majority population.) "Ethnic Persians" and "native speakers of Persian" are not necessarily equivalent categories, given that some native speakers are part of other ethnic groups. Persians are found in sizable numbers throughout Iran, unlike any other ethnicity, although they reside primarily in the central plateau, to the north and west of the great deserts and away from the borderlands.

Iran's Turkic peoples, native speakers of various Turkish languages, are the country's second largest ethnicity (a third of the population). Similarly, "ethnic Turks" and "native speakers of Turkish" are not necessarily equivalent groups. Turks in Iran are geographically dispersed but not to the same extent as are the Persians. They are divided into different, variously sized, specific, sub-ethnic, national minority, and tribal groups, unlike Iran's Persians. Persians are characterized by regional, urban, and rural distinctions (often marked by dialects and accents) rather than by any explicit or specific sub-ethnic or sociopolitical classifications. Just as identity for Iran's Persians is often not well defined, such is also the situation for any subgroups among them.

For centuries, rulers in Iran have tried to control certain territories and their populations by sending agents (often Persians) from state and provincial capitals to govern them, exploit resources and labor, and dominate vital markets, industries, trade routes, border crossings, and ports. Other Persians accompanied these governors as military officers, soldiers, judges, civil servants, merchants, teachers, and religious personnel. These arrivals (mostly Persians) changed the population dynamics of areas that were economically and politically important to the rulers, such as the oil and natural-gas fields of Iran's southwest during the past century.

Likewise, Iran's rulers have viewed certain tribal and ethno-political groups as risks to their power and have dispersed and relocated some of them (or some segments) to other parts of the country, especially its far reaches.[105] They have also deployed such groups to police and defend the borders. Some Kurds are still found in northeastern and southeastern Iran, far from their homelands to the west, because of these policies. Only in the twentieth century, when a modernizing nation-state was emerging, were these and other often-outlying peoples perceived as minorities. As rulers attempted to form a national identity, they confronted conflicting identities and nationalities developing throughout the country and along its borders.[106]

Persians as a group, because of their majority standing, differed from other ethnic groups, which have lived under and coped with Persian domination. People who were not Persians asserted distinctive identities as a strategy to unify them while they coped with minority status and the economic, political, and social disadvantages that often accompanied it. These other ethnic and national minority identities are to be seen in relation to Persian identity; one of them helped to create the others, if only by the extent of their perceived differences. If these peoples had not been minorities in a Persian-majority state, their identities would not have taken the forms or intensities that they did.

Persians have often seemed oblivious to other ethnic peoples in Iran, or they disregarded them, considered them inconsequential, made sarcastic or malicious jokes about them, or viewed them as foreign tourists might have done.[107] They tended to equate Iranian identity—an Iran-

[105] John Perry, "Forced Migration in Iran," *Iranian Studies*, 8 (1975), pp. 199–215.

[106] Firoozeh Kashani-Sabet, *Frontier Fictions: Shaping the Iranian Nation, 1804–1946*, Princeton: Princeton University Press, 1999.

[107] Some middle-class urban Persians have been attracted to the colorful folkloric traditions of Iran's ethnic minorities; see Lois Beck and Julia Huang, "Manipulating Private Lives and Public Spaces," *Comparative Studies of South Asia, Africa and the Middle East*, 26 (2006), pp. 303–25. During their travels in Iran, Per-

wide sense of the state's nationality—with Persian identity. Such a construction, often intended to diminish the significance of the other identities, makes it difficult to describe "a Persian culture" as compared to other cultures in Iran. People in Iran who were not Persians might have spoken the Persian language (facilitated, even mandated by, schools, governmental functions, and media exposure) and expressed some loyalty to Iran as a country—all factors complicating the definition of a Persian culture.

When Iraq's Saddam Hussein attacked Iran in 1980, he unleashed patriotic, nationalistic sentiments throughout the country. Later, many people who were not Persians regretted their emotional response to this territorial incursion when they saw how Iran's ruling clergy was exploiting and prolonging the war in order to defeat its internal enemies, centralize power, and reinvigorate now-ebbing revolutionary fervor by channeling it toward the hostilities. Khomeini, other clerics, and their supporters utilized the war to help them confront the problems also faced by every other post-revolutionary regime—that is, how to routinize revolutionary leadership, institutions, goals, and enthusiasm.

Iran's minority peoples experienced firsthand how destructive to human life the Iraq–Iran War turned out to be and how it had ruined Iran's economy and substantial portions of vital infrastructure. Some Persians regarded the war in similar ways, but they were more invested than many non-Persians were in protecting Iran's sovereignty and territoriality against Saddam Hussein's aggressions. Iran's Arabs, Lurs, and Kurds, many of whom lived near and along the border with Iraq, suffered more directly from the war than did some other minorities (and more directly than most of Iran's Persians). Iran's minorities mourned their sons, lost in a war that had little or nothing to do with them as minority communities.[108] By the time of the war's ceasefire (1988), nei-

sians purchased handcrafted decorative and utilitarian items (textiles, ceramics, and baskets) said to represent local and regional groups.

108 Like the Pahlavi shahs, the Islamic Republic's army and revolutionary-guard corps conscripted soldiers from all the country's minority groups, including Bahais and other religious minorities (with certain restrictions applying only to them). Some other nation-states prohibited some of their minorities from serving in the military because they perceived their presence as a threat. Some Persian Gulf states excluded Shi'i Muslims from serving in the military and police (Gengler, this volume).

ther Iraq nor Iran had achieved any positive results. The territorial border remained as it had been eight grueling years earlier.[109]

Since the Islamic regime took power, the non-Persian minorities have associated it with the Persian majority, and many of them have come to blame Persians for the state's oppressions, obsessions, failings, and mistakes.[110] Just as the Islamic Republic has undercut the attachment of many Iranians to Islam, so too had the pursuit of war turned many non-Persians against those who had drawn out the war for their own political and economic gain.

The Sunni and non-Muslim minorities have critiqued the ruling regime in a different way than the non-Persians have done. They have not focused, as have the ethno-linguistic minorities, on Persians being the responsible party for destruction, injustice, and inequality. Instead, they viewed Shi'i Muslims (and not Persians per se) as the primary cause of the regime's abuses and considered the hardships that these minorities have suffered to be the regime's fault. As religious minorities, they faced discrimination because of their faiths. In turn, they blamed the dominating, ruling religious group (Shi'i Muslims). Some non-Muslim minorities, including the Bahais, Jews, and Zoroastrians, are native Persian-speakers and identify themselves as such. Yet their primary identity comes from their religion, and they too faulted Shi'i Muslims (and not Persians per se) for the intolerance and persecution they have endured.[111]

Notions of "Iran" and Iranian nationalism may not be relevant to the lives of many non-Persians, non-Muslims, and Sunni Muslims in Iran. Or these notions may be only situational, depending on the extent of people's integration in the country, their knowledge of wider events, and the ways these circumstances directly or indirectly impact them.[112] Such

[109] Some journalists had viewed the Iraq–Iran War as a conflict between Sunni Muslims (Iraq) and Shi'i Muslims (Iran), often without understanding that both countries had sizable numbers of each group. Some had seen the war as one between Arabs (Iraq) and Persians (Iran), also without comprehending that both countries were ethnically diverse.

[110] The non-Persian minorities had expressed similar opinions about the Pahlavi regimes, which had discriminated against them and neglected their territories during modernization.

[111] Armenian, Assyrian, and Chaldean Christians have been less likely than Bahais, Jews, and Zoroastrians to consider themselves Persians. They had their own languages and took their ethno-religious identities as their primary ones.

[112] Non-Persians, non-Muslims, and Sunni Muslims are, respectively, 51, 1–2, and

recent situations include the popular uprising against Mohammad Reza Shah, Saddam Hussein's military attacks against Iranian territory, US bombings in neighboring Afghanistan (resulting in the influx of refugees), Iran's verbal threats against Israel (and any ensuing retaliation), and confrontations between Iran's rulers and foreign powers over the Islamic Republic's right to develop its nuclear industry despite near-universal condemnation.[113] How have each of these major events affected Iran's minorities and played a role in forming their identities? How have such events also impacted the identities of Iran's Shi'i Muslims and Persians and the identity of the nation-state?

A young Turkman tribesman, conscripted by Iran's national army in 2005, understood that he was now part of an Iran-wide entity. When he ended his compulsory service and returned home to his kin and tribal groups in northeastern Iran, he resumed his primary affiliations as a Turkish-speaking, Sunni, Turkman tribesman. Little or nothing about his time in the military had given him reason to be patriotic to the nation-state. In fact, his experiences turned him against Iran and its ruling majorities (Shi'i Muslims and Persians), such as maltreatment by officers and persistent hazing from fellow soldiers about his Eurasian ("Chinese") facial features, backward customs, and poor knowledge and pronunciation of Persian.[114]

A nation-state's nationalism differs from other kinds of identities, including those of Iran's national minorities who hold specific grievances

---

9–11 percent of Iran's population (with some overlapping members), numbers too significant to ignore.

[113] Even some Iranians highly critical of the Islamic regime and its policies support the right of Iran to pursue its nuclear ambitions (just as Israel, Pakistan, and India have done). The Islamic regime in 2012–13 hoped that its efforts to cope with international sanctions and to face the world's opprobrium would enhance national unity and enable the government to sustain power and defeat its internal and external enemies. It had exploited the Iraq–Iran War for similar ends.

[114] Mohammad Reza Shah and the Islamic Republic have sent conscripted soldiers of minority backgrounds to serve in territories distant from their homelands so they could not ally with their compatriots there against the state. They also attempted to prevent minority soldiers from intensifying their common affiliations during their service. Some of Iran's prisons have tried to keep minority inmates apart from one another but could not always do so because of chronic overcrowding. Prisoners in Iran, often highly politicized, have activated the ties and allegiances they formed in prison during ensuing struggles against the regime in power.

against the Islamic regime (and its predecessors) and who define themselves partly in these terms. Notions of nationalism reflect the virtues of patriotism, loyalty, and solidarity. Patriotic songs and slogans and the colors and symbols depicted on national flags summarize these ideals.[115]

Perhaps Persians can be defined as those who are patriotic toward Iran, support its territorial and political integrity, and respect Iran's right to choose its regional and international alliances. Yet, other traits, especially the Persian language, also define this ethnic group. For the vast majority in Iran, the beliefs and practices of Shi'i Islam have been central to Persian identity. (This component of Persian identity seems to be diminishing, due to the many Iranians who reject or distance themselves from Islamic beliefs and practices, express their spirituality privately—such as through meditation—and lean toward secular values.) Also, many of Iran's Shi'i Muslims already have explicit, primary ethnic identities as Azeri Turks, Gilakis, Lurs, Qashqa'i, and others. Almost all of Iran's Sunni Muslims (except for the Persians among them) have strong identities as Kurds, Arabs, Baluch, or Turkmans, for example, and their religious sect and their ethnicities preclude them from being regarded as Shi'is or Persians, two central components of Iran's national identity. A focus on Shi'i affiliation (as it relates to a Persian identity) also excludes people who are not Muslims. Yet, many Bahais, Jews, and Zoroastrians identify themselves as Persians as well as members of their religious communities.

Increasing numbers of Persians define themselves as opponents of monarchical and/or theocratic oppressive rule and as resisters against tyranny, in ways, perhaps ironically, that match the long-standing attitudes of Iran's minorities toward centralized state rule. This dimension of Iranian identity grew during the popular protests against Mohammad Reza Shah in 1977–9, then under an increasingly repressive Islamic regime, then in response to the fraudulent presidential election in 2009, and most recently under debilitating international economic sanctions

[115] Flags under the Qajar dynasty and the Pahlavi shahs depict the Lion and the Sun, each having its own evolving identity; see Afsaneh Najmabadi, *Women with Mustaches and Men without Beards: Gender and Sexual Anxieties of Iranian Modernity*, Berkeley: University of California Press, 2005. "Allah" (Iran's new emblem) is depicted in Arabic script in the center of the Islamic Republic's flag, and "Allah akbar" (God is great) is written in Arabic twenty-two times between the green and white stripes and the red and white stripes.

and internal economic crises. Such a new concordance of negative views against a regime in power may be diminishing the political gap between Persians and some other Iranians, with consequences yet to be actualized and understood.

Tohidi notes that most Iranians who speak the diverse languages of Iran (other than Persian) "perceive their ethnic identity as a complement to their national identity."[116] She and others seem to ignore the subordinate position and second-class status of the minorities in Iran and the ways they regard their disadvantaged situation, caused by governmental programs offering the minorities few rights and entitlements, little or no political representation, and economic and social exclusion. If any minorities do have positive sentiments about Iranian nationality, what are the bases for this notion? What do they gain from this attachment? How are they disadvantaged if they adhere to such an idea? How do their own linguistic, religious, ethnic, national minority, and tribal identities fit with those of the nation-state? Are they, or can they be, compatible?

Iran's ethnic groups are relatively distinctive but they are also often situated within regional contexts where commonalities exist between and among them. Many regions of Iran have characteristic features that are also apparent in the sociocultural groups that reside there, including those of Persians. Some examples are the lush littoral of the Caspian Sea, the rugged mountains of Kurdistan in the northwest, the well-watered agricultural plains of Khuzistan in the southwest, the long and sparsely populated Persian Gulf coast, and the desolate deserts of Baluchistan in the southeast. The specific features of the physical environment in each locale, and the range of economic activities that are possible (or impossible) there, affect the residents, regardless of their linguistic, religious, ethnic, national minority, and tribal identities. Thus a particular livelihood, technological complex, residential type, or settlement pattern may be more attributable to the geographic region and its physical features than to any specific ethnic or other sociocultural traits. Several qualifications regarding these points are necessary. Shi'i Muslims and Persians still seem to be favored in these regions, over people of other religions and ethnicities. Governmental programs and facilities there reached and

[116] Nayereh Tohidi, "Iran: Regionalism, Ethnicity and Democracy," 28 June 2006, http://www.opendemocracy.net/democracy-irandemocracy/regionalism_3695.jsp

benefitted them more directly than other citizens. Also, tribal organizations and affiliations assist people in their adaptations to certain physical environmental conditions and give them an advantage over the non-tribal people there.

A regional perspective also demonstrates how ethnic groups within their locales are often differentiated by their livelihoods and how inequalities and hierarchies emerge among them. Occupational specialization sometimes marks an ethnic group and distinguishes it from others in a region. Each ethnicity influences and is influenced by other ethnicities, as seen in their regional interactions (such as between Gilakis and the Talysh in Gilan). Some of Iran's non-Persian ethnicities are related to similar ethnicities across international borders (including the majority ethnicities there), while others are found only in enclaves within Iranian territory.

For many Persians, the cities (and perhaps regions) they consider home are part of their sociocultural (and perhaps economic and political) identities. Shirazis exemplify such an attachment. Isfahan is "half of the world," as the centuries-old adage proclaims. Those who regard Tehran as their home often stress the supremacy of this location, compared with backwater provincial ones, while Yazdis say they benefit from an urban environment without having to suffer from the crime, overpopulation, and pollution that typify Tehran. People in these cities (and regions) who are not Persians are more likely to emphasize their other, non-locational identities, unless ethnicity and place are closely interconnected.

Some small occupational and caste-like groups in Iran have unique cultural and even physical features. They lack large populations, but they are still a distinctive feature of Iran's human landscape. They demonstrate many traits that Iran's larger ethnic groups also have.

Known by different names in Iran, "gypsies" live dispersed throughout the country (and around the world).[117] Often itinerant, Iran's Romani people tend to reside in small groups and engage in specialized tasks such as metal-working and music. They speak variants of Romani and Domari (both "gypsy" languages) and regional Indo-Iranian languages. Their lifestyles, physical appearance, and sometimes pariah sta-

[117] Common names in Iran are *ghorbat* and *koli*, which others apply often pejoratively.

tus often lead other Iranians to assume that they are the poorest members of local ethnic groups.

People with dark skin and other physical features that appear to derive from African immigrants (including slaves) also reside in Iran, especially along the Persian Gulf coast. Many work as fishermen, date cultivators, and weavers of utilitarian objects from palm fronds. As with gypsies, they tend to marry only within their own groups. Some of them still engage in religious and curing rituals of African origins.

National Minorities

Many Iranians, especially those who are part of the linguistic, religious, ethnic, and tribal minorities, hold grievances against Iran's government because of the inequitable and discriminatory distribution of national resources (oil income, modern industry and infrastructure, and educational institutions), political power, and sociocultural status. Many of them lack even basic services, such as clean water, electricity, modern healthcare, schools, and vehicular roads.[118] Not all of these citizens have the means to protest effectively against this inequality. Minorities who are not Muslim especially have to exercise caution in any activism outside their communities, to avoid further discrimination and persecution.

Each of Iran's many national minorities (Table 8.6), including those who are also Sunni Muslims, has a sense of being a "nation" that differs from that of Iran's "nation."[119] Its members have focused their attention and efforts on three or four levels. First, internal to the group, they cultivated leaders, formed unifying institutions (including rituals and ceremonies), politicized their identities, and defended their interests. Second, they managed their regional ties by cooperating with neighboring groups and competing over access to scarce resources. Third, in relation to the state, they sought beneficial services, made demands, and tried to prevent detrimental incursions. Some of them agitated for

[118] First a governmental agency and then a ministry, Jihad-e Sazandegi (Crusade for Construction) has brought some services to areas that the Pahlavi shahs had intentionally neglected.

[119] Rasmus Elling discusses Azeri Turks, Kurds, Arabs, and Baluch in Iran in the post-revolutionary period (with a focus on 2005–7); *Minorities in Iran: Nationalism and Ethnicity after Khomeini*, New York: Palgrave Macmillan, 2013. His book was published after I completed this chapter.

Table 8.6: National Minorities in Iran

Group[120]	*Location in Iran*	*Population Figure*	*Language*	*Tribally Organized*
Azeri Turks (Turkic)	northwest, Tehran	11.2–19.4 million	Turkic	none
Kurds	northwest, west, northeast, southeast	5–7.5–10 million	Kurdish	some
Lurs	west, southwest	2.6–4.7 million	Luri	all
Gilakis	Caspian coast	3–4 million	Gilaki	none
Mazandaranis	Caspian coast	3–4 million	Mazandarani	none
Arabs	southwest, Gulf coast, northeast	1.3–1.6–2.1 million	Arabic	some
Qashqa'i (Turkic)	southwest	1.5–1.8 million	Turkic	all
Baluch	southeast	1.2–1.6 million	Baluchi	all
Turkmans (Turkic)	northeast	1–2 million	Turkic	all
Bakhtiyaris (Lurs)	central southwest	1–2 million	Luri	all
Talysh	Caspian coast	430,000	Talyshi	none
Shahsevan (Turkic)[121]	northwest	130,000–310,000	Turkic	all
Armenians[122]	northwestern, central	200,000–250,000	Armenian	none

[120] Groups are listed according to approximate population figures.
[121] The Shahsevan may be too small of a group to warrant status as a national minority.
[122] Armenians are often listed instead as an ethno-religious or ethnolinguistic group.

greater rights, even autonomous status within a new federal state, while a few saw no alternative except independence. And fourth, many of them cooperated with compatriots across international borders, and some allied with neighboring states (or their opponents) and wider entities such as nationalist and Islamist movements and foreign powers. These collective efforts and the related organizations, institutions, and ideologies differentiate the national minorities from other sociocultural, even sociopolitical, groups in Iran and cause any ruling regime concern.

Religious institutions and leaders are key attributes of some national minorities. Sunni Muslims hold greater grievances against Iran's Shi'i-led government than people who are Shi'i Muslims. Their supportive religious structures are often not found among the Shi'i minorities. Sunnis are potentially more vulnerable to the regime because these institutions and leaders pose threats to state power, but Shi'is are also vulnerable to the state if they lack such mediating, buffering agencies.

Institutional leadership among Iran's religious minorities, national minorities, and tribes is a key factor in characterizing these entities, compared with less politicized linguistic and ethnic groups. Leaders of religious minorities are especially important in mediating between the practitioners and the state's authorities and providing representation for people who are otherwise powerless in such often hostile environments.

Iran's national minorities have general and specific aspirations and demands. They want Iran's government to treat them in the same fashion as it does citizens who have full rights; they do not want to be victimized because of their minority linguistic, religious, ethnic, and tribal identities. Yet wider, extenuating circumstances complicate their situation. The Islamic regime has denied full legal and civil rights to increasing numbers of citizens since 1979—not only the minorities but also some Shi'is and Persians, most secular individuals, all women, and a large part of the youth—and this escalation poses a crisis for practically every Iranian there. Still, Iranians who oppose the current regime's intensification of power and expansion of authority seem more focused on ways to improve conditions for the Shi'i and Persian majorities and for women than for any minorities.

The minorities want representation at the national level as cabinet ministers, other high-level officials, and parliamentarians.[123] They

[123] Iran's six elected presidents (1979–2013, through the second term of Mahmud

expect dominant roles in local governance as policymakers, administrators, mayors, and judges, and need control over the police and other security forces. These groups desire access to television and radio broadcasts, newspapers, and magazines in their languages. They hope for the freedom to express their cultures in publications and public forums, such as weddings and heritage celebrations. Communities want their students at all levels to receive instruction in their native languages, parallel to instruction in Persian so they can be linguistically equipped to pass national university-entrance examinations, find jobs, and participate in the wider Iranian society. Religious minorities expect to practice their faiths in ways they choose, without being mistreated because of their religious beliefs.

Many of Iran's ethno-linguistic minorities (including Sunni Muslims) are located in the least advantaged and developed regions and at great distances from Tehran and other major urban and industrial centers. Efforts by the government to improve their conditions, if it were so motivated, would be challenging, especially because of persisting infrastructural deficits. The government assesses these situations in terms of how it could benefit by providing services beyond the minimum.[124] It also has to consider the consequences if it continues to disfavor or ignore these regions and groups, especially if foreign powers, neighboring states, or compatriots in neighboring countries decide to intervene.

Iran's government is troubled by the prospects of Iran's many "nations" becoming independent and forming their own nation-states, perhaps in concert with compatriots across borders.[125] External powers,

---

Ahmadinejad) have chosen only one Sunni Muslim as a cabinet minister or deputy minister, despite Sunnis comprising 9–11 percent of the country's population. Several presidents have selected one or two members of ethnic minorities (but not any non-Muslims).

[124] Early in his rule, Ayatollah Khomeini expressed interest in providing remedial goods and services to Iran's many dispossessed peoples (*mostazafin*), whom he viewed as the unfortunate victims of discriminatory policies by two Pahlavi shahs. He regarded them as fellow Muslims only, and not as ethnic, tribal, or minority peoples. After a few years he abandoned this goal. Ahmadinejad resurrected the idea of assisting the poor when he ran for the presidency in 2005 (and for reelection in 2009), but since 2005 other issues distracted him.

[125] Despite the critical stance of many Iranian scholars about the dismal failures of Iran's rulers over the past century, they still support the territorial and political

including the United States, European states, the EU, and all of Iran's neighbors, including the Persian Gulf countries, are also concerned about such possible developments. Yet only Kurds and Azeri Turks have recently (1945–6) achieved some independence; their success was short-lived, and their efforts were influenced or directed by foreign powers, which soon withdrew their support.[126] Except for some Kurds, none of Iran's minority groups was actively pursuing independence from Iran in 2013. They all want better economic, political, social, and cultural opportunities, including a share of Iran's oil income, but no Iranian government in the twentieth and early twenty-first centuries has made this effort a priority. As time progresses, the non-sovereign ethnicities and nationalities of Iran will likely be further excluded and neglected, with consequences yet to be determined.

If Iran's government is unwilling or unable to improve conditions for them, most national minorities would support a federal system of autonomous regions. The autonomous Kurdish Region in northern Iraq offers an example for them. In a federal Iran, the central government could handle defense, foreign affairs, telecommunications, and currency, and each region could rely on local individuals as officials and agents and control local policies and administration.[127]

Iran's largest, most prominent national minority consists of the Turkish-speaking Azeris. Located primarily in the northwest, Azeri Turks are possibly a quarter or even a third of Iran's total population, with significant numbers in the capital of Tehran and other large urban centers.[128]

---

integrity of the country. They reject ideas about regional secession, even knowing that Iran's governments have made little effort to improve these areas and ease the hardships that so many people there endure.

[126] The Kurdish Republic of Mahabad and the Democratic Republic of Azerbaijan were formed in 1945–6. See Nader Entessar, *Kurdish Politics in the Middle East*, Lanham, MD: Lexington, 2010; and Touraj Atabaki, *Azerbaijan: Ethnicity and the Struggle for Power in Iran*, London: I.B. Tauris, 2000.

[127] Each potentially autonomous region in Iran contains residents who do not belong to the majority ethnic group there, often by the explicit design of prior and current regimes, and they would need to have their legal and civil rights respected. Also, some ethnic and minority groups do not have contiguous territories.

[128] Azeri Turks are perhaps half of Tehran's population; they are the major non-Persian group there. Most of Tehran's poor have come as migrants from Turkish-speaking regions; see Asef Bayat, *Street Politics: Poor People's Movements in Iran*, New York: Columbia University Press, 1997, p. 30.

Unlike many of Iran's national minorities, they are not tribally organized. Their high numbers, strong urban presence, lack of tribal institutions, and Shi'i affiliation help them to be more integrated and assimilated in the nation-state than any other minority.[129] They may be the least likely to want independence from Iran. They have already made substantial economic, political, and social investments in the nation-state.

As Turks, Azeris suffer some linguistic and ethnic discrimination in Persian-dominated Iran. A condescending cartoon in an official Iranian government newspaper in 2006—which equated Azeris with cockroaches that needed to learn to speak Persian—resulted in outrage, demonstrations, jailings, and deaths.

When Azerbaijan declared its independence as a republic after the collapse of the Soviet Union in 1991, Iran's Azeris were further politicized, and they sought greater rights in Iran. Neighboring independent nation-states, where the languages, religions, and cultures of some of Iran's diverse peoples are preserved and formally recognized, help Iran's minority linguistic, religious, and ethnic communities and their identities to survive and flourish. These states include Azerbaijan, Turkey, Iraq, Turkmenistan, and Armenia. The region's press writes about North Azerbaijan (the new nation-state) and South Azerbaijan (currently part of Iran). The two areas have been historically connected, and some people hope for greater unification of this ethno-linguistic region.[130] If Iran were to break up into separate independent or autonomous sectors, Iranian Azerbaijan would constitute the most populous, unified, and economically self-sufficient one. It is strategically positioned near coun-

[129] Writers on Iran emphasize that the country's supreme leader (1989–), Ali Khamenei, is an Azeri Turk, as if to say that ethnic discrimination does not and could not occur in Iran. Yet his identity as the highest-ranking cleric in Iran supersedes his Azeri origins, and his interests focus on supreme power in Iran, not on local or regional sectarian issues. Iran's Azeris do not view him as an ally when they compete for greater access to Iran's wealth and power. Iranians joke that Khamenei has three ethnic identities. As a sayyid, a reputed descendant of the Prophet Muhammad, he has Arab ancestry. His father is an Azeri Turk, and his mother is presumably a Persian. Mir-Hossein Mousavi, a front-runner in the disputed 2009 presidential election, is also an Azeri Turk.

[130] Iran has more Azeri Turks as citizens than does the Republic of Azerbaijan. Turkey shares ethno-linguistic features with the new republic and with Iran's Azeris, as do other Turks in the Caucasus and Central Eurasia. Notions of pan-Turkism inspire millions of Turks in the wider region.

tries that would be supportive, and its infrastructure (including transnational trade routes) is already developed.

The Kurds are Iran's second most prominent national minority, and they have many compatriots in neighboring Turkey, Iraq, Syria, and elsewhere.[131] Their political and military connections across borders are more developed than those of other minority groups in Iran (except the Baluch). The Islamic regime worries about the extent of the Kurds' loyalty to Iran, and the autonomous Kurdistan Region in northern Iraq troubles multiple countries in the area. The Kurds are more likely than Iran's other national minorities to witness the birth of an independent state, but Iran's Kurds would not necessarily be able to join it. Rulers in Iran have attempted to subjugate the Kurds, and in a more aggressive, violent fashion than for the other minorities. Some Kurds are tribally organized, and internal linguistic, religious, and cultural diversity is more extensive than in Iran's other national minorities. The Kurds' vast numbers in multiple nation-states, their long history as a separate people, their periodic expulsions and relocations by imperial and modern states, and the relative isolation of many local communities in rugged mountainous terrain contribute to the development and persistence of diversity. More than Iran's Shi'i Kurds, Iran's Sunni Kurds are oriented toward their own communities and are distanced from the Shi'i regime. Shi'i Kurds having Ahl-e Haqq, Alevi, Yazidi, and Sufi affiliations are similar to the Sunnis in this regard.

Iran's Baluch, residents of Iran's southeastern region, are largely Sunni Muslims but they also have some Zikri members. Many compatriots live across the borders in Pakistan and Afghanistan and in the wider Persian Gulf region and are a factor in the politics of many countries.[132] The

[131] The world population of Kurds is 28–35 million: Turkey (14–19 million), Iran (5–10 million), Iraq (4.3 million), Syria (2 million in 2013), and elsewhere. Kurds are the fourth largest ethnic group in the Middle East (after Arabs, Persians, and Turks), but they share more cultural traits than each of the three other groups do. For maps, see: http://gulf2000.columbia.edu/images/maps/Kurd_Distribution_in_Mid_East_lg.jpg, and http://gulf2000.columbia.edu/images/maps/Kurdish_Tribal_Confederacies_lg.jpg

[132] Selig Harrison, *In Afghanistan's Shadow: Baluch Nationalism and Soviet Temptations*, New York: Carnegie Endowment, 1981; and Martin Axmann, "Phoenix from the Ashes?" in *The Baloch and Others* focus on the wider political context for the Baluch. Nine million Baluch live in Pakistan (6.2 million), Iran (1.8 million), Afghanistan (300,000), and Oman (250,000). They make up 10–13 per-

Baluch are tribally organized and possess leadership and other institutions for political and military activism in Iran and in cooperation with Baluch elsewhere.[133] They have participated in local and regional nationalist and Islamist movements, including Jundullah. In Pakistan, the Baluch constitute "the most serious, effective, and militant ethno-nationalist force," a level of activity that impresses their compatriots in Iran.[134]

Iran's Baluch occupy a large, sparsely inhabited territory that is limited in natural resources and modern infrastructure, a situation increasing poverty there but also affording the residents space for relatively unimpeded political and economic activities. Some Baluch profit by trafficking in commodities and people.[135] Baluchistan is a major route for Iranians emigrating illegally. The Baluch have long needed economic assistance from Iran's government, which has resisted giving them any priority. Recent governmental efforts for the province (and not for the Baluch specifically) include developing three urban areas, including the Indian Ocean port of Chabahar and its free-trade zone.[136] Many Baluch from Iran and its neighbors are migrant workers in the Persian Gulf states to the west and southwest, travel between the two areas, and renew their ethno-linguistic, religious, and tribal ties in both. These international connections enhance their sophistication in matters of local, national, regional, and Islamist politics, and the politicization of this population in Iran has more potential than found among the other national minorities

---

cent of Oman's population (John Peterson, this volume). For a map, see: http://gulf2000.columbia.edu/images/maps/Baluch_Ethnic_Distribution_lg.jpg

[133] The literature on Baluch politics in Iran in the 1990s and early 2000s sometimes mentions "non-tribal" Baluch participants such as university students and middle-class civil servants. Authors seem to assume, incorrectly in my view, that whenever any Baluch receive higher education and attain new occupations, they are no longer a part of tribal society. To continue to espouse tribal affiliations is a response to modernizing times, just as learning computer technology is. Most writers disparage "tribalism" and consider any "tribal" connections to be a manifestation of pre-modern "traditional" society and thus having no contemporary significance.

[134] Axmann, "Phoenix," p. 286.

[135] Multiple regimes in Iran and Pakistan have attempted to defeat Baluch insurgents. They distort the rebels' political goals by claiming that they are only "bandits" and "smugglers" exploiting the open border for economic profit.

[136] Hassan Afrakhteh, "Social, Demographic and Cultural Change in Iranian Balochistan," in *The Baloch and Others*.

(excluding the Kurds).[137] Influential Baluch leaders reside in Dubai, Kuwait, and London and impact the wider community.

Most Arabs in Iran are found in two areas, Khuzistan province at the head of the Persian Gulf and all along the Persian Gulf coast. Other Arab communities are located in Khorasan in northeastern Iran. Iran's Arabs are not as concentrated and their territories are not as contiguous as some other minorities. As with Iran's Kurds, some of Iran's Arabs are Shi'i Muslims, and others are Sunni Muslims. Iran's Arab communities trace tribal and cultural connections to Iraq and the opposite shore of the Persian Gulf. Some are still tribally organized and are often more politicized than their neighbors in Iran.

The Arabs in Khuzistan share a border with Iraq and are historically connected to that area. Some Arabs in Iran have agitated for an independent "Arabistan" while others have lacked interest, and few have wanted to align with Arab-dominated Iraq (especially during Saddam Hussein's rule and after his demise). Iran's government has relocated Persians to Khuzistan since the discovery of oil in 1908 and, to dilute further the Arab presence there, has encouraged neighboring ethnic and tribal groups (Lurs in particular) to join the growing industrial work force. The area is now a mixture of people (some say 50 percent Persian), which has made regional autonomy less feasible for the Arabs there. When Saddam Hussein began his military assault against Iran in 1980, he expected that Iran's Arabs, especially along the war's front line, would challenge Iran's government and even join Iraq's military forces. He was mistaken. Saddam also underestimated how much his brutality against Iraq's Shi'i Arabs would alarm Iran's Shi'i and Sunni Arabs.

Communities of Arabs in Iran are also located along the Persian Gulf coast and just inland, and are linked economically and socially to the Gulf's western and southern shore and the Arab peoples and states there. Many have migrated to these regions for work since 1979.[138]

Iran's Turkmans enjoy the advantage of having a new, compatible nation-state along their northern border. Turkmenistan acclaims the same kinds of linguistic, religious, ethnic, and tribal affiliations that are

[137] Stéphane Dudoignon, "Zahedan vs. Qom?" in Denise Aigle et al. (eds), *Miscellanea Asiatica*, Sankt Augustin, Germany: Institut Monumenta Serica, 2010.

[138] Shahnaz Nadjmabadi, "Arab Presence"; Shahnaz Nadjmabadi, "Cross-Border Networks," *Anthropology of the Middle East*, 5 (2010), pp. 18–33.

found among Iran's Turkmans.[139] Turkmans in both areas are Sunni Muslims. Those in Iran have a strong sense of their common ethnicity, which they demonstrate through their Turkish language, religion, and material culture, including unique dwellings (felt yurts) and a rich array of handwoven textiles. Many Turkmans have physical features similar to those of people in Central Eurasia to the north and east and are identifiable in Iran when they leave their region.

The Qashqa'i, another of Iran's many Turkish-speaking peoples, are better known inside and outside of Iran than some other groups. Yet they have received less attention as a national minority than the Azeri Turks, Kurds, Baluch, Arabs, and Turkmans, primarily because they do not reside along Iran's often-troublesome international borders or have compatriots across them, unlike these other peoples. Qashqa'i territory is an enclave in southwestern Iran, and the people are Shi'i Muslims. Qashqa'i tribal leaders have participated in national politics during the twentieth century, and the group was one of the few in Iran to raise an insurgency against the newly declared Islamic regime. Paramilitary forces defeated them in 1982.[140] Early on, some Kurds, Baluch, Arabs, and Turkmans had also resisted the rule of the new government but in less coordinated and focused fashion than the Qashqa'i. Hostilities among these other peoples against the state have continued to simmer since 1979.

Within Iran, as is the case with all the other national minorities, the Qashqa'i have distinctive cultural features, which outsiders often consider quaint and exotic. Iran's governments under the shah and the ayatollahs have exploited the Qashqa'i in their efforts to project a softer and less-threatening national image abroad, for external political and economic purposes. They expected that photographs and videotapes exhibiting expressive and vibrantly dressed Qashqa'i women migrating on horseback, weaving textiles, and dancing at weddings would dispute the notion that Iran is a prison for subordinated, secluded, veiled, and sullen women. Qashqa'i writers promote various facets of their culture though books and specialized magazines, and poets, musicians, and weavers organize cultural festivals.[141]

[139] Adrienne Edgar, *Tribal Nation: The Making of Soviet Turkmenistan*, Princeton: Princeton University Press, 2004.

[140] Lois Beck, *The Qashqa'i of Iran*, New Haven: Yale University Press, 1986.

[141] Under the cover of highlighting a seemingly innocuous "culture" (*farhang*), these

Independence or even greater autonomy does not seem likely for the Qashqa'i, unless the central government collapses and other minority groups act on behalf of their own interests. Somewhat reluctantly, the Qashqa'i depend on the institutions and services of the Iranian state. They say they lack other options if they want to improve the conditions of their lives. By accepting this assistance, they acknowledge that they are becoming more integrated in Iran. Many Qashqa'i do try to avoid cultural assimilation in Persian-dominant Iran by emphasizing and elaborating the attributes of their Turkish heritage. Their social ties outside their groups are most often with other regional ethnic and tribal peoples and less often with the non-tribal Persians who reside in the vicinity's villages, towns, and cities. Many Qashqa'i are more socio-economically mobile than members of some other Muslim minorities. They embraced formal education sooner than many of Iran's other rural, tribal, nomadic peoples and have benefitted by taking advantage of new economic opportunities.

The southern coast of the Caspian Sea and the provinces of Gilan and Mazandaran there contain a rich array of ethnic groups. Two of them, the Gilakis and Mazandaranis, can also be considered national minorities. They are Shi'is. Their identities are based more on distinctive linguistic and other cultural traits than on political organization and activism. The relative lushness of their physical environment, along the rain-watered coast, and their livelihoods based on fish, rice and tea cultivation, silk production, and tourism contribute to their economic success. Many residents lack the economic reasons to oppose the Persian-controlled state that other national minorities accentuate. Although Persians joke about and ridicule them, Gilakis and Mazandaranis are not socially discriminated against in the ways that some other minorities are.

A third ethnic group along the Caspian coast, near the Gilakis and just north of them, consists of the Talysh. Many Talysh were previously

---

festivals serve as arenas for the greater politicization of the attendees. Expressions of cultural resurgence also occur among Iran's other ethnic, national minority, tribal, and regional groups, with the Islamic regime's approval or at least without its prohibition. The government's Organization for Nomads' Affairs facilitates these efforts for Iran's *ashayer* (meaning nomads, but also referring to tribes). For political reasons and to avoid further harassment and persecution, Iran's non-Muslim peoples have tried to maintain a low profile by not engaging as publicly in such cultural events.

Sunni Muslims but some converted to Shi'i Islam, a process that paralleled the spread of the Azeri-Turkish language in the area. The Talysh have a fierce pride in their ethnic identity. They have a distinctive language and have become increasingly politicized since 1979. Unlike the Gilakis, the Talysh have substantial numbers of compatriots outside the province of Gilan and beyond Iran's border in the Republic of Azerbaijan. Some activists in Iran have pressed for their own province.

Iran's Lurs in western and southwestern Iran are Shi'i Muslims. They are divided into separate northern, central, and southern sections, with few direct political ties between and among them. Most if not all of them are tribally organized in their specific localities. The territory of the northern Lurs lies near and alongside Iraq.[142] The two other Lur territories are farther inland, and Persian, Arab, and Qashqa'i communities are in close proximity. These Lurs do not have affiliates across borders. Language and other cultural traits unite each of the three Lur areas and "greater Luristan" as well.

As a separate entity between the northern and southern sections, the Bakhtiyari have created interrelated features that the other Lurs have not: a tribal confederacy led by powerful khans, lucrative links with foreign powers, and activism in Iran's national politics in the late nineteenth and early twentieth centuries. The Bakhtiyari are better known as a group than Iran's other Lurs.[143] As a polity, the Bakhtiyari faded from the national scene after the rise of Reza Shah in 1925, and they no longer seem to possess the leadership, institutions, and aspirations that would enable them to reemerge as a significant national minority in the near future. Their cultural attributes still remained strong in 2013 and

142 Mehdi Karroubi, former speaker of parliament and a front-runner in the disputed 2009 presidential election, is a Lur from northern Luristan. As a prominent clergyman and politician for decades, he has created an identity that supersedes his non-Persian ethnicity, especially as a Lur. He probably could not have attained high, state-level positions, especially outside of Luristan, if he had not been a cleric and if the regime had not been clergy-run.

143 Arash Khazeni, *Tribes and Empire: On the Margins of Nineteenth-Century Iran*, Seattle: University of Washington Press, 2009. Gene Garthwaite wrote a book about Bakhtiyari history without mentioning anywhere that the people are Lurs and part of a large ethno-linguistic minority; see *Khans and Shahs: A Documentary Analysis of the Bakhtiyari in Iran*, Cambridge: Cambridge University Press, 1983. I read the last draft of the manuscript and suggested that he ought to include these important facts; he did so.

helped to preserve the people as a distinctive sociocultural group. Many descendants of the formerly influential khans reside abroad and are well assimilated there.

The Shahsevan, another of Iran's many Turkish-speaking groups, are similar in features to the Qashqa'i, including tribal organization and a history of nomadic pastoralism. Oral histories link the two peoples. Residing in northwestern Iran, the Shahsevan share some linguistic and other cultural traits with Azeris and other Turks in the region. They too are Shi'i Muslims. Their comparatively small size and lack of prominent leaders in 2013 made them less viable as an autonomous group.

The Armenians are the final group considered here. Unlike all the other groups, these people are Christians. Scholars do not usually include the Armenians among Iran's national minorities, in part because of their relatively few numbers and their geographic dispersion, but the people do share some similarities with the others. They have many compatriots in neighboring countries, including the Republic of Armenia, and in a worldwide diaspora. Writers usually consider Iran's non-Muslim minorities as religious or ethno-religious groups instead. Armenians occupy a special place in Iran's recent economic and cultural history due to their mercantilism and artistic achievements. The Republic of Armenia, another new nation-state along Iran's borders, lacks territorial contiguity with Iran's dispersed, largely urban Armenian minority, although it potentially offers a place of refuge for Iran's Armenians if political conditions in Iran worsen for them.[144]

Several scholars draw attention to Iran's peripheral populations and their participation in national politics through elections.[145] The combined votes of these peoples (many of them Iran's national minorities) are increasingly affecting the outcome of the government's presidential elections. Also, every district (*shahrestan*) in Iran is represented in the national parliament, and the majority of parliamentary deputies come

[144] Armenia has become a popular destination for Iranians during the New Year holiday, a nearby location where they can escape from many of the social and cultural constraints they experience at home.

[145] Ali Gheissari and Kaveh Sanandaji, "New Conservative Politics and Electoral Behavior in Iran"; Nayereh Tohidi, "Ethnicity and Religious Minority Politics in Iran"; and Kaveh Ehsani, "Urban Provincial Periphery in Iran"; all in Ali Gheissari (ed.), *Contemporary Iran: Economy, Society, Politics*, Oxford: Oxford University Press, 2009.

from rural, provincial, minority, and border territories. Many of these representatives are part of Iran's diverse regional, linguistic, religious (Sunni Muslim), ethnic, national minority, and tribal populations. As these deputies rise to speak in parliament, they usually begin by identifying themselves in one or more of these terms, and they and their constituencies become known in the body and beyond through media coverage. Some of these individuals wear the clothing distinctive to their groups. Such strong minority representation has shocked the urban, Shi'i, Persian deputies each time election results were announced and new sessions were convened. They had expected to control parliament, just as urban Shi'i Persians dominated practically all other centralized state institutions and powerful para-statal foundations.[146]

Shahriyar Qermezi, parliamentary deputy in 1996–2000 for the mountainous, rural district of Semirom in southern Isfahan province, exemplifies the multiple, complex identities of many deputies. He represented the district, province, Qashqa'i tribal confederacy, Qashqa'i ethnicity and national minority identity, and Turkish-speakers. As a former nomadic pastoralist, he personified socio-economic mobility and modernity. As a teacher, he embodied the importance of formal education in securing new occupations. As a wounded veteran of the Iraq–Iran War, he stood for fellow veterans, families of martyrs, and their sacrifices for the country. And as a (moderate) hezbollahi, he exhibited religious piety and support for the supreme leader and the Islamic Republic.

Tribes

Iran's tribal peoples include many also listed according to their languages, religions, ethnicities, and national minorities. Their tribal affiliations are only one part of their identities, and these connections increase or decrease in importance depending on local and wider circumstances. Some of Iran's large tribal groups (Table 8.7) have played

[146] More than any other Iranians who are not Persians, Azeri Turks have played a role in parts of the central government (the supreme leader since 1989 being the most prominent example). Some parliamentary deputies have formed subgroups to represent their regions and/or ethnic and minority communities; see Samii, "The Nation and its Minorities." Five Qashqa'i deputies in 1996–2000 allied to support measures that benefitted their group and region, and twelve Sunni deputies in 2012 petitioned the supreme leader.

Table 8.7: Tribal Populations in Iran

Group[147]	*Population in Iran*	*Population in Other States*[148]	*Religion*
Kurds[149]	5–10 million	millions (in many states)	Sunni Islam (75%) Shi'i Islam Ahl-e Haqq (Yarsan) Alevi Yazidi
Baluch[150]	1.2–1.6 million	millions (in Pakistan, Afghanistan, Persian Gulf)	Sunni Islam Zikri
Qashqa'i	1.5–1.8 million	none	Shi'i Islam
Bakhtiyari	1–2 million	none	Shi'i Islam
Lurs	2.6–4.7 million	a few (in Iraq)	Shi'i Islam
Turkmans	1–2 million	millions (in Turkmenistan, Afghanistan)	Sunni Islam
Shahsevan	130,000–310,00	none	Shi'i Islam
Arabs[151]	1.3–1.6–2.1 million	millions (in many states)	Shi'i Islam (80%), Sunni Islam
Khamseh	400,000	none	Shi'i Islam (majority), Sunni Islam

147 Each tribal group listed has its own named sections, which are not included here.
148 This category does not include tribal people who are part of the recent Iranian diaspora.
149 Some but not all Kurds in Iran are tribally organized.
150 More Baluch are migrant workers outside of Iran than any other tribal group.
151 Some but not all Arabs in Iran are tribally organized.

Hazaras	283,000	millions (in Afghanistan)	Shi'i Islam
Afshars	200,000	some	Shi'i Islam
Aimaq (incl. Timuris)	170,000–200,000	some (in Afghanistan)	Sunni Islam
Pashtuns	113,000	millions (in Afghanistan, Pakistan)	Sunni Islam
Khalaj	20,000–48,000	some	Shi'i Islam

roles in Iran's recent history. Iran's tribes have drawn the attention of anthropologists (mostly foreigners) more than any other category in Iran, and more detailed information is known about them than for many other segments of Iranian society.[152]

Anthropologists often define tribes by their sociopolitical characteristics.[153] These entities of various sizes are organized by ties of political affiliation to hierarchies of groups and leaders. Tribally organized people form flexible local groups according to kinship and marriage ties and compatibility. Their wider ties are sociopolitical and connect them to lineages, clans, subtribes, tribes, and sometimes tribal confederacies. These hierarchical structures and the leaders associated with them are the principal attributes of tribally organized people (and they distinguish them from people who are not tribally organized). These wider systems do not operate continuously; instead, they emerge and reemerge during times of external or internal crises and threats.[154] Distinctive ceremonies,

[152] Major anthropological studies, listed chronologically, include Fredrik Barth, *Nomads of South Persia: The Basseri Tribe of the Khamseh Confederacy*, London: Allen and Unwin, 1961; William Irons, *The Yomut Turkmen*, Ann Arbor: University of Michigan Museum of Anthropology, 1975; Richard Tapper, *Pasture and Politics: Economics, Conflict and Ritual among Shahsevan Nomads*, London: Academic Press, 1979; Black-Michaud, *Sheep and Land*; Daniel Bradburd, *Ambiguous Relations: Kin, Class, and Conflict among Komachi Pastoralists*, Washington, DC: Smithsonian, 1990; Beck, *Nomad*; Martin van Bruinessen, *Agha, Shaikh and State: On the Social and Political Structures of Kurdistan*, London: Zed Books, 1992 (he also discusses non-tribal Kurds); and Philip Salzman, *Black Tents of Baluchistan*, Washington, DC: Smithsonian, 2000. For a tribal map of Iran color-coded by environmental factors (mountains, steppes, wooded lowlands, and deserts), see: http://gulf2000.columbia.edu/images/maps/Iran_Tribes_and_Environment_lg.jpg

[153] Lois Beck and Julia Huang, "Tribes," in Emad El-Din Shahin (ed.), *Oxford Encyclopedia of Islam and Politics*, Oxford: Oxford University Press, 2013; Lois Beck, "Tribes and the State in Nineteenth- and Twentieth-Century Iran," in Philip Khoury and Joseph Kostiner (eds), *Tribes and State Formation in the Middle East*, Berkeley: University of California Press, 1990.

[154] The Qashqa'i provide a recent example; see Beck, *Qashqa'i of Iran*. Reza Shah executed the Qashqa'i *ilkhani* (paramount leader) in 1933. When Allied forces drove the shah from power in 1941, the *ilkhani*'s sons resumed Qashqa'i leadership. Mohammad Reza Shah exiled these sons in 1954. The sons returned to leadership when the revolution expelled the shah in 1979. Iran's paramilitary forces defeated them in 1982.

rituals, and symbols help to unify people in their relationships with these leaders and groups.

Historians, political scientists, and others sometimes define the tribes of Iran as kinship groups. All people in Iran have kinship systems (a universal trait), and thus kinship alone cannot define a tribe. Even the elaborate genealogies of some tribal groups are charters constructed for political purposes and are not maps of actual kinship ties. Kinship links are one of the central organizing principles of tribal people at the local level, just as they are for many non-tribal Iranians, including those in villages and urban quarters.

Alone or together, other traits are associated with Iran's tribal groups but do not define tribes. They are found as well among many non-tribal people in Iran.

Tribal groups in Iran often have a distinctive language; only rarely is this language Persian. Where tribal people do speak Persian as a first language, they appear to have adopted it recently, and the usage stems from their accelerating contact with towns and cities, governmental agencies, military service, markets, religious institutions, and agricultural communities. Ancestors of the people in these groups probably spoke other languages, especially if their history includes nomadic pastoralism (which would have connected them with tribes of diverse linguistic backgrounds).[155]

Some tribes in Iran consist of Sunni Muslims, and others are Shi'i Muslims, the sects of Islam appealing to their ancestors and leaders according to their geographical locations and prior histories. Sufi Islam and some heterodox Shi'i sects are present in some tribal groups, especially the Kurds, and some Baluch are Zikris. Iran's other religious minorities (excluding Sunni Muslims) are not represented among the tribes of Iran. These non-Muslim minority religions have been primarily urban phenomena with centralized institutions, while members of Iran's tribes have tended to be dispersed and located far from cities.

Tribes in Iran also have distinctive cultures, some traits of which they may have in common with wider ethnic groups. The Kurds share some cultural characteristics regardless of having tribal affiliations or not. The

[155] Nomadic pastoralism and tribal organization often coexisted. Tribal structures helped nomadic pastoralists to gain access to seasonal pastures, schedule their migrations, and mediate their relationships with settled society.

Kurds are an identifiable ethnic group in Iran, and some of them are associated with tribes.

Yet other traits—ones associated with the people's locations, survival strategies, and economic practices—also characterize most of Iran's tribal populations. These traits too do not define tribes per se; each of them is also found among many non-tribal people in Iran. Iran's tribes are often located in rural and peripheral regions and in mountainous, steppe, and remote territories. Each group has developed strategies for surviving in these sometimes harsh environments, and their patterns are distinctive and identified with certain groups. The material culture associated with their livelihoods and survival patterns has distinguishing traits.[156] Many of Iran's tribal groups have relied on nomadic pastoralism, and some have also adopted agriculture, in part to produce fodder for their livestock. Most of Iran's tribal peoples in 2013 subsisted on some combination of animal husbandry, agriculture, wage and salaried labor, and textile production. Even people who have settled in towns and cities to work there have retained strong ties to their tribal groups, frequently visited their territories (often seasonally based), participated in group ceremonies and rituals, and followed customary traditions in their new places of residence.[157]

Many tribal groups are also part of Iran's national minorities (Tables 8.6, 8.7). The political affiliations within some national minorities stem in part from tribal structures, organizations, and ideologies, all of which strengthen these minorities and tribes as political entities and make them competitive with governmental institutions. In Iran's past, tribal polities had both supported and opposed regional leaders and external powers. Empires and states rose and fell due in part to their rulers' alliances with and hostilities against tribal groups, and some new states had tribal origins. Similar to Iran's shahs, the rulers of the Islamic Republic fear the political and military potential in the country's tribally based groups.

156 Even the ornate handwoven straps (*tangs*) that Iran's nomadic tribes use to fasten their possessions on camels and other pack animals during the seasonal migrations are distinctive for each group; see Dareshuri and Beck, "Bands."

157 I detail these processes for Qashqa'i tribespeople in Lois Beck, *Nomads Move On: Qashqa'i Tribespeople in Post-Revolutionary Iran*, London: Routledge (forthcoming, 2014).

Members of Iran's tribes value the ability to support and defend their interests, and many are sophisticated in the use of weapons, knowledge of military strategies, skills for handling horses and camels, abilities to adapt to rugged conditions, and techniques to evade detection and capture. Soon after Iraq attacked Iran in 1980, President Bani-Sadr and Ayatollah Khomeini appealed to Iran's tribesmen to help defend the country. Tribes were and still are Iran's leading armed units, other than the government's armed forces.[158] State efforts to disarm Iran's tribesmen have not progressed beyond the planning stages.

Various Perspectives on Iran's Minorities

I approach the issue of Iran's minorities by way of the five interlinking categories: languages, religions, ethnicities, national minorities, and tribes. In this chapter I have sought to demonstrate how each of these categories can be separately examined and analyzed and how they can also be combined with others to form composite identities. The literature on Iran tends to essentialize and reify each of these categories, as if each one is sufficient for understanding one or more sectors of Iran's population. Few authors demonstrate how identity is instead a composite of features and is complex, flexible, situational, and contextual, with one feature (among others) replacing another as settings and circumstances change. People politicized key attributes of their identities, created fluid symbols and meanings for them, and adapted their responses to frequently changing contexts.

In this final section I raise relevant overarching and underlying topics, without which no discussion of Iran's diversity is complete. I phrase many of these topics and subtopics in the form of questions (as I have also done elsewhere in this chapter), to demonstrate that we currently lack sufficient information and that do not yet have adequate answers. (The issue of Iran's ethnic Persians who are also Sunni Muslims is a case in point.) The questions also suggest possible avenues for future research. The answers to each question are complex and multifaceted and would

158 Iran's paramilitary forces, especially the volunteer *basij* militia, rely on violence, surveillance, and intimidation, unlike the way Iran's tribes engage in military action. The US Marine Corps in 2005 commissioned studies of Iran's major ethno-linguistic and tribal groups for a program titled "Cultural Intelligence for Military Operations: Iran," to prepare for US military action in Iran.

probably differ for each of the communities we would consider. The task of generalization hinges in large part on having new research results and doing further case-study and comparative analysis.

The Iranian nation-state, its ties with its citizens, and its sense of national identity relate to a discussion of Iran's minorities. Minorities are defined by their relationships with the Iranian state, from which they take some of their characteristics and against which they formulate their opposition and resistance. Detailed historical and contemporary studies of each of Iran's minority communities would help us to understand them, the wider contexts including their ties to state structures, and the ways they have changed from one regime to the next. With this information, we could assess the status of Iran's minorities under the first Pahlavi regime, under the second one, during the 1978–9 revolution, and under the Islamic Republic. Mohammad Reza Shah promulgated notions of a secular Iranian nationalism based on the Persian language and literature and the historical achievements of Persians since pre-Islamic times.[159] Khomeini and the Islamic regime redirected nationalist constructions to the unity brought about by adherence to Twelver Shi'i Islam. Each perspective had a different impact on the various components of Iran's diverse citizenry and alienated some people.[160]

A focus on centralizing states and possibly defiant minority communities includes information on the constitutional and other legal rights of citizens and on state institutions, ideologies, and policies. How do such attributes of the state actually affect people's lives? The wording of laws is one issue; knowing if, where, and how these laws are applied is another.[161] We rely on the perspectives of people whom the state impacts; such information derives from local-level studies and personal encoun-

[159] Amanat, "Iranian Identity Boundaries."

[160] Nikki Keddie, "The Minorities Question in Iran," in Shirin Tahir-Kheli and Shaheen Ayubi (eds), *The Iran–Iraq War: New Weapons, Old Conflicts*, New York: Praeger, 1983; and Kaveh Bayat, "The Ethnic Question in Iran," *Middle East Report*, 35 (2005), pp. 42–5. My intention to be more analytical and anthropological has prevented me from offering a more historical overview of the topic. Also, I emphasize recent, post-revolutionary circumstances.

[161] Iran's governments have not always observed constitutional protections for religious minorities, nor have they respected legal rights to use languages other than Persian, Arabic, and English in schools. The Arabic taught in schools is part of the formal study of Islam and the Qur'an and is not a response to the demands of Iran's Arabic-speakers for instruction in their spoken and written language.

ters. What are the state's mechanisms for integrating and assimilating people? How does the state try to promote national unity and citizen solidarity and create a sense of national identity? How are minorities organized to confront state institutions and ideologies, and how effective are they in the short term and the long term? What techniques do they develop to resist state encroachment? How do they also try to benefit from some state programs, such as educational services and regional security? What kinds of internal leadership do they have, and how are these leaders connected with the state?

The economic and socio-economic underpinnings of Iran and its minority communities are central topics.[162] How do state policies determine the distribution of resources, labor, and wealth within Iran and among these groups? How do rulers justify inequitable practices? When are minorities disadvantaged or advantaged? What paths are available for socio-economic mobility, and how do the minorities fare? Several of Iran's socio-economic classes flourish under new educational and occupational opportunities; others are hindered and fall further behind. Iran's rulers have favored the middle and upper classes of the dominant religious and ethnic communities, which often meant depressed conditions for the lower classes, especially in minority communities.[163]

The Islamic Republic has faced severe and escalating economic, political, social, and cultural problems since 1979, including war, an influx of refugees, international economic and political sanctions, external as well as self-imposed global isolation, diverted oil income, rising inflation, unemployment, socio-economic inequality and deprivation, underdevelopment, governmental corruption and pervasive bribery, a lack of democracy, weak (and state-impeded) civil society, lawlessness, a lack of political and civil liberties, human rights abuses, and restrictions on the rights of women. Many of these problems concern all citizens, not only the minorities, but some societal segments are better placed than the minorities to handle detrimental conditions and can perhaps even profit

162 Akbar Aghajanian, "Ethnic Inequality in Iran," *International Journal of Middle East Studies*, 15 (1983), pp. 211–24; and Leonard Helfgott, "Structural Foundations of the National Minority Situation," *Iranian Studies*, 13 (1980), pp. 195–214.

163 The wealthy and professional middle classes among the non-Muslim religious minorities benefitted under the last shah but lost this privileged position soon after the Islamic regime took power.

by them. What grievances do Iran's minorities have, and how do these issues relate to the country's other problems? How does the treatment of minorities compare with the experiences of Iran's other citizens? What difference does it make to the lives of Iranians if they are part of the Shi'i-dominating and Persian-dominating sectors of society or if they are not? When do issues of socio-economic class prevail over those of minority-group affiliation?

How do the ideologies and activities of Iran's oppositional movements relate to the minorities? Where do activist groups stand on minority rights? If the ruling regime permitted its citizens greater freedoms, many entities could form part of a vibrant civil society in Iran: the Green Movement, secularists, Islamic reformists (including those who oppose state rule by the clergy), women's rights activists, human rights advocates, leftists, intellectuals, writers, publishers, filmmakers, artists, students, trade unions, and workers could all play a part in a more pluralistic Iranian society. Some oppositional groups say that minority rights is an issue they will consider later, after they have achieved specific goals (such as freedom of the press) relating to the current regime (or, as they hope, its subsequent one). Women's rights advocates heard the same promises from a wide spectrum of the opposition during the 1978–9 revolution and were disheartened by subsequent events when their rights, one after another, were taken away or denied them. At the time of the revolution and afterward, leftists of different ideologies and affiliations had encouraged anti-regime activism among Iran's national minorities (especially those that were tribally organized) but made no effort to improve their conditions.[164] Minority group activists have tried to convince oppositional groups to include minority issues in their platforms. Middle-class urban Persians who support a West-leaning secular democracy may pay attention to minority rights, or, more likely, they may regard the issue as inconsequential when compared to others.

Issues of geography suggest other topics. How do Iran's neighbors and the region as a whole affect the regime's attitudes toward its diverse citizenry? Where are Iran's minority communities concentrated or dispersed, and what kinds of contacts do their members have with one another and

[164] Leftists had been attracted by the military expertise and relative political autonomy of these minority groups and by their geographical locations, which offered them protection while they engaged in their own anti-regime activities. Subsequently, the state punished these minorities for this contact.

with people across international borders?[165] How do changes in Iran's physical environment affect minorities, such as water shortages and desertification? Iran's administrative divisions (provinces and districts) do not match the borders of defined ethnic and minority groups, and the government since 1979 has intentionally complicated the issue by dividing existing provinces and creating new ones. How are minorities represented and administered according to these new divisions?

What roles do Iran's large diaspora communities play, especially people who originated in Iran's minority groups? How does this external presence affect people who remain in Iran?

Non-sectarian, transversal, cross-societal mobilizations in society—based on socio-economic class, religious ideology (such as fundamentalism), and other ideologies (such as democracy and secular nationalism)—underlie and overlap with sectarian identities. A more complete discussion of Iran's minorities would give fuller weight to these other issues. Just as sectarian identities rise and recede according to changing situations and contexts, so too do these cross-societal factors, and sometimes in concert with sectarian ones.

Some writers approach the issue of Iran's diverse peoples by choosing one or several groups as examples. Others include lists or charts but without much detail. Some authors study one group found in multiple nation-states. Others examine how another state developed policies for and handled its multiethnic peoples, with implications for Iran.[166] Some writers take a specialized topic such as tribe–state interrelationships and compare and contrast multiple places.[167] Others select a region (the Persian Gulf) and a topic (sectarianism) and draw on comparative information relating to each country there.

Scholars of Iran could include, and not ignore, issues concerning languages, religions, ethnicities, national minorities, and tribes in their works, where relevant.[168] These topics form part of larger discussions of

[165] Nadjmabadi demonstrates how Arabs on both shores of the Persian Gulf maintained contact; "Arab Presence" and "Cross-Border Networks."

[166] William McCagg and Brian Silver, the editors, explain in *Soviet Asian Ethnic Frontiers*, New York: Pergamon, 1979, how the Soviet Union dealt with its ethnic minorities in Central Eurasia.

[167] Richard Tapper (ed.), *Conflict of Tribe and State in Iran and Afghanistan*, London: Croom Helm, 1983.

[168] Fred Halliday, *Iran: Dictatorship and Development*, New York: Penguin, 1979; and Nikki Keddie, *Modern Iran: Roots and Results of Revolution*, updated edn,

Iran's history, politics, societies, and cultures. Some researchers focus on women's status so they can influence more general studies on Iran, which may not at first glance appear to be gender-related. So too can scholars of Iran's diversity expand the perspectives of other writers on Iran, to encourage them to consider issues—such as politicized social identities—that may be significant in their own studies.

New Haven: Yale University Press, 2006 demonstrate how these issues can be written into general historical studies and become essential parts of the authors' arguments.

BIBLIOGRAPHY

Abrahamian, Ervand, *The Iranian Mojahedin*, New Haven: Yale University Press, 1989.

Abu Hakima, Ahmad, *History of Eastern Arabia, 1750–1800: The Rise and Development of Bahrain and Kuwait*, Beirut: Khayats, 1965.

Afrakhteh, Hassan, "Social, Demographic and Cultural Change in Iranian Balochistan: Case Studies of the Three Urban Regions of Zahedan, Iranshahr and Chabahar," in Carina Jahani, Agnes Korn, and Paul Titus (eds), *The Baloch and Others: Linguistic, Historical and Socio-Political Perspectives on Pluralism in Balochistan*, pp. 197–224, Wiesbaden: Reichert, 2008.

Aghaie, Kamran, *The Women of Karbala: Ritual Performance and Symbolic Discourses in Modern Shi'i Islam*, Austin: University of Texas Press, 2005.

Aghajanian, Akbar, "Ethnic Inequality in Iran: An Overview," *International Journal of Middle East Studies*, 15, 2 (1983), pp. 211–24.

Ahmadi, Hamid, "Unity within Diversity: Foundations and Dynamics of National Identity in Iran," *Critique*, 14, 1 (2005), pp. 127–47.

Ahmed, Hassan, *Qiyam al-Dawla al-Zaydiyya fi al-Yaman* [The Rise of the Zaydi State in Yemen], Cairo: Madbouli Bookstore, 1996.

Alavi, Nasrin, *We are Iran: The Persian Blogs*, Brooklyn, NY: Soft Skull Press, 2005.

Al-Alawi, Hassan, *Al-Ta'thirat al-Turkiya fi al-Mashro'o al-Qawmi al-Arabi fil Iraq* [The Turkish Impact on Arab Nationalism in Iraq], London: Dar al-Zawra'a, 1988.

——— *Al-Shi'a wal Dawla al-Qawmiya fi al-Iraq 1914–1990* [The Shi'a and the National State in Iraq 1914–1990], Qom: Dar Al-Thaqafa, 1990.

Al Bakri, Yasin, *Bunyat al Mujtama'a al Iraqi: Jadaliyat al Sulta wal Tanawu'u* [The Structure of Iraqi Society: The Dialectic of Power and Plurality], Baghdad: Masr Murtadha, 2011.

Al-Hasan, Hamza, *Al-Shi'a fi al-mamlaka al-'arabiyya al-sa'udiyya*, vol. 1, *Al-'ahd al-turki 1871–1913*; vol. 2, *Al-'ahd al-sa'udi 1913–1991* [The Shia in the Arab Kingdom of Saudi Arabia, vol. 1, The Turkish Period 1871–1913; vol. 2, The Saudi Period 1913–1991], n.p.: Mu'assasat al-Baqi' li Ihya al-Turath, 1993.

Al Hasan, Hasan Tariq, "Bahrain Bids its Economic Reform Farewell," Open Democracy, 8 July 2012, http://www.opendemocracy.net/hasan-tariq-al-hasan/bahrain-bids-its-economic-reform-farewell

——— "Labor Market Politics in Bahrain," in Steffen Hertog (ed.), *National Employment, Migration, and Education in the GCC*, pp. 117–61, Berlin: Gerlach Press, 2012.

——— "The Role of Iran in the Failed Coup of 1981: The IFLB in Bahrain," *The Middle East Journal*, 65, 4 (2011), pp. 603–17.

——— "The Socio-Economic Foundations of Bahrain's Political Crisis," Open Democracy, 20 Feb. 2012, http://www.opendemocracy.net/hasan-tariq-al-hasan/socio-economic-foundations-of-bahrain%E2%80%99s-political-crisis

Al-Hasani, Abdul Razzaq, *Tarikh al Wizarat al Iraqiya* [The History of Iraqi Ministries], 7th edn, 8 vols, Baghdad: Dar al-Shu'oon al Thaqafiya al Ama, 1988.

Al Jaza'iri, Zuhair, *Harb al 'Ajiz* [The Invalid's War], Beirut: Al Saqi, 2009.

Al-Kadhem, Nader, *Isti'malat al-dhakira fi mujtama' ta'aduddi mubtala bi al-tarikh* [Uses of Memory in a Multicultural Society Burdened with History], Manama, Bahrain: Maktaba Fakhrawi, 2008.

Al-Khaburi, Jawad, *Al-Adwar al-'Umaniyya fi al-Qara al-Hindiyya: Dur Bani Sama bin Lu'ay—Ahl Lawatiyya* [The Omani Role on the Indian Continent: Role of the Bani Sama bin Lu'ay—The Lawatiyya], Beirut: Dar al-Nubala', 2001.

"Al-Mas'ala al-Ta'ifiyya wal Ithniya: al-Iraq Namuthaj" [The Sectarian and Ethnic Question: The Iraqi Example], *Oriental Affairs*, 1, Special Issue (2008).

Al-Mdayris, Falah Abdallah, *Al-Haraka al-Shi'iya fi Kuwait* [The Shi'a Movement in Kuwait], Kuwait: Qurtas, 1999.

Al-Najjar, Baqir Salman, *Al-Harakat al-Diniyah fi al-Khalij al-Arabi* [Religious Movements in the Arabian Gulf], London: Dar al-Saqi Press, 2007.

Al-Rasheed, Madawi, "God, the King and the Nation: Political Rhetoric in Saudi Arabia in the 1990s," *The Middle East Journal*, 50, 3 (1996), pp. 359–71.

——— (ed.), *Transnational Connections and the Arab Gulf*, London: Routledge, 2005.

Al-Salimi, Muhammad, *Nahda al-A'yan bi-Hurriya 'Uman* [The Notables' Renaissance in the Liberation of Oman], Cairo: Matabi' Dar al-Kitab al-'Arabi bi-Misr, 1961.

BIBLIOGRAPHY

Alshayji, Abdullah K., "Mutual Realities, Perceptions, and Impediments between the GCC States and Iran," in Lawrence G. Potter and Gary G. Sick (eds), *Security in the Persian Gulf: Origins, Obstacles, and the Search for Consensus*, pp. 217–37, New York: Palgrave, 2002.

Al-Ta'ifiyya fil Iraq [Sectarianism in Iraq], Beirut: Al-Aref, 2008.

Amanat, Abbas, "Iranian Identity Boundaries: A Historical Overview," in Abbas Amanat and Farzin Vejdani (eds), *Iran Facing Others: Identity Boundaries in a Historical Perspective*, New York: Palgrave Macmillan, 2012.

Amanat, Mehrdad, *Jewish Identities in Iran: Resistance and Conversion to Islam and the Baha'i Faith*, London: I.B. Tauris, 2011.

Anderson, Benedict, *Imagined Communities: Reflections on the Origin and Spread of Nationalism*, London: Verso, 1983.

Anderson, Lisa, "The State in the Middle East and North Africa," *Comparative Politics*, 20, 1 (1987), pp. 1–18.

Asgharzadeh, Alireza, *Iran and the Challenge of Diversity: Islamic Fundamentalism, Aryanist Racism, and Democratic Struggles*, New York: Palgrave Macmillan, 2007.

Aslanian, Sebouh, *From the Indian Ocean to the Mediterranean: The Global Trade Networks of Armenian Merchants from New Julfa*, Berkeley: University of California Press, 2011.

Atabaki, Touraj, *Azerbaijan: Ethnicity and the Struggle for Power in Iran*, London: I.B. Tauris, 2000.

Axmann, Martin, "Phoenix from the Ashes? The Baloch National Movement and its Recent Revival," in Carina Jahani, Agnes Korn, and Paul Titus (eds), *The Baloch and Others: Linguistic, Historical and Socio-Political Perspectives on Pluralism in Balochistan*, Wiesbaden: Reichert, 2008.

Badalkhan, Sabir, "Zikri Dilemmas: Origins, Religious Practices, and Political Constraints," in Carina Jahani, Agnes Korn, and Paul Titus (eds), *The Baloch and Others: Linguistic, Historical and Socio-Political Perspectives on Pluralism in Balochistan*, pp. 293–326, Wiesbaden: Reichert, 2008.

Bahry, Louay, "The Socio-Economic Foundations of the Shiite Opposition in Bahrain," *Mediterranean Quarterly*, 11, 3 (2000), pp. 129–43.

Bailey, Frederick G., *Stratagems and Spoils: A Social Anthropology of Politics*, Oxford: Blackwell, 1969.

Baluch, Muhammad Sardar Khan, *History of Baluch Race and Baluchistan*, 2nd edn, Quetta: Gosha-e-Adab, 1977.

Banuazizi, Ali, and Myron Weiner (eds), *The State, Religion, and Ethnic Politics: Afghanistan, Iran, and Pakistan*, Syracuse: Syracuse University Press, 1986.

Barfield, Thomas, "Afghanistan's Ethnic Puzzle: Decentralizing Power before the U.S. Withdrawal," *Foreign Affairs*, 90, 5 (2011), pp. 54–65.

Barth, Fredrik, *Nomads of South Persia: The Basseri Tribe of the Khamseh Confederacy*, London: Allen and Unwin, 1961.

——— *Sohar: Culture and Society in an Omani Town*, Baltimore: Johns Hopkins University Press, 1983.

Bayat, Asef, *Street Politics: Poor People's Movements in Iran*, New York: Columbia University Press, 1997.

Bayat, Kaveh, "The Ethnic Question in Iran," *Middle East Report*, 35, 4 (2005), pp. 42–5.

——— "Iran and the 'Kurdish Question'," *Middle East Report*, 38, 2 (2008), pp. 28–35.

Bayart, Jean-François, *The Illusion of Cultural Identity*, trans. Steven Rendall, Janet Roitman, and Jonathan Derrick, London: Hurst, 2005.

Bayart, Jean-François, and Peter Geschiere, "J'étais là avant: problématiques politiques de l'autochtonie" [I Was Here Before: The Politics of Nativism], *Critique Internationale*, 10 (2001).

Beblawi, Hazem, "The Rentier State in the Arab World," in Giacomo Luciani (ed.), *The Rentier State: Nation, State and Integration in the Arab World*, vol. 2, London: Routledge, 1987.

Beck, Lois, *Lords of the Mountains: Qashqa'i Tribal Insurgency in Post-Revolutionary Iran*, unpublished book manuscript.

——— *Nomads Move On: Qashqa'i Tribespeople in Post-Revolutionary Iran*, London: Routledge, 2014.

——— *Nomad: A Year in the Life of a Qashqa'i Tribesman in Iran*, Berkeley: University of California Press, 1991.

——— *The Qashqa'i of Iran*, New Haven: Yale University Press, 1986.

——— "Revolutionary Iran and its Tribal Peoples," *MERIP Report*, 87 (1980), pp. 14–20.

——— "Tribes and the State in Nineteenth- and Twentieth-Century Iran," in Philip Khoury and Joseph Kostiner (eds), *Tribes and State Formation in the Middle East*, pp. 185–225, Berkeley: University of California Press, 1990.

Beck, Lois, and Julia Huang, "Manipulating Private Lives and Public Spaces in Qashqa'i Society in Iran," *Comparative Studies of South Asia, Africa and the Middle East*, 26, 2 (2006), pp. 303–25.

——— "Tribes," in Emad El-Din Shahin (ed.), *Oxford Encyclopedia of Islam and Politics*, Oxford: Oxford University Press, 2013.

Beeman, William, *Language, Status, and Power in Iran*, Bloomington: Indiana University Press, 1986.

Bellier, Irène, "Les peuples autochtones aux Nations Unies: un nouvel acteur dans la fabrique des normes internationals" [Indigenous Peoples at the United Nations: A New Actor in the Fabric of International Norms], *Critique Internationale*, 54 (2012), pp. 61–80.

Bennigsen, Alexandre, and S. Enders Wimbush, *Muslims of the Soviet Empire*, Bloomington: Indiana University Press, 1986.

BIBLIOGRAPHY

Bestor, Jane, "The Kurds of Iranian Baluchistan: A Regional Elite," MA thesis, Department of Anthropology, McGill University, Montreal, 1979.

Black-Michaud, Jacob, *Sheep and Land: The Economics of Power in a Tribal Society*, Cambridge: Cambridge University Press, 1986.

Blok, Anton, *Honour and Violence*, Oxford: Polity Press, 2001.

Bosworth, Clifford Edmund, "Ajam," *Encyclopædia Iranica*, 1 (1985), pp. 700–1, http://www.iranicaonline.org/articles/ajam

Boyce, Mary, *A Persian Stronghold of Zoroastrianism*, Oxford: Oxford University Press, 1977.

Bradburd, Daniel, *Ambiguous Relations: Kin, Class, and Conflict among Komachi Pastoralists*, Washington, DC: Smithsonian Institution Press, 1990.

Bromberger, Christian, *Un autre Iran: Un ethnologue au Gilan* [Another Iran: An Ethnologist in Gilan], Paris: Armand Colin, 2013.

——— "Eating Habits and Cultural Boundaries in Northern Iran," in Sami Zubaida and Richard Tapper (eds), *Culinary Cultures of the Middle East*, London: I.B. Tauris, 1993.

——— "GILAN xv. Popular and Literary Perceptions of Identity," *Encyclopædia Iranica*, 2011, http://www.iranicaonline.org/articles/gilan-xv-identity

——— *Habitat, Architecture and Rural Society in the Gilan Plain (Northern Iran)*, Bonn: Ferd. Dümmlers Verlag, 1989.

——— "Ta'zie (le theatre religieux) vs Noruz (la nouvelle annee et ses rituels): les enjeux de la politique du patrimoine immateriel de l'humanite en Iran" [Ta'zie (religious theater) vs. Noruz (the new year and its rituals): The Political Challenges of an Intangible Heritage for the People of Iran], *Etnografica*, 16, 2 (2012), pp. 407–17.

Bruckner, Pascal, *The Tyranny of Guilt: An Essay on Western Masochism*, Princeton: Princeton University Press, 2010.

Bucar, Elizabeth, "Saving Face: Navigating Land Mines with Ritual Politeness in Iran," *History of Religions*, 52, 1 (2012), pp. 31–48.

Buckley, Jorunn Jacobsen, "The Mandaeans: Ancient Texts and Modern People", *Encyclopædia Iranica*, (2002).

——— "Mandaeans iv. Community in Iran," *Encyclopædia Iranica*, 2005, http://www.iranicaonline.org/articles/mandaeans

Chandra, Kanchan, *Why Ethnic Parties Succeed*, Cambridge: Cambridge University Press, 2004.

Chehabi, Houchang E., "Ardabil Becomes a Province: Center–Periphery Relations in Iran," *International Journal of Middle East Studies*, 29, 2 (1997), pp. 235–53.

——— "Iran and Iraq: Intersocietal Linkages and Secular Nationalisms," in Abbas Amanat and Farzin Vejdani (eds), *Iran Facing Others: Identity Boundaries in a Historical Perspective*, pp. 191–216, New York: Palgrave Macmillan, 2012.

Cole, Juan R.I., *Sacred Space and Holy War: The Politics, Culture and History of Shi'ite Islam*, London: I.B. Tauris, 2002.

Collett, Nigel A., "Baluch Service in the Forces of Oman: A Reflection of Makrani Society and an Impetus for Change," *Newsletter of Baluchistan Studies*, 2 (1985), pp. 8–15.

Cooper, Merian C., and Ernest B. Schoedsack, *Grass: A Nation's Battle for Life*, DVD released 28 Mar. 2000, running time seventy-one minutes, Paramount Pictures, 1925.

Corstange, Daniel M., "Institutions and Ethnic Politics in Lebanon and Yemen," PhD dissertation, University of Michigan, 2008.

Crystal, Jill, *Kuwait: The Transformation of an Oil State*, Boulder: Westview Press, 1992.

——— *Oil and Politics in the Gulf: Rulers and Merchants in Kuwait and Qatar*, New York: Cambridge University Press, 1995.

——— "Patterns of State-Building in the Arabian Gulf: Kuwait and Qatar," PhD dissertation, Harvard University, 1986.

Dareshuri, Naheed, and Lois Beck, "Bands, Ropes, Braids, and Tassels among the Qashqa'i of Iran," in Fred Mushkat (ed.), *Warp-Faced Bands and Related Weavings of Nomadic Pastoralists in Iran*, unpublished book manuscript.

Davis, Eric (ed.), "The Question of Sectarian Identities in Iraq," *International Journal of Contemporary Iraqi Studies*, 4, 3 (2010).

Delgado, Richard, and Jean Stefancic, *Critical Race Theory: An Introduction*, New York: New York University Press, 2001.

Digard, Jean-Pierre, *Techniques des nomades Baxtyari d'Iran* [Techniques of Bakhtiari Nomads of Iran], Cambridge: Cambridge University Press, 1981.

Douglas, Leigh, *The Free Yemeni Movement 1935–1962*, Beirut: The American University of Beirut, 1987.

Dresch, Paul, *A History of Modern Yemen*, Cambridge: Cambridge University Press, 2000.

——— *Tribes, Government, and History in Yemen*, Oxford: Oxford University Press, 1989.

Dudoignon, Stephane, "Zahedan vs. Qom? Les Sunnites d'Iran et l'emergence du Baloutchistan comme foyer de droit hanafite, sous la monarchie Pahlavi" [Zahedan vs. Qom? Iran's Sunnis and the Emergence of Baluchistan as a Source of Hanafi Law, under the Pahlavi Monarchy], in Denise Aigle et al. (eds), *Miscellanea Asiatica*, Sankt Augustin, Germany: Institut Monumenta Serica, 2010.

Dyer, Richard, "The Matter of Whiteness," in Les Back and John Solomos (eds), *Theories of Race and Racism: A Reader*, pp. 538–48, London: Routledge, 2000.

Edgar, Adrienne, *Tribal Nation: The Making of Soviet Turkmenistan*, Princeton: Princeton University Press, 2004.

Ehsani, Kaveh, "The Urban Provincial Periphery in Iran: Revolution and War in Ramhormoz," in Ali Gheissari (ed.), *Contemporary Iran: Economy, Society, Politics*, pp. 38–76, Oxford: Oxford University Press, 2009.

Eickelman, Dale F., "Identité nationale et discours religieux en Oman" [National Identity and Religious Discourse in Oman], in Gilles Kepel and Yann Richard (eds), *Intellectuels et militants de l'Islam contemporain* [Intellectuals and Militants of Contemporary Islam], pp. 103–28, Paris: Le Seuil, 1990.

——— "Kings and People: Information and Authority in Oman, Qatar, and the Persian Gulf," in Joseph A. Kechichian (ed.), *Iran, Iraq, and the Arab Gulf States*, pp. 193–209, New York: Palgrave, 2001.

Elling, Rasmus C., *Minorities in Iran: Nationalism and Ethnicity After Khomeini*, New York: Palgrave Macmillan, 2013.

Entessar, Nader, *Kurdish Politics in the Middle East*, Lanham, MD: Lexington, 2010.

Eriksen, Thomas Hylland, *Ethnicity and Nationalism: Anthropological Perspectives*, London: Pluto Press, 1993.

Esfandiari, Haleh, *Reconstructed Lives: Women and Iran's Islamic Revolution*, Baltimore: The Johns Hopkins University Press, 1997.

Fakhro, Munira, "The Uprising in Bahrain: An Assessment," in Lawrence G. Potter and Gary G. Sick (eds), *The Persian Gulf at the Millennium: Essays in Politics, Economy, Security, and Religion*, pp. 167–88, New York: St. Martin's Press, 1997.

Fandy, Mamoun, *Saudi Arabia and the Politics of Dissent*, London: Macmillan, 1999.

Fanon, Franz, *Black Skin, White Masks*, 2nd edn, London: Pluto Press, 2008.

Farhadi, Asghar, *A Separation* [Joda'i-ye Nader az Simin], motion picture, running time 123 minutes, Iran: Asghar Farhadi Productions, 2011.

Fattah, Khaled, "Tribes and Terrorism: Myth and Reality," Canadian International Council, 2012, http://www.opencanada.org/features/the-think-tank/tribes-and-terrorism

Fibiger, Thomas Brandt, "Engaging Pasts: Historicity and Political Imagination in Bahrain," PhD dissertation, Aarhus University, Denmark, 2010.

Flaskerud, Ingvild, "Redemptive Memories: Portraiture in the Cult of Commemoration," in Pedram Khosronejad (ed.), *Unburied Memories: The Politics of Bodies of Sacred Defense Martyrs in Iran*, pp. 22–46, London: Routledge, 2013.

Freitag, Ulrike, *Indian Ocean Migrants and State Formation in Hadhramaut*, Leiden: Brill, 2003.

Friedl, Erika, "State Ideology and Village Women," in Guity Nashat (ed.), *Women and Revolution in Iran*, pp. 217–30, Boulder: Westview Press, 1983.

——— "Women in Contemporary Persian Folktales," in Lois Beck and Nikki Keddie (eds), *Women in the Muslim World*, pp. 629–50, Cambridge: Harvard University Press, 1978.

——— *Women of Deh Koh: Lives in an Iranian Village*, Washington, DC: Smithsonian Institution Press, 1989.

Friedland, Roger, "Religious Nationalism and the Problem of Collective Representation," *Annual Review of Sociology*, 27 (2001), pp. 125–52.

Fromanger, Marine, "Variations in the Martyrs' Representations in South Tehran's Public and Private Spaces," in Pedram Khosronejad (ed.), *Unburied Memories: The Politics of Bodies of Sacred Defense Martyrs in Iran*, pp. 47–67, London: Routledge, 2013.

Fromherz, Allen J., *Qatar: A Modern History*, Washington, DC: Georgetown University Press, 2012.

Fuccaro, Nelida, *Histories of City and State in the Persian Gulf: Manama Since 1800*, Cambridge: Cambridge University Press, 2009.

Garthwaite, Gene, *Khans and Shahs: A Documentary Analysis of the Bakhtiyari in Iran*, Cambridge: Cambridge University Press, 1983.

Geertz, Clifford (ed.), "The Integrative Revolution: Primordial Sentiments and Civil Politics in the New States," in *Old Societies and New States: The Quest for Modernity in Asia and Africa*, pp. 105–57, London: Free Press of Glencoe, 1963.

Gengler, Justin J., "Are Bahrain's Sunnis Still Awake?" in *Sada: Analysis of Arab Reform*, Washington, DC: Carnegie Endowment for International Peace, 2012.

——— "Bahrain's Sunni Awakening," Middle East Report Online, 17 Jan. 2012, http://www.merip.org/mero/mero011712

——— "Ethnic Conflict and Political Mobilization in Bahrain and the Arab Gulf," PhD dissertation, University of Michigan, 2011.

——— "Royal Factionalism and the Securitization of 'the Shi'a Problem' in Bahrain," *Journal of Arabian Studies*, 3, 1 (2013), pp. 53–79.

Ghabra, Shafeeq, "Kuwait and the Economics of Socio-Economic Change," in Barry M. Rubin (ed.), *Crises in the Contemporary Persian Gulf*, pp. 105–26, New York: Frank Cass Publishers, 2002.

Ghamari-Tabrizi, Behrooz, *Islam and Dissent in Postrevolutionary Iran: Abdolkarim Soroush, Religious Politics and Democratic Reform*, London: I.B. Tauris, 2008.

Gheissari, Ali, and Kaveh-Cyrus Sanandaji, "New Conservative Politics and Electoral Behavior in Iran," in Ali Gheissari (ed.), *Contemporary Iran: Economy, Society, Politics*, pp. 275–98, Oxford: Oxford University Press, 2009.

Gingrich, Andre, "Review of 'The Hadrami Diaspora: Community-Building on the Indian Ocean Rim' by Leif Manger," *Social Anthropology*, 2 (2012), pp. 113–15.

Goldberg, Jacob, "The Shi'i Minority in Saudi Arabia," in Juan Cole and Nikki Keddie (eds), *Shi'ism and Social Protest*, pp. 231–6, New Haven: Yale University Press, 1986.

Goodell, Grace, *The Elementary Structures of Political Life: Rural Development in Pahlavi Iran*, New York: Oxford University Press, 1986.

Gruber, Christiane, "The Martyrs' Museum in Tehran: Visualizing Memory in Post-Revolutionary Iran," in Pedram Khosronejad (ed.), *Unburied Memories: The Politics of Bodies of Sacred Defense Martyrs in Iran*, pp. 68–97, London: Routledge, 2013.

Haddad, Fanar, *Sectarianism in Iraq: Antagonistic Visions of Unity*, London: Hurst, 2011.

——— "Sectarian Gulf," *Critical Muslim: Fear and Loathing*, 1, 3 (July–Sep. 2012), edited by Ziauddin Sardar and Robin Yassin-Kassab, pp. 105–19. London: Hurst and the Muslim Institute, 2012.

Haider, Najam, "Zaydism: A Theological and Political Survey," *Religion Compass*, 4 (2010), pp. 436–42.

Halliday, Fred, "The Formation of Yemeni Nationalism: Initial Reflections," in James Jankowski and Israel Gershoni (eds), *Rethinking Nationalism in the Arab Middle East*, pp. 26–41, New York: Columbia University Press, 1997.

——— *Iran: Dictatorship and Development*, New York: Penguin, 1979.

Hameed, Ala'a, "Al Ayquna al Shi'iya: Qira'ah fi Dala'il al Suwar al Ramziya li A'imat al Shi'a" [The Shi'a Icon: Analyzing the Symbolic Images of the Shi'a Imams], *Masarat*, 15 (2011), pp. 116–20.

Harrison, Selig S., "Ethnicity and Politics in Pakistan: The Baluch Case," in John Hutchinson and Anthony D. Smith (eds), *Ethnicity*, pp. 294–301, Oxford: Oxford University Press, 1996.

——— *In Afghanistan's Shadow: Baluch Nationalism and Soviet Temptations*, New York: Carnegie Endowment for International Peace, 1981.

Hashim, Ahmed S., *Insurgency and Counter-Insurgency in Iraq*, London: Hurst, 2006.

Haykel, Bernard, *Revival and Reform in Islam: The Legacy of Muhammad al-Shawkani*, Cambridge: Cambridge University Press, 2003.

Hegland, Mary, "Aliabad of Shiraz: Transformation from Village to Suburban Town," *Anthropology of the Middle East*, 6, 2 (2011), pp. 21–37.

——— "Aliabad Women: Revolution as Religious Activity," in Guity Nashat (ed.), *Women and Revolution in Iran*, pp. 171–94, Boulder: Westview Press, 1983.

——— "Islamic Revival or Political and Cultural Revolution? An Iranian Case Study," in Richard Antoun and Mary Hegland (eds), *Religious Resurgence:*

Contemporary Cases in Islam, Christianity, and Judaism, pp. 194–219, Syracuse: Syracuse University Press, 1987.

Helfgott, Leonard, "The Structural Foundations of the National Minority Situation in Revolutionary Iran," *Iranian Studies*, 13, 1–4 (1980), pp. 195–214.

——— "Tribalism as a Socioeconomic Formation in Iranian History," *Iranian Studies*, 10, 1–2 (1977), pp. 36–61.

Herb, Michael, *All in the Family: Absolutism, Revolution, and Democracy in the Middle Eastern Monarchies*, Albany, NY: SUNY Press, 1999.

Higgins, Patricia, "Minority–State Relations in Contemporary Iran," in Ali Banuazizi and Myron Weiner (eds), *The State, Religion, and Ethnic Politics: Afghanistan, Iran, and Pakistan*, pp. 167–97, Syracuse, NY: Syracuse University Press, 1986.

Ho, Engseng, *The Graves of Tarim: Genealogy and Mobility across the Indian Ocean*, Berkeley: University of California Press, 2006.

Hobsbawm, Eric, and Terence Ranger (eds), *The Invention of Tradition*, Cambridge: Cambridge University Press, 1983.

Holes, Clive, "Dialect and National Identity: The Cultural Politics of Self-Representation in Bahraini *Musalsalat*," in Paul Dresch and James Piscatori (eds), *Monarchies and Nations: Globalization and Identity in the Arab States of the Gulf*, pp. 52–72, London: I.B. Tauris, 2005.

Hooglund, Eric, "Letter from an Iranian Village," *Journal of Palestine Studies*, 27, 1 (1997), pp. 76–84.

Horowitz, Donald L., *Ethnic Groups in Conflict*, Berkeley: University of California Press, 1985.

Hourani, A.H., *Minorities in the Arab World*, London: Oxford University Press, 1947.

Hourcade, Bernard et al., *Atlas d'Iran* [Atlas of Iran], Paris: Reclus, La Documentation Française, 1998.

Howarth, Anthony, *People of the Wind*, motion picture, running time 110 minutes, New York: Milestone Films, 1976.

Huang, Julia, "Integration, Modernization, and Resistance: Qashqa'i Nomads in Iran since the Revolution of 1978–79," in Dawn Chatty (ed.), *Nomadic Societies in the Middle East and North Africa: Entering the 21st Century*, pp. 805–39, Leiden: Brill, 2006.

——— *Tribeswomen of Iran: Weaving Memories among Qashqa'i Nomads*, London: I.B. Tauris, 2009.

Hurewitz, J.C., "The Minorities in the Political Process," in Sydney N. Fisher (ed.), *Social Forces in the Middle East*, pp. 205–21, Ithaca, NY: Cornell University Press, 1955.

Hussein, Abdul Khaliq, *Al Ta'ifiyyah al Siyasiyah wa Mushkilat al Hukm fil Iraq* [Political Sectarianism and the Problem of Governance in Iraq], Baghdad: Mesopotamia House, 2011.

Ibn Khaldun, *The Muqaddimah: An Introduction to History*, trans. Franz Rosenthal, Princeton, NJ: Princeton University Press, 1980.

Ibrahim, Fouad, "Shi'at al Iraq: Inbi'ath Hawiya Maqmu'a wa Tahadiyat Muraga'at al Dhat" [The Shi'a of Iraq: The Revival of a Suppressed Identity and the Challenges of Self-Critique], *Masarat*, 15 (2011), pp. 74–89.

International Crisis Group, "Iraq's Civil War: The Sadrists and the Surge," *Middle East Report*, 72 (2008), http://lynx.csusm.edu/adp/ICGbriefingonIraq.pdf

Irons, William, *The Yomut Turkmen: A Study of Social Organization Among a Central Asian Turkic-Speaking Population*, Ann Arbor, MI: University of Michigan Museum of Anthropology, 1975.

Isaacs, Harold R., "Power and Identity: Tribalism and World Politics," *Headline Series*, 246. New York: Foreign Policy Association, 1979.

Ismael, Jacqueline, *Kuwait: Social Change in Historical Perspective*, Syracuse: Syracuse University Press, 1982.

Izady, M.R., "The Gulf's Ethnic Diversity: An Evolutionary History," in Lawrence G. Potter and Gary G. Sick (eds), *Security in the Persian Gulf: Origins, Obstacles, and the Search for Consensus*, pp. 33–90, New York: Palgrave, 2002.

Jahani, Carina, "State Control and its Impact on Language in Balochistan," in Annika Rabo and Bo Utas (eds), *The Role of the State in West Asia*, pp. 151–63, London: I.B. Tauris, 2006.

Jahani, Carina, Agnes Korn, and Paul Titus (eds), *The Baloch and Others: Linguistic, Historical and Socio-Political Perspectives on Pluralism in Balochistan*, Wiesbaden: Reichart Verlag, 2008.

Jawad, Ghanem, *Al Shi'a wal Intiqal al Dimocrati* [The Shi'a and Democratic Transition], Damascus: Dar al Hasad, 2011.

Jayaram, N., "Identity: A Semantic Exploration in India's Society and Culture," in *Key Words: Identity*, series editor Nadia Tazi, pp. 125–48, New York: Other Press, 2004.

Jetly, Rajshree, "Baluch Ethnicity and Nationalism (1971–81): An Assessment," *Asian Ethnicity*, 5, 1 (2004), pp. 7–26.

Jones, Toby Craig, "Rebellion on the Saudi Periphery: Modernity, Marginalization, and the Shi'a Uprising of 1979," *International Journal of Middle East Studies*, 38, 1 (2006), pp. 213–33.

Kamalkhani, Zahra, *Women's Islam: Religious Practice among Women in Today's Iran*, London: Kegan Paul, 1998.

Kamrava, Mehran, "Royal Factionalism and Political Liberalization in Qatar," *The Middle East Journal*, 63, 3 (2009), pp. 401–20.

Kamrava, Mehran, and Manochehr Dorraj (eds), *Iran Today: An Encyclopedia of Life in the Islamic Republic*, vols 1–2, Westport, CT: Greenwood, 2008.

Kashani-Sabet, Firoozeh, *Frontier Fictions: Shaping the Iranian Nation, 1804–1946*, Princeton: Princeton University Press, 1999.

Kaufman, Stuart J., *Modern Hatreds: The Symbolic Politics of Ethnic War*, Ithaca: Cornell University Press, 2001.

Keddie, Nikki, "The Minorities Question in Iran," in Shirin Tahir-Kheli and Shaheen Ayubi (eds), *The Iran–Iraq War: New Weapons, Old Conflicts*, pp. 85–108, New York: Praeger, 1983.

——— *Modern Iran: Roots and Results of Revolution*, New Haven: Yale University Press, 2006.

Kedourie, Elie, "Anti-Shi'ism in Iraq under the Monarchy," *Middle Eastern Studies*, 24 (1988), pp. 249–53.

Keshavarz, Fatemeh, *Jasmine and Stars: Reading More than Lolita in Tehran*, Chapel Hill, NC: University of North Carolina Press, 2007.

Khajehpour-Khoei, Bijan, "Mutual Perceptions in the Persian Gulf Region: An Iranian Perspective," in Lawrence G. Potter and Gary G. Sick (eds), *Security in the Persian Gulf: Origins, Obstacles, and the Search for Consensus*, pp. 217–37, New York: Palgrave, 2002.

Khalaf, Abdulhadi, "Contentious Politics in Bahrain: From Ethnic to National and Vice Versa," paper presented at The Fourth Nordic Conference on Middle Eastern Studies: The Middle East in a Globalizing World, Oslo, 13–16 Aug. 1998, www.hf.uib.no/smi/pao/khalaf.html

Khalaf, Abdulhadi, "What the Gulf Ruling Families Do When They Rule," *Orient*, 44, 4 (Dec. 2003), pp. 537–54.

Khalaf, Sulayman, "Poetics and Politics of Newly Invented Traditions in the Gulf: Camel Racing in the United Arab Emirates," *Ethnology*, 39, 3 (Summer 2000), pp. 243–61.

Khazeni, Arash, *Tribes and Empire: On the Margins of Nineteenth-Century Iran*, Seattle: University of Washington Press, 2009.

Khosravi, Shahram, *"Illegal" Traveller: An Auto-Ethnography of Borders*, New York: Palgrave Macmillan, 2010.

Khosronejad, Pedram, "Introduction: Unburied Memories," in Pedram Khosronejad (ed.), *Unburied Memories: The Politics of Bodies of Sacred Defense Martyrs in Iran*, pp. 1–34, London: Routledge, 2012.

——— (ed.), *Unburied Memories: The Politics of Bodies of Sacred Defense Martyrs in Iran*, London: Routledge, 2012.

Khoury, Philip S., and Joseph Kostiner (eds), *Tribes and State Formation in the Middle East*, Berkeley: University of California Press, 1990.

Khuri, Fuad I., *Tribe and State in Bahrain: The Transformation of Social and Political Authority in an Arab State*, Chicago: University of Chicago Press, 1980.

Kohlberg, Etan, "Some Zaydi Views on the Companions of the Prophet," *Bulletin of the School of Oriental and African Studies*, 39 (1976), pp. 91–8.

Kolsto, Pal, "The 'Narcissism of Minor Differences' Theory: Can it Explain

Ethnic Conflict?" *Filozofija i Društvo* [*Philosophy and Society*, Belgrade], 2 (2007), pp. 153–71.

Koohi-Kamali, Farideh, *The Political Development of the Kurds in Iran: Pastoral Nationalism*, New York: Palgrave Macmillan, 2003.

Kraetzschmar, Hendrik Jan, "The First Democratic Local Elections in Saudi Arabia in 2005: Electoral Rules, the Mobilization of Voters and the Islamist Landslide," *LSE Public Policy Group Working Paper*, 6, London: London School of Economics, 2011.

Lewis, Bernard, *The Political Language of Islam*, Chicago: University of Chicago Press, 1988.

Lewis, M. Paul, *Ethnologue: Languages of the World*, 16th edn, Dallas, TX: SIL International, 2009, http://www.ethnologue.com

Loeb, Laurence, *Outcaste: Jewish Life in Southern Iran*, New York: Routledge, 1977.

Loeffler, Reinhold, "The Ethos of Progress in a Village in Iran," *Anthropology of the Middle East*, 6, 2 (2011), pp. 1–13.

——— *Islam in Practice: Religious Beliefs in a Persian Village*, Albany: State University of New York Press, 1988.

Longva, Anh Nga, "Nationalism in Pre-Modern Guise: The Discourse on *Hadhar* and *Bedu* in Kuwait," *International Journal of Middle East Studies*, 38, 2 (2006), pp. 171–87.

Longva, Anh Nga, and Anne Sofie Roald (eds), *Religious Minorities in the Middle East: Domination, Self-Empowerment, Accommodation*, Leiden: Brill, 2011.

Louër, Laurence, "The Political Impact of Labor Migration in Bahrain," *City & Society*, 20, 1 (2008), pp. 32–53.

——— "Shi'i Identity Politics in Saudi Arabia," in Anh Nga Longva and Anne Sofie Roald (eds), *Religious Minorities in the Middle East: Domination, Self-Empowerment, Accommodation*, pp. 221–43, Leiden: Brill, 2011.

——— *Transnational Shia Politics: Religious and Political Networks in the Gulf*, New York: Columbia University Press, 2008.

Lu'aibi, Shakir, *Tasawir al Imam Ali* [Depictions of Imam Ali], Beirut: Riad El-Rayyes Books, 2011.

Luciani, Giacomo, "Allocation vs. Production States: A Theoretical Framework," in Hazem Beblawi and Giacomo Luciani (eds), *The Rentier State: Nation, State and Integration in the Arab World*, pp. 63–82, London: Croom Helm, 1987.

Mad'aj, Abd al-Muhsin, *The Yemen in Early Islam*, London: Ithaca, 1988.

Madelung, Wilfried, "Islam in Yemen," in Werner Daum (ed.), *Yemen: 3000 Years of Art and Civilizations in Arabia Felix*, pp. 174–7, Frankfurt: Umschau-Verlag, 1989.

Mahdavi, Pardis, *Passionate Uprisings: Iran's Sexual Revolution*, Stanford: Stanford University Press, 2009.

Mahdavy, Hossein, "Patterns and Problems of Economic Development in Rentier States: The Case of Iran," in M.A. Cook (ed.), *Studies in the Economic History of the Middle East: From the Rise of Islam to the Present Day*, pp. 428–67, London: Oxford University Press, 1970.

Makdisi, Ussama, *The Culture of Sectarianism: Community, History, and Violence in Nineteenth-Century Ottoman Lebanon*, Berkeley: University of California Press, 2000.

Marschall, Christin, *Iran's Persian Gulf Policy: From Khomeini to Khatami*, London: Routledge Curzon, 2003.

Matin-asgari, Afshin, "The Academic Debate on Iranian Identity: Nation and Empire Entangled," in Abbas Amanat and Farzin Vejdani (eds), *Iran Facing Others*, pp. 171–90, New York: Palgrave Macmillan, 2012.

Matthiesen, Toby, "Hizbullah al-Hijaz: A History of The Most Radical Saudi Shi'a Opposition Group," *The Middle East Journal*, 64, 2 (2010), pp. 179–97.

——— "A 'Saudi Spring?' The Shi'a Protest Movement in the Eastern Province 2011–2012," *Middle East Journal*, 66, 4 (Autumn 2012), pp. 628–59.

——— *Sectarian Gulf: Bahrain, Saudi Arabia, and the Arab Spring that Wasn't*, Stanford: Stanford University Press, 2013.

McCagg, William, and Brian Silver (eds), *Soviet Asian Ethnic Frontiers*, New York: Pergamon Press, 1979.

McDowall, David, *A Modern History of the Kurds*, London: I.B. Tauris, 2004.

Mermier, Franck, "De l'invention du patrimoine omanais" [On the Invention of Omani Heritage], in Marc Lavergne and Brigitte Dumortier (eds), *L'Oman contemporain: Etat, territoire, identité* [Contemporary Oman: State, Territory, Identity], pp. 245–60, Paris: Karthala, 2003.

Messick, Brinkley, *The Calligraphic State: Textual Domination and History in a Muslim Society*, Berkeley: University of California Press, 1993.

Milani, Abbas, *Eminent Persians: The Men and Women Who Made Modern Iran, 1941–1979*, 2 vols, Syracuse: Syracuse University Press and Persian World Press, 2008.

Mir-Hosseini, Ziba, "Breaking the Seal: The New Face of the Ahl-e Haqq," in Krisztina Kehl Bodrogi, Barbara Kellner Heinkele, and Anke Otter Beaujean (eds), *Syncretistic Religious Communities in the Near East*, pp. 175–94, Leiden: Brill, 1997.

——— "Faith, Ritual and Culture among the Ahl-e Haqq," in Philip Kreyenbroek and Christine Allison (eds), *Kurdish Culture and Identity*, pp. 111–34, London: Zed, 1996.

——— "Inner Truth and Outer History: The Two Worlds of Ahl-e Haqq of

Kurdistan," *International Journal of Middle East Studies*, 26, 2 (1994), pp. 267–85.

——— "Redefining the Truth: Ahl-e Haqq and the Islamic Republic of Iran," *British Journal of Middle Eastern Studies*, 21, 2 (1994), pp. 211–28.

Mir-Hosseini, Ziba, and Richard Tapper, *Islam and Democracy in Iran: Eshkevari and the Quest for Reform*, London: I.B. Tauris, 2006.

Moaveni, Azadeh, *Lipstick Jihad: A Memoir of Growing Up Iranian in America and American in Iran*, New York: PublicAffairs, 2005.

Mojab, Shahrzad, and Amir Hassanpour, "The Politics of Nationality and Ethnic Diversity," in Saeed Rahnema and Sohrab Behdad (eds), *Iran After the Revolution: Crisis of an Islamic State*, pp. 229–50, London: I.B. Tauris, 1995.

Momen, Moojan, *An Introduction to Shi'i Islam: The History and Doctrines of Twelver Shi 'ism*, New Haven: Yale University Press, 1985.

Muttar, Saleem, *Al-Dhat al-Jareeha* [The Wounded Self], Beirut: Al-Mu'asasa al Arabiya lil Dirasat wal Nashr, 1997.

Naby, Eden, "The Iranian Frontier Nationalities: The Kurds, the Assyrians, the Baluchis, and the Turkmens," in William McCagg and Brian Silver (eds), *Soviet Asian Ethnic Frontiers*, pp. 83–114, New York: Pergamon Press, 1979.

Nadjmabadi, Shahnaz R., "Travellers between the 'World' and the 'Desert': Labor Migration from Iran to the Arab Countries of the Persian Gulf," paper presented at the Bellagio Conference on Transnational Migration in the Gulf, Bellagio Center, Italy, 20–25 June 2005.

Nadjmabadi, Shahnaz, "The Arab Presence on the Iranian Coast of the Persian Gulf," in Lawrence G. Potter (ed.), *The Persian Gulf in History*, pp. 129–45, New York: Palgrave Macmillan, 2009.

——— (ed.), *Conceptualizing Iranian Anthropology: Past and Present Perspectives*, New York: Berghahn Books, 2009.

——— "Cross-Border Networks: Labour Migration from Iran to the Arab Countries of the Persian Gulf," *Anthropology of the Middle East*, 5, 1 (2010), pp. 18–33.

Naficy, Hamid, *An Accented Cinema: Exilic and Diasporic Filmmaking*, Princeton: Princeton University Press, 2001.

——— *A Social History of Iranian Cinema, Volume 3: The Islamicate Period, 1978–1984*, Durham, NC: Duke University Press, 2012.

——— *A Social History of Iranian Cinema, Volume 4: The Globalizing Era, 1984–2010*, Durham, NC: Duke University Press, 2012.

Nafisi, Azar, *Reading Lolita in Tehran: A Memoir in Books*, New York: Random House, 2003.

Najmabadi, Afsaneh, *The Story of the Daughters of Quchan: Gender and National Memory in Iranian History*, Syracuse: Syracuse University Press, 1998.

——— *Women with Mustaches and Men without Beards: Gender and Sexual Anxieties of Iranian Modernity*, Berkeley: University of California Press, 2005.

Nakash, Yitzhak, *Reaching for Power: The Shi'a in the Modern Arab World*, Princeton: Princeton University Press, 2006.

——— *The Shi'as of Iraq*, Princeton: Princeton University Press, 1996.

Nakhleh, Emile A., *Bahrain: Political Development in a Modernizing Society*, Lanham, MD: Lexington Books, 2011.

Nash, Manning, *The Core Elements of Ethnicity*, Chicago: Chicago University Press, 1989.

Nasr, Vali, "If the Arab Spring Turns Ugly," *New York Times*, 28 Aug. 2011.

——— *The Shia Revival: How Conflicts within Islam Will Shape the Future*, New York: Norton, 2007.

——— "When the Shiites Rise," *Foreign Affairs* (July–Aug. 2006), pp. 58–74.

Natali, Denise, "Syrian Kurdish Cards," Middle East Research and Information Project Online, 2012, http://www.merip.org/mero/mero0320122

Nicolini, Beatrice, "The Baluch Role in the Persian Gulf during the Nineteenth and Twentieth Centuries," *Comparative Studies of South Asia, Africa and the Middle East*, 27, 2 (2007), pp. 384–95.

——— *Makran, Oman, and Zanzibar: Three-Terminal Cultural Corridor in the Western Indian Ocean (1799–1856)*, Leiden: Brill, 2004.

Noraiee, Hoshang, "Change and Continuity: Power and Religion in Iranian Baluchistan," in Carina Jahani, Agnes Korn, and Paul Titus (eds), *The Baloch and Others*, pp. 345–64, Wiesbaden: Reichert, 2008.

Oberling, Pierre, and Bernard Hourcade, "Arab iv. Arab Tribes of Iran," *Encyclopædia Iranica*, 2 (1987), pp. 215–20, http://www.iranicaonline.org/articles/arab.

Perry, John, "Forced Migration in Iran during the Seventeenth and Eighteenth Centuries," *Iranian Studies*, 8, 4 (1975), pp. 199–215.

Peters, J.R., *God's Created Speech: A Study in the Speculative Theology of the Mu'tazili Qadi-l-qudat Abul-Hasan bin Ahmed al-Hamadani*, Leiden: Brill, 1976.

Peterson, J.E., "Bahrain: Reform, Promise, and Reality," in Joshua Teitelbaum (ed.), *Political Liberalization in the Persian Gulf*, pp. 157–85, New York: Columbia University Press, 2009.

——— *Historical Muscat: An Illustrated Guide and Gazetteer*, Leiden: Brill, 2007.

——— "Oman's Diverse Society: Northern Oman," *Middle East Journal*, 58, 1 (2004), pp. 32–51.

——— *Oman's Insurgencies: The Sultanate's Struggle for Supremacy*, London: Saqi, 2007.

——— *Yemen: The Search for a Modern State*, London: Croom Helm, 1982.

Planhol, Xavier de, *Minorités en Islam: Géographie Politique et Sociale* [Minorities in Islam: Political and Social Geography], Paris: Flammarion, 1997.

Potter, Lawrence G. (ed.), *The Persian Gulf in History*, New York: Palgrave Macmillan, 2009.

——— "The Persian Gulf: Tradition and Transformation," *Headline Series*, 333–4, New York: Foreign Policy Association, 2011.

——— "Religion in World Politics: Why the Resurgence?" in *Great Decisions*, New York: Foreign Policy Association (1986), pp. 75–85.

Potter, Lawrence G., and Gary G. Sick (eds), *Iran, Iraq, and the Legacies of War*, New York: Palgrave Macmillan, 2004.

"Power and the Politics of Difference: Minorities in the Middle East," Special Issue, *Middle East Report*, 200 (July–Sep. 1996).

Price, Massoume, *Ancient Iran*, Vancouver: Anahita Productions, 2008.

——— *Iran's Diverse Peoples: A Reference Sourcebook*, Santa Barbara, CA: ABC-CLIO, 2005.

——— *Medieval Iran*, Vancouver: Anahita Productions, 2012.

Randeree, Kasim, "Workforce Nationalization in the Gulf Cooperation Council States," CIRS *Occasional Paper*, 9. Doha, Qatar: Center for International and Regional Studies, Georgetown University School of Foreign Service in Qatar, 2012.

Reicher, Stephen, "The Context of Social Identity: Domination, Resistance and Change," *Political Psychology*, 25, 6 (2004), pp. 921–45.

Ringer, Monica, "Iranian Nationalism and Zoroastrian Identity: Between Cyrus and Zoroaster," in Abbas Amanat and Farzin Vejdani (eds), *Iran Facing Others*, pp. 265–75, New York: Palgrave Macmillan, 2012.

Rizvi, Sajjad H., "From Communalism to Communitarianism: Imagining Communities, Nations and their Fragments in South Asia and Beyond," paper presented at Princeton University Workshop, "Rethinking Sectarianism," 22 May 2008.

Rosen, Nir, *Aftermath: Following the Bloodshed of America's Wars in the Muslim World*, New York: Nation Books, 2009.

Roy, Olivier, "Groupes de solidarité au Moyen-Orient et en Asie Centrale: États, territoires et réseaux" [Solidarity Groups in the Middle East and Central Asia: States, Territories and Networks], *Cahiers du CERI*, 16 (1996).

——— "Patronage and Solidarity Groups: Survival or Reformation?" in Ghassan Salamé (ed.), *Democracy without Democrats? The Renewal of Politics in the Muslim World*, pp. 270–81, London: I.B. Tauris, 1994.

Saeed, Haider, *Siyasat al Ramz: An Nihayat Thaqafat al Dawla al Wataniya fil Iraq* [The Politics of the Symbol: On the End of Culture of the National State in Iraq], Beirut: Al Mu'assasa al Arabiya, 2009.

Saghiya, Hazim (ed.), *Nawasib wa Rawafidh* [Nawasib and Rafawidh], Beirut: Dar al-Saqi, 2009.

Salih, Kamal Osman, "The 1938 Kuwait Legislative Council," *Middle Eastern Studies*, 28, 1 (1992), pp. 66–100.

Salih, Qassim Hussein, *Al Mujtama'a al Iraqi: Tahlil Sikosociology Lima Hadath wa Yahduth* [Iraqi Society: A Psycho-Sociological Analysis to what Happened and is Happening], Beirut: Arab Scientific Publishers, 2008.

——— *Al Shakhsiya al Iraqiya: Al Madhhar wal Jawhar* [The Iraqi Persona: The Appearance and the Essence], Baghdad: Dhefaf, 2011.

Salmoni, Barak A., Bryce Loidolt, and Madeleine Wells, *Regime and Periphery in Northern Yemen: The Houthi Phenomenon*, Santa Monica, CA: Rand National Defense Research Institute, 2010.

Salzman, Philip, *Black Tents of Baluchistan*, Washington, DC: Smithsonian Institution Press, 2000.

Samii, A. William, "The Nation and its Minorities: Ethnicity, Unity and State Policy in Iran," *Comparative Studies of South Asia, Africa and the Middle East*, 20, 1–2 (2000), pp. 128–42.

Sanasarian, Eliz, *Religious Minorities in Iran*, Cambridge: Cambridge University Press, 2000.

——— "State Dominance and Communal Perseverance: The Armenian Diaspora in the Islamic Republic of Iran, 1979–1989," *Diaspora*, 4, 3 (1995), pp. 243–65.

Satrapi, Marjane, *Persepolis: The Story of a Childhood*, New York: Random House, 2004.

Shahbazi, A. Shapur, Erich Kettenhofen, and John R. Perry, "Deportations," *Encyclopædia Iranica*, 7 (1994), pp. 297–312.

Sharan, Timor, and John Heathershaw, "Identity Politics and Statebuilding in Post-Bonn Afghanistan: The 2009 Presidential Election," *Ethnopolitics*, 10, 3–4 (2011), pp. 297–319.

Sharma, Sunil, "Redrawing the Boundaries of *Ajam* in Early Modern Persian Literary Histories," in Abbas Amanat and Farzin Vejdani (eds), *Iran Facing Others*, pp. 49–62, New York: Palgrave Macmillan, 2012.

Sluglett, Marion F., and Peter Sluglett, "Some Reflections on the Sunni/Shi'a Question in Iraq," *The Bulletin of the British Society for Middle Eastern Studies*, 5 (1978), pp. 79–87.

Smith, Anthony, *Chosen Peoples: Sacred Sources of National Identity*, Oxford: Oxford University Press, 2003.

——— *The Ethnic Origins of Nations*, Oxford: Blackwell, 1986.

——— *Myths and Memories of the Nation*, Oxford: Oxford University Press, 1999.

——— *The Nation in History: Historiographical Debates about Ethnicity and Nationalism*, Cambridge, UK: Polity Press, 2000.

Sreberny, Annabelle, and Gholam Khiabany, *Blogistan: The Internet and Politics in Iran*, London: I.B. Tauris, 2010.

Steinberg, Guido, "The Shiites in the Eastern Province of Saudi Arabia (al-

Ahsa), 1913–1953," in Rainer Brunner and Werner Ende (eds), *The Twelver Shia in Modern Times: Religious Culture and Political History*, pp. 236–51, Leiden: Brill, 2001.

Suleiman, Yasir, *The Arabic Language and National Identity: A Study in Ideology*, Edinburgh: Edinburgh University Press, 2003.

Tabrizi, Kamal, *Marmulak* [The Lizard], motion picture, running time 115 minutes, Iran: Barian Entertainment Ltd, 2004.

Tadros, Mariz, "Sectarianism and Its Discontents in Post-Mubarak Egypt," *Middle East Report*, 259 (Summer 2011), http://www.merip.org/mer/mer259/sectarianism-its-discontents-post-mubarak-egypt

Tapper, Richard (ed.), *The Conflict of Tribe and State in Iran and Afghanistan*, London: Croom Helm, 1983.

——— *Pasture and Politics: Economics, Conflict and Ritual among Shahsevan Nomads of Northwestern Iran*, London: Academic Press, 1979.

——— "Some Minorities in the Middle East," Centre of Near and Middle Eastern Studies *Occasional Paper*, 9. London: University of London, School of Oriental and African Studies, 1992.

——— "Who are the Kuchi? Nomad Self-Identities in Afghanistan," *Journal of the Royal Anthropological Institute*, 14, 1 (2008), pp. 97–116.

Tapper, Richard, and Nancy Tapper, "'Thank God We're Secular!' Aspects of Fundamentalism in a Turkish Town," in Lionel Caplan (ed.), *Aspects of Religious Fundamentalism*, pp. 57–78, London: Macmillan, 1987.

Teitelbaum, Joshua, *Holier than Thou: Saudi Arabia's Islamic Opposition*, Washington, DC: Washington Institute for Near East Policy, 2000.

Tohidi, Nayereh, "Ethnicity and Religious Minority Politics in Iran," in Ali Gheissari (ed.), *Contemporary Iran: Economy, Society, Politics*, pp. 299–323, Oxford: Oxford University Press, 2009.

——— "Iran: Regionalism, Ethnicity and Democracy," Open Democracy, 2006, http://www.opendemocracy.net/democracy-irandemocracy/regionalism_3695.jsp

Tsadik, Daniel, "Identity among the Jews of Iran," in Abbas Amanat and Farzin Vejdani (eds), *Iran Facing Others*, pp. 219–42, New York: Palgrave Macmillan, 2012.

Valeri, Marc, "High Visibility, Low Profile: The Shi'a in Oman Under Sultan Qaboos," *International Journal of Middle East Studies*, 42 (2010), pp. 251–68.

——— "Nation-Building and Communities in Oman since 1970: The Swahili-Speaking Omani in Search for Identity," *African Affairs*, 106, 424 (2007), pp. 479–96.

——— *Oman: Politics and Society in the Qaboos State*, London: Hurst, 2009.

Vali, Abbas, "The Kurds and Their 'Others': Fragmented Identity and Fragmented Politics," *Comparative Studies of South Asia, Africa and the Middle East*, 18, 2 (1998), pp. 82–95.

Van Bruinessen, Martin, *Agha, Shaikh and State: On the Social and Political Structures of Kurdistan*, London: Zed Press, 1992.

Van Engeland-Nourai, Anisseh, "Repatriation of Afghan and Iraqi Refugees from Iran: When Home is No Longer Home," *International Journal on Multicultural Societies*, 10, 2 (2008), pp. 145–68.

Vandewalle, Dirk, "Political Aspects of State Building in Rentier Economies: Algeria and Libya Compared," in Hazem Beblawi and Giacomo Luciani (eds), *The Rentier State: Nation, State and Integration in the Arab World*, pp. 159–71, London: Croom Helm, 1987.

Varisco, Daniel, "Making 'Medieval' Islam Meaningful," *Medieval Encounter*, 13 (2007), pp. 385–412.

Vaziri, Mostafa, *Iran as Imagined Nation: The Construction of National Identity*, New York: Paragon House, 1993.

Visser, Reidar, and Gareth Stansfield (eds), *An Iraq of Its Regions*, London: Hurst, 2007.

Volkan, Vamik, *Blood Lines: From Ethnic Pride to Ethnic Terrorism*, Boulder: Westview Press, 1998.

Vom Bruck, Gabriele, "Evacuating Memory in Post-Revolutionary Yemen," in Madawi Al-Rasheed and Robert Vitalis (eds), *Counter-Narratives: History, Contemporary Society, and Politics in Saudi Arabia and Yemen*, pp. 229–45, New York: Palgrave Macmillan, 2004.

——— *Islam, Memory, and Morality in Yemen*, Hampshire, UK: Palgrave Macmillan, 2005.

Watson, Patty Jo, *Archaeological Ethnography in Western Iran*, Viking Fund Publications in Anthropology 57, Tucson: University of Arizona Press, 1979.

Wedeen, Lisa, *Peripheral Visions: Publics, Power, and Performance in Yemen*, Chicago: University of Chicago Press, 2008.

Wehrey, Frederic, *Sectarian Politics in the Gulf: From the Iraq War to the Arab Uprisings*, New York: Columbia University Press, 2014.

Weiner, Myron, and Ali Banuazizi (eds), *The Politics of Social Transformation in Afghanistan, Iran, and Pakistan*, Syracuse: Syracuse University Press, 1994.

Weir, Shelagh, "A Clash of Fundamentalisms: Wahhabism in Yemen," *Middle East Report*, 204 (1997), pp. 22–3.

——— *A Tribal Order: Politics and Law in the Mountains of Yemen*, Austin: University of Texas Press, 2007.

Weiss, Max, *In the Shadow of Sectarianism: Law, Shi'ism, and the Making of Modern Lebanon*, Cambridge: Harvard University Press, 2010.

White, Benjamin Thomas, *The Emergence of Minorities in the Middle East: The Politics of Community in French Mandate Syria*, Edinburgh: Edinburgh University Press, 2011.

Whitley, Andrew, "Minorities and the Stateless in Persian Gulf Politics," *Survival*, 35, 4 (Winter 1993), pp. 28–50.

Willis, John, "Leaving Only Question Marks: Geographies of Rule in Modern Yemen," in Robert Vitalis and Madawi Al-Rasheed (eds), *Counter-Narratives: History, Contemporary Society, and Politics in Saudi Arabia and Yemen*, pp. 119–49, New York: Palgrave, 2004.

Wimbush, S. Enders, "Divided Azerbaijan: Nation Building, Assimilation and Mobilization Between Three States," in William McCagg and Brian Silver (eds), *Soviet Asian Ethnic Frontiers*, pp. 61–81, New York: Pergamon Press, 1979.

Windfuhr, Gernot, "Dialectology," *Encyclopædia Iranica*, 7 (1996), pp. 362–70.

——— (ed.), *The Iranian Languages*, London: Routledge, 2009.

Wirsing, Robert G. (ed.), "South Asia: The Baluch Frontier Tribes of Pakistan," in *Protection of Ethnic Minorities: Comparative Perspectives*, pp. 277–312, New York: Pergamon Press, 1982.

Wright, Steven, "Generational Change and Elite-Driven Reforms in the Kingdom of Bahrain," *Durham Middle East Papers*, 81, Durham: Durham University, June 2006.

Wright, Steven M., "Fixing the Kingdom: Political Evolution and Socio-Economic Challenges in Bahrain," CIRS *Occasional Paper*, 3, Doha: Center for International and Regional Studies, Georgetown University School of Foreign Service in Qatar, 2008.

Yates, Douglas A., *The Rentier State in Africa: Oil Rent Dependency & Neocolonialism in the Republic of Gabon*, Trenton, NJ: Africa World Press, 1996.

Yegen, Mesut, "'Prospective-Turks' or 'Pseudo-Citizens:' Kurds in Turkey," *The Middle East Journal*, 63, 4 (2009), pp. 597–615.

Zubaida, Sami, "The Fragments Imagine the Nation: The Case of Iraq," *International Journal of Middle East Studies*, 34, 2 (2002), pp. 205–15.

——— *Law and Power in the Islamic World*, London: I.B. Tauris, 2005.

INDEX

INDEX